The Encyclopedia of
PROFESSIONAL WRESTLING

2ND EDITION

100 Years of History, Headlines & Hitmakers

Kristian Pope & Ray Whebbe Jr.

Published by

700 East State Street • Iola, WI 54990-0001
715-445-2214 • 888-457-2873
www.krause.com

Our toll-free number to place an order or obtain a free catalog is 800-258-0929.

Library of Congress Catalog Number: 2001086363

ISBN: 0-87349-625-6

Designed by Jamie Griffin

Edited by Tracy Schmidt

Printed in USA

ACKNOWLEDGMENTS

For those of you who read our first two books, *Professional Wrestling Collectibles* and *The Encyclopedia of Professional Wrestling*, we say thank you for stopping by again. For our new readers, we would like to extend a warm welcome.

This second edition of *The Encyclopedia of Professional Wrestling*, offers an updated view on the incredible history of professional wrestling. You'll find an expanded Slamographies chapter, which includes mini biographies for over 1,500 wrestling stars, both past and present.

Throughout the writing of this book, our focus was to give new fans an entry point into the rich history of the sport, while giving true-blue fans a refresher course on the last century of professional wrestling. Part of the challenge in putting a wrestling history book together is in answering one question: Where do you start? That question is one that drove both of us crazy at times.

Truly, the entire, unabridged history of professional wrestling is so incredibly vast that no book could ever do it justice. Upon closer examination of the industry, it is apparent that every year has enough new twists and turns to warrant its own guide.

What you will find here is a trip down memory lane. You will read about names you already know that, through fabulous photography, are made new again.

Of course, we believe the photos from the archives of Norman Kietzer tell a story all their own. If you look closely, we think you'll agree that no words say more about wrestling history than Kietzer's photographs. The support we've received as a result of our first two efforts have been tremendous. A sincere and heartfelt thanks goes to everyone who cared to send a letter of encouragement, browse a copy at their local bookstore or, even better still, buy one to keep as a reference at home.

So many people deserve credit for making this book possible. Thank you to Norm Kietzer, Dr. Mike Lano and the "Nighthawk," Ron Thomas. Thanks also goes to Tracy Schmidt and Paul Kennedy and the entire Krause family for their guidance and friendship. We'd also like to send our appreciation to: Pat Hollis, Eddie Sharkey, Mick Karch, Terry Katzman at Garage D'Or Records in Minneapolis, Dave Meltzer and Alex Marvez from the *Wrestling Observer Newsletter*, Royal Duncan, Adnan Al-Kaissey, Bruce Hart, Derrick Dukes, Ricky Rice, Fancy Ray McCloney, and Dr. Greg Olson.

Most importantly, we would like to thank our families. To the Whebbe and Pope families, your love and support has meant everything to us.

So there you have it. We can only hope you enjoy reading this book as much as we enjoyed writing it. Of course, we love hearing from wrestling fans, just like us, from all over the world. If you have any comments, questions, complaints or corrections, send them to kristianpope@earthlink.net.

Until next time,

Kristian Pope and Ray Whebbe Jr.

TABLE OF CONTENTS

Ray Whebbe Jr. asked a young man in the mid-1980s to help him complete a project that would be the one thing in his life he had always wanted, but had not yet been given the chance to see realized.

For several years, in his free time, Ray had written accurate, detailed career histories of hundreds of professional wrestlers whom he had seen, read about, met, promoted, jeered, and admired since he was a teen. He wrote the biographies by hand on 3x5 cards, bound them in rubber bands and boxed them away to hopefully be used one day.

Like a lot of Ray's dreams, that project, which he wanted to turn into a book, was temporarily shelved despite great efforts on his part to send out proposals and letters to publishers, who, at the time, weren't interested in history books about wrestling.

Nearly two decades later, and those cards having been misplaced, Ray and I began to write from scratch. What you see here in this book is just a sampling of what Ray wanted his original dream to be. But he was happy knowing one of his contributions in life would be fulfilled.

That story is recounted for you because in reading this book you helped Ray realize one of his true passions before he died in August 2003, at age 48, from health complications. One of the last things he did before he passed away was read the final manuscript of what you see here.

It's been hard to grasp that Ray is gone. But he leaves an extraordinary list of accomplishments. After overcoming drug addiction in the 1970s, he devoted his life to sobriety and extending a helping hand. He promoted pro wrestling, trained professional and amateur boxers, directed youth boxing gyms in the Twin Cities, founded several community newspapers and hosted an award-winning cable television show.

More than that, he was a fountain of wisdom for many. His phone would sometimes ring constantly from people who needed his help. Even as his health deteriorated in the years and months leading to his death, he obliged his friends.

Wrestling and baseball were the two things Ray followed since he was a teenager. He even sometimes borrowed the rarely mentioned, but honorable, personality traits of the wrestlers he got to know on a personal level. He admired how Bruiser Brody always looked out for the little guy, how Terry Funk always did it his way, how Michael Hayes used flair to put a smile on people's faces and how guys like Ricky Rice and Derrick Dukes stayed true to themselves in pursuit of their own dreams. All of those traits were things Ray identified with and held onto tightly.

I'm happy to know I was the person Ray chose to help with his first book. Only a teenager at the time, I wasn't ready for such an undertaking. When the opportunity to write this book came my way a few years ago, there is no way it would have been possible without Ray.

One of the things Ray taught his friends was to always be thankful. He was grateful for his chance to write three different books on wrestling. Even more he was thankful for the fans and readers who cared enough to share the enjoyment of his work.

But the real debt of thanks goes to Ray, without whom, we'd all have missed something special.

-Kristian Pope

INTRODUCTION

One hundred years of professional wrestling: The mere thought can leave someone as drowsy as a fallen wrestler after a sleeper hold. Chronicling 100 years of anything, let alone professional wrestling, poses serious questions and challenges.

What is professional wrestling? Is it sport or entertainment? Or is it both? Who watches wrestling and why? How does it affect those involved in the phenomenon like fans and performers? How does the history of wrestling affect the product we see today on television? Is there a way to connect all the dots?

In this second revised edition we will try to answer some of those questions by starting from the industry's beginnings to where it is today. Since our last printing, the landscape of pro wrestling

Rob Van Dam, left, and The Rock have followed in the footsteps of Woody Strode and Tor Johnson and have moved from the ring to the big screen.

Former WWF champion Bret Hart.

athleticism and entertainment. All of us are enamored watching someone like daredevil Jeff Hardy fall 15 feet through a table in a World Wrestling Entertainment ring. And everyone can certainly appreciate the pure talent of former Olympic wrestler Kurt Angle delivering a suplex to his foes. Throughout 100 years, wrestling has changed from a carnival act to a sport to curiosity to entertainment. We may be attracted to professional wrestling for different reasons. But we are all in agreement that there is no greater show on earth.

Through the use of classic photographs from wrestling historian Norman Kietzer's library, different tales of the sport can be told. Whether it's an image of high-flying originator Antonino Rocca throwing his amazing barefooted drop kick, or a snapshot of the classy Lou Thesz appearing majestically with his jeweled National Wrestling Alliance world title belt, the true story of our appeal to wrestling can be explained. The pictures allow us to be up close and personal with the stars, and help us feel the magnitude and importance of the event. Pictures, particularly ones taken up to the 1970s, when the use of a camera was the best way to preserve memories, most accurately display the history and evolution of professional wrestling.

We'd again like to thank all those important people who helped make

has changed dramatically. And as its recent history has shown, there are surely more changes to come.

A look at one-hundred-year history of sports like baseball, or even the automobile, show numerous trends in changes. To tackle this wonderful world of professional wrestling will be our task. Because wrestling's roots are both regional and global, its history is subject to different viewpoints. A fan growing up in Omaha, Neb., has different beliefs and preferences than do fans from New York. Followers from Japan have completely different opinions than domestic fans.

But one common thread binds all of us. As wrestling fans, the sport has touched our hearts for different reasons. While those who will share their experiences with us through this book come from different walks of life, we all are alike in our desire to witness wrestling's amazing display of

Goldberg checks his press coverage in the Japanese magazines.

this project happen. For the use of their photographs, a debt of gratitude goes to Kietzer and the excellent work of Dr. Mike Lano and Ron Thomas. Both Lano and Thomas are the types of fans that wrestling needs more of. Their appreciation for the immense lore of this ring sport, not to mention their eye for the perfect picture, is unparalleled. To our families and friends, your support made you all the most valuable players in our minds.

So let's get to the ring. One hundred years of professional wrestling. From shoots to works, carnies to crushers, and heroes to villains, it's all here in a bold and colorful manner, which only the grand industry of professional wrestling would dare to reveal.

Kristian Pope and *Ray Whebbe Jr.*

Steve Austin is arguably wrestling's most charismatic star of all-time.

CHAPTER 1

WHY BE A PRO-WRESTLING FAN?

"To those who believe in the beauty of professional wrestling, nothing needs to be said.
For those who don't appreciate wrestling, nothing could be said to change their minds."

—*Vincent K. McMahon Jr., owner of World Wrestling Entertainment*

Heroes, villains, winners, and losers. Pro wrestling has it all. And that's why we love it.

Despite computer graphics, mainstream publicity, pyrotechnic tricks, and slick television production, the core of pro wrestling really hasn't changed much over 100 years. And neither have the fans, who retain an insatiable desire for the sport.

From closet fans to impassioned viewers, we all share a love for wrestling. At times, we're fans whose eyes gaze in wonderment at the spectacle. Remember when nearly 60,000 fans jammed the Toronto Sky Dome for Wrestlemania 18 to witness Hulk Hogan versus The Rock? At other times, we're cheerleaders. Who can't be affected by the raw, unbridled charisma of the performers? Sometimes we're critics. We get frustrated with storylines that make no sense, or mad at gimmicks that rub us wrong. It's all part of being a fan.

Little had been published about pro wrestling until a boom in the 1980s. But why? Despite a business downtrend since 2000, wrestling still embarrasses real sports like Major League Baseball and college athletics in cable television ratings.

World Wrestling Federation fans show their passion for various grapplers, including The Rock.

Vince McMahon is the most profitable wrestling promoter of all time.

It seems more books are written about America's favorite pastime, baseball, in one year's time than have been written about the "Sport of Kings" in 100 years. The media seemed to only take potshots at wrestling. As a result, promoters felt snubbed by the media and press. In turn, they were protective of their business.

The notion of exposing the business, or admitting that pro wrestling had predetermined outcomes, was a mortal sin in a wrestler's mind. Based largely on tradition from wrestling's late 19th-century carnival days, no one was allowed to know about wrestling's facade. Aside from inner-circle wrestlers and promoters, only a chosen few were allowed to be part of the backstage fraternity. That privilege came only after a process of paying dues and a so-called security check that would make the KGB proud.

The word "fake" has caused more than a few involved in wrestling to be upset with the press. In 1985, Hulk Hogan, who was America's most famous wrestling hero, demonstrated a

chokehold on actor Richard Belzer that sent him into oblivion. Belzer was knocked out and needed stitches. Some say Hogan played rough because earlier, Belzer called wrestling fake during their interview together.

A year earlier, Hogan's rough, Southern pal, Dr. D. David Schultz, cracked ABC investigative reporter John Stossel upside the head. The journalist was left with permanent ear damage for questioning the reality of wrestling. Apparently, being part of the media covering professional wrestling can be a serious hazard to one's well being. That fact, combined with the long-standing book publisher's comical belief that wrestling fans didn't care to read, helps to explain why so few truthful books about pro wrestling have been written. Until now, anyway.

For most of the modern day, fans of wrestling history were shunned by the public for enjoying wrestling. Those who found joy in it were seemingly forced to hide their knowledge and would have to meet other wrestling fanatics in backyards, ball fields, and basements. Every neighborhood had wrestling fans, but its detractors were plenty. Those who stuck together had a common bond. Their demand for more information grew and underground avenues, like fan clubs, provided the best way to get ring gossip.

From 1940 to 1980, when a wrestler succeeded in garnering mainstream coverage, we all shared in the glory. If an Associated Press photo was published in the daily newspaper, we all cheered. When a wrestler was seen on a television show or a film, we all watched. As soon as the mainstream jumped on wrestling's popularity and rode its coattails for profit, we all wondered, "What took them so long?"

Even Elvis Presley was a wrestling fan. Here he discusses some business with Whipper Billy Watson.

At one time, wrestling magazines gave the only look into its wackiness. In the 1950s, youths could only wonder if Mongolians really had big muscles and odd haircuts. They wondered if Sicilians all looked like Tony Altamore and Captain Lou Albano? What kind of match would the then World Wide Wrestling Federation world champion, Bruno Sammartino, have against the National Wrestling Alliance champion Lou Thesz? Prior to videotapes, the only place to gain information about other wrestling leagues was through the newsstand magazines. Playing to promoter's fears about revealing the truth, magazines covered up wrestlers' real names and backgrounds and wrote only what they thought promoters and fans wanted to read. Nobody, so it seemed, was to be let in on the secrets.

By the early 1980s, videotape-trading fans bonded through the mail. All of a sudden, because of video, news traveled a lot faster in the mail than what was found through newsstand magazines. Today, those footprints of trading info are found through sources on the Internet. Prior to 1985, any official information offered about a wrestler was standard drivel and, often times, fabricated. For many fans, the thirst for truth was a driving force in their lives, so they pursued accurate information.

Eventually, fans were let in on the real information. Through newsletters, which boasted regional focuses, fans in Tacoma, Wash., could be in tune with what was happening in Tallahassee, Fla. Soon, with an emerging younger generation of wrestlers, editors of the newsletters began to garner access to backstage gossip and news. Newsletters like Dave Meltzer's *Wrestling Observer* and Steve Beverly's *Matwatch*, read like miniature trade magazines. Nowadays, backstage information flows so freely

that most ardent followers get their scoops from Web sites and newsletters as the news happens.

To be sure, a lot has changed when it comes to information and exposure. Today, wrestlers are everywhere. The Rock sat next to President George W. Bush at the Republican National Convention in 1999. Chyna and Sable were once *Playboy* magazine cover models. It's not unusual to see mainstream personalities like Jay Leno of "The Tonight Show," comedian Jimmy Kimmel, country crooner Toby Keith, and should-be Hall of Fame baseball player Pete Rose appear on wrestling television programs. In fact, wrestlers themselves are regarded as mainstream. The WWE has earned gold records with its music CDs, and The Rock has been in box-office-hit motion pictures.

"Is it real or isn't it? What is tough and does it really matter? Wrestling is about giving fans a product they love and will pay to see."

—Norman Kietzer, six-decade wrestling journalist and historian

Fans love Rob Van Dam.

A lot of the ring action is pre-rehearsed, but the pain on Buh Buh Dudley's face looks all too real, as he gets smashed by Balls Mahoney and Masato Tanaka.

Mick Foley as Captain Jack.

Despite the dwindling media snub, we can't deny wrestling's firm connection to pop culture. It may appear to only be a modern-times spectacle, but wrestling has always been imbedded in pop culture. In Mexico, El Santo and the Blue Demon made countless movies between them, and were treated like gods by the public. East Coast legend Antonino Rocca cut an album in the 1950s. Minneapolis' Verne Gagne once hawked vitamins in 1960s. In Japan, the popular Tiger Mask wrestling character was actually derived from a children's cartoon program. You name it, when it comes to professional wrestlers, they truly have done it all.

Those successes can all be traced to the fans. Whatever your background, wrestling has made its impact on your soul. The young watch in hypnotic-like wonderment. Older folks watch with a childlike faith. There are no stereotypical wrestling fans. In Japan, many high-society members grab the front row seats similar to the chosen few who are invited to the opening of a Broadway play. The only difference between all of us lies in the passion. For some, being a fan is enough. However, there are those daring few who are bitten by the wrestling bug and become collectors, writers, promoters, referees, photographers, announcers, part of the ring crew, or Webmasters. A few even don the tights and become wrestlers themselves.

The mystery is what draws us in. In reality, every fan knew that Bruiser Brody could beat a wimpy foe like Greg Gagne into a bloody pulp. Despite reality telling us differently, we cheered on Gagne anyway. Deep down, few fans believed the scrawny Bob Backlund could hold back the cadre of 400-pound challengers sent from eerie places by their evil managers, the Grand Wizard and Fred Blassie, to challenge his championship. But we chose to make believe. Most knew the Road Warriors and Abdullah the Butcher were fellow human beings, but none of us wanted to believe we could see them at the local grocery store. Perhaps that was, and still is, the beauty of professional wrestling, and why we're all fans.

Hawk goes toe-to-toe with the Warlord.

The Rock continues the wrestling tradition started by his father Rocky Johnson. The Rock, far right, poses with his father, mother, and wife Dani.

CHAPTER 2

WRESTLING'S ROOTS

Wrestling's beginnings obviously extend farther back than the 100 years allowed in these pages, but to see where the sport is today, it's worthwhile to witness its true and honorable beginnings.

Wrestling's roots can be traced to Biblical times. Not surprisingly, every part of the world embraced and participated in wrestling, the sport. Early European cave dwellings dating back nearly 20,000 years show different holds and counter holds that are still used in the New Millennium. The early Greeks grappled and contested in feats of strength in historic coliseums before throngs of spectators. That Greek style was very rugged, based on rules that could be compared with today's Ultimate Fighting Championships and mixed martial arts. It is believed their wrestling, called Pancration, allowed hitting, kicking, and submission maneuvers. Thousands of years later, in 2000, a group of worldwide warriors and Japanese business leaders called their pseudo-wrestling promotion "Pancrase" in honor of the Greek battle mongers.

The first Olympic Games to offer wrestling took place in 704 B.C. At one point, the Greeks had a six-time Olympic champion named Milon. In the 1940s and 1950s, Mighty Milo, named in honor of the Greek forefather, was often copied as a wrestling gimmick. The real Milon was said to be so powerful, he trained for his contests by lifting cattle. Wrestling evolved further with the expansion of the Roman Empire. It was during that time, during the 2nd century B.C., that catch-as-catch-can wrestling spread its influence in Europe. The Roman Empire is noted for its impressive grapplers and strongmen. As the Olympics evolved, the Greco-Roman style was honored. Europeans, with their knowledge of wrestling combat, immigrated to North America in the 1700s, and by the 1800s a myriad of wrestling styles existed in the United States.

Soldiers entertained each other by grappling during the Civil War, and those in attendance were treated with a very eclectic sporting contest. Carnivals

Strangler Lewis gets friendly with a Native American during a photo opportunity.

John Perrelli of New York was a typical early-century grappler.

Gus Sonnenberg helped solidify wrestling's image.

and traveling entertainment troupes honed in on America's love of strength and combat. From pre-Civil War times to the late 1950s, carnivals loved to "work" crowds with wrestling, meaning they would fake out the spectators with a contrived contest. Hometown strongmen would bet hard-earned pay to beat the carnival champion, who often showed vulnerability in the faked match, with a touring pal beforehand. The carnies, who were the promoters and managers, would milk the scenario for side bets and occasionally "mark" a cash prize if they could defeat, or even last, just 10 minutes with the carny. Needless to say, few regular folk were up to the task.

The ascension of "Honest Abe"

Prior to the Civil War, a lanky, 6-foot-4 genius named Abraham Lincoln took up wrestling and made a name for himself in his native Illinois. Honest Abe, as he was nicknamed later, quietly won the title of Sangamon County wrestling champion in New Salem, Ill., in 1831 at the age of 21. He did this by beating the town tough-guy, Jack Armstrong. Lincoln, the country's 16th President (1861-1865), certainly was the precursor to the likes of people like Jesse Ventura who served a term as the Governor of Minnesota (1999-2002). Despite Lincoln's profound public deeds during the Civil

Bull Montana is looking sharp.

War, his stand on slavery, and subsequent brutal murder, it was only recently that the public realized the glory of Abe's grappling success. The International Wrestling Institute and Museum in Newton, Iowa, has dedicated an entire exhibit to Lincoln.

Muldoon becomes an icon

Many historians enjoy debate about when wrestling turned from being a legitimate contest between two competitors, to a fixed show. Lou Thesz wrote in his book, *Hooker,* that he believed midway through the 1800s is when the shift occurred. Thesz also claimed that even in the early 1900s, legitimate contests happened occasionally with one wrestler wanting to show up the other unexpectedly. By the later 1880s, inklings of true professional wrestlers were popping up in most communities. Saloon frequenters and ship workers were recipients of some early battles that were known to last hours on end.

The first wrestling mega-star was William Muldoon. Muldoon was probably the sport's first pure professional and he was a superstar known throughout the land. After the Civil War, the former Union frontline soldier, drummer, and wrestler joined the rugged New York Police Department. To keep his grappling skills sharp, he leased his services on the weekends to the highest-bidding tavern proprietor and challenged all comers. In 1887, Muldoon was featured on one of the first trading cards ever made. That Allen and Ginters endorsement deal may have been the first recorded deal of that kind.

Muldoon's first championship, called the U.S. Greco-Roman Title, came earlier in 1883 when he defeated England's Edwin Bibby in New York City. Now he was truly the sport's first traveling

"Sandpit" matches were common in India during the early 1900s. This one pitted Great Gama versus Stanislaus Zbyszko.

Everett Marshall strikes a dashing pose.

Farmer Burns often displayed his amazing neck strength by putting himself in a hangman's noose.

Mustapha Pasha, a lightweight from Turkey, throws a smile.

champion. Eventually, news of Muldoon's exploits were heard globally. Contenders from Japan and Scotland, followed by England's Tom Cannon, ventured to the United States with hopes of winning Muldoon's gold. But all went home empty-handed. German strongman Carl Abs and the first Dr. Bill Miller were the only ones to challenge Muldoon, and even they merely held the illustrious champion to draws. His match with Miller reportedly lasted nearly 10 hours. Muldoon retired undefeated from championship competition in 1891.

Some reports say Muldoon actually christened as the next champion, the barely known Ernie Roeber. For Roeber, following a true-life hero like Muldoon would be an insurmountable task. Certainly, Roeber was worthy of the title—he held it for several years—but he didn't grab America's hearts like Muldoon had. Prior to his retirement, Muldoon formed an alliance with the first modern-day boxing champion, John L. Sullivan. Along with other boxers and wrestlers, the twosome's touring troupe took ring sports around the country. They broke the sport's stigma by bringing the action out of saloons and farmlands and brought it into the mainstream. The alliance with Sullivan was perhaps the greatest career move for Muldoon. It allowed him to quit dodging bullets as a cop in the streets of New York. By Muldoon teaming with Sullivan, the two legitimized both boxing and wrestling.

The Farmer opens the barn door

Martin "Farmer" Burns, an Iowa native, had few equals. Over his impressive career, which took him all over the country, Burns achieved as many as 6,000 victories and he was twice regarded as the United States champion in the late 1800s. Burns wasn't huge—he was reportedly 150 pounds at his peak—but there are tall tales of his prowess on the mat. When it came to mat generalship and technique, Burns was

This is a classic cartoon describing the famous, Ed "Strangler" Lewis.

A guard keeps a careful watch over the world title to hype an upcoming match between Jim Londos and Oki Shikina in Hawaii, circa 1939.

Promoter Jack Curley crowns new champion, Danno O'Mahoney.

Jim Londos takes a moment to be with his many fans.

Dick Shikat and Everett Marshall tangle in a 1934 bout.

unmatched. He was fast, well-conditioned, and deserving of recognition, along with the celebrated Muldoon, as one of the greats of the day.

Those tales of athleticism extended beyond the ring for Burns. In fact, Burns was so tough, it is said that his 20-inch neck could withstand the lurch of being dangled from a hangman's noose. He even performed the stunt, and had photographers capture the image in film, to prove his toughness. Seeing that image of Burns gritting his teeth while being strangled from a noose probably

sent shock waves through any future opponent. How's that for trash talking?

With Muldoon gallivanting around the world with Sullivan, Burns was one of many recognized as the champion of the day. Tom Cannon, Tom Jenkins, and Burns were the top grapplers. Burns was the easiest to sell, even though some folks had difficulty knighting a man named Farmer. Even so, Burns was recognized by most to be the champion. But back in Iowa, Burns stumbled on a young, ex-high school jock who had even more talent than he possessed. Despite his own admirable talent as a wrestler, this find by Burns would eventually mark the real success of his own career.

While barnstorming through his home state, the wise Burns watched in awe as a small-town lad from Humboldt, Iowa, tossed wrestlers around a rickety ring, like rag dolls. Burns, already tiring of living in Muldoon's shadow, knew this youngster had the goods to go far, and signed him to a contract. Burns brimmed with confidence. He was sure he could make this Iowan the best wrestler in the world. That young man happened to be the great Frank Gotch, who just may have been the most unbeatable and brutal ring warrior in wrestling history.

Burns instilled everything he knew in Gotch, taking him all over the nation in search of challengers. In August 1901, Gotch earned a then-record purse of $10,000 by embarrassing Silas Archer for the Yukon Gold title. The match lasted nearly 20 minutes, and was so gripping miners threw nearly $9,000 in gold nuggets into the ring to honor the champion, whom they had accepted as one of their own.

Gotch's name gathered steam around the country and even across the Atlantic Ocean. Meanwhile, across the globe, it was a fairly chaotic time in wrestling from an administration standpoint. Without any sanctioning bodies, grapplers throughout the world continued to lay claim to their own championships. From Germany to England to the United States, champions were everywhere. But given the chance, most of them refused to enter the same state, let alone the same ring, as the feared Gotch.

In May 1901, longtime championship claimant and Muldoon nemesis Tom Jenkins geared up to prove his superiority by facing European sensation George Hackenschmidt in New York City for the first recognized world heavyweight championship. Over 100 members of the media were in attendance at the mega-match. The suit, tie, and top-hat crowd was bountiful on that night. In the smoke-filled air, the European champion, Hackenschmidt, prevailed over the recognized North

American champion, Jenkins. Hackenschmidt had already beaten then-British champion, Cannon, in England. The two victories made a solid case for Hackenschmidt to be the real world champion.

In 1901, with championship claimants still plentiful, dozens of top-flight sports promoters banded together to form the National Wrestling Association. With one champion recognized by the Association, promoters believed they would be able to keep the sport productive, vital, and true. The majority of sportswriters agreed. Through Hackenschmidt's decisive wins over Cannon and Jenkins, and wins over other top contenders, he was widely regarded as the world champ by the Association.

Hackenschmidt, also dubbed the Russian Lion, defended the world title belt and his other European belts nobly. Waiting in the wings, though, was a fine Midwest boy—the Farmer's protégé.

In 1905, Gotch beat Jenkins for one version of the world title. But Gotch knew that to be the real world champion, he must face the Russian Lion, who, at the time, was destroying all comers across Europe and other challengers from America. While Hackenschmidt took on most competition, he ducked Gotch, which brewed contempt inside of the Iowan and his manager. Did Hackenschmidt know his fate already?

Finally, in April 1908, Gotch got his chance to fight the Russian nightmare. Gotch took advantage of his once-in-a-lifetime opportunity before a reported crowd of close to 10,000 frenzied spectators in Chicago by winning the NWA world title. Gotch reportedly defeated Hackenschmidt in a straight-up legitimate fight. It is widely known

Bill Longson demonstrates his famous piledriver move on Everett Marshall.

Strangler Lewis shows off his notorious headlock machine.

George Hackenschmidt, the first recognized world's champion.

Joe Stecher was a fearsome foe to many competitors.

Fred Beell shows a menacing pose.

Gotch was a monster in the ring, regularly hurting his opponents for the sheer joy of it. This night was no exception. The outcome was somewhat controversial, as Hackenschmidt cried foul play on Gotch's part.

Despite the humiliating loss, Hackenschmidt insisted on a rematch, but he would wait three years for his second chance. Hackenschmidt may deserve his spot among the all-time greats, but after the ring war he had that night in the Windy City with Gotch, athletically, and perhaps mentally, the Russian Lion was never the same.

Life was good for Gotch as a champion. He opened several Iowa-based businesses, picked up numerous endorsement deals, and toured the world before standing-room-only crowds with a theatrical play about his experience winning the Yukon Gold title. Burns, meanwhile, never appreciated Hackenschmidt for dodging Gotch in the first place. Burns and Gotch made Hackenschmidt wait until 1911 for a rematch, again in Chicago. This time, Gotch punished the Russian Lion severely in the two-out-of-three falls bout. Later it was discovered that Hackenschmidt was injured in a pre-match workout and he wanted to pull out before getting crushed by the vengeful Gotch. But because promoters had sold many tickets already, Hackenschmidt was persuaded to go on as scheduled. The European forced one caveat if he did go through with it: he demanded that Gotch must allow him to win one fall to make him look good.

Gotch apparently agreed, but once the two warriors got in the ring, the Iowan pulled a double-cross and took Hackenschmidt for two-straight falls. Gotch pinned Hackenschmidt in the first fall, and after absorbing two hours of punishment to his body in the second fall, Hackenschmidt wearily conceded the match to Gotch. Up to that date, it was the largest paid gate in United States wrestling history at $73,000 before a reported crowd of over 30,000 people.

Gotch, later recognized by the Association as the world title holder, was a fighting champion who respected all global forces and foes. He held back German Jess Westerguard, the Middle East's Mahout Yussif, and other top-rated opponents throughout the world. Charlie Cutler, who seemed to be everyone's favorite top contender, gave a good outing against Gotch. Over a five-year span, Gotch, an expert at submission holds, retired as an undefeated champion. His last title defense was against George Lurich in 1913, and he vacated the title thereafter. Sadly, several years after walking away a winner, Gotch died due to kidney failure at the age of 39 in his hometown. Doctors, knowing Gotch lived a clean life, linked the breakdown of his damaged kidney to the severe pounding he took while training under Burns, and from his years of ring wars.

The Gotch-Hackenschmidt I clash in 1908 was to that era what Joe Frazier-Muhammad Ali was in 1971. Films of the historic match-up were sold to movie houses around the world. The match may have taken years to procure, but the two must have appreciated the wait. Afterwards, a local picture company out of Chicago sold state's rights to own the film. The company certainly knew how to sell a fight. Advertisements released by the film company asked, "Was Hackenschmidt yellow?" and "Did the Russian lay down?" Though the wars that Gotch had in the ring were far different by today's standards, make no mistake—Gotch was, above all, a professional wrestler.

CHAPTER 3

THE BELTS

Wrestling's main organizations crowned their champions and molded the 1900s. With Gotch's influence, the foundation for wrestling's future was set. And through much of the first half of the 20th century, that one world title, despite claims to other ill-regarded belts, was the sport's pinnacle. However, it was at this point in history when different world titles began to splinter off as battle lines for regional territories were drawn.

Few would question that wrestling's glorious honor and prestige comes from the history of the world championship.

For the better part of the 1900s, one organization, the NWA (still named the National Wrestling Association at this time) was the premiere organizing body for professional wrestling. As the century reached its midpoint, other organizations like the American Wrestling Association (AWA) and the World Wide Wrestling Federation (WWWF) crowned their own champions. Still, before titles promoted by Vince McMahon and Ted Turner, the NWA-sanctioned title was the preeminent title in North America, although its early lineage is not an unbroken chain of predecessors.

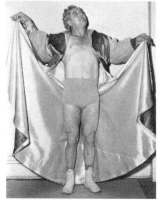

The pioneering legend who started wrestling's gimmicks was Gorgeous George.

Bulldog Brower gives Mighty Igor a powerful punch.

Barking challenges was a daily routine for Killer Kowalski.

This first NWA was an offshoot promotion formed by a conglomerate of promoters. It was first known as the National Boxing Alliance and continued to sanction throughout World War II. With boxing becoming the nation's sport, the public kept wrestling on the back burner.

The NWA crowned many champions. Within all of those title changes, wrestling historians can track important trends in the sport. More importantly, the early 1900s were essentially the years where professional wrestling, as we know it, began. It was the NWA which tried to make sense out of the disorder that was wrestling during the early 1900s. At the time, numerous men claimed to be the holders of other titles. The title of wrestling champion went back and forth between numerous stars of the past, and often via controversial circumstances. Oftentimes, these disputed decisions weren't universally recognized by all states and promoters.

After Hackenschmidt had beaten the world's best to be recognized as the champion in 1901, Gotch then went on to defeat Hackenschmidt in 1908 to become the undisputed champion and first recognized NWA champion. At the time, other stars may have laid claim to a belt, but few wanted to get into a match with the great Gotch. After Gotch's retirement, many legends of the sport made their runs. In 1920, Earl Caddock and Joe Stecher flip-flopped the title. Then, in December 1920, Ed "Strangler" Lewis, a

Famed strongman Reggie Parks demonstrates his stomach muscles in this stunt in which he allowed a van to drive over him.

Lord James Blears waves to the crowd.

Danny O'Shocker, a star from the 40s, blows a tune during some free time.

Luther Lindsay, left, takes on feared German Karl Von Steiger.

master of the sleeper hold, beat Stecher for the gold. Stanislaus Zbyszko, Gus Sonnenberg, and Wayne Munn all held the belt throughout the 1920s.

Despite the friction between all the different titleholders, world title matches were enormous happenings around the country. They were no-frills contests and very athletic. Today, former champions like Jim Londos and Sonnenberg are still remembered for their toughness. Londos, a Greek descendent, was a fluid fan favorite. Amid much controversy, Dick Shikat defeated the "Golden Greek" in Philadelphia in August 1929 to capture his first title. Londos got his revenge by winning a rematch with Shikat, also in Philadelphia, in 1930. A would-be third match between the two in 1932 never took place because Londos refused an order by the New York Athletic Commission to fight Shikat. Instead, Lewis beat Shikat.

Shikat, Londos, Sonnenberg, Lewis, Joe Savoldi, Henri DeGlane, and Ed Don George all held versions of this title through the 1930s. Danno O'Mahoney, after defeating the likes of Londos, George, and Lewis all within one month in 1935, claimed the universally recognized world title at this time. However, in 1936, Shikat rose again to beat O'Mahoney.

Because there was no television, news traveled slowly. Ali Baba beat Shikat in 1936, and the film footage became a penny arcade attraction. A machine had clips of the event and a customer plunked in a penny, turned the crank, and picture-by-picture viewed the event. In June 1936, a handsome, but cagey, Everett Marshall beat Baba. However, later that year, the NWA didn't recognize Marshall as its heavyweight champion. In turn, the administration awarded the crown to John Pesek.

By the end of the 1930s, fewer disputed branches of the belt were recognized, and by 1937, when a young, 21-year-old Lou Thesz got his chance to be champion, there was a sense of some

Silver screen star and wrestler, Lenny Montana.

Mike Padousis was one of many ex-football players to enter the ring.

In this classic bout, Antonio Inoki takes on world champ, Lou Thesz.

Who can argue that Lou Thesz wasn't the greatest world champion ever?

American sensations Lou Thesz and Karl Gotch sign autographs for fans in Japan.

Even royalty have enjoyed wrestling. The U.K.'s Prince Phillip talks with wrestlers Alfred Hayes and Jack Pallo during a pre-match ceremony in Royal Albert Hall during 1968.

stability in the heavyweight ranks. Also due to Thesz's popularity at the box office, Thesz would become arguably the most admired and respected NWA champion ever. On December 29, 1937, Thesz captured the title for the first time. Through his career, Thesz would carry the prestigious belt six times. That was in a day when title switches were not common. But with his help, the NWA survived a chaotic time for contenders and often-weak ticket sales. The best days of the NWA—and the entire sport— lay ahead.

Wrestling's Golden Age

As much as anything in its history, professional wrestling owes a debt of thanks to television for its lasting position in modern pop culture. When sports on television first became available in the mid-1940s, wrestling seemed like the perfect partner. Along with sports like baseball and boxing, wrestling came through better than any programming available. A minimal number of cameras were needed, and the action was centrally located and easy to follow. The fact that it aired live and was cheap to produce helped, too.

The advent of television was thought to be merely a communications tool for the government. Really, who wanted to sit at home and watch something through a fuzzy, five-inch screen? And pay, to boot? In 1948, it is said that

Americans owned close to 200,000 television sets. But with sports, which were aired to garner the new medium interest, nearly one-half million sets were in homes by 1950. Television, too, owes some thanks to wrestling for giving it the kick-start it needed.

Professional wrestling was one of the first shows available when the original two networks, the DuMont Network and NBC, hit the airways. By 1948, three of the four networks running full programming schedules included wrestling. DuMont, most noted for its affiliation with comic Jackie Gleason's first television show, carried wrestling from the Marigold Arena in Chicago and several sites in New York, including the Jamaica Arena in Queens.

DuMont's show was a rival to NBC's popular "Gillette Cavalcade of Sports." In 1948, NBC got in the act. It aired live wrestling from the Rainbow Arena in Chicago. On some evenings, networks aired only a few hours of programming. With wrestling as one of the shows to fill that time, it helps explain the unique partnership between the tube and the sport.

Wrestlers like Gorgeous George, Whipper Watson, Mighty Atlas, Primo Carnera, and Antonino Rocca became as well known on television as their movie screen counterparts. At first, matches were basic exhibitions of grappling. Eventually, things became a bit more theatrical. Ironically, its theatrical aspects both killed off network-aired wrestling shows and livened up live attendance at the arenas.

By the mid-1950s, the networks stopped airing wrestling nationally because television executives felt the sport was too low-brow for the tastes of sponsors. From that point, wrestling

began to air on local channels and has been on ever since.

Early wrestling programmers should be recognized for creating several cross-over stars. Hard Boiled Haggerty became a television and film bit actor because of

Wrestler and film star Mike Mazurki, at left, in a promo photo for an NBC television show, "Timothy Heist."

Having fun are two former world champions, the great Lou Thesz and Terry Funk.

Boxing heavyweight champion Joe Louis, who donned the tights later in his career, throws a shoulder block against Jim Bernard in Detroit, circa 1956.

his experience in the ring. Several wrestling announcers went on to big things as well. Chicago's Jack Brickhouse, who is in the baseball Hall of Fame in Cooperstown, got his announcing start on the DuMont wrestling program, where he hosted and did play-by-play every Saturday night from the Marigold Gardens.

Another DuMont announcer, Dennis James, was the New York-area announcer from Queens and White Plains. His signature line, "Okay, Mother," which he created on the wrestling show, was later used as the

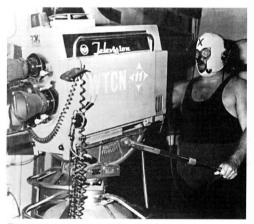

The man behind the mask—and the camera—is none other than Mr. X, Dick Beyer.

name of a quiz show he hosted on the network. Could James be the forefather of catch-phrases like "Do you smell what The Rock is cooking?" Thanks to his wrestling days, James also was the co-host of the famous, "Jack Benny Show."

Television made its own superstars, the first being Gorgeous George, one of the all-time greatest gimmicks. George Wagner, his real name, was a tough guy to be sure. Born in Seward, Neb., he worked as a laborer by day and wrestled by night. But as a non-entity in the ring, he just couldn't earn a living. He gave himself a complete make-over, nicknamed himself the "Human Orchid" and suddenly became Gorgeous George.

As the Gorgeous One, he dyed his hair platinum blonde, donned a purple silk cape, and was ushered into the ring with his wife. He later added a hairdresser to accompany him to the ring who would roll out a red carpet and disinfect the ring with an atomizer before the match began. On is way to the ring, George tossed 24 karat gold-plated bobby pins, or sometimes roses, to spectators to give the illusion of his riches.

Wagner became the man fans loved to hate and, in doing so, he became the top drawing attraction of the 1940s. Some would say he was the first "must-see" performer. Wagner was the first wrestler to play into homophobia and the rouse worked. His outrageousness spawned wrestling's era of extravagance. Boxing legend Muhammad Ali once said it was after seeing Gorgeous George that he decided to display an outrageous persona.

In 1949, Wagner reached the pinnacle of wrestling stardom by headlining at Madison Square Garden in a win over Ernie Dusk on the first card at that arena

Dick the Bruiser absorbs a dropkick from Antonino Rocca.

in 12 years. Wagner later legally changed his name to Gorgeous George. For 20 strong years, few wrestlers filled the seats like Wagner. To this day, performers who push the envelope owe a nod and a wink to the one and only "Human Orchid."

Beauty and the Beast: Hard Boiled Haggerty takes a moment with the 1948 Miss America winner, Bebe Shopp.

Three main belts take shape in the United States

Ironically, during 1948, the same year that television wrestling spread its wings, the National Wrestling Alliance, as we know it most famously, began. With television ready to go, and programmers needing shows to fill airtime, wrestling promoters were ready to take advantage of the new medium. Most promoters saw the future, and there was big money to be had through television. As a result, live attendance was increased around the country at the start of the 1950s.

This NWA differed from the Association of the early 1900s, because the new group was a conglomerate of wrestling promoters who were picking up steam in cities across America, rather

Chief White Owl cheers up some children while in a Pittsburgh hospital.

Jackie Fargo and Ray Stevens show off their tag-team titles in June 1958.

The television boom in the 1950s led to many new gimmicks, like incense belching from an urn courtesy of Princess Salima.

President John F. Kennedy talks politics with wrestler Hard Boiled Haggerty.

Dave Levin, a world champion in the 1930s, is honored at the Cauliflower Alley Club with Mike Mazurki, left.

than a committee of regulators and commissioners from different states. The new NWA claimed that its titleholders were direct descendants of the days of

Frank Gotch. Lou Thesz, it was decided, would be the flagship of the Alliance, and he was anointed champion in 1948. Thesz's last title reign ended in 1966, but he carried the belt continuously from 1947 to 1956 before he lost it to Whipper Watson. After that loss, Thesz would have another day and another run.

Soon, with the first Association waning, the entire country got behind the Alliance. Thanks to Thesz's title reigns, the new NWA highlighted the sport's growing appeal and helped pave the way for fellow champions like Ric Flair, Terry Funk, Harley Race, Ricky Steamboat, Jack Brisco, and Giant Baba. The champion, in this case, Thesz, would be the crown jewel of the Alliance. Promoters who belonged to the NWA voted for which wrestler would be champion and carry the belt. And, as protection for the promoters of the NWA, the champion had to put up his own money as a bond just in case he refused to drop the strap, or miss a booking in defiance of the promoters.

While Thesz was busy working around the globe, other challengers came to the forefront. After some initial stability, the Alliance showed signs of dissent. With the blond-haired original, "Nature Boy" Buddy Rogers, now stomping through the Northeast with the NWA title, which he won from Pat O'Connor in 1961, there were rumblings of some trouble among the promoters. The NWA had begun to grow tired of Northeast promoter Toots Mondt, and how he was seemingly stealing the champion away from bookings around the rest of the country. In 1962, it was decided by the NWA that Rogers would lose the title. Naturally, they looked to the reliable Thesz for help to re-establish some stability.

Initially, Rogers dodged the attempts to put a match together against Thesz. Rogers, you see, had no designs on losing the belt. But when the NWA threatened to take away the bond money he put up for the belt, Rogers reluctantly agreed to a match against Thesz. In January 1963 in Toronto, Thesz regained his championship at age 46. Knowing he wasn't happy about losing the title, Thesz was ready to take back the belt in whatever way he saw fit. If that meant decking Rogers for real, he would have. Thesz and the NWA had good intentions, and with the win, most everyone basked in their glory. But that title switch set in motion a chain of events, which would shape the industry forever. Disgruntled over the loss by his man, Rogers, Mondt, and a fellow named McMahon formed the World Wide Wrestling Federation, and with it, their own version of the world title.

Sammartino, the Garden and the McMahons

Madison Square Garden is one of America's sports Meccas. From its earliest days to the present, it has been a haven for professional wrestling. Joe Frazier and Sugar Ray Robinson headlined shows there, but it was an Italian immigrant-turned-pro wrestler, named Bruno Sammartino, who really owned the Garden. Throughout most of the 1960s, the strongman from Abruzzi, Italy, played to sold-out crowds at the Garden and major arenas throughout the East.

Sammartino can thank the promoters in the East, and their battles with the NWA, for his chance to shine in the Big Apple. New York area promoter Vince McMahon, Sr., Philadelphia's Willie Gilzenberg, and many others had previously played under the auspices of the NWA and used its champion as their own. The arrangement seemed to work, but when business picked up, naturally money became an issue. Soon, the East's promoters grew tiresome of the constant politicking and getting what they thought were leftovers. The Thesz win cemented their belief.

So, in 1963, they founded the WWWF, the forefather of today's World Wrestling Entertainment. McMahon's son, Vince Jr., initially got his feet wet in the family business by running errands, making posters, and announcing for his pop. Junior was given the town of Bangor, Maine, to promote and fared well. It was during these humble beginnings when Vince Jr. began his plans for the future. When the younger McMahon finally took the reigns from his father in the 1970s, he shortened the WWWF acronym to World Wrestling Federation.

That's Gene Kiniski sporting his trademark crewcut.

Legendary strongman, Bert Assirati.

Bob Orton Sr. is in a battle with Eddie Graham (right).

On May 17, 1963, just a month removed from Rogers being proclaimed the WWWF champion, Sammartino dethroned Rogers at Madison Square Garden in less than 60 seconds. To this day, Sammartino claims the match was real. Rumors circulated that Rogers was suffering from a bad heart and wanted it over quickly. Sammartino denies the story. By defeating a top foe like Rogers so convincingly, Sammartino shook the world of wrestling.

Awaiting their world title match are Lou Thesz and Danny Hodge.

Known for his dropkick, Antonino Rocca sends Verne Gagne flying.

Through the rest of the 1960s, he went undefeated and held back the challenges from a veritable "Who's Who" list of wrestling's elite contenders. Sammartino's specialty was destroying the monsters of the ring. Gorilla Monsoon, Russian Nikolai Volkoff, and the strange-looking Killer Khan gave their best efforts only to go home with a loss against Bruno. Sammartino is remembered as the master of the bear hug maneuver, and he may be the only man ever to bodyslam the nearly 600-pound Haystacks Calhoun.

Sammartino's reign wouldn't last forever, as there were many greats waiting to hold the belt. The times finally caught up to Sammartino, and in January 1971, "Russian Bear" Ivan Koloff defeated the Italian for the company's crown. Pedro Morales beat Koloff two weeks later and held the belt for nearly three years until he fell victim to Stan Stasiak at the Spectrum in Philadelphia. Nine days later, Bruno outclassed Stasiak at the Garden to reclaim the world belt. He held the title for the next three years, before losing to "Superstar" Billy Graham.

When Sammartino's final reign as the WWWF champion ended in 1977, many fans cried. At one time, the popular Italian rivaled Mickey Mantle as New York's top sports icon. He was so popular that, when national television did a series on sports legends, Sammartino was included. He also was one of the few dual champions. Besides holding back all challenges for the company's world heavyweight title, he held the world tag team titles for over two years with Greek technician Spiros Arion. Sammartino and Arion defeated Lou Albano and Tony Altamore to win the tag belts. Albano, later the greatest tag-team manager of any league, dedicated his life to dethroning

Sammartino of the singles' crown, but never succeeded.

Sammartino was a true gentleman in and out of the ring, and he set the bar for champions in the 1960s and 1970s. He was tirelessly active with numerous charities, often wore a suit and tie in public, and never shied away from the responsibilities of being a role model. Everyone who lived in the East, whether they were wrestling fans or not, seemed to have a favorite memory of Bruno.

The American Wrestling Association holds its own for three decades

World titles were not limited to the NWA and WWWF. Politics of deciding who would carry the title caused major rifts among some deserving wrestlers even beyond the Thesz versus Rogers affair. In 1963, Midwest promoters became antsy. A 30-year-old former football and wrestling standout at the University of Minnesota named Verne Gagne had been campaigning for himself throughout the wrestling world. Still, major title shots and victories seemed to elude the Golden Gopher alumnus.

Gagne rivaled Thesz as being the Upper-Midwest's top-drawing attraction. As legend has it, Gagne, who held the Omaha World title in 1963, maneuvered to gain his own belt by aligning with a handful of promoters. They bought the rights to the Minnesota territory, and Gagne was immediately named the first American Wrestling Association champion. Gagne claimed he had to do this because Thesz refused to meet him in an NWA title match. With promoter Wally Karbo's brilliant sense of booking and Gagne's innate sense of getting along with people, wrestling in Minnesota spawned another new era for the sport.

Lou Thesz, here against Japanese hero Antonio Inoki, was a popular attraction in the Orient.

Classic manager Red Berry talks strategy with Gorilla Monsoon.

For the better part of 30 years, the AWA ruled the Midwest and parts of Canada and Japan. The superstars included the Crusher, Jim Brunzell, Rick Martel, Greg Gagne, the Hennigs, and the one and only Baron Von Raschke. The territory prided itself on having a solid in-ring style, but added a unique sense of humor. Fans from the area can't shake memories of Mad Dog Vachon building a casket for Jerry Blackwell. The group allowed newcomers like Ric Flair, the Iron Sheik, and Ricky Steamboat to have a chance to get their feet wet. It supported tag teams like Jim Brunzell

Homer O'Dell with Southern tag-team champions, Bronco Lubich (left) and Aldo Bogni (right).

The unforgettable, Fred Blassie.

and Greg Gagne, and Jesse Ventura and Adrian Adonis.

It also promoted legends like Nick Bockwinkel, Johnny Valentine, Ernie Ladd, the Freebirds, and the Road Warriors. Usually, the AWA delivered the goods to fans. The champions of the AWA were strong technicians who ventured as far as Japan and defended their honor in wrestling hotbeds like St. Louis, Amarillo, Memphis, Chicago, Indianapolis, Denver, San Francisco, and Winnipeg. Through the years, Minneapolis was always home for the AWA. When the WWF broke territorial truces in the 1980s, the promotion fell victim to poor business deals, and wound up with an inferior product.

For a time, though, the AWA was a highly respected organization whose champion was one fitting the title of world champion. Gagne was the first

champion, and son-in-law, Larry Zbyszko, was the promotion's last when the title was vacated in 1990, prior to the group's closing in 1991. The greatest legacy left by the AWA are its memories. It was recognized in all corners of the world and its wrestlers are some of the industry's all-time greats. Gagne had a good run to be certain.

El Santo: Wrestling's first true cross-over star?

With the popularity of wrestling on television in the 1950s, the groundwork had been laid for stars to crossover into other more lucrative mediums. Ever since wrestlers were seen as multitalented stars, American film producers have hired them to play a variety of characters. But film producers have never caught on film the charisma wrestlers display on television or in person.

Although Hollywood has been in the dark trying to recapture the best of what fans enjoy most in pro wrestling, Mexico has been enormously successful in making movies that feature wrestling stars. El Santo (The Saint) is by far the most popular wrestler/actor of all time. He has appeared in dozens of films and television shows. His movies were over dubbed in English for American consumption by exploitation master K. Gordon Murray who renamed the wrestler, Samson, in the English versions.

El Santo was a true crossover star and far ahead of his time. Can you imagine if John Wayne were ever a wrestler? That would give the American audience a taste of the impact El Santo had in Mexico. Born Rodolfo Guzman Huerta in 1917, he was also known as the "Man in the Silver Mask" and fought all challengers in, and out, of the ring.

In the ring, El Santo held numerous titles such as the Mexican welterweight title, the NWA world middleweight title, and the National tag-team title. He made his wrestling debut as a 25-year-old in

1942. Sixteen years later, he transcended to the silver screen for the first time, and became one of the world's purest matinee idols.

There are over 200 movies starring Mexican wrestlers, and El Santo was clearly the most successful. His films alone, made mostly in Cuba, total near 60. Blue Demon, Mil Mascaras, Dos Caras, and others were involved in Mexican box office hits, too. The plots of these campy films were basic, but enjoyable. One needn't be multilingual to understand their plots.

Because of their wide appeal, the heroes under the masks have become part of Mexican pop culture. Part of their appeal is that these heroes are themselves. They're not like the dapper Brit, James Bond, nor are they perfectly groomed like Hollywood heroes. On screen they show the world that they are just as good as any other country's

Woody Strode, a great wrestler and a super Hollywood actor.

Klondike Bill knew precisely what a choke from Mr. Ota felt like.

Pat O' Connor was regarded as one of the finest technicians to hold the NWA world title.

heroes. El Santo and Blue Demon were never seen without their hoods—in the movies and in real life. Santo was even buried in his silver mask. To Americans, it's quite campy to see a masked wrestler in a suit and tie at a wedding or laying on a table at an emergency room, but somehow it all works on film.

They were classic good versus evil. In addition to zombies and vampires and werewolves, El Santo fought his main rival, Blue Demon, who was also a ring star. El Santo often bested the Blue Demon, but many of his foes were too large for the sport of wrestling. Santo's first epic film, *Brain of Evil* was made in 1958. His last, the *Fury of the Karate Experts*, was produced in 1982.

Most critics of the genre say the Mexican wrestling film phenomenon ended around 1977. In 1984, when The Saint diedfrom a heart attack at age 67, thousands mourned. Legend has it that so many people attended the funeral that it took an hour for pallbearers to reach the mausoleum with the casket carrying the star. The world was a better place because of him.

Ted Lewin shows his skills as an artist.

Once the 1970s began, American culture saw things on a grand scale. Planes flew across the country on a daily basis, and people's lives were sped up to meet ever-growing demands. Wrestling went right along with the times. Wrestlers were getting bigger and promoters were thinking big. Really big.

It's no wonder that in America's grandest city, New York, promoters wanted to book the grandest shows ever.

And there was only one venue adequate to hold these mega-events.

In New York City, the then-modern Shea Stadium was the home of professional baseball's New York Mets. The building had already become synonymous with large-scale events. In 1965, the Beatles hosted one of their last

That's second-generation star, Bob Orton Jr.

Reggie Parks hurls Russian Ivan Koloff into the turnbuckle.

It's a champion's roll call: Harley Race, left, Fabulous Moolah and Nick Bockwinkel.

Terry Funk uses a bull rope to choke his opponent, Dusty Rhodes.

No fan at ringside was safe when Bobo Brazil and the Sheik tangled.

concerts there, drawing 55,000 people. Boxing champion Muhammad Ali slugged it out with Ken Norton Sr. in 1976 in a heavyweight title fight. And the Amazing Mets went from being baseball's laughing stocks to World Series champions at Shea in 1969. New Yorkers always had Yankee Stadium to gloat over, but the Bronx Bombers were the team everybody loved to hate. The Mets, meanwhile, were the world's lovable underdogs. It all seemed to make the perfect place for promoter Vince McMahon Sr.

Venues with stadium seating were often used for wrestling in the Roaring 1920s. But New York stadiums had not staged wrestling for several decades. All of a sudden the WWWF had just the right man, champion Bruno Sammartino, who could help fill the seats. The promotion staged events at Shea Stadium three times. From 1972 to 1980, they promoted there every four years,

Hector Guerrero was a member of a great wrestling family.

Terry Funk proudly displays his NWA world title.

just like an Olympic schedule. Sammartino, their Italian-born star, was the main event attraction for each card. In all, over 100,000 fans paid to see the three Shea Stadium events.

Before the first card there, Pedro Morales defeated Ivan Koloff in August 1971, to become the fourth WWWF champion ever. Sammartino, the group's first, and arguably best-drawing champion ever, wanted to regain the title he had lost earlier that year after a seven-year reign. However, few promotions pitted fan favorites against each other. Morales was nearly as popular as Sammartino. Finally, the group came to its senses and booked the match.

When Morales finally met Sammartino, no building could hold the expected crowd. In September 1972, over 30,000 paid to see Morales and Sammartino tangle to a 75-minute draw in a clash of two championship-caliber titans. The only other championship match of the day saw the women's champion, the Fabulous Moolah beat Debbie Johnson. Jack Brisco, an NWA attraction, beat Mr. Fuji and WWWF regulars Gorilla Monsoon, Ernie Ladd, John Studd, Jay Strongbow, Lou Albano, and others filled out the show.

In June 1976, the federation returned to Shea in a co-promoted event that was aired in theaters and auditoriums around the world. In addition to the live show, it was promoted in conjunction with the epic match pitting Ali versus Japanese judo star, Antonio Inoki, which would be seen via closed-circuit television from Tokyo's Budokan Hall. The star of the day, however, was Sammartino, who defended the title on the live show at Shea against one of his stiffest competitors, future AWA champion Stan Hansen.

ROCKY (SOULMAN) JOHNSON
Rocky Johnson, the father of The Rock, throws a dropkick.

Nick Bockwinkel and Bob Orton Jr. escape the mayhem and head to the locker room.

Also at Shea, which drew a then-record-setting house of 42,000, heavyweight boxer Chuck Wepner hit the wrestling ring for a match with Andre the Giant. Wepner lost via count out. In an accompanying tag-team title match, the popular Billy White Wolf and partner Strongbow retained their belts by holding back the challenge of the

Jesse Ventura strikes a famous pose in his wrestling days.

The friendly, but fearsome, NWA world champion, Jack Brisco.

Known for his scientific wrestling was the classy, Dory Funk Jr.

Executioners (John Studd and Killer Kowalski under masks).

Those first two cards were just precursors for the promotion, now called the WWF. Shea Stadium's most dramatic card was held in August 1980, before 41,000 fans. After months of trash talking, Sammartino's one-time protégé, Larry Zbyszko, met him in a cage match.

Sammartino was coined the "Living Legend." It was during this match-up that Zbyszko lifted the name from Sammartino, despite losing to Bruno. As expected, Sammartino left Zbyszko in a bloody heap and beat him cleanly. Also, as expected, Zbyszko never shut up again.

Promotions from several countries sent wrestlers to represent them on this

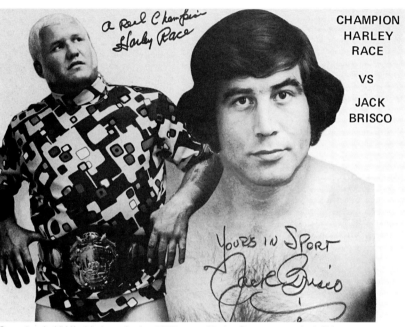

One classic NWA title bout in the 1970s was Harley Race versus Jack Brisco.

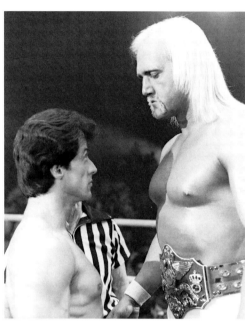

"Rocky 3" highlighted an appearance by Hulk Hogan as Thunder Lips.

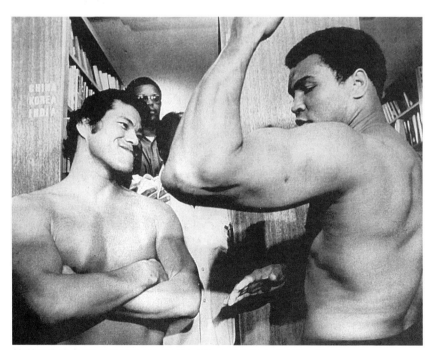

Hyping their famous match are Japanese legend Antonio Inoki and boxing star, Muhammad Ali.

Nick Bockwinkel chokes his frequent partner and nemesis, Ray Stevens.

show. The National Wrestling Federation champion, Inoki, defeated Larry Sharpe in a mixed martial arts match. Japanese superstar and junior heavyweight champion, Tatsumi Fujinami, defeated Texas superstar Chavo Guerrero. The AWA pitched in by sending Greg Gagne, who beat Rick McGraw.

In a match that followed years of controversy and blood, Andre the Giant cleanly beat a young Hulk Hogan. WWF champion Bob Backlund and Morales beat the Samoans for the tag-team championship. In an Intercontinental title match, Ken Patera beat bodybuilder Tony Atlas.

The card was monumental, as well as dramatic, as over $500,000 was taken at the gate. Stadiums were used for wrestling before and certainly after. Many a Wrestlemania has been staged before a stadium crowd. From North Korea to Milwaukee and from Chicago to Tokyo, some events simply demand stadium seating. But few demanded or produced the aura of Sammartino and the WWF.

Paul Boesch: The life lived of many

Although former Houston promoter, the late Paul Boesch, was most noted for his wrestling connection, he was also a World War II hero, lifeguard, author, radio and television commentator, and memorabilia collector. Before Boesch died in 1989 at age 76 from a heart attack, he lived the lives of many different people.

Boesch, a Brooklyn, N.Y., native, began wrestling in Bronx smokers and, shortly thereafter, headlined bouts everywhere by the 1930s. His career took him all over the world, and he was just as popular in New Zealand as he was in New York. He even had a series of

matches with former NWA champion Dick Shikat, in which he held him to time limit draws of 90 and 120 minutes. He was even credited with showing Verne Gagne the sleeper hold, which Gagne used to win the AWA championship.

By the early 1940s, he tried his hand at promoting. In the Northwest, he once promoted a card and accidentally invented the mud-wrestling match. He set up a Hindu-styled match between Gus Sonnenberg and India's Harnam Singh. Loads of dirt were added to the ring to simulate the common sandpit matches that took place in India. Water was added, but the ring was flooded accidentally and turned it all to mud.

While competing as a wrestler, the war broke out and Boesch was called to active duty. He spent three years in the Army and returned to America a hero. On the battlefield he won numerous medals, including a silver star, bronze star, and purple heart.

Once he returned home, Boesch quickly hit the ring. But in 1947, the world traveler was involved in a car

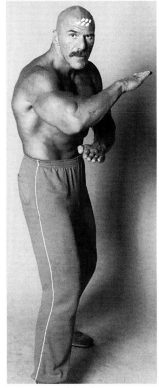

Billy Graham later revitalized his career as a karate expert.

Houston promoter, Paul Boesch, is considered a legend in wrestling history.

Ripped strongman, the famous "Superstar" Billy Graham.

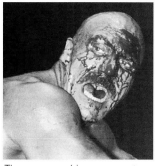

There was no bigger superstar than Billy Graham.

Even Billy Graham suffered deep cuts during his matches.

accident in Texas. Although he did return for a brief stay after he mended, the accident changed his focus for good. With the television explosion ahead, and with his previous radio experience, he became an ideal candidate to host the Houston-area wrestling program. And for many of those years he was matchmaker and assistant promoter with Houston's legendary boss, Mo Sigel. In 1967, after Sigel passed away, Boesch took over control of Houston.

He learned valuable lessons from Sigel. Boesch once said of promoting, "Give the fans men who produce action, make sure they get their money's worth, and always give what you promised." Boesch became highly respected. In an era where promotions often disallowed cross-pollinated shows, Boesch simply used the best available talent. His shows would often have both the AWA and NWA titleholders on the same card. In later years, he promoted with Bill Watts (Mid-South), Jim Crockett Sr. (Mid-Atlantic), and the McMahons. Through the years, Boesch helped expose stars like Count Billy Varga, LeRoy McGuirk, and Wild Red Berry to Texas crowds.

Promoter Paul Boesch, who never turned down a challenge, arm-wrestles Billy Graham on televison.

The high school dropout was also a published author. He wrote a book of poetry, a wrestling autobiography, and, at the time of his death, he was finishing a biography based on his wartime exploits.

Among his Texas pals, he regarded former President George Bush a good friend. In fact, when Boesch promoted his last card in 1987, Bush wrote him a telegram, which was published in the last Houston program. Said Bush: "Wrestling will never be quite the same without [Boesch's] firm, principled leadership."

Billy Graham's calling card: "The Superstar says it all!"

Throughout wrestling history, promoters have been obsessed with creating stars out of football players, boxers, weightlifters, and bodybuilders. Football players could usually figure to make the transition. There isn't much else a 6-4, 265-pound man can do, right?

Boxers, by the time they hit the wrestling ring, were generally too old to make in impact. Weightlifters were often slow, plagued with injuries, and were often dull. Bodybuilders would seem a natural choice. They have an inflated sense of identity, enjoy looking good on camera, and play well to crowds. But wrestling was a whole new game, and they were sometimes clumsy and uncoordinated in the ring.

"Superstar" Billy Graham (Wayne Coleman) broke that barrier in a big way. Adopting the popular and widely used name, Graham, probably didn't hurt. Dr. Jerry (the only real Graham), Crazy Luke, and Eddie Graham preceded the Superstar, and all earned solid reputations. But this chiseled bodybuilder-turned-wrestler likely would have been popular if his name was Smith. Nobody in the business was as well built as Superstar. With a nickname that said it all, Graham was one of the superior talkers of any era and backed up his image.

Through most of the early 1970s, the Superstar rode his biceps around the country. Unlike others who joined the wrestling ranks from other sports, he enjoyed learning the ropes and especially enjoyed interviews. Although he was most often billed as a rule breaker, he also became the anti-hero whom many fans could not help but laugh along with. Some fans called him a must-see attraction. Promoters were often in a quandary as to how touse him. In the end, that was a small problem considering his appeal at the turnstiles.

Graham was wrestling's first true-life hippie. He wore tie-dyed shirts, wild sunglasses, and feathered boas. He bragged of his movie-star looks and hard rocking friends. Wrestling fans perked up whenever Superstar arrived. His charisma brought non-wrestling fans out to see him. During Graham's early years, he often feuded with Dusty Rhodes. The two Hall of Fame stars also teamed to battle forces of evil as the "American Dream Team."

As a heel, he was cheered. As a fan favorite, he lost much of his charm. The World Wide Wrestling Federation wasn't the least bit confused how to exploit the star. They saw money and were right on target. In April 1977, iconoclastic Graham defeated the undeniably popular Bruno Sammartino to become the world champion. The live crowd in Baltimore was shocked. Graham's victory helped to signify a new era as Sammartino would never be a major title threat again.

Graham just looked unbeatable, especially when his photo was compared alongside the other champions of the day. Nobody could deny that Verne Gagne, Jack Brisco, Terry Funk, or Nick Bockwinkel were shoo-ins for the Hall of Fame, as they were superior technicians. But when fans saw a 200-pound, balding Gagne pictured next to Graham, there was no comparison. The Superstar looked invincible, and his looks told the world he was the best.

Graham's career was cut short, sadly. He lost the belt less than a year after winning it in a loss to Bob Backlund. Shortly after, Graham took time off to heal. The steroids he used to build his body into a Greek god seemed to work on him like a new paint job on a Cadillac. It looked good, but....

He made several comebacks, but he would never regain the health or status he had in the 1970s. He briefly appeared in the WWF, Florida, and Texas as a ninja-type, which added depth to his character. But by the 1980s, another new era emerged, which Graham helped introduce: the era of the muscle head.

Inside his body, the steroid abuse was ravaging his sculpted frame. He's had dozens of minor injuries and surgeries because of the damage from drugs. He's had multiple artificial hips, has shattered both ankles like glass and has a collapsed spine. Because of hepatitis C, he was searching for a liver transplant.

Graham has warned anyone within earshot about the evils of steroid abuse. The steroids changed Graham's appearance, but his success as an attraction due to the drugs changed the face of wrestling. As much as Superstar helped bring in a new batch of wisecracking underdogs, he brought in the muscles. Many of the current muscle-toned ranks of wrestlers and anti-heroes owe something to Billy Graham.

Muhammad Ali blasts a stare at his opponent, wrestler Antonio Inoki, during their match from 1976.

Inoki versus Ali: Boxing and wrestling cross their similar paths

Wrestling promoters have seemingly always had an affection for pro boxing. Some pre-World War II promoters hosted both boxing and wrestling shows. Chris Dundee of Miami promoted wrestling for several decades. During the late 1940s and early 1950s, Dundee supplanted his boxing penchant with profits made through wrestling. His brother, Angelo, finally hit pay dirt in the 1950s, and the Dundees guided Willie Pastrano to the world's light heavyweight title. Angelo hit it big in the 1960s as Muhammad Ali's corner man.

Muhammad Ali, who highly respected wrestlers, speaks to Bobo Brazil backstage.

Dundee later co-trained Sugar Ray Leonard, and was with the Olympian during his Hall of Fame fights.

Both Ali and Leonard crossed paths with professional wrestling. Leonard, in one of his numerous comebacks, battled Canadian Donny Lalonde in a fight co-promoted by Vince McMahon Jr. Ali's foray into wrestling was both glorious and tainted. Ali said he took a page out of Gorgeous George's playbook. Ali, after he saw that George made money with his flair, decided to copy some of the wrestler's style.

Did the greatest boxer ever really know Gorgeous George? Ali said in interviews that he and George once appeared together on a Las Vegas television show and, after seeing George, invented his own persona that day. Historians doubt the meeting ever took place, because George was out of the limelight before Ali ever became a pro. But who knows?

Ali's wrestling career was unique to say the least. In 1976, he bit the bait that Japanese promoters had dangled in front of him when he agreed to a multi-million dollar fight in Tokyo against the Brazilian-trained judo and karate star, Antonio Inoki. After being out of boxing for several years, due to his suspension for refusing to enter the draft, Ali needed an influx of cash. And Inoki needed the boost that Ali would give him in Japan. Fans in that country were still recovering from the murder of pro-wrestling pioneer Rikidozan in 1963, and the only other star was Inoki's former stable mate, Giant Baba. Baba ran All-Japan wrestling. Inoki and partner Seiji Sakaguchi were promoting through the rival group, New Japan wrestling.

To prime himself and pump some enthusiasm into the match-up, Ali went on a public relations blitz throughout the United States. His first challenge was against AWA cult heroes Kenny Jay and Buddy Wolfe. Fred Blassie helped as Ali's corner man, and Verne Gagne refereed. The match-up was held before a standing-room-only crowd. As always, Jay gave it his best, but he lost an early round knockout by Ali. Shortly after, Ali battled Gorilla Monsoon just prior to the Tokyo match. Things got out of control when Monsoon threw Ali out of the ring.

The Ali versus Inoki bout, which took place in June 1976 from Budokan Hall in Tokyo, was seen globally on closed-circuit television. In Japan, fans paid around $1,000 to sit ringside. Shown as part of a joint card at Shea Stadium in New York, a crowd of 32,000 witnessed the broadcast. Was it real? Was it fixed? Was it both? What exactly happened between the two that evening will be something a privileged few take to their graves. Most insiders contend the famed mixed martial arts match was 100-percent real. Others, such as the hometown Japanese fans, called it a real phony.

Most viewers were bored and felt ripped off. Visually, it was one of the most boring events ever staged. Up until bell-time, the rules were contested. It is said that Ali was allowed to grapple, punch, and use takedowns. Inoki, though, was barred from using leg dives and tackles, his main arsenal. And the language barrier was clearly evident.

Both camps felt double-crossed by the other. Ali supposedly agreed to a wrestling-styled match and finish while Inoki wanted a rumble. One insider theory suggests that Ali was prepared to back out of the match, but at the last minute, he convinced Inoki not to use his hands.

If that is true, Inoki indeed cooperated. Rather than stand tall and trade any type of hand-to-hand combat, he lay on his back for the entire 15 rounds. The strategy rendered Ali defenseless and offenseless. In fact, Ali looked clueless as Inoki simply kicked away at Ali's legs and thighs. The match was declared a draw. To this day, Ali complains that he was injured by Inoki's offense.

As boring as it was, the match-up created a life of its own through the years, despite the fact there was zero demand for a rematch. Inoki faced a lot of criticism in his home for the apparent fix. In the end, Inoki got what he wanted, and it eventually made him a legend.

Antonio Inoki kicks boxing star Muhammad Ali in their legendary bout from 1976.

The 1980s was a funky decade. Television sensation, MTV, and the cable explosion turned one-hit wonders into short-term pop culture icons. A by-product of the 1970s, wrestling territories still permeated the country. At its peak, the territorial system, in which promoters around the country respected each other's areas to promote in, made up nearly 30 distinct places a wrestler could find work. Though the system was about to be discarded with the help of cable television, it was a good time for wrestlers and fans. Business was up and everyone was happy.

Most every major city was tied to a territory. In Portland, Don Owens kept things going. In the Midwest, Verne Gagne handled Minnesota, the Dakotas, Nebraska, and Wisconsin. Roy Shire promoted California. Jim Crockett's Mid-Atlantic group made waves in Virginia and the Carolinas. Jerry Jarrett was in charge of Tennessee and the surrounding region. And on it went.

There is no easy explanation for the demise of the territories. Most point to Vince McMahon Jr., who took his New York-based World Wrestling Federation nationally. McMahon's strategy was to put every regional promoter out of business by stealing their top name talent. Some of the original names he pried away include Jesse Ventura and Hulk Hogan from the AWA, and Roddy Piper from the Mid-Atlantic group.

Cable television was another reason. For the first time, programs from other parts of the country, which fans never saw before, built an aura of competition. It was an interesting time to be a fan. If you lived in Chicago, you had watched Fred Kohler's wrestling. Then, suddenly for the first time, different groups headed to Chicago. Fans had a chance to see new stars, and it happened everywhere. The old-time promoters felt the squeeze in their hometowns.

In other cases, promoters unwittingly burned their loyal fan bases. After delivering top-shelf shows for nearly 25 years, nonsensical storylines and a dismal corps of wrestlers caused Gagne's American Wrestling Association

Nick Bockwinkel was one of the classiest wrestlers to wear the AWA world title.

The greatest team ever, Michael Hayes and Terry Gordy, interviewed by Harry Thornton.

to pull the plug. Although Gagne's son, Greg, was an exceptional technician, fans no longer believed that at 35 years old and 180 pounds he could beat a 280-pound monster like Bruiser Brody. Verne himself made comeback and retirement tours so often, that any credibility he had with his fans was lost.

The Gagnes were not alone. Regional promoters had ample opportunity and resources to compete with McMahon's WWF. Those other groups simply made bad business decisions; decisions that made it hard for fans to root for the home team any longer. The wrestlers who had stuck around through loyalty could no longer sail on a sinking ship.

Failing to change with the times wasn't the only problem facing promoters of the 1980s. In Dallas, the family-run business led by Jack Adkisson reached empire status. Adkisson, who wrestled as Fritz Von Erich, had success himself. Before his wrestling days, he was a football player at Southern Methodist University. In the ring, he played the part of a German-sympathizer, complete with goose step

Jerry Lawler drops his famed closed fist on a motionless foe.

and a finishing move called the iron claw. He promoted Texas, but, after a falling out with the National Wrestling Alliance, he founded World Class Championship Wrestling in Dallas. Von Erich, as he was known publicly, envisioned an entertainment group unparalleled in wrestling. He had the booking and media savvy. Most of all, he had his family to present to the public.

At one time, World Class was seen on dozens of television networks worldwide. Von Erich had five wrestling sons and all were groomed as hometown boys. They were presented as dynamic, good-looking family members who epitomized small-town America. Aimed at the teenager market, the Von Erichs took over the state. Sons Kevin, David, Mike, Kerry, and Chris were all, at one time, the oyster in the eye of Dallas teenagers.

Sold-out crowds were a weekly guarantee at the Sportatorium and annual Super Cards at sold-out major venues followed. The wrestling sons cultivated fan worship to a new level. The boys were John Travolta, Elvis, and the Dallas Cowboys all rolled into one.

Through much of the 1980s, World Class was as hot as any promotion in America. The Fabulous Freebirds, Michael Hayes, Terry Gordy, and Buddy Roberts had career performances there and cemented their place in history as the greatest working unit in wrestling history. Veterans like Iceman Parsons, Bill Irwin, Ken Mantel, Skandor Akbar, Gary Hart, Jimmy Garvin, One Man Gang, Chris Adams, the Fantastics, and Eric Embry found homes for themselves working for Von Erich. Newcomers like the Simpsons, the Dingo Warrior, Jack Victory, John Tatum, Precious, Sunshine, and later, Steve Austin, all received opportunities to hone their skills in the territory at one time.

Though the outside of the Von Erich phenomenon looked great, no one envisioned the turmoil that lay inside. Family problems of the largest magnitude caused the territory's early and tragic demise. The family was an American success story. But overnight, it turned into a nightmare. The problems began with the death of wrestler Gino Hernandez in 1984, at age 29. News that his death was due to a drug overdose went public and started a ripple effect that would hit the family hard.

Adkisson's first son, Jack Jr., died from electrocution in a farm accident in 1959. The family then went a quarter century before facing adversity again. Once the adversity came, it never stopped. Things began to cave in February 1984, with the death of David Von Erich, at age 25, from acute enteritis while on tour in Japan. Papa Fritz, bordering on good taste, made fans in Dallas pay $5 each to attend his son's memorial service. Later, the family profited greatly from the memorial show, called the Parade of Champions, in May 1984. On that card, the sterling Kerry Von Erich, wearing the yellow rose of Texas to honor his fallen brother, won the NWA world title from Ric Flair before a crowd of 40,000 at Texas Stadium.

The family was rocked by David's death. Rumors that David died of a drug overdose circulated. Then, in 1987, Mike Von Erich, 23, committed suicide after learning he would never wrestle again because of a bout with toxic shock syndrome. In September 1991, the youngest son, Chris, took his own life at age 21.

Kerry, who was the most successful of the five siblings, had a tumultuous career. His ring accomplishments were many and he reached the top with his

In this corner, is WWE announcer, Howard Finkel!

Many female fans loved the dashing Rick Martel.

win over Flair. Later on, in the early 1990s, he wrestled for Vince McMahon and won that group's Intercontinental title. A massive injury in the late 1980s, suffered in a motorcycle accident, left him with his foot partially amputated. Though the amputation was kept well hidden for several years, Kerry became addicted to pain relievers. His dependency led to him forging prescriptions. Just days after being indicted for drug possession in 1993, Kerry took his own life at age 33.

Only Kevin, the eldest son, remains. He, like Kerry, had a brilliant wrestling career. He was a multi-time regional champion and he also had several NWA world title matches. Kevin quit the wrestling profession shortly after Kerry's death. He resides with his family in Texas, where they embrace their Christian faith to bring them through tough times. In 1998, Fritz Von Erich passed away at age 68 from a bout with cancer.

By the mid-1990s, Fritz Von Erich handed over control of his promotion to several promoters who tried to save it. Memphis promoters Jerry Jarrett and Jerry Lawler bought the company, merged it with their own United States Wrestling Association, and aired programs on the ESPN network. The Global Wrestling Federation, run by former announcer Joe Pedicino, gave a valiant effort to jumpstart the area after Jarrett gave up. Global focused on ring work, and is noted for giving opportunities to wrestlers like Sean Waltman, Jerry Lynn, Raven, and Marcus Bagwell. It was a chance for the little guys to show their wares on the main stage. Eventually, any promoter there had to accept the inevitable death of the territory.

The Freebirds in their famous shot sporting Dixie war paint.

In Canada, Bruce Hart tried to keep his father's Stampede promotion afloat. After a mid-1980's buyout, the group lost most of its proven stars to the World Wrestling Federation. Badd Company (Hart and Brian Pillman), the powerhouse Larry Cameron, and technician Chris Benoit did their best to save the fledgling territory. In 1991, poor box office attendance forced the Hart family to end the six-decade old group. Down but not out, Hart revived the Calgary territory again on a limited basis.

Passion and excitement defined Jim Ross, shown here in his Mid-South announcing days.

Out West, one of the oldest surviving groups was Owens' Portland Championship Wrestling. During the years it operated, a laundry list of wrestling greats traveled through the area. Roddy Piper cut his teeth there. Buddy Rose, Jesse Ventura, Dutch Savage, Col. DeBeers, and others wrestled for the group, which was an ally of the NWA. Somewhere, the small-town appeal of the group was lost with the fans. Eventually, the lack of solid television exposure forced Owens to say goodnight.

And fans said goodnight in return, to a territorial system that had dominated North America.

Davey Boy Smith and Dynamite Kid made up the duo, the British Bulldogs.

Jerry Lawler sports his classic "King" outfit, which brought thousands of fans through the turnstiles.

The makings of a wrestling champion

Champions are the biggest focal point of any wrestling group. Throughout history, the holder of the belt, and the chase to capture the belt, have been points of interest for the masses. Today's wrestling builds larger-than-life stars with movie-like storylines. But is there a more compelling drama than that of the chase for the championship?

Champions in wrestling have to be larger-than-life. The gold they wear cements their status. World-class football players, weightlifters, karate stars, amateur wrestlers, boxers, and other sports stars have tried to chase pro wrestling titles, and most of them fail. For every amateur standout like Kurt Angle who succeeds, there seems to be a number of Laurent Soucies who don't make the transition to being a professional.

For every celebrated football player, such as Bill Goldberg and Ron Simmons, there are hundreds of ex-gridiron greats like Lawrence Taylor and Reggie White who could barely lace up their boots. For every world-class weightlifter, like Mark Henry or Ken Patera who do make it as wrestlers, there are men like Bill Kazmeier who simply don't make the grade.

Wrestling champions are rare breeds. Few in any field are as talented at what they do. They must adhere to long or short-term feuds, be loyal employees, be uniquely charismatic, and have athletic talents. Wrestling champions truly earn their moniker as the kings of sports. To become a champion, wrestlers have to be special people.

Sex appeal is important, too. In the men's ranks, a wrestler has to be appealing to women, but not too intimidating to other men. There must also be the illusion that he can be beaten any night. It's easy to build a monster contender, but in grooming a champion, the fan must be able to believe the match they are witnessing could be a title change. That's what makes fans pay to see them. Baseball philosopher Branch Ricky once said, "You're only as good as your opponents, and just a bit better than those you beat." In wrestling, that theory couldn't be more appropriate.

In music, the greatest of the greats are known by their first or last name: Sinatra, Michael, Elvis, Garth, Madonna. In pro wrestling, the name says it all: Thesz, Bruno, Race, Inoki, Flair, Hogan, and Austin. Declaring who is the greatest is subjective. Baseball, boxing, and football have stats to gauge the best, but even they can be tweaked to make a case. Wrestling doesn't have that luxury. We generally gauge the greats by their longevity, impact, and gate appeal. It also comes down to our individual preferences.

For added legitimacy in the 1980s, you needn't look further than Ric Flair for inspiration. As the total package, Flair had everything one dreams of. Few men in any sport can claim the success that Flair has had in wrestling. Whether it's 12, 14, or 16 world titles—who is keeping count? He's one of the most celebrated champions of all time. It was through hard work and countless miles of traveling around the world that made him a great one. After breaking into the business as a pudgy, 250-pound rookie in the early 1970s, Flair looked better suited for another career.

After suffering a broken back in an October 1975 plane crash in North Carolina, Flair worked at rehabilitating himself. When he returned, he earned, and kept, his main-event status up to the Millennium. Because the National Wrestling Alliance belt was still recognized globally throughout the 1980s, Flair, as the NWA champion, was in more top-level feuds than any other wrestler alive. Take all of the top names of the 1980s, throw them in a hat, and Flair has probably wrestled them at one time or another.

Crossing the generational gap became an art for Flair. His wars with Ricky Steamboat, Wahoo McDaniel, Harley Race, Bruiser Brody, Ivan Koloff, Ron Garvin, Dusty Rhodes, Sting, the Funks, the Von Erichs, the Briscos, and others kept NWA promoters alive. In the 1990s, Flair ventured briefly to the World Wrestling Federation where he expanded his list of opponents and cemented his name in the history books. His feuds with Bret Hart, Randy Savage, Curt Hennig, and Roddy Piper were classics. He returned to World Championship Wrestling in 1995 where he feuded with Kevin Nash, Big Van Vader, Diamond Dallas Page, and Rick Rude.

Was Flair the greatest ever? Even better than Thesz? As a pure technician, Thesz would win hands down. Based on professional wrestling qualifications, a strong case can be made for either.

Flair wore versions of the world title 17 times over a 30-year career. Thesz, a champion from a different era where title changes happened sporadically, is merely a six-time NWA titleholder. Both Flair and Thesz were global champions. Thesz's longest title run was from 1948 to 1954. Flair, on the other hand, had his longest title reign of 26 months from May 1984 to July 1986. Thesz's unbeatable days would seem to dwarf Flair's many reigns. Even The Rock, with just several years as a pro, has been the world champion at least seven times.

In his prime, Flair wrestled in a harder-paced style of the day. That style also left him vulnerable to injuries, however, but he stayed relatively healthy. Flair also fended off threats by muscled-up powerhouses. Many champions of yesteryear couldn't have stayed afloat in today's brand of wrestling. Athletically, Thesz probably could have, but he likely would have been forced to add bulk to his frame.

Thesz holds victories over world champions over a five-decade span. He remarkably had wins over Gorgeous George, Pat O'Connor, Killer Kowalski, Bill Watts, Verne Gagne, Leo Nomellini, Whipper Watson, Dick the Bruiser, Bob Orton Sr., Buddy Rogers, Karl Gotch, Fritz Von Erich, and virtually every star of the NWA. He also held wins over England's Lord Layton, and Japan's Giant Baba and Antonio Inoki on their home turf.

Flair's career was never based around the Orient like Thesz's was, but Flair had successful tours in Japan. In the case of Flair, he transcended styles and trends. No matter how hard the powers-that-be tried to cast off the Charlotte native, Flair always rose above the

Former UWF heavyweight champion, Terry Gordy, had a productive career.

On the set of his breakout film "Predator" is Jesse Ventura.

That's Brutus Beefcake in his days as Dizzy Ed Boulder.

Larry Zbyszko shows Sgt. Slaughter who's the boss.

Mean Gene speaks to the crowd.

turmoil. Fans who grew up watching wrestling in the 1980s have vivid memories of the prestigious-looking Flair holding the NWA world title. He became the wrestler by which all other champions were measured.

Flair lived his gimmick, arriving to arenas in limousines and always carrying his 10 pounds of gold that was the NWA world title. He wasn't limited to just being a gimmick wrestler, though. In the ring, not many came close to Flair's ability. He could chain wrestle, brawl if he had to, and he never lost control of a match. He was in charge at all times. Who else could have five-star performances with Steamboat one afternoon, and then bring a muscled-out freak like Road Warrior Hawk to an exciting bout the next night?

Because Flair was the NWA champion, and many smaller regional groups still recognized the NWA title as their own, Flair traveled around the country reminiscent of the good old days. He may have been in Gainesville, Ga., one night and Dallas the next. Flair was regularly taking bookings in Missouri, Georgia, Texas, Oregon, and Japan.

Lawler and Kaufman stage wrestling's best trick ever

"I'm from Hollywood," was the repeated mantra of comedian Andy Kaufman on the weekly Memphis wrestling programs in 1982. The television star, known for his unpredictability, was intrigued by wrestling. He always appreciated the talent wrestlers had in duping the public. Wrestling, Kaufman figured, was the perfect place for him to be himself.

At first, Kaufman joked around and seemed intent on only wrestling women. Within weeks, he was the headline attraction at the Mid-South Coliseum and involved in one of the most talked about wrestling feuds in history. His feud with Jerry "The King" Lawler would change the face of both men's careers. Even twenty years removed, it's still remembered for its brilliance.

Kaufman sold the feud like his life depended on it. The viewing public was baffled by Kaufman's bits. He would show up on talk shows and variety shows and openly challenge women to wrestle. Prior to his battles in Memphis, Kaufman claimed to have beaten hundreds of women. Kaufman was unorthodox in his ring style and looked gangly, if not sick, in his wrestling gimmick. He was having fun, to say the least. Kaufman reportedly had a wrestling ring in his basement, which he took on his standup tours. Even close friends like Robin Williams thought Kaufman had lost his mind.

Kaufman certainly met his match in Lawler. At the time, Lawler was one of Memphis' most-recognizable figures. He had a local talk show and was a former disc jockey. Lawler also headlined most of the Coliseum's weekly cards. Matchmaker Eddie Marlin chose from a wide array of talent to fit the Monday night cards. In those days, few wrestlers around the country faced a more beastly cadre of characters as Lawler did. From Armstrong to Zukoff, the King battled them all. He wasn't about to let a Hollywood type like Kaufman show him up.

Kaufman first came to the Coliseum offering $5000 to any woman who could pin him in 10 minutes. After beating a few women on the weekly shows he upped the ante to $10,000, and his hand in matrimony, if he lost. He claimed to pick his opponents anonymously. Folks just shook their heads at the whole spectacle.

When Kaufman began to rub his opponents' faces into the canvas mat, Lawler decided it was time to put the whole mess to a halt. He entered the ring, warned the comic to lighten up and shoved him. In an angle a four-year-old could have seen coming, the first Lawler versus Kaufman match was scheduled for April 1982.

The build-up to the main event was straight out of Wrestling Promoting 101. Kaufman insulted Memphis fans and attacked everything from their hygiene to their country ways. Lawler, in turn, promised to shut Kaufman's mouth.

With around 8,000 fans watching, Lawler entered the ring to the theme from *Rocky*. Kaufman came out with his friends and manager, Jimmy Hart, who was a long-time nemesis with Lawler. Kaufman stalled for 10 minutes even before he entered the ring. When the two finally entered the ring it was over in less than a minute.

Lawler allowed Kaufman to take the lead with a headlock. The King reversed it into a suplex and Kaufman was out cold. To further punish the "Taxi" co-star,

Lawler gave him a piledriver. When the King gave him a second piledriver for good measure, the crowd sat in wonderment.

Kaufman was carried out and taken to nearby St. Francis Hospital. That night, local newscaster Jack Eaton even reported that Kaufman was in traction. The media attention eventually led to an appearance on the "David Letterman Show." Like so many had reacted already, Letterman didn't know what to make of the whole ordeal. Kaufman went into a tirade and threw water on Lawler. Lawler threw a huge slap at the neck brace-wearing Kaufman. Lawler and Kaufman clearly duped the world.

This was still an era when most fans were in the dark about what they were seeing. While only a few fans truly believed wrestling was real, most others still believed a certain portion. The mainstream media coverage added attention and believability to the angle.

After the first battle, the two were just getting warmed up. The grudge match aftermath lasted for several months. Kaufman continued to wear the neck brace and insult Memphis. He even accompanied other foes against the King. The Masked Assassins, a goon named Colossus, and former Olympian Ken Patera arrived in Memphis to collect on Kaufman's bounty he placed on Lawler.

Jerry Lawler sports his battle gear to rile fans.

Tonga Kid and Roddy Piper had a memorable feud in the WWF.

Two Georgia broadcast legends, Gordon Solie and Freddy Miller.

Ric Flair was often turned upside down by his many opponents.

Austin Idol looks for revenge.

Who was the bigger beast? The Swamp Thing or Bam Bam Bigelow?

Kaufman's television co-stars, Tony Danza, Marilu Henner, and his manager, Bob Zmuda, still wonder about the comic's sanity, even years after his death from cancer in 1984 at age 35. There was one thing Zmuda didn't question, though. He said he never saw Kaufman happier than when he was in Memphis. The general feeling with Kaufman was, "you never know." Real or contrived, it doesn't much matter. The King and the Man on the Moon put together one of the most memorable wrestling gimmicks of modern times.

Road Warriors explode on the scene

When the Road Warriors burst on the scene in 1982, they became the most successful phenomenon in the history of professional wrestling. Not only were they huge draws on television and at the gate, they became one of the most emulated gimmicks since Gorgeous George. Promoters scrambled to find other muscular youngsters to push, and literally everyone at one time employed wrestlers who wore face paint.

Prior to the Roadies' first appearance on cable channel WTBS and its "Georgia Championship Wrestling" program, few wrestlers wore face paint. There were Kabuki sightings here or a Mongol sighting there, but once the Warriors hit the scene, their paint became as essential to their gimmicks as their haircuts and motorcycle boots. They were a hot commodity and trendsetters that caused sellouts everywhere. Not bad for two guys who barely knew each other.

By the end of their major run, the Road Warriors held world tag-team titles in three major organizations. The team's beginning was more humble. The 6-1, 250-pound Mike Hegstrand was known throughout the tough Minneapolis areas and had boxing experience. He hardly

would have been picked as most likely to succeed.

The 5-11, 265-pound Joe Laurinidas was called too short for football. Though he was academically literate, he was no bookworm. After dismissing football as a career, he tried his luck as a bar bouncer, where he met Hegstrand. It was at a Minneapolis bar where trainer Eddie Sharkey discovered the two. Laurinidas was tentative about wrestling at first, but after taking a few bumps at a local gym, he was eager to give the ring sport a try. Hegstrand was all for it.

In 1981, Laurinidas and Hegstrand trained at Sharkey's gym. Rick Rood (Rick Rude), Scott Simpson (Nikita Koloff), and Barry Darsow (Krusher Kruschev/Demolition) all graduated from the class. Ted Russell (Savannah Jack), Scott Norton, and a handful of other wrestlers stopped in from time to time. When it was time to graduate from the camp, Hegstrand was the first to find work with a small promotion. But Laurinidas got the first call to big-time wrestling.

By 1982, Ole Anderson, a longtime ally of Sharkey's, had recently earned the position to organize the WTBS Superstation wrestling show. Anderson loved using pop culture and hit films for ideas to use in wrestling. After seeing Mel Gibson's first mega hit, *The Road Warrior*, Anderson was sure he had a gimmick that would lead his group into the future. He was impressed with what he saw in Laurinidas, and was especially impressed with his toughness. The rookie was known to pop his own knee back into place if it dislocated at wrestling workouts. Anderson took notice.

Anderson booked Laurinidas for the Georgia program and called him the

Road Warrior. In his first appearance, he looked more like an outcast from the Village People. Soon, his speed, aggression, and size made him an exciting newcomer. Anderson decided to make Hegstrand, who had an unsuccessful stint as Headsick Hegstrand in British Columbia, the second Road Warrior. He simply expanded on the Headsick gimmick, added face paint, and the Hawk was born. Fellow Minnesotan Paul Ellering was included as their manager, and the Legion of Doom soon started their trip as the fastest rising tag team in history.

With Ted Turner declaring WTBS to be his national superstation, the Road Warriors couldn't have been invented at a better time. Teens were enamored by the duo, and afforded them a type of hero worship saved for pop-culture icons. Even older, disillusioned fans etched watching the Georgia wrestling program into their weekly routine.

Every wrestling magazine put the Road Warriors on their cover. People couldn't get enough of them. They weren't just originators, they were impact draws. Hawk's running clothesline and the tandem's top-rope spike demonstrated their ability to portray a dangerous team. Animal's power moves (he once body slammed King Kong Bundy and Jerry Blackwell, a combined 700 pounds, in consecutive moves) were feats of strength not seen in wrestling since the days of Bruno Sammartino. Animal's double gorilla press slam of Terry Gordy will forever be watched in awe.

The Road Warriors were limited in their ring experience, but their muscular stature, power moves, and intense interviews brought an air of excitement, reality, and danger to the television screens. The duo seemed unbeatable, and

Stu Hart has his hands full with Bengal tiger, Chi-Chi.

Kerry Von Erich, en-route to winning the world title, locks in his famous claw hold on Ric Flair.

the demand for them was high. For many, they were must-see performers. The Road Warriors could only be in one place at one time. They had gotten to most regional territories, but there weren't enough dates on the calendar to meet the demand. In the later 1980s, promoters created their own Road Warrior-like concoctions.

Ric Flair shows his paycheck following a big win over Dusty Rhodes at Starrcade.

Mr. T and Hulk Hogan prepare for their appearance at Wrestlemania I.

Barely trained and face-painted beginners sprouted everywhere. Midgets, women, monsters, maniacs, and even main-event attractions like the Freebirds wore face paint at one time. Some of the copycats caught on. Sting and the Ultimate Warrior, after a brief run in the Mid-South as the Blade Runners, caught on as single wrestlers. Chiseled frames seemed to become a mandatory element to be a wrestler. The look remains prevalent today.

Face paint gave the Missing Link (Dewey Robertson) and Jim Harris (Kimala) new life. The Terminators, the New Breed, Rick Link, and countless others fell by the wayside. Demolition (Bill Eadie and Darsow) survived the shakeout and won World Wrestling Federation tag-team titles. Even though promoters had been excited to use bodybuilders, once the Road Warriors hit the scene, wrestling was never the same. Even the high-flyers Davey Boy Smith and Dynamite Kid had to bulk up before they started with the WWF.

The 1980s were wild and fast times. Cable television, MTV, the WWF explosion, rock videos, special effects, and 24-hour sports networks all made impacts. The Road Warriors enjoyed being part of the fast changing times and helped bring wrestling into the next era.

Hulkamania was built

The film *Rocky* made the perennial underdog, Sylvester Stallone, a household name. He once said the movie was adapted from his own struggle as an aspiring screenwriter. In making the preceding "Rocky" flicks, he reserved numerous roles for would-be stars and he had a keen eye for potential. Burgess Meredith and Talia Shire became household names due to their parts in the *Rocky* cast. He also helped former football star Carl Weathers, kick boxer

Dolph Lundgren, toughman contest winner Mr. T, and then-struggling pro wrestler Hulk Hogan get their starts in Hollywood.

Weathers became a serviceable actor with solid efforts in *Predator* and *Happy Gilmore*. Lundgren became an action star and was commendable with Brandon Lee in *Showdown in Little Tokyo*. Mr. T became a cult favorite in the "A-Team" series and played an important part in Wrestlemania I and II. And the then-gawky Hogan went on to appear in dozens of films. Before all that happened, Hogan's performance as Thunderlips in *Rocky III* made the wrestling world take notice.

Hogan had already toured Japan and many American territories in the Southeast. In 1979, he debuted in Vince McMahon Sr.'s, World Wide Wrestling Federation as Sterling Golden. Sometimes he worked a promotion as the brother of Ed Boulder, who later wrestled as Brutus Beefcake. In Tennessee, Hogan's paydays were allegedly so small that he had to sleep on a couch at the apartment of fellow wrestler Wayne Ferris. Ferris was later known as the Honky Tonk Man.

Hogan had arrived in the American Wrestling Association in 1981, as a heel alongside manager Johnny Valiant. At around this time, he agreed to work in Stallone's movie. While in the AWA, Hogan was a curiosity. Fans liked him, but he was promoted as a rule breaker. The territory used John Studd, Andre the Giant, and Billy Graham in the past, but never for long stints. The AWA concentrated on wrestling skills and never really pushed bigger men. And for good reason; many of them could not perform well in the ring.

When *Rocky III* was released in 1982, fans began to clamor for Hogan. The promoters were forced to use him more and listened to the fans' demands. Valiant and Hogan's heel act was exited stage left. Once Hogan was allowed to build his persona, which was in part Thunderlips, things began to click for him. Hogan began to play the part fans wanted to see: the 6-6 movie star with 22-inch pythons. By 1983, Hulkamania was well on its way.

Hogan enjoyed a special on-camera relationship with announcer Gene Okerlund. Okerlund could sell a card with the best. As part of an all-star cast that included Nick Bockwinkel, Jesse Ventura, Mad Dog Vachon, and Baron Von Raschke, Hogan was involved in numerous sold-out crowds in the AWA. He coined the St. Paul Civic Center the "House that Hogan built." Hulkamania did run wild. He developed an insanely campy six-man team with Buck Zumhoff and Raschke and often faced a band of heels presented by manager Bobby Heenan.

By 1983, fans demanded the opportunity to see Hogan break out as a singles star. Even during the slower moments of the summer, Hogan drew sold-out crowds in St. Paul. Eventually, a series of title matches were scheduled for Hogan against the world champion, Bockwinkel. The wily Bockwinkel was in his third AWA title reign and possessed enough ring savvy to draw money with the challenger. The AWA's promoters had big plans for Hogan. They feuded for nearly a year, with matches ending in count-outs and disqualifications.

Hulkamania created an unprecedented buzz around the circuit. In April 1983, it reached a new level. On a card named Super Sunday, Bockwinkel and Hogan packed 18,000 frenzied fans

into the Civic Center, and another 10,000 fans jammed into an adjacent building on closed-circuit television. Hogan originally won the title, but the decision was reversed which caused a lot of fan frustration.

Despite his undeniable popularity and strength at the box office, Hogan never was awarded a title in the AWA. Bockwinkel was a noble champion, but he also knew how to put his own ego aside for the good of the business. Allegedly, Hogan was actually penciled in to win the AWA title at the 1983 Christmas show. Hogan no-showed the card. He admits he left because he wanted the chance to wrestle in Japan for

Buddy Roberts, Michael Hayes and Terry Gordy made up the unmistakable Fabulous Freebirds trio.

Roddy Piper and actor Keith David pose for a moment while filming John Carpenter's They Live.

Joe Pedicino with wife, Bonnie Blackstone, during a taping of "Pro Wrestling This Week."

Jimmy Hart was adamant about crossing out Jerry Lawler in their classic 80s feud.

Andre the Giant in his memorable role in the film, The Princess Bride.

One crossover to the silver screen was the brash, Rowdy Roddy Piper.

Today, the feud between Jesse Ventura and Hulk Hogan, continues to be waged.

No rings were big enough to hold the egos of Hulk Hogan and Jesse Ventura.

Hulk Hogan sizes up his No. 1 nemesis, Jesse Ventura, in an AWA struggle.

Muhammad Ali reaches for Roddy Piper at Wrestlemania I in 1985.

big paydays in addition to his work in the AWA. But Gagne wouldn't allow it unless he shared in the profits. So Hogan bolted. Some say that when Hogan left, it spelled the end for the AWA. It never was the same, and in 1990, the promotion closed forever.

Naturally, Hogan left for greener pastures. He entered the WWF in January 1984, during a hostile time. Owner Vince McMahon Jr., was breaking territorial lines and raiding talent from all over the country. A full-fledged wrestling war was declared. On January 23, 1984, Hogan officially declared Hulkamania by defeating the Iron Sheik at Madison Square Garden for the WWF crown. The WWF was arguably the most powerful U.S. promotion. Past champions like Bruno Sammartino, Bob Backlund, and Superstar Graham were all stellar attractions. Hogan followed their large footsteps and became an internationally known star.

Hogan held versions of the world title 11 times. Over the course of his career, he helped create a character that seemed bulletproof and took wrestling to places only McMahon envisioned. After leaving the AWA, Hogan hung out with Hollywood power brokers, endorsed hundreds of products with his likeness, appeared on major talk shows, starred in a cable television series, "Thunder in Paradise," and enjoyed being part of sold-out crowds over three decades.

Stallone could have used any one of a thousand wrestlers to appear in *Rocky III*. As history shows, his decision to use Hogan was a wise one. For Hogan, the opportunity was a gift from God. Joining the AWA was a stroke of luck, and leaving it was a stroke of brilliance. It changed pro wrestling forever, and made Hulk Hogan one of America's most recognizable celebrities.

Carlos Colon and The Invader, once a popular tandem in Puerto Rico.

Standing with his manager, Andy Kaufman, is the mean Ken Patera, which shows the comic's role in wrestling was no joke.

Ric Flair sports his "ten pounds of gold," the NWA world championship.

Two wild men, T-Joe Khan and the Barbarian, while filming the cult classic, Body Slam.

In his younger days, is svelte, Savannah Jack.

Before his Texas wrestling days, Fritz Von Erich was known for having a hated German gimmick.

The ladies loved Kerry Von Erich. Here, he thrills the St. Louis Cardinals cheerleaders.

Three legends of Memphis: Jerry Jarrett, left, Tojo Yamamoto and Jackie Fargo.

Wrestlemania I, which showcased a tag-team match including Hulk Hogan and Roddy Piper, put the WWE on the map in 1985.

The face-painted Road Warriors, Hawk and Animal.

6

THE WWF AND WCW WARS

When the 1980s ended, professional wrestling was like a starlet in need of a makeover. The decade of Wrestlemania, and the emergence of two main organizations—the World Wrestling Federation and World Championship Wrestling—brought the industry to its most profitable days. Just a few years away, some major cosmetic changes were about to take place.

Suddenly, as the early 1990s appeared, wrestling wasn't cool to the masses anymore. At one point in 1993 and 1994, arenas that had often been filled were drawing less than 1,000 people at the gate. The cartoon and comic-book acts that had permeated wrestling were turnoffs.

Under the surface, things were about to bubble over in a big way. For two decades, wrestling was known as the home of the big man. The Ultimate Warrior, Rick Rude, Davey Boy Smith, Hercules, Billy Jack Haynes, Ken Patera, and Brutus Beefcake were the muscled icons of Vince McMahon Jr.'s, WWF. For years, the size of that group's roster became an insider joke. Surely they must be on steroids, everyone thought. Even to non-fans, it seemed that to be a successful wrestler, you must be freakishly big.

Sure enough, years later, wrestlers admit to having taken steroids to enhance their appearance. But at the time, everyone denied it. Even Hulk Hogan himself, on an episode of the "Arsenio Hall Show," said he was clean of drugs. The steroid controversy was met head on, in 1993, when McMahon and his company were indicted on charges of steroid distribution. McMahon says the indictments were part of a larger plan to cripple the WWF, in what he has called a "witch hunt" by the federal government.

Whatever the reason behind the charges, it served to bring the apparent drug scandal to the forefront. In 1994, McMahon was put on trial. Several wrestlers who had worked for him, including Hogan, Jim Hellwig (Ultimate Warriors), and Rude had to testify against McMahon. After a two-week

A man of many faces, Sting.

D-Lo Brown, left, with Al Snow and Val Venis.

The goofy Red Rooster, Terry Taylor.

Dr. Death, Steve Williams, was an amateur star in college at Oklahoma.

Tom Horner stops by with Brian Pillman and Tom Zenk during a WCW card.

The Rock gets a hold on the legend, Jerry Lawler.

trial, McMahon was acquitted of the charges. Had he been found guilty, the scandal almost surely would have toppled his empire. Even with the acquittal, it nearly did.

No one figured fans would react negatively to McMahon's troubles with the law, but that's what happened. His business dropped to all-time lows. There were even rumors the multi-media juggernaut was close to filing bankruptcy. The WWF never closed its doors and continued to promote nationwide. It scaled back its operations and retooled its business plan a bit to accommodate the new climate in wrestling.

The struggles suffered by the WWF opened a window of opportunity to its only competitor, WCW. While the WWF was forced to rid itself of big money talent like Hogan and Savage, WCW, with the money backing of then-owner Ted Turner, hired all the castaways. Leading the way behind the scenes was an unlikely person to wage war with the WWF. As it turned out, some of the biggest changes in wrestling came from an ex-coffee boy.

Eric Bischoff, like so many power brokers in wrestling, grew up in Minnesota. He was known to be somewhat athletic, but his brains and savvy served him best of all. At 5-8, his athletic possibilities were limited, although he did excel in martial arts. He claims to be a black belt and says he has several kick boxing fights to his credit.

He joined the American Wrestling Association, in Minneapolis, during the late, tumultuous 1980s. He spent time politicking with the bosses and hustling new advertising accounts. He was also instrumental in earning the group a renewed deal with 24-hour sports network ESPN.

Only in professional wrestling could a Bischoff-like story be told. When the AWA filed for bankruptcy in 1990, Bischoff wisely looked for work elsewhere. He tried out for an announcing position with the WWF, but was under-qualified. He found takers in WCW. Immediately, his eagerness to do any task was rewarded. He worked tirelessly as an event coordinator, ad salesman, commentator, and assistant television producer. After helping coordinate several tightly run pay-per-views, Bischoff was made the senior producer of television wrestling.

In the fall of 1995, his brightest idea was developing the "Monday Nitro " television concept to battle head-to-head with the WWF's "Monday Night Raw " program. First seen as suicide—who would challenge McMahon straight up?—"Nitro" worked. Rather than get crushed, it was suddenly seen as an alternative product. Bischoff gained power and, with it, the ability to sign talent. He went on a spending spree never seen before in wrestling.

In 1994, Bischoff made one of his biggest hires when he grabbed Hogan from early retirement and brought him to WCW. On his first WCW show, Hogan captured the WCW world title from Ric Flair. As the ratings wars heated up, all eyes were on wrestling. WCW gave new life to retread characters like Hogan, Randy Savage, Roddy Piper, and Paul Orndorff.

With signs of success, Bischoff strutted around WCW's headquarters at CNN Center in Atlanta like a victorious general. The WWF responded by filing lawsuits. The basis of one of the suits stemmed from WCW's illegal usage of television airwaves aimed at destroying the WWF's program on Monday. McMahon also took potshots at Turner by mocking Hogan, Savage, and Turner in a series of tacky, but humorous, skits about "Billionaire Ted."

To make the wars even wilder, Bischoff successfully signed Scott Hall and Kevin Nash, who were toiling in the WWF as Razor Ramon and Diesel. Bischoff called them the Outsiders, and promoted them as invaders from the "other" promotion. And in a stroke of genius, Hogan was convinced to play a rule-breaker character and team with the fresh Hall and Nash. Together, the trio called itself the New World Order. The gimmick made WCW explode in popularity. For the first time ever, WCW was must-see television. Bischoff was given a raise, more power, and the credit for rebuilding the once-floundering company. No one could deny what Bischoff had done.

The success of WCW spawned the greatest television war ever. For over a year, from 1996 to 1997, "Nitro" not only beat "Raw," but also embarrassed the WWF in the ratings. Armchair drop kickers were as intrigued with Tuesday morning ratings results as they were with the action in the ring. Wrestling became so powerful on Monday nights, sometimes garnering a combined audience of 10 million, that even the ratings for "Monday Night Football"

were affected. Many bars and bowling alleys dumped football on television in favor of "Raw" and "Nitro."

Led by WCW, wrestling dominated the cable ratings and dwarfed professional basketball, baseball, boxing, and car racing in numbers. Bischoff hired his pals, like Ernest Miller, and a cadre of ex-WWF standbys like Jim Duggan, Ted DiBiase, Curt Hennig, and Rick Rude. He combined big name stars with some of the best technical wrestling in the world by bringing in Dean Malenko, Ultimo Dragon, Rey Mysterio Jr., Juventud Guerrera, and Eddie Guerrero. The roster was stockpiled with the most expensive and talented wrestlers anywhere.

His show's ratings were built on inspiration. Fans were inspired by the newfound energy of the group. His new ideas in television production and booking were appreciated by the fans.

A young X-Pac, right, then known as Lightning Kid, has a tug-of-war with Jerry Lynn over a title belt.

Brian Pillman takes a moment with friend, Scott Norton.

Chris Benoit challenges a foe.

Boxer Mike Tyson stepped into the ring as a troubleshooting referee.

Marcus Bagwell was once a popular star for WCW.

Randy Savage proudly displays his WCW world championship belt on his way to the ring.

Later, Bill Goldberg and new stars like Dallas Page and Booker T ascended to the top. When the new ideas became standard fare, WCW was left with a whole bunch of unmotivated wrestlers who were more concerned with keeping their million-dollar contracts than the company's well-being. Once at the top of the world, WCW crashed fast.

By summer 1998, Bischoff's WCW was quickly on shaky ground. His pay-per-view match with Jay Leno and recruitment of other non-wrestlers like basketball players Dennis Rodman and Karl Malone netted headlines, but were ill-received by the pure wrestling fans. At times, Bischoff was more concerned with his own celebrity status than continuing the company's growth.

Meanwhile, the WWF was lifting itself out of the doldrums of the steroid scandal. Forced to fight back, the WWF responded to WCW's onslaught by focusing on younger talent. Led by Shawn Michaels and Bret Hart, who became one of the WWF's all-time top champions, fresh faces like Triple H, Mankind, Owen Hart, Road Dogg, and

Steve Austin were allowed to shine. The WWF held tight, although that was really its only option. They lacked star power temporarily, but their pay-per-views were consistently better than WCW's.

Having faced near bankruptcy, McMahon changed his style of promoting. For years, his group was portrayed as the red, white, and blue, All-American company. Forced to change, he borrowed ideas and successes from all over.

First, he copied the hardcore, in-your-face style of Extreme Championship Wrestling, and called it "WWF attitude." He allowed new scriptwriter Vince Russo to inject some raciness into their shows. Most importantly, the company listened to the fans and built itself around the rugged Austin, who was repackaged as "Stone Cold."

One of the moves McMahon made was to lure boxing icon Mike Tyson to be involved as the guest referee at Wrestlemania 14. He also gave monster pushes to former WCW castoffs like Foley, who appeared as Mankind and Cactus Jack, Dustin Rhodes, Marc Mero, Ron Simmons, Triple H, and X-Pac. Austin, who was also castoff from WCW, became wrestling's hottest star by feuding with McMahon himself. By throwing new stars like Chyna and the up-and-coming Rocky Maivia into the mix, the WWF once again became the viewer's choice. By the end of 1998, "Raw" was consistently back on top.

WCW's biggest years in the ratings were clearly while Bischoff was at the helm. In 1997, WCW's net worth was valued at nearly $100 million. Four years later, McMahon bought Turner's old group for pennies on the dollar. Some reports valued the sale at a mere $1.5 million. Under normal circumstances, Bischoff would likely never have been heard from again. But wrestling is far from normal. After Bischoff pitched Hollywood on several ideas for television shows, Bischoff resurfaced in wrestling again in 2002, as an on-air talent in McMahon's group, now called World Wrestling Entertainment.

As it was in the courts and in the now-famous Monday night wrestling wars, Bischoff was again battling Vince.

A look at wrestling's First Family

Former World Wrestling Federation champion Bret Hart was born to be a professional wrestler. That could be said for just about all eight male siblings of the Hart family, which is without a doubt, the most famous of wrestling families.

Father, Stu Hart, born in 1915, was a wrestling machine in his heyday, who could out hustle the best on the mat. In the 1940s, after a solid amateur career, Stu turned professional. Word soon got around that he was one of the toughest men in the business. He was a master at recognizing nerve points.

After Stu Hart's pro days were over, he turned to training his sons and anyone who wanted to learn the craft. Well into his 80s, the avowed "shooter" continued to try new wrestling holds on newcomers. More than a few have winced in pain by simply shaking hands with Stu. Though he was an outstanding wrestler, he was in his glory when in his family mansion's wrestling gym. Stu called it the "Foothills Athletic Club." Wrestlers who dared stop by and train there knew it by one simple term: the dungeon.

Growing up in the Hart family must have been a surreal thing for the 12 sons and daughters of Stu and Helen Hart. Normal families sit down to dinner together and enjoy conversations in front of the fire—not Stu's family. Bret Hart, the eighth child, remembers as a child hearing the cries of unsuspecting wrestlers down in the dungeon begging for their lives as Papa Stu had them tied up with a painful wrestling hold. There is even rumored to be audiotape proof.

Young guns who dared train with the Harts likened the family's mansion to the "Addams Family." Made in Gothic architecture, it sits atop the city of Calgary, Canada, on highly prized land. To get there, one drives up a winding, dirt road that stretches for miles. That's just enough time to get any approaching students scared for their lives. The street that takes people to the mansion can be a

Announcer Joey Styles heads to the ECW Arena for a card.

Bill Goldberg was a crossover star, having appeared in films like Ready to Rumble, *with David Arquette.*

Sting sports his updated look, a.k.a. the Crow.

Lance Storm is a proud Canadian talent in WWE.

Jesse James Armstrong wrestles his friend, Jeff Jarrett.

road to success or one of agony and utter torment. The choice is theirs.

As you get nearer the house, a wrestler's fears come to the surface. Former Calgary Stampede champion Ricky Rice once recalled his first visit, "I was broke, several thousand miles from home and just a kid," he said. "When we got close to that creepy mansion, we all worried. A large number of dogs, Dobermans I think, came barking at the car. I didn't know if it was a joke or what. To stay on the safe side, I gave the dogs the last four turkey sandwiches I had stashed."

Once past the dogs, a Hart family member answers the door. Most guests are given a look-see inspection by Stu himself. Helen Hart, the matriarch of the family, who died in November 2001, once commissioned a painter to compose a huge mural in the house around 10-feet tall that depicted each of her eight wrestling sons and four daughters. When

you enter the door to the dungeon, the "Addams Family" comparisons come to life. The wrestling room is very dark and dingy.

The family's wrestling group, called Stampede Promotions, was a world of its own. Most of the wrestlers who succeeded there went on to become mega-stars. Abdullah the Butcher, Big Daddy, Sylvester Ritter, Bad News Allen, Jake Roberts, Hiro Hase, Carlos Colon, Sabu, Tiger Jeet Singh, Rick Martel, Davey Boy Smith, Jim Neidhart, Dynamite Kid, Don Muraco, Brian Pillman, Dan Kroffat, Bulldog Brown, Johnny Smith, Rhonda Singh, and Chris Benoit led a whole litany of wrestlers who performed there. The list reads like a "Who's Who" of wrestling. Somehow, they all survived the dungeon.

The stars were the sons. Bret is the most famous of the wrestling Harts. The Hitman, as he was called, had a deep history with the World Wrestling Federation. He and his brother-in-law, Neidhart, were one of the league's top tag teams ever. As the Hart Foundation, the tandem won its first championship in 1987 over the British Bulldogs, and again in 1990, against Demolition.

The singles division beckoned Bret. In 1991, Bret beat Curt Hennig for his first of two Intercontinental titles. His biggest claim to fame was as the world champion. Few champions battled as many diverse characters as Hart. In 1992, he defeated the legendary Ric Flair to win his first of five WWF heavyweight championships. In 1994, he had a second run at excellence by defeating Yokozuna at Wrestlemania 10. In 1995, he regained the coveted belt over Diesel. On two separate occasions in 1997, Hart beat the Undertaker to win the title. His sharpshooter was a classic finishing move that won him many accolades.

Known as someone who could apply any style in the ring, Hart is arguably the greatest WWF champion of all-time.

Bruce Hart largely gave up his career to watch over the family's estate and promotion. He was a superb tag-team wrestler and master ring psychologist. Brothers Smith (the oldest), Dean, Ross, Wayne, and Keith also wrestled or refereed or promoted. Ross and Keith had moderate success as wrestlers in Hawaii, England, and Canada. Dean passed away in 1990 from a kidney ailment.

The baby of the family, Owen, may have been the most talented. Owen was a collegiate wrestler at the University of Calgary in 1983. Stu desperately wanted to have a son become an Olympic champion, and his youngest was the last shot at that dream. At that time, no professionals were allowed in the Olympics. To protect his amateur status while in college, Owen wrestled pro under a hood, refereed, or was part of Stampede's ring crew. Owen hid his identity the best way he could.

In 1986, Owen officially joined his brothers in the pro ranks. He rose quickly up the wrestling ladder and won titles in Mexico, England, Germany, and Japan. He also won a bevy of belts and honors in Calgary Stampede. Owen was one of the most popular wrestlers among insider fans and writers. He had a style which he and Bruce worked on that utilized the best of Mexican, Japanese, and American styles. Prior to Owen's entry to the pro ranks, few, if any, wrestlers employed such a diverse style. His junior heavyweight win in Japan in 1988 over Hase is still considered to be a classic. Many of Owen's matches were.

Naturally, Owen would one day join his brother Bret in the WWF. He floundered on his first tour, in 1988, because the promotion never got behind his character. The promotion tied him with a masked gimmick, called the Blue Blazer. Compared to his days in Calgary, he seemed like a fish out of water. He was considered too small, and few of the muscular stars could keep up with his high-flying style. Gone from the WWF, Owen took the Blue Blazer gimmick throughout Europe, Japan, and Mexico with great success. In 1994, with the WWF's federal steroid trial looming, Owen fit the group's new focus on smaller stars. Also, he wasn't saddled with a mask any longer. The real Owen began to break out.

Once he became a solid member of the WWF family, Owen earned his keep. Whether he was part of the Nation of Domination or feuding with his brother, Bret, Owen was now a full-fledged employee. He was a two-time Intercontinental champion and three-time tag-team champion.

In 1999, the most horrific tragedy fell on the Harts. Owen died in a ring accident in Kansas City during a live broadcast of the WWF's "Over the Edge"

Crowbar throws a menacing pose.

That's 3-Count, Shane Helms, Evan Karagis and Shannon Moore.

Hulk Hogan on the set of his former television show, "Thunder in Paradise."

Former WCW and WWE star, Lex Luger.

Chris Benoit, left, hangs out with Chris Jericho pre-show.

Now you can see why Scott Steiner got the nickname, "Big Poppa Pump."

McMahon later explained that he didn't want Hart, who was intent on leaving for WCW, stealing away his federation's belt. Bret maintains that he was "screwed" in front of his fans. McMahon later claimed the controversy was acted out as a favor. Was it a plot to get WCW to hire Hart away with a big money contract? In the end, Hart did receive a dream contract from WCW. But he still speaks passionately against McMahon.

Hart stayed in WCW for over two years winning the U.S. title, and later, the world championship. His tenure in WCW was muddled and cloudy. He did win the belts, and received one of the biggest paydays in wrestling history. But he was also riddled with injuries and dealings with backstage politics. As the result of a fall he took at the hands of Bill Goldberg, Hart legitimately suffered a concussion and short-term memory loss which caused his early retirement. In 2002, Hart suffered another setback. He had a bicycle accident and suffered a mild stroke and partial paralysis. After a brilliant ring career, Hart was left picking up the pieces.

In 2003, the Hart family's impact in wrestling is still felt. Thanks to Bruce Hart, Stampede Promotions is alive in Calgary on a limited basis. There, nephew Ted Hart, and Harry Smith, the son of the late Davey Boy Smith, are the main event stars. Wrestlers still train with the Harts. Away from the ring, Owen's death and Bret's hatred for McMahon have caused friction in the family. Diana Hart wrote a book titled *Under the Mat*, but it was pulled from stores after a lawsuit filed by Owen's widow, Martha. To say the Harts have had a painful life would be an understatement. But there is much to be proud of.

pay-per-view. Owen was supposed to rappel nearly 70 feet down from the ceiling into the ring. But his equipment failed and he fell to his death. To this day, the WWF still answers questions as to why it continued the production of the show, despite its knowledge of Owen's death before the show ended.

The death of Owen hit the Hart family hard. The wrestling world took it nearly as hard. Bret Hart blasted the WWF both publicly and in his *Calgary Sun* newspaper columns. Earlier, in 1997, Bret broke his ties with the WWF after a controversial match with Shawn Michaels in Montreal. Hart was furious over the match's ending, in which he submitted to Michaels. Hart claims the ending was a double-cross by promoter Vince McMahon Jr., but everyone else claims otherwise. If you look close, the ending is shady at best. While it's been the topic of heated and prolonged discussion for years, no one really knows for sure what happened. After the match, Hart allegedly punched McMahon in the face before he quit the WWF, and left for WCW.

Heyman took the long route to get home

Paul Heyman never really knew what path his life would take, but he knew where he always wanted to end up. He began as a teenaged ringside photographer at events in New York run by Vince McMahon, Sr. Over his career, he's held a litany of jobs in wrestling, and is now a major player for Vince McMahon Jr.'s World Wrestling Entertainment. But what a road it has been.

Heyman, born in Scarsdale, New York, was hooked on pro wrestling by the time he was in grade school. At the age of 12, he began shooting photos of his favorites in the World Wide Wrestling Federation. He'd often give those photos to Vince Sr., who enjoyed the kid's spunkiness. It is said the elder McMahon promised young Heyman he would always have a job in the WWF if he needed one. Eventually, that offer would come true.

The overzealous New York native continued to shoot photos like crazy and he submitted them to most wrestling magazines of the day. His photos of the Freebirds, complete with Road Warrior-like war paint, may be the most widely circulated pictures of the legendary tag team. He also published a cult classic, *Paul Heyman Scrapbook*, from his family's basement. Wrestling certainly kept the eager teen busy.

While most of Heyman's school friends graduated and went to top colleges, he opted for wrestling's school of hard knocks. After viewing one-time photo wiz Jim Cornette's work in *Wrestling News* as a manager, Heyman put the camera aside. He realized only a few could make a living in wrestling photography, and decided to follow Cornette into wrestling managing.

Heyman invented the "Paul E. Dangerously" gimmick and went to work.

As "Paul E.," Heyman began working small Eastern promotions. Before 21, he had built a following for himself. Heyman created a wave in Memphis in the mid-1980s, when he became involved in a feud with Jerry Lawler. The opportunity was ripe and it brought Heyman fame. It didn't bring him big money though. After working in many matches, including a famous cage bout, Heyman was paid peanuts. Dismayed with his payoffs, he bolted for the Midwest group called the American Wrestling Association.

In the AWA, the cell-phone wielding Heyman rode a wave into fame. The AWA had an ESPN deal and was the viewer's choice in some parts of the country. While there, he managed the Original Midnight Express (Dennis Condrey and Randy Rose) to tag-team gold. Even with established managers like Bobby Heenan, Jimmy Hart, and Cornette grabbing the attention nationally, by the late 1980s, Heyman was one of the top young managers around. After a falling out with the AWA, Heyman toiled briefly in a few minor league groups. But his big call to the big leagues was just around the corner.

Heyman finally got his chance to shine when promoters in WCW came knocking. The young manager had a chance to work with stars he had idolized as a youth. He was also afforded the chance to develop his announcing skills and sit in on production meetings. For a short time he was ruling the roost. He helped manage an upstart Mark Calloway (the future Undertaker) and was brilliant on commentary with Jim Ross.

Shane Douglas is a former ECW world champion.

Former ECW rebel, Paul Heyman, was once a manager named Paul E. Dangerously.

A bloody Hollywood Hogan with the WCW title.

Tommy Rich, center, with Perry Saturn, left, and John Kronus, who were tag-team champs The Eliminators.

WWF champ Mankind (Mick Foley).

Underneath that veneer, Heyman was reaching a boiling point. It's unclear whether it was Heyman's youthful bliss or his own short fuse, but he became frustrated. Once again, he bolted. The television announcers said Heyman had been suspended, insiders said he was fired and he claimed he quit. So he went back home to New York.

In Philadelphia and other Eastern cities, independent shows were gaining a lot of attention for their talent and vociferous crowds. Some of the shows were under the banner of Eastern Championship Wrestling. The group was offering a second chance to burned-out stars and also was a platform for underdeveloped talent that fell below the radar. Heyman knew what it was like to be held back. All those that competed in ECW were given the green light to go all the way. Those deemed too fat or too small found a home there. Heyman was hired as the booker for ECW promoter Tod Gordon, and immediately plied his education in promoting and developing talent which he had learned around the country for nearly 10 years.

ECW, which had developed a new extreme feel that was seen in Japan for several years already, was now called Extreme Championship Wrestling. Quickly, the group became the choice of the underground. Heyman also played to a growing Internet crowd who had knowledge of overseas styles, and were resentful of the cartoon-like WWF and WCW. Veterans like Cactus Jack, Terry Funk, Shane Douglas, Eddie Guerrero, Brian Pillman, Chris Benoit, Steve Austin, and countless others found new careers in ECW at one point.

ECW was also exceptionally wise with its own creations. The beer-swilling Sandman, cane-swinging Tommy Dreamer, table-crashing Sabu, and the chair-heaving team of Public Enemy were also created, at least in part, by Heyman's genius. Heyman, though, was never seen on camera. He gave the television time to his characters to develop. But people knew that Heyman was the man who made the group go.

Heyman did a lot of things properly in ECW. He played to all the desires that fans had through the decade of exposure to WWF and WCW. By using new stars and an abrasive style on camera, ECW caught on nationally. The group even found itself a home on national television and pay-per-view. His extreme style was even copied by the WWF. The influence that ECW had on the business can't be denied. Independent promotions everywhere have emulated the ECW style with hardcore matches. But sadly, ECW would barely see its fifth year anniversary. Mounting debts, erratic crowd turnouts, and slow payments from pay-per-view hurt Heyman's efforts. Bankruptcy was inevitable, and in 2001 it closed shop.

But as he had done throughout his career, Heyman landed on his feet.

Whether it was Vince Sr.'s promise, or Vince Jr.'s belief in his work, Heyman finally got his chance to be part of the biggest wrestling group in the world when he was hired by the WWE as a television scriptwriter.

By 2002, Heyman re-emerged as a manager again, this time guiding the mammoth Brock Lesnar. It was reminiscent of the old managers like the Grand Wizard and Fred Blassie who managed larger-than-life figures, and who Heyman grew up idolizing. At the 2002 Summer Slam, Lesnar won the world title with Heyman by his side.

It's been a wild ride for Heyman. He is now positioned as the right-hand man for McMahon in the WWE. Only Heyman knows for sure if it's the position he planned all along when he sat next to Vince Sr. with his camera so long ago.

How Jesse shocked the world

Jesse "the Body" Ventura shocked the world in 1999 when he snuck on the Independent ticket to become Governor of Minnesota. While the Democratic and Republican candidates became involved in an embittered catfight, Ventura rallied the non-voters, the young, and thousands of others who were disgusted with the political status quo to rally behind his candidacy. Needless to say, Ventura became the first major American politician to wear purple boas.

As a politician, Ventura, the "Rock & Roll Governor," caused many emotions in his constituency. He confused, startled, angered, and sometimes motivated the masses in his four-year term. To the approval of many, he refused to raise taxes and gave residents tax rebate checks. He also cut several costly programs that led to cheaper auto license plate fees. To their dismay, he

failed, though, to do proper math. On his way out of the office in 2002, Minnesota was at least $2 billion in the hole, and its education system was a complete mess. After-school programs were slashed and class sizes doubled in some cases.

Ventura, though, put his home state on the map. As Governor, he traveled to China, Japan, and Cuba. He joked with the Dali Lama, was a White House pop star, penned two best-selling books, saw a network television movie made about his life, appeared on most U.S. media talk shows, and was generally well-received nationally for his outspoken, truthful comments.

As to be expected, controversy surrounded Ventura. He battled the media over his decision to referee at the 1999 Summer Slam and announce weekly XFL football games on NBC. He called the media jackals and claimed they were only interested in entertainment and not news. He also shocked some Minnesotans by admitting to going to cathouses while in the military.

It was a wild ride in which, at times, he seemed to bait the public and the media. Whatever game he was playing, most of his constituency believed he disrespected the Governor's seat. His approval rating bounced from a high of 82 percent to a low of 35 percent. Yet, had he chosen to run for a second term, Ventura may have pulled an upset win again.

Born Jim Janos, Ventura is a son of a World War II hero. He graduated from a South Minneapolis High school and met his wife Terry, years later, at a nearby watering hole, the Schooner. Upon graduation he went to junior college and tried his luck with football. With a cloudy future ahead, the 6-3 Janos

X-Pac is about to drop Jerry Lynn with a piledriver.

The Maestro.

Al Snow shows off one of his most precious commodities.

Former WCW champ Booker T.

entered the Navy where he became a member of the elite team called SEALs. Ventura was proud of his Navy work. But controversy swirled about his past as a seaman. Navy records prove that he was a trained member of the SEALs. But he brags that he was akin to a modern day hand-to-hand warrior. Ventura begs off the discussion by saying his experiences are confidential. No one questions his toughness, though.

The Navy man had no career plans when he left the military. While walking around a Minneapolis tough area, he stumbled into a boxing gym. After watching boxers warm up, the adventurous SEAL challenged a local fighter to spar. The boxer turned Janos over to the proprietor who happened to be professional wrestling trainer, Eddie Sharkey. Sharkey believed he had the wares to make a champion out of Janos. In one of Sharkey's first groups of students, he taught a young Bob Backlund and the future Jesse Ventura.

Backlund and Ventura were complete opposites. Backlund was a small-town boy, and a fine amateur wrestling champion while at North Dakota State. Ventura was all bright lights and big city. Once he turned pro, he was quickly a main-event star in the Oregon and Hawaii territories. Like his favorite wrestler, Superstar Graham, Ventura's biggest assets were his body and mouth, and those two strengths helped him forge his wrestling career.

As "the Body," Ventura became an icon in the Midwest. He won the American Wrestling Association tag-team championship with Adrian Adonis. Because of his superb verbal skills and minimal in-ring capabilities, Ventura was best suited for tag-team wrestling. On his home turf in the AWA, Ventura

expounded on his greatness, but always infused it with a bit humor.

When the World Wrestling Federation exploded nationally in 1984, Ventura went with it. It was a good fit for him, as it was focusing on characters. In 1985, while on the road, Ventura fell ill. He was diagnosed with a lung ailment and was pulled from active wrestling. To this day, Ventura regrets stopping. He was scheduled to face Hulk Hogan in a series of upcoming title bouts, and he believed it was his time to shine. He certainly had big paydays ahead in his clashes with Hogan. He claims he would have answered a lot of critics had he been able to utilize his time in the spotlight.

The ailment, in turn, became a victory for the WWF and Ventura. The group made him their No. 1 television commentator alongside Gorilla Monsoon and Vince McMahon Jr. This new job allowed Ventura to take advantage of his strength: talking. Some believe Jesse's television work was just as much a part of the WWF's success as Hogan was in the ring. Ventura wound up as a commentator for the rest of the 1980s and early 1990s. He later took his chances as a commentator for the NFL's Tampa Bay and Minnesota franchises.

With his Governorship now behind him in Minnesota, Ventura has returned to the private sector, but is once again in familiar territory. In early 2003 he signed a deal to host his own show on the cable network MSNBC. The man who once believed his body would be his ticket to fame, now relies on his mental prowess 100 percent of the time. Now how is that for shocking the world?

CHAPTER 7

HEROES AND TOUGH GUYS

What is a hero? Does someone have to enter a burning building or save a life to be called a hero? Or can it be a simple deed? Does rescuing a fellow wrestler from a serious beat-down count? Probably not. But wrestlers do some pretty heroic things in the minds of wrestling fans. Whatever makes a hero, there is no denying they always become larger-than-life figures. World Wrestling Entertainment owner Vince McMahon Jr. calls his wrestlers "live action heroes." He is right on.

While McMahon's outlook on his industry fits, early 20th century wrestlers were simple, honest folk. The heroes of wrestling's earliest days were part John Wayne, part Lionel Barrymore, and part Gary Cooper. They were good-looking fellows who, while kind-hearted away from the ring, could deftly battle any size monster that promoters threw at them. To be a well-rounded pro wrestler in any era, one needs to be physically and mentally tough. Wrestlers must be extremely talented and have the ability to tell a story. The best heroes of the ring told a story through their matches, much like a Hollywood movie.

The parallels between Hollywood and wrestling are striking. The industry makes a habit of taking some elements of movie fantasy and translating them into the ring. As movie heroes became more flawed—take Marlon Brando, James

Gridiron star Leo Nomellini posed a challenge to many in the 60s.

Few wrestlers were as rowdy as the indignant Roddy Piper.

Gene Kiniski is taken down by Pat O'Connor.

Heroes And Tough Guys ◆ 71

Bruiser Brody is considered by some to be the toughest wrestler of all time.

Dean, and Clint Eastwood for example— so went the heroes of wrestling. From the beginning days of world champions through the 1960s, heroes generally played their part to a tee. Add an amateur wrestling background and a star was born.

One thing needs to be pointed out: Professional wrestling is not a legitimate, athletic contest. It only looks that way. But make no mistake, part of the allure of wrestling, particularly in tough guys and heroes, lies in their believability. If fans actually believe the hero is tough enough to battle any wild man, he could

go far. Most believe wrestling's days of Frank Gotch were a time of honestly contested fights. However, some believe those fights were also staged.

But if those bouts were real (shoots), precisely when wrestling changed to pre-determined outcomes (works) is difficult to say. In Japan, fights are often sold as real in promotions like Pride F/C and K-1, although those groups aren't exactly pro wrestling. If the century, indeed, began with the majority of wrestling matches being legitimate, by the end of the century, the industry has done a complete turn from its roots.

Texas native, Tully Blanchard, was a champion in the Southwest territory.

Jesse Ventura takes down his opponent, the hulking Hulk Hogan.

Fans have become better educated through insider publications and the Internet. Information has opened things up to where wrestlers and promoters, who no longer have connections to the old days, openly talk about the inner workings. Even so, there is still an aura of "what's real and what isn't." That's one reason why people keep coming back.

Toughness is a big sell, too. Bill Goldberg's power and Steve Austin's defiance are versions of new-age toughness. Former promoter Bill Watts was legendary for having tough guys in his Mid-South territory. Watts loved to utilize amateur standouts or barroom brawlers like Steve Williams, Jim Duggan, Nord the Barbarian, and Rick Steiner. Watts once joked he had only one concern about hiring these characters. "I didn't care if they got into a bar fight," he said. "But if they lost, I fined them on the spot."

Oklahoma great Danny Hodge is considered a legendary tough guy. The former pro wrestler was a three-time national college champion at the University of Oklahoma and is the only person to hold national amateur wrestling and boxing championships simultaneously. He pulled off that feat in 1958. Prior to becoming a pro wrestler, he recorded eight wins in 10 fights as a pro boxer. But there was no money in boxing, so he turned his attention to wrestling.

Remembered as the finest light heavyweight wrestling champion of all time, Hodge had a career filled with historic one-hour-long matches. Often, he gave up 30 pounds to his opponents in the heavyweight division. He was rarely pinned cleanly. Hodge is also remembered for what he didn't do—but was certainly capable of—in the ring. If

Bruiser Brody puts a chin lock on an unwilling Harley Race.

he had chosen to, he could have legitimately hurt his opponents. Mostly, he spared them from significant injury. That perceived violence typifies the attraction fans have to wrestling.

Although good-guy champions have a harder edge now, they are basically the same wrestlers who performed as Gotch and Hodge. Austin and The Rock are heroes for the new age with multi-layered personalities. Through interviews and matches, they convey a certain aura. Austin is a hero for his confidence and defiance of authority. The Rock is a hero for his unwavering

Adnan Al-Kassey dressed, in his pre-Sheik days, as Billy Whitewolf.

Former WWWF tag-team champions, Jay Strongbow and Billy Whitewolf, with interviewer, Vince McMahon Jr.

Angle's beginnings are as humble as any pure Midwesterner. The Pittsburgh native is the youngest of four Angle brothers. From a young age, Kurt stood out from the rest. Angle won his high school state wrestling championship before heading to Clarion College in Pennsylvania, where he emerged as a national challenger and eventually won the NCAA heavyweight title in 1992. All that was mere prologue for the future World Wrestling Entertainment superstar.

In 1996, Angle won an Olympic gold medal at the Atlanta games. A staunch amateur with tremendous pride in his skills, Angle scoffed at the idea of turning pro. But there is no money or worldwide fame in Olympic-style wrestling. Besides, Angle had a light inside him to be something more.

Though he had constantly fought against the idea of going pro, in 1998 Angle became intrigued. Ironically, before he turned pro, he once made an appearance as an announcer at an Extreme Championship Wrestling show in Philadelphia and was so disgusted by what he saw that he walked out of the building.

So he looked to Vince McMahon Jr. and Eric Bischoff who, at the time, was running the now-defunct World Championship Wrestling. Angle expressed interest in becoming a pro and needed a place to train. Angle quickly signed a lucrative multi-million dollar deal with McMahon. At the time, the move was criticized. Just prior to Angle's signing, the WWE had signed Olympic weightlifter Mark Henry to a huge money deal and he hadn't panned out. Would Angle succumb to the same pressure of becoming a pro?

Terry Funk builds up his next match in an interview with Les Thatcher.

bravery. Goldberg is a hero for his power and simplicity in the ring.

All-American boys become stars

Few amateur athletes make the transformation into a superb professional wrestler. In the world of wrestling, the odds are even greater. For every Danny Hodge there is a Laurent Soucie. For every Scott Steiner there is a Sylvester Turkay. Few credentialed amateur grapplers have made the transition to the pros look as smooth as former Olympian Kurt Angle. Angle is truly an American success story. Although his on-screen persona is grating and antagonistic, in reality, Angle has been a leader.

The WWE sent Angle to its developmental territory in Memphis, where he appeared on local television every week. Admittedly, he was unimpressive in his first efforts. He was almost like a throwback. He had no flare, no style, and was rather boring in the ring. But the WWE and Angle kept at their project and over time he got better. As a rookie, Angle played the fan favorite, which can sometimes hide a wrestler's real potential as a marketable talent. No one could deny that Angle had all the physical tools to be a decent wrestler, but the jury was still out as to his future in the WWE.

Angle made his debut in November 1999, with a persona that contradicted his reputation. Instead of wrestling as a pure baby face, Angle came out and gloated over his past athletic achievements, and immediately fans booed him. Angle reacted with a certain amount of disdain for the fans. It was wildly entertaining. All of a sudden, Angle had a persona he could work with, and by that time, his in-ring skills were surpassing even some veterans. Just like that, the industry had a new star.

In just his rookie year, Angle won all three major singles titles: the Intercontinental, European, and world championships. Since then, Angle, a three-time world champion, has established himself as a true superstar. His years of experience have taught him a superb sense of comic timing, and his in-ring exploits have drawn comparisons to some of the greatest pro wrestlers of all-time. Will he exceed Lou Thesz and Ric Flair in that department? It may be unfair to compare him in that way, but Angle is a special talent.

Although there were brief rough spots for Angle along the way, Angle

made the transition from the amateur ranks to the pros seem like child's play. No one, it was thought, could make the switch as cleanly as he. That was until college standout and South Dakota native Brock Lesnar came along.

The second that most professional wrestling fans got a look at Lesnar, he was dubbed "the next big thing." After mere months in the WWE, he proved the scouts correct in their assessment at the 2002 Summer Slam. In one of the most important matches of the new millennium, Lesnar beat The Rock for the WWE heavyweight championship. At 25 years old, he became the youngest holder of the most coveted belt in all of wrestling.

Lesnar has put the tiny town of Webster, S.D., on the map. Dairy farming, the main source of income in Webster is not for wimps. But "the next big thing" almost missed the boat. In high school, he fought hard to reach 200 pounds. He may have enjoyed wrestling,

Jerry Lawler once considered running for mayor of Memphis.

Bruno Sammartino congratulates Pedro Morales after a hard-fought match at Madison Square Garden.

Former WWWF champion, the great Bruno Sammartino of Abruzzi, Italy.

Bruiser Brody poses after a tough-fought win in Japan.

Murdered in 1988, Bruiser Brody's legend will always loom large.

Terry Funk calls Texas, the birthplace of many wrestlers, his home.

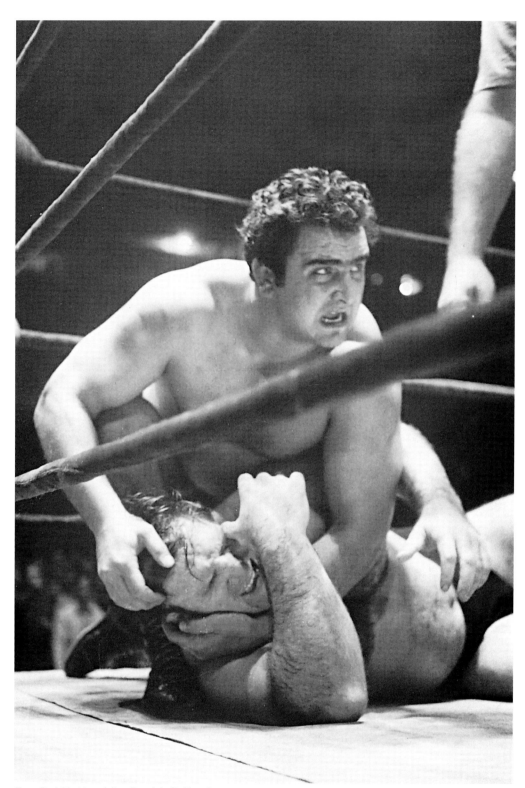

Tony Parisi holds a fallen Dominic DeNucci.

but he was more driven to weightlifting and bodybuilding. Eventually, his frame filled out, and the outline for a future champion was drawn.

When Lesnar graduated from high school, he ventured off to Bismark (N.D.) Junior College to wrestle, where he was discovered by University of Minnesota wrestling coach J. Robinson. After Lesnar won the junior college nationals in 1998, Robinson recruited him to be the University's top dog. By now, the 6-4, 285-pound behemoth was ready for primetime. He threw opponents around like bales of hay. He seemed unbeatable, and became a unique collegiate attraction.

He was pulled in several directions while in college. The Olympics hung over his head, but he was a natural for the pros. He was also even offered bodyguard and pro football positions. The offbeat owner of the Washington Redskins, Daniel Snyder, was reportedly interested in him, but with limited gridiron experience, Lesnar wisely avoided the offer to try out.

During his senior season, when he won the NCAA heavyweight title in 2000, he garnered calls from promoters worldwide. They all wanted to secure

Lesnar's services for the future. But Robinson had a hunch and contacted his former college teammate, who happened to be WWE talent agent Gerald Brisco. Brisco, a former NWA tag-team champion, signed Lesnar to a multi-year deal. Rumors circulated that he had signed for no less than a six-figure bonus. For Lesnar, the Olympics were out and the pros were in.

The first order of business, once he turned pro, was to begin training with former ring technician Brad Rheingans. By late 2000, Lesnar was ready to get his skills going. He started in the WWE's developmental area called Ohio Valley Wrestling. Because of his size and power moves, Lesnar was eased into the ring as a tag-team wrestler. He and fellow Gophers standout Shelton Benjamin teamed as the Minnesota Wrecking Crew.

He's the "King," Jerry Lawler.

Baby-faced WWF champion Bob Backlund was a hero is every sense.

Two strongmen who posed quite a challenge were Ken Patera and Chris Taylor.

Second-generation star Ted DiBiase was a star, even in his younger days.

Champ Kevin Nash.

Former Olympic medalist Chris Taylor splashes a hapless foe.

Hulk Hogan is arguably the greatest mainstream attraction in wrestling history.

Fujinami and Ric Flair at a match signing in Tokyo in 1991, prior to their title-vs.-title match.

By 2001, Lesnar was chomping at the bit and moved to singles competition. After a dozen matches off television, the WWE fans demanded to see the newcomer and the WWE complied. Soon, Lesnar became a phenomenon. He has a neck like a pit bull and muscles in places most humans never use. Just like the respect he earned as an amateur, fans were in awe looking at the monster wrestler.

En route to winning the WWE title, Lesnar was unbeatable. He toyed with the likes of the Undertaker and destroyed the icon, Hulk Hogan. That's a lot of learning for a man under 30 years of age. Certainly, the world looks to be Lesnar's oyster. But neither the world nor any oyster are safe around this massive champion.

From the pros to pro wrestling

There are no tougher athletes than wrestlers and football players. Find someone who is adept at both and you have something special. Football players have always had a deep connection to professional wrestling. Promoters have used ex-gridiron stars for one-time main events, or as regular performers to boost attendance. Hall of Fame fullback Bronko Nagurski is perhaps the most celebrated pro-football-player-turned-pro-wrestler of all time.

In between his football seasons with the Chicago Bears in the 1930s and 1940s, Nagurski wrestled for extra money.

Often called the greatest football player to ever live, Nagurski won versions of the world championships three times. History books note Nagurski mostly for his playing days, but in wrestling, he was more than just an oddball attraction. He was one of the great wrestlers, too.

Through the years, many football players have turned to wrestling. Gus Sonnenberg was a tackle at Dartmouth college, before he turned pro in 1928. He utilized football techniques in the ring such as the flying tackle. Although promoters clearly pushed his All-American status, he was known to fans as the "Human Torpedo."

Leo Nomellini was also an All-American who played 14 seasons with the San Francisco 49ers and is also in the Hall of Fame. Ed "Wahoo" McDaniel, one of the all-time great Native American stars, played for the New York Jets and Miami Dolphins, and wrestled during the off-season. After the football seasons were finished, McDaniel trained with Dory Funk Sr. in Texas, and enjoyed a 20-year career as a wrestler.

Even today, many stars have football backgrounds. The Rock was a back up at the University of Miami, Bill Goldberg played with the Atlanta Falcons, and Steve Austin played at North Texas. Some others have included Farooq (Florida State), Darren Drozdov (Denver Broncos), the Funks (West Texas State), Greg Gagne (Wyoming), Lex Luger (Penn State), and Steve Williams (Oklahoma). Goldberg became an icon in wrestling, and Drozdov was settling into his career when an injury in the ring sadly paralyzed him from the chest down.

Other big name football players have tried their hands at wrestling in recent years to varying degrees of success like Lawrence Taylor (New York Giants), Steve McMichael (Chicago Bears), Kevin Greene (Pittsburgh Steelers), and Reggie White (Green Bay Packers). Hall of Fame defensive end, Taylor, was the main-event star of Wrestlemania 11 against Bam Bam Bigelow. Super Bowl champion and one-time Four Horsemen member, McMichael, teamed with Greene at the 1996 Great American Bash against Ric Flair and Arn Anderson. White, one of the game's greatest defensive ends, made his debut in 1997 at Slamboree in a loss to McMichael.

"They're the originators of the sport"

Native Americans are truly heroic figures in wrestling. Not only for their talents in the ring, but for their battles against stereotyping that has long permeated the industry. Their opportunities were met with classic stereotyping. Billy Red Cloud, Sonny War Eagle, Don Eagle, Wahoo McDaniel and Tiny Mills were Native Americans who did not have a choice except to play up their heritage. If promoters decided McDaniel was to be called "Wahoo," McDaniel had few options. Once Native Americans got in the ring, it was magical. They lit up crowds from coast to coast.

McDaniel was perhaps the greatest of all. Over the course of his career, McDaniel was a star in Florida, the Midwest, and the Mid-Atlantic region where he feuded with Ric Flair. Years later, McDaniel realized he would be best suited in tag-team competition. He brought Jules Strongbow to the NWA with him and had success. Prior to that, Vince McMahon Sr. used Billy White Wolf as Strongbow's partner in the World Wide Wrestling Federation. Together, they were a very popular team.

During his main event days, Austin Idol called his popularity, "Idol Mania."

One of the toughest NWA champions was "Handsome" Harley Race.

El Canek, wearing a Japanese banner, was a top Lucha Libre attraction.

Over half of the so-called Native Americans who entered the ring were not even 1/16 true Indians. But if promoters could convince fans that Maurice Vachon was a "Mad Dog," convincing fans that a darker-skinned wrestler with a headdress was an Indian wasn't far-fetched. Many Native American wrestlers were actually Mexicans. Even though Mexican wrestlers could headline in their home country, few made the kind of money American wrestlers were taking in the U.S. When second-generation wrestlers Mark and Chris Romero were at a crossroad, they allowed promoters to turn them into "Youngbloods."

Ironically, a Native American with an Hispanic name, Chris Chavis, was the top-drawing Indian in the 1990s. As Tatanka—a name given to him after the movie *Dances With Wolves*—he was the World Wrestling Federation Intercontinental champion. After touring with the WWF, he stayed active on the independent circuit.

Steve Gatorwolf was a WWF preliminary performer in the mid-1980s, and later ran a training facility in Arizona. Whether it's McDaniel or Tatanka, Native Americans have added something special to wrestling. Hollywood is beginning to throw away old stereotypes and hopefully pro wrestling will bring some respect to Native Americans in the future.

An original, a governor, and a giant

In Japan, Rikidozan, Antonio Inoki, and Giant Baba were the three biggest heroes ever. Rikidozan was a former Sumo wrestling star who rose to power in the 1950s, and is credited with being the father of pro wrestling in that country. In 1953, Lou Thesz traveled to Japan to capture the first Japan Wrestling Association NWA International belt. Five years later, Rikidozan became the champion and wrestling in that country escalated to new heights.

Rikidozan later became a promoter in Japan, and brought in top challengers from around the world to wrestle. His matches with the Destroyer and Fred Blassie were classic bloodbaths. Blassie was relentless in his pursuit of Rikidozan's belt and tried to bite his way to victory.

By the early 1960s, Rikidozan slowed and turned his attention to grooming his successors-to-be, Giant Baba and Antonio Inoki. In 1963, Japan mourned when the Korean-born Rikidozan was murdered. His death meant a void, and thankfully, he had been busy training Baba and Inoki. They were ready to keep professional wrestling strong in Japan.

Baba, at 6-9, 260 pounds, was a gangly-looking wrestler who turned to the ring when he failed to become a professional baseball player. Baba first won the JWA/NWA title in 1965. He lost the belt to Bobo Brazil in 1968, only to win it back two days later in Tokyo. In the fall of 1972, Baba left the promotion to form his own group, All-Japan, where he won five All-Japan titles.

Baba's name was immortalized in America when he won the NWA world championship three times, beating Jack Brisco and Harley Race in 1974, 1979, and 1980. He competed into the 1990s before his death from stomach cancer in 1999. His funeral was carried on live television and attended by 50,000 who wanted to pay their respects to the fallen hero.

Inoki has been a cultural icon since the 1970s. In his own promotion, New Japan, the judo-expert Inoki held a

The many moods and makeup of Sting.

variety of belts and was active wrestling numerous boxers and martial artists. He once beat former boxing champion Leon Spinks. In 1983, he defeated Hulk Hogan in a tournament for the first Grand Prix belt. Inoki's career took on new meaning when he entered politics. Actually, Inoki beat Jesse Ventura to the punch. In 1989, Inoki was elected to the Japanese Diet, an equivalent of the United States Senate. While Baba was no politician, he was Inoki's equal in terms of being an icon.

In the late 1980s, Inoki battled ultra-villain Masa Saito in an "island match." Saito had just returned to Japan after a two-year prison sentence on an assault charge. Saito was back to dethrone and embarrass Inoki. A ring was set up on a nearby island and both competitors were ushered there by boat and helicopter. In the dramatic made-for-television show, the two wrestlers camped in tents for nearly a day until the match began. The only people who attended this survivor-ish battle were press members and

fellow wrestlers. More than the match itself, the event was promoted as a four-hour television special. Inoki prevailed and the video is a cult favorite.

Through the years, Japan has been a fertile land in supplying the U.S. with talented opponents. Mitsu Arakawa, Kabuki, Kendo Nagasaki, Harold Sakata, Mr. Fuji, Ryuma Go, Toru Tanaka, the Great Muta, and a host of others have been an integral part of wrestling lore in America.

Asian wrestlers have been some of the most talented found anywhere, but sadly, like virtually all ethnic backgrounds, the Asian stars have been stereotyped into roles as heels. Rather than allow them to shine, American promoters were simply happy to let them be jeered. Even recent stars like Kaientai, Kaz Hayashi, and Magnum Tokyo were relegated to small parts.

Japanese promoters have had the last laugh. With the shoe on the other foot,

Mouthy and brash, that's what Don Muraco was in his heyday.

Some great amateurs made even better pros, such as Verne Gagne.

Dr. Death, Steve Williams, was a tough brawler in his prime.

Strongman Mighty Igor shows his Polish might.

Former University of Minnesota stars, Brock Lesnar and Shelton Benjamin, wearing the OVW tag-team titles.

Americans had to work twice as hard to be accepted in Japan and three times harder to go over with the crowds. Many Americans who toured there had to lose to Japan's hometown heroes.

Morales, Colon, and the best of Puerto Rico

There have been numerous wrestlers of Puerto Rican heritage, but the biggest stars to come from the island are Pedro

Andre the Giant hoists a bevy of beauties. Few wrestlers had more world-wide appeal than Andre.

Terry Funk was a spry wrestler in his younger days.

Sabu and Onita promoting their feud in XPW.

Sid Vicious has size and power behind him.

Morales and Carlos Colon. Morales captured the hearts of American fans in 1971, by winning the WWF championship from Ivan Koloff at Madison Square Garden. Morales fended-off any challenge thrown at him: everything from bullies to monsters to weirdos. Eventually, he was dethroned by Stan Stasiak in 1973.

Seven years later, in 1980, Morales beat Ken Patera to become the Intercontinental champion, a title that he would trade back-and-forth with Don Muraco between 1981 and 1983. At one time, Morales was the first man to hold all three of the WWF's main belts; the World, Intercontinental, and Tag-team titles. In an era when former champion Bruno Sammartino left large shoes to fill, Morales kept crowds enthused.

Colon traveled throughout the U.S. in the 1970s. Was he learning his trade or actually scouting talent? Stateside success eluded Colon, but when he returned to Puerto Rico he passed all wrestlers as the top drawing card. In the World Wrestling Council, which he owned part of, Colon won the championship on many occasions. He regularly fought American challengers, which he had run across when in the U.S., like Harley Race, Ric Flair, Junkyard Dog, Jerry Lawler, Eddie Gilbert, and Dutch Mantel.

Although Colon did well against technicians like Rick Martel, he was best suited battling the strong heels. Colon made brawling outside the ring with his opponents a trademark of Puerto Rican wrestling. Action in Puerto Rico was ultra-extreme. His rivalries with heels Dick Murdoch, Dusty Rhodes, Bruiser Brody, Gorilla Monsoon, Kimala, Randy Savage, Hercules Ayala, and Abdullah the Butcher were all bloody, mat classics.

Brody's senseless murder

In July 1988, Frank Goodish was murdered in Puerto Rico. Famed sportswriter Scott Ostler wrote a syndicated column about the incident called, *The Night Wrestling Died*. Goodish, who was more popularly known as Bruiser Brody, was an international icon who was the main event in virtually every territory he ever appeared in. He was a man who listened to his own tune, and a man who created his own history. Stan Hansen, Jimmy Snuka, and Nord the Barbarian were taught by Brody.

In locker rooms, the kind-hearted Brody favored the veterans, but gravitated toward the young. He was never shy to talk about who he was, how others saw him, or his role as wrestling's last dinosaur. He was the last of the truly independent and free wrestlers.

The story of the night when Brody was killed is both cloudy and chilling. Brody always fought for his rights as a wrestler. On this night, he allegedly got into an argument over being owed several hundred dollars. One of the wrestlers, Jose Gonzales, who wrestled as Invader III, said that Brody acted like a madman, and that Brody came after him in a violent tirade. Gonzales, in an apparent act of self-defense, stabbed Brody, which led to his death.

The facts speak for themselves. Brody was left to lay for several hours in a pool of blood before medical help ever arrived. Brody died later in a hospital bed. The American wrestlers there were scared for their lives, and sadly never spoke on the record about what they saw. Gonzales beat the subsequent murder rap and went home a free man.

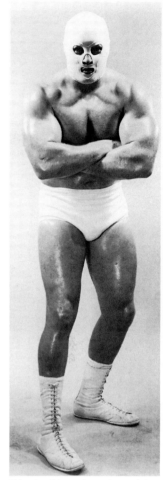

Wearing his trademark mask is Mr. Wrestling.

Showing off his fabulous haircut is the Tennessee legend, Jackie Fargo.

But the legend of Brody lives on. And what a legend it is.

Brody reportedly had put his first million dollars in the bank prior to his death. Pre-Brody ruffian Ox Baker once said he talked with Brody before his murder, and had indicated his family was set. Although he traveled the world, some claim Brody's favorite promotions, in addition to Japan, were the independently-run groups. In the independents, he could create his own rules. Early in his career he realized he wasn't a corporate type or a backstage politician.

Terry Funk once added that with Brody, what you saw was what you got. Japanese and American fans still watch

Jumbo Tsuruta is ranked among the all-time greats in Japan.

the 1982 match between Terry and Dory Funk Jr., against Brody and Stan Hansen in the All-Japan Real World tag-team tournament. Nearly a quarter century after that match, Brody's impact is still felt.

Abdullah the Butcher was another whom Brody often teamed or feuded with. Long considered to be over the hill, Butcher's career took on an additional 20 years, thanks, in part, to Brody. Their bloodbaths spawned legions of hardcore wrestling fans. Butcher and Brody were huge stars in Puerto Rico and had one of the longest running feuds in history.

Brody began wrestling in the 1970s, for Fritz Von Erich in Texas. He met Von

Ric Flair helps Sting work his abs.

Erich while he was in college at West Texas State. Von Erich thought Brody, a football player, had the "it" factor. The 6-5, 265-pound Brody, however, had dreams of becoming a sports journalist. Still wanting to be a writer, he decided to give wrestling a try, if for nothing else, to stay in shape and make some quick money.

The street-smart Goodish quickly realized professional wrestling was where the money was. Not wanting to be part of the norm, he transformed himself into the wild-eyed Bruiser Brody character. Although he was one of the most intelligent men in the business, his Brody act was unbelievably realistic.

Brody looked like a bearded wild man. When allowed, he swung chairs and dismantled entire rows of chairs as part of his act, as he made his way to the ring. His entrance alone was worth the price of admission. In Japan, his fury unleashed on the way to ringside was a scene out of a *Godzilla* movie. Brody wasn't shy about shoving people out of the way, and the Japanese fans even felt a sense of honor to be part of one of Brody's staged attacks.

Once in the ring, he barked like a dog and paced around like a lunatic. He was the best brawler of his time. Maybe too real. Ringside fans witnessed his late 1980s cage match in Florida against Lex Luger in which the muscled Luger actually begged to get out for real. As good as he was at brawling, Brody was also adept at an old-fashioned wrestling match. He was a purist who appreciated wrestling's vast history. In St. Louis, the site of many classic bouts, Brody shined. He always honored the Gateway City's tradition of solid ring work.

Brody wasn't everyone's cup of tea, but he did draw money. He would often

Star of Lucha Libre, Mil Mascaras.

be brought to places to help sagging attendance. He helped build up the crowds more than once in St. Louis, Texas, Georgia, and Japan. In Japan, he was so wildly popular that he helped build followings in both All-Japan and New Japan. At the time of his death, he was offered a record purse of $100,000 to lose to Japanese star Antonio Inoki. His memory in Japan is immortalized by an annual memorial tournament.

For all his craziness, Brody will be most remembered as a man among men. He rightly fought the system, created his own market, and earned his keep. At heart, his in-ring persona belied a gentle, focused, and honest man. He truly was the most successful free agent of all-time.

Pioneering high-flyer, Tiger Mask, was a sensational wrestler.

Jesse Ventura always made sure people knew how strong he was.

One star who had tons of potential was Terry Taylor.

Chavo Guerrero was a popular Latino attraction in the Southwest.

Jack Brisco brought respectability to the NWA world title.

Sensational Sting in his youthful days in the Mid-South area.

Andre the Giant was first a star in his native France before heading to the U.S.

The smiling "Sailor" Art Thomas takes a breather in the weight room.

Koko B. Ware, looking good, as usual.

Bronko Nagurski is another football star turned wrestling champion.

Rocky Johnson shows his muscular attributes.

Ken Patera, an accomplished weightlifter, gets buffed up.

Magnum T.A. was a sensational 1980s attraction.

Paul Orndorff puts a hold on tough Texan Stan Hansen.

The wacky Grand Wizard had bad guys like Stan Stasiak at his disposal.

Rocky Johnson strikes a pose.

Mick Foley as Mankind.

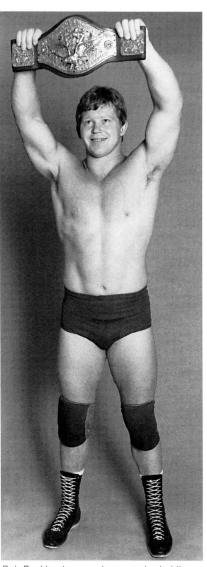

Bob Backlund seems happy to be holding the WWF world title.

Ricky Steamboat gave opponents great matches around the world.

Diamond Dallas Page converted from managing to wrestling.

Japanese star Masato Tanaka.

Jerry Lawler had many tough matches in Tennessee over his Southern heavyweight title.

Classic comic Joey Bishop shares a laugh with Andre the Giant.

Japanese hardcore legend Atsushi Onita.

Andre the Giant, always gentle, shows jockey Bill Shoemaker what it's like to be over 7-feet tall.

The WWF had many popular stars in the 1970s like Bob Backlund and Chief Peter Maivia.

What a star-studded team: Dusty Rhodes and Andre the Giant.

Hulk Hogan often appeared on television shows with stars like Joan Rivers.

Always popular in Japan is Dory Funk Jr., here with a young Tenyru.

Dory Funk Jr. (right) with pal Dennis Stamp in Amarillo.

Managed by Gary Hart, the Dingo Warrior was a quick-rising star in World Class.

CHAPTER 8

GREAT WRESTLING GIMMICKS—

ODDBALLS, FREAKS, AND MONSTERS

Wrestling wouldn't be much without gimmicks. From the bland to the bizarre, and from the mundane to the magnanimous, professional wrestling, and the promotional gimmicks to get its fans interested, are made for one another.

Gimmicks are wrestling's ties to the carnival days when human oddities and human feats of strength were lures to the big tents in small towns everywhere. Promoters would give their wrestlers strange names and contrive stories as to their origin. Sometimes, the story was so sensational, legends were born.

Yousouf the Terrible Turk was billed as a monster from Turkey, who was in North America to take the world championship back to his homeland. In actuality, the Terrible Turk was from France. Far be it for a wrestling promoter to tell the truth. Some gimmicks are just plain tacky. In World Wrestling Entertainment, Mark Calloway was handed the Undertaker gimmick with the premise that he had once worked in a funeral home. In reality, not true. Later in his career, Undertaker was linked by bloodlines to Kane. Storytellers wrote that Kane, played by Glen Jacobs, had been burned in an accidental fire when he was a kid by none other than his brother, the Undertaker. Not only are they not brothers, but if Jacobs took off his Kane mask, fans would know the truth about that fire, too. Few fans

actually believed the tale. But it's part of the story, and no matter how wildly conceived the story is, wrestling fans are always ready to be entertained.

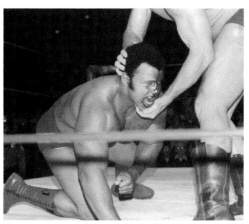

The Stomper gets an upper hand on Rocky Johnson.

Tiger Jeet Singh was a menace in Japan.

Carlos Colon puts a pounding on Dutch Mantel.

Tiger Jeet Singh (left), Kurt Von Hess, and Mr. Hito share a workout.

quick time, he added another 10 years onto his career. Dewey Robertson was a solid amateur wrestler before he broke into the professional ranks. But he never hooked on as a marketable talent until he painted his face green and blue, cut patches out of his hair, and called himself the Missing Link. With his new gimmick, Robertson was a main-event star in the early 1980s. Robertson actually continued wrestling at age 50, an age when wrestlers are usually retired.

Often the best gimmicks are simply an extension of a wrestler's real life. Steve Austin likes his beer and Shawn Michaels was a ladies' man. Maybe that's why their gimmicks were so successful. Gimmicks, like the tough guy Stan Hansen and out-of-control Bruiser Brody, were successful because of their realism. Before cable television, there was mystery. Pampero Firpo's wild hair and the theater offered by the Mummy had to be seen to be believed. Because fans from some parts of the country never saw these wrestlers live, the mystery added to their mystique.

Riding high is Mexican film star Mil Mascaras.

Look at those mugs! It's Mick Foley and Ox Baker.

How real or fake a gimmick is can add mystique to the character. Some gimmicks were ideas spun off from movies and comic books. Chris Champion played Teenaged Mutant Ninja Turtle. The Road Warriors were born from the Mel Gibson film of the same name. Some wrestlers just don't make it on their own and need gimmicks to get over. Maybe they are too tall or too short. Then, when given a unique gimmick, their career blossoms.

Jim Harris was once told by doctors he had a bad heart and he wouldn't be able to wrestle for more than five minutes at a time. When promoters gave him the gimmick, Kimala, which called for him to demolish his opponents in

Like bad movies, almost everyone has a guilty pleasure. Outback Jack and Red Rooster added laughs to weekly shows. Today's gimmicks are more sophisticated with the use of technical glitz and pyrotechnics. Kevin Sullivan was a master at creating wild characters that were too bad not to like. Sullivan created Purple Haze, played by Mark Lewin in Florida, and also a bevy of strange beings in the now-defunct World Championship Wrestling, like the Shark and the Zodiac. There is no reason why we should enjoy these characters, but we do. Isaac Yankem was no Ric Flair. Bastion Booger was no Rey Mysterio Jr. But for some reason, they were just as entertaining as their technical counterparts.

Dr. D. David Schultz was a fearsome foe.

Having a manager could help a wrestler become successful. Managers could take a wrestler with little ability and make him a star just by talking for him. When John Studd and King Kong Bundy teamed up, their manager, Bobby Heenan, made them sound like they could end the world if they got angry. Managers also helped a wrestler's gimmick by making it seem that his protégé would be the man to dethrone the baby-faced champion. Jimmy Hart had a whole stable of freaks and monsters in Memphis to take down Jerry Lawler in the early 1980s.

Some gimmicks are so ridiculous, that all we can do as fans is laugh. In South America, a genius promoter even sold someone named the Invisible Man. His opponent must have appeared dim-witted. All a wrestler did against the Invisible Man was move around the ring like he was getting beat up by a phantom wrestler. In WCW, the Ding Dongs were actually a rip-off of the fun-loving Bushwackers. When the Ding Dongs hit the ring, bells that were attached to their outfits fell off and trickled around the mat. Thankfully that gimmick was short lived.

Sometimes, even one part of a wrestler's body or personality can be turned into a gimmick. Wild Bull Curry looked like a maniac with his wild eyebrows, and caused riots wherever he went. Just a glance at the glaring eyes of Abdullah the Butcher could send a youngster running for the exits.

Some wrestlers were too good to be true. Maurice Tillet brought fame to Sweden in the 1940s with the wrestling name, the French Angel. In real life, he had a handicap few overcome, called acromegaly. It is a disease that causes extreme body growth. In America, when promoters glanced at Tillet, they saw big

potential at the box office. But American fans refused to jeer a real-life human oddity. Instead he was cheered and Tillet enjoyed a very successful ring career.

Leave it to promoters to capitalize on a good thing. With Tillet's success, promoters often used the Angel character. After Tillet there was the Polish Angel, Swedish Angel, Czech Angel, Irish Angel, Golden Angel, the Canadian Angel, and even a Lady Angel. Tor Johnson, the Swedish Angel, later

Bearcat Wright, dressed for success, was once the WWA world champion.

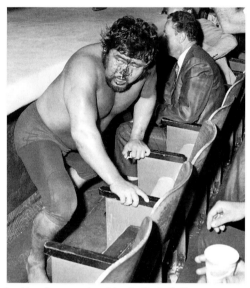

Looking for cover is a bloody Kevin Sullivan.

Live from England, here's Quasimodo!

Thunderbolt Patterson takes a hit from Abdullah the Butcher.

A classic monster, George "The Animal" Steele.

added Super to his name. Johnson was a main-event performer in the 1950s, and parlayed his ring talents into opportunities in Hollywood. Johnson was a classic movie villain, and hung out with the likes of Ronald Reagan. But he also had a unique sense of humor and appeared in Ed Wood's classic B-film, *Plan 9 from Outer Space*, with Bela Lugosi.

Do you believe King Kong Bundy once had a full head of hair?

Dusty Rhodes introduces Harley Race to a chair.

The barrel-chested Ox Baker is one of the only villains who battled into the future. The bald menace, who was known for his thick mustache and heart punch maneuver, reached the future in a death match against the Kurt Russell-played character Snake Plissken in *Escape from New York*. Although Baker won't be remembered as a tactical wizard in the ring, his ugly mug kept him a touring main-event star from 1950 to 1980.

Gimmick matches take center stage

Gimmick matches are nothing new. From Battle Royals to Bunkhouse Stampedes, wrestling has always been filled with a large number of gimmick matches. Non-traditional matches have become a widely-used technique to attract fans. Projecting fear builds the mystery behind gimmick matches. Letting the fans see every movement the wrestler makes portrays the feeling of danger. It's similar to a maestro with a wand.

By the late 1990s, "hardcore" became a household word in professional wrestling. The World Wrestling Federation put a hardcore title on Mick Foley in a move that seemed temporary. Foley, as Mankind, took on all challengers in the strangest of places— trash bins, boiler rooms, bathrooms, parking lots, and locker rooms. His matches were unbelievably entertaining, and he usually enhanced his surroundings by using blunt objects to hit his opponent. Everything was allowed, from fire extinguishers, plungers, and stop signs to garbage cans and other assorted garage-sale leftovers. To the masses, the matches were unique. They caught on with the fans, and a new division was born. Since then, hardcore bouts have become a staple on television. Their influence has trickled to promotions all over the world. While

Carlos Colon takes aim for Frankie Lane.

Foley brought it to a national phenomenon, hardcore matches were hardly original.

The idea has been passed down from previous generations. In the United States, the now-defunct Extreme Championship Wrestling made hardcore matches a way of life. Wrestlers used garbage can lids in bouts almost routinely. The late Eddie Gilbert, who was known as a matchmaking mastermind, first picked up on that style. It was being used to violent extremes in Japan during the early 1990s. Gilbert, it is believed, is the one who first brought the idea to America. ECW cultivated the idea further by using Foley, Terry Funk, Tommy Dreamer, Sabu, and the Public Enemy to scar their bodies in hardcore matches. As ECW hit its stride, in the late 1990s, the WWF used the idea to juice up its own shows. That's when Mankind became the Federation's first hardcore champ. And the rest is history.

Long-time fans will take issue with hardcore being created in the 1990s. The Original Sheik was hardcore 25 years earlier. In 1978 in Tupelo, Miss., a now-famous match between Jerry Lawler and Bill Dundee against the Moondogs spilled over into a nearby concession stand. The wrestlers used jars of mustard, mops, and popcorn containers as foreign objects, and sent the fans into a frenzy. Is that where hardcore was born?

For much of the 1990s, Japan's Frontier Martial Arts group was the king of extreme promotions. In 1990, Atsushi Onita's promotion became a popular Japanese alternative. That summer, he organized the first-ever, no-rope, barbed wire, exploding death match. Onita has become a legend for his essays in violence. He was hospitalized numerous times, and has received so many stitches

Roddy Piper with his favorite bullwhip.

A classic Florida feud: Kevin Sullivan and Dusty Rhodes in a chain bout.

Greg Valentine tries to survive after a brutal ring battle.

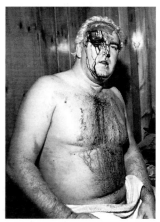

Crazy Luke Graham was no stranger to ring battle scars.

A strange man indeed, the bizarre T-Joe Khan.

for his wounds, he would probably be the Guinness Book's uncrowned stitch king. The promotion's death matches were the talk of wrestling. Foley, then known as Cactus Jack, traveled to FMW for almost three years to partake in some of the group's most brutal matches. Funk, Tarzan Goto, Ricky Fuji, Mike

The talented Vampiro.

Sputnik Monroe challenged promoters to desegregate wrestling arenas in Tennessee.

Jesse Ventura tests his own strength in the ring.

Cadillac tournament	
BOB ARMSTRONG	
BOBO BRAZIL	
CHARLIE COOK	
ROBERT FULLER	
RON FULLER	
DORY FUNK Jr.	
RONNIE GARVIN	
THE GLADIATOR	
JIMMY GOLDEN	
DON KERNODLE	
THE GREAT MEPHISTO	
DICK SLATER	
RIP SMITH	
MIKE STALLINGS	
THE STOMPER	
LOUIE TILLET	
KARL VON STEIGER	
KURT VON STEIGER	
MR. WRESTLING II	
RON WRIGHT	
TORA TANAKA	

Gimmick matches, like tournaments, are always popular. Here, Les Thatcher shows off the special seedings.

Three classic stars: Bugsy McGraw, Superstar Graham, and Bruiser Brody.

Awesome, the Original Sheik, Sabu, and Horace Boulder became instant legends for their daringness to be involved.

Promoters will try anything as long as it's unique and entertaining and sometimes absurd. The latter was accomplished in the WWF when Rick Martel took on Jake Roberts in a blindfold match at Wrestlemania 7. It was the first-noted attempt of this type. Both Roberts and Martel wore blindfolds—fans insist the fabric was see-through—and the two stammered around the ring for 10 minutes. Another absurd match was the WWF's Hell in a Kennel bout between Al Snow and Big Bossman. The wrestlers were locked inside a regular cage and dogs were locked inside a barrier outside the first cage. In theory, the dogs would attack the wrestlers if they got out of their cage. The result was both horrible and laughable. The wrestlers did their part to make the match tolerable. But the dogs just stood and barked at each other. Promoters haven't tried this match again. During the 1950s, wrestling bears were a popular attraction. Women wrestlers Alma Mills, Lulu LeMar, and Mae Young were all known for wrestling live bears.

One crazy match that reached wide appeal in the 1980s was the scaffold match. Bill Dundee, a former trapeze artist in Australia, knew it would take something unique to get his character accepted. In 1983, Dundee met Koko Ware in what is believed to be the first scaffold bout. High above, stretched across the whole ring, was a 3-ft.-wide scaffold. The object of the match was to throw your opponent off the scaffolding. In the 1986 Starrcade, the scaffold match reached its pinnacle when the Jim Cornette-led Midnight Express fought the Road Warriors. The Express and Cornette all took the 20-foot-plunge from atop the scaffold. Cornette even injured his knee badly as a result.

In Puerto Rico, known as the island of blood, fire was used for the first time. To culminate his feud with Hercules Ayala, Carlos Colon promoted a Ring of Fire match where the ring ropes were doused with flammable liquid and set ablaze. Colon tried to burn Ayala while attending fans sat in awe. While it is a dangerous bout for obvious reasons, the wrestlers are careful not to burn each other accidentally. In later years, fire became increasingly accepted as a regular match. The WWF even promoted a hybrid of the Colon-styled match to settle the Undertaker-versus-Kane feud. Promoters realize that no matter the danger, craziness is best.

Cage matches have offered fans some of the most memorable bouts. Seeing Jimmy Snuka leap from atop a cage in his feud with Bob Backlund at Madison Square Garden, made such an impression on a young Foley, that he wanted to become a wrestler the moment he saw it. When there is a cage match, fans can almost be assured they will see blood. When there isn't blood, they're disappointed. The National Wrestling Alliance promoted a few War Games. The idea was solid. Two rings surrounded by one giant cage. Inside there were two, five-man teams. Unfortunately, the cage took over 40 minutes to assemble and often those matches were short, bloodless, and boring.

Gimmick matches are often used to settle a feud. Indian strap matches gave Wahoo McDaniel and Jay Strongbow years of main-event status. Billy White Wolf may have engaged in the first strap match in 1962 against Tony Borne. The two wrestlers were bound together with a 10-foot leather strap. To win, one man had to drag his foe to all four corners of the ring. Of course, the strap was used as a weapon.

Lots of wrestlers lay claim to originating different gimmick matches. The late Boris Malenko was the originator of the Russian chain match. Similar to the strap match, here, a long chain was used instead. Dusty Rhodes was the so-called father of the bull-rope match. And don't forget the Jim Duggan versus Ted DiBiase tuxedo match, or the

coal miner's glove and brass knuckles matches.

Battle Royals were first popular in the 1960s. The match, used on special occasions, would sometimes determine the No. 1 contender for the singles championship. Promoters dubbed Battle Royals the most dangerous of any match. But many wrestlers saw the attraction as a night off, because it didn't require them to work very hard. In later years, the Battle Royal evolved. The NWA featured

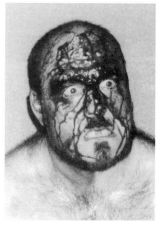

Look at that fear-inducing pose from Mad Dog Vachon.

Dusty Rhodes after a bloody war.

The only ballet star turned wrestler, Ricky Starr, shows his moves for the ladies.

Cactus Jack (Mick Foley) and Ox Baker.

A mysterious masked man named Dr. Death wrestled in the 60s.

The king of midget wrestlers, Lord Littlebrook.

With a crazy look in his eyes, Terry Funk wields a flaming branding iron.

Watch out, Ox Baker will take you home on a stretcher.

Sweet Daddy Siki tries to escape the wrestling bear.

the Bunkhouse Stampede match, which was an "anything-goes," mid-1980s Battle Royal.

Of late, table and ladder matches have been a hit. The Dudley Boyz brought the table match from ECW with them to the WWF. Throwing an opponent through a folding table is the only way to win that type of spectacle. Edge, Christian, and the Hardy Boys have been highly innovative with the maneuvers they have dreamt of in ladder

matches, where ladders are used as weapons.

From parts unknown: wrestlers from faraway places

Prior to the 1980s, wrestling fans were left in the dark as to the what, where, and why about their favorite wrestlers, particularly villains. What were they really about? Where did they live? Did they have families? Why did they choose wrestling as a career? Those were honest questions to ask. After all, fans only saw one side of the wrestler, the one on television. Was the wrestler named Kabuki really a Ninja warrior from Japan? Was the Iron Sheik really a national hero in his native Iran? Were these stories that fans heard on television real?

Until the late 1980s, promoters believed that if the fans really knew that Gorilla Monsoon hadn't been found in some Asian village, as was said about him on television, nobody would pay to see him wrestle. Most of the wrestlers that used foreigner gimmicks from foreign lands were actually from North America. Baron Von Raschke played a goose-stepping heel from Germany. Actually, he was from Nebraska. Sabu was promoted as a descendent of the Sheiks from the Middle East. Actually, he is from Michigan. And on it goes.

Racial stereotyping has been a way of life in Hollywood for years. Should it be expected that it would be any different in wrestling? Performers from Germany and Russia fit right in. With the knowledge of Adolph Hitler's brutal reign in the 1930s, it was easy to jeer a wrestler using a Nazi gimmick. When World War II was finally over, the emotion of those years spilled over into wrestling arenas. Germans became the ring's biggest villains.

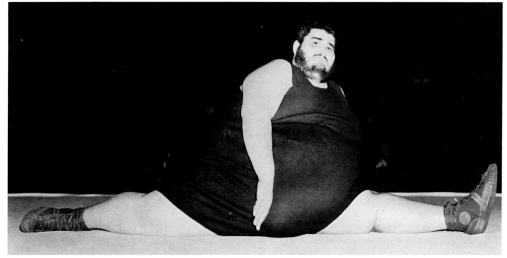

From the 1950s, the "Human Blimp" Martin Levy weighed nearly 700 pounds.

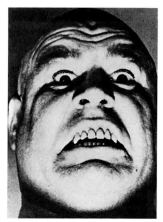

The Swedish Angel, a.k.a. Tor Johnson, was also a B-film star.

Raschke was a wrestling and football star in college at the University of Nebraska. Former Midwest promoter, Verne Gagne, loved to hire former All-American athletes with amateur backgrounds similar to his own. As himself, Jim Raschke was dull and he knew that his career was going nowhere fast. After touring with colorful men like Dick the Bruiser and the Crusher, Raschke changed his life forever. He shaved his head, borrowed mannerisms from fellow German character Fritz Von Erich, and changed his name to the Baron. As a monster heel, he challenged many champions like Bruno Sammartino and Antonio Inoki. Towards the end of his career, when he aligned himself with fan favorites, the Baron was revered by fans.

In the 1970s, Russian gimmicks allowed fans an opportunity to hate the heels and be patriotic towards America. One such star, who played the part of a Russian, was George Gordienko. For much of his career, Gordienko's character was a rugged Russian. The Volkoffs, Koloffs, and Zukoffs were easy to get riled over.

The Samoans, Afa and Sika, are seemingly related to every islander who

Wire fence matches, like this one between Kevin Sullivan and Mike Graham, were substitutes for cage matches.

The flamboyant Jimmy Valiant rides his hog to the matches.

Ernie Ladd, right, gets a nose job from Dick the Bruiser.

The cigar-smoking Bruiser was once the WWA champion.

The Outlaw and Don Wayt were an ugly duo.

One of the tallest wrestlers ever was Sky Hi Lee.

Giant Baba reaches to bloody a mean Sheik.

has stepped into the ring. Wrestlers they weren't. Instead, they were wild-eyed, bona fide butt kickers. Afa and Sika were hardcore before hardcore was cool. Sometimes they were seen eating raw fish or talking in some strange dialect no one understood. In their wake, others followed—Rikishi, Tonga Kid, Samu, and the late Yokozuna all made an impact in wrestling.

The Rock, too, is related to the Samoan family tree. His dad, Rocky Johnson, is a former WWF tag-team champion, and his mom is the daughter of "High Chief" Peter Maivia, one of the WWF's top draws in the 1970s. Jimmy Snuka may have been the top island star. He was a legitimate brawler, who had a reputation with other wrestlers for being one of the toughest men to step foot in a ring.

Don Muraco left the island of Hawaii with the good looks of Tom Selleck and the sculpted body of Rick Rude. In the early 1970s, he worked most available circuits with only mid-level success. Once he gained weight, turned on the fans, and declared himself to be "Magnificent," Muraco became a main-event-caliber star. As he shuffled down the aisle in a cocky manner, he would grab a microphone to insult the fans. Muraco became a one-of-a-kind character and won't be forgotten. Into the 1980s, few threw insults or worked the crowd like Muraco. Prior to his final years in the industry, he was a heel for the ages. Part 1950s, part 1980s, and 100-percent box office, that was Magnificent Muraco.

Arab stars were some of the most unique and mystical characters in wrestling. But there was more to their personalities than a turban and pointed boots. Sheiks have popped up in virtually every territory at some time.

Some were legit Arabs and others just saw it as a gimmick to make money.

There were many Sheiks in wrestling, going back to some of the earliest days of the business. Ali Baba was one of the first. In 1936, he defeated Dick Shikat for the National Wrestling Association title in Detroit. Wild Bull Curry was actually an American with Lebanese lineage. His attitude could instigate a riot at the drop of a hat. He began boxing and wrestling at the age of 14 in carnivals. Later, he had a main-event war at Madison Square Garden with Antonino Rocca that was out-of-control mayhem. Ironically, when Curry settled down in Connecticut, he worked in law enforcement.

Adnan Al-Kaissey and Kozrow Vaziri (The Iron Sheik) are two Middle East-born wrestlers with amateur backgrounds. Vaziri represented Iran as a weightlifter in the Mexico City Olympic Games in 1968, and Al-Kaissey was a scholarship athlete at Oklahoma State. Al-Kaissey first heard cheers from the crowd as a Native American named Billy White Wolf. He returned to his native Iraq for almost seven years before heading back to the United States in the early 1980s, playing a Sheik. Both he and Vaziri became hated men in wrestling. The Iron Sheik won the WWF world title from Bob Backlund in December 1983 and later led a heel, Sgt. Slaughter, to the WWF gold in January 1991.

Perhaps the most famous of all Arabs is the Original Sheik, Ed Farhat. Born of Lebanese heritage, Farhat began grappling in the 1950s. He continued to slice and dice foes in Japan at an age when many others have long since put their boots to rest. Oddly, he and real-life nephew Terry Brunk (Sabu) seemed to imitate a person from India rather than the Arab nations. By dropping the

"Araby" from the moniker and instilling pure mayhem into his arsenal, the Sheik became a powerful headline attraction in the United States and Canada during the 1970s.

Haystacks Calhoun throws his foe back in the ring for more punishment.

Mystery always surrounded The Mystic, wherever he wrestled.

Don Eagle, in a scene from the "Osceola Story" with fellow wrestler Billy Two Rivers.

Many wrestlers have worn face paint, such as Rick Link.

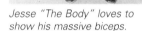

Jesse "The Body" loves to show his massive biceps.

Thunderbolt Patterson was a popular star in the South.

Sheik regularly headlined Toronto's Maple Leaf Gardens and Detroit's Cobo Hall. He would maim himself and opponents' foreheads, shoulders, and arms with gashes from a fork or razor blade. Nobody was safe from the Sheik's apparent terror. His feuds with Bobo Brazil, Dusty Rhodes, and Terry Funk carried on throughout the U.S. and eventually Japan. In Japan, the Sheik and his feuding partner, Tiger Jeet Singh, became maestros in blood. The Sheik wore out his welcome in Detroit, where crowds dwindled from 12,000 to 1,200. However, as long as he was willing to

The Mongol and King Curtis were scary looking wrestlers.

Mad Dog Vachon takes a bite from Sheik Kaissy.

wreak havoc on himself and others, the Sheik was always welcome in Japan. In 1992, Sheik was involved in his last match there at age 68.

In India, the name Singh is more common than Smith in America. The name has religious overtones and has been around since the country's inception. Few wrestlers from India have ventured outside their homeland. One who dared to cross the ocean was Singh.

In South Africa and India, Singh and Dana Singh were the top draws in the 1960s and 1970s. Later on, Gama Singh hit U.S. rings. But Tiger made the biggest impact of them all. In Japan, he had bloodbaths against the Sheik and Antonio Inoki. Brute force and guaranteed blood were his calling cards. Tiger, like the Sheik, was active into the 1990s when he helped usher in a decade of decadence for FMW.

One of the great oddities, Maurice Tillet, wrestled as the French Angel. Here, he is with manager Carl Pojello.

Reluctantly entering the steel cage is George "The Animal" Steele.

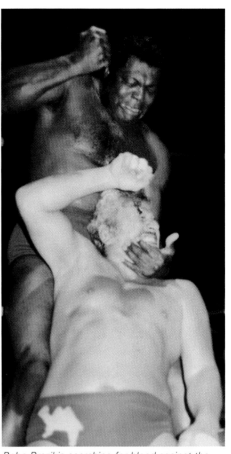

Bobo Brazil is searching for blood against the Sheik.

Sabu sets up a table for an unsuspecting foe.

WCW star, Rick Cornell.

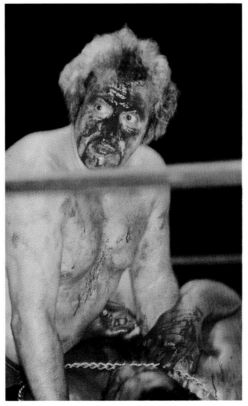

They come no more evil than the Original Sheik.

In England, Jackie Pallo called himself Mr. T.V.

Bobo Brazil had hundreds of matches against the Sheik in Detroit and every one was a battle.

New Jack, left, Tommy Dreamer (atop ladder) and Spike Dudley celebrate after a ladder match.

The Grand Wizard with his charge, the menacing Ox Baker.

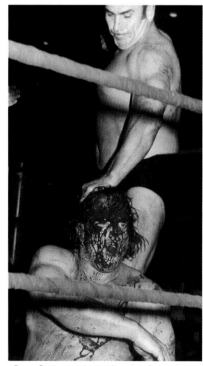

Buzz Sawyer takes a beating from the Mongolian Stomper.

Sabu and Terry Funk in a chain match.

Randy Savage tries to recuperate after a blow.

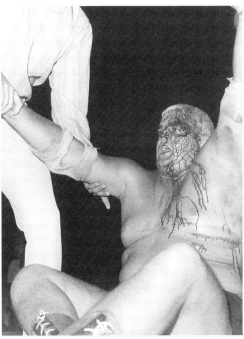

Hulk Hogan tries his hand at acting, here as Thunder Lips in "Rocky 3."

A youthful Dusty Rhodes tries to recover after a beating.

Bad News Allen grabs George Wells in a judo match.

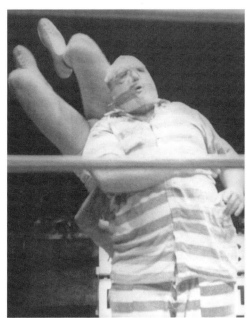

Happy Humphrey could have eaten anyone out of house and home.

Wearing a different face is the Convict, a.k.a Uncle Elmer.

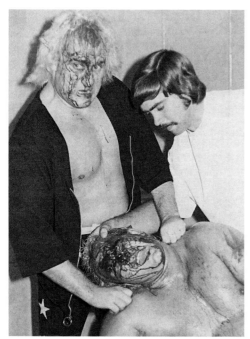
The Valiant Brothers following a bloody tussle.

Midget superstar, Sky Low Low, kicks Jaye Russell.

Abdullah attempts to unmask his opponent.

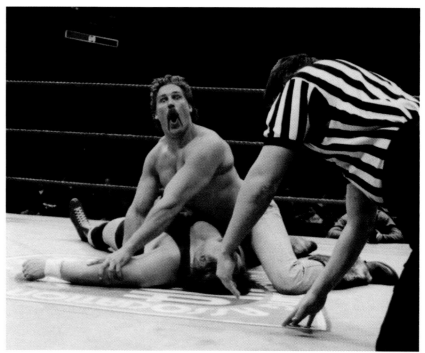
Nord the Barbarian looks happy to get the pin.

Harold Sakata had a role in "Goldfinger" as
Oddjob.

One of the great talents from Japan to
have success in the U.S. was Kabuki.

One of the great gimmicks was the
ragtag Mummy.

The sensational, intelligent Destroyer.

Little Bruiser looked up to his idol, Dick
the Bruiser.

Many wrestlers have donned the
gimmick known as Lord Humongous.

Perry Saturn gets ready to throw a chair.

Adrian Baillargeon is tied up in an interesting Boston Crab move.

Abdullah the Butcher and Gary Hart made a great tandem.

CHAPTER 9

TAG TEAMS AND FAMILY FEUDS

From look-alike wrestlers to brothers to ex-rivals coming together, tag-team wrestling is an important aspect to any wrestling show. One of the first tag-team matches was held in Houston in 1937 that included Whiskers Savage and Milo Steinborn against Fazul Mohammed and Tiger Daula.

Promoted by Mo Sigel, the matches followed Texas Tornado rules, meaning all four men were in the ring simultaneously. The idea caught on. But promoters felt more comfortable with the concept of having partners tag each other in, like how it's done today.

The best tag teams have a certain chemistry together. In the recording industry, Glen Frye and Don Henley were magical together in the band, the Eagles. History shows some of the great wrestling tag teams are comprised of individuals who complement one another in different ways.

Since the early days, tag teams have evolved. Over time, some of the best tag-team partnerships were brother combinations, and fathers and sons. Even identical ring attire can tie two together. Some of the first tag teams to wear matching ring outfits were the Bastien Bros. and the Fabulous Kangaroos. Certainly, having the two dress alike made them more marketable, and gave the wrestlers' careers longer life.

Sibling combinations have a life all their own. The Funks (Dory Jr. and Terry) and the Briscos (Jack and Jerry) were real blood brothers while others, like the Road Warriors and the Valiant Bros., were just partners in war.

And though brother acts were typically hero types, most turned heel eventually. Brothers who were not actually related were relegated to heel roles. The Valiants (Johnny, Jimmy, and Jerry), Fargos (Jackie and Don), Beverly Brothers (Blake and Beau), Strongbows (Jules and Jay), the Andersons (Gene, Lars, and Ole), Grahams (Crazy Luke,

Del Wilkes and Paul Diamond teamed up to win the AWA tag-team championship.

Jesse Ventura, Bobby Heenan, Ken Patera, and Blackjack Lanza join forces for an eight-man tag match.

Dr. Jerry, Eddie, and Superstar), Dudleys (D-Von, Bubba Ray, and Spike), and Kane and the Undertaker never shared family picnics together to be sure. But the idea of their relationship attracted fans. Fans went crazy at the thought of them looking out for their partners at all costs.

Look-alike tandems do well at the box office. The Masked Interns, the Superstars, the Yukon Lumberjacks, the British Bulldogs, the Hart Foundation, The Rock & Roll Express, the Midnight Rockers, Bad Company, the Assassins, the Southern Boys, Too Cool, Skip and Zip, Public Enemy, and Demolition all projected the feeling they were together for a reason. Promoters push them like they were part of a family.

To promoters, tag teams mix things up on a card and create more interest. Plus, they allow them more material to work with. As the years have passed, tag teams have stayed popular for other reasons. Often a tag team will combine two wrestlers who, when wrestling alone, have little charisma.

Ricky Morton and Robert Gibson made up the popular Rock & Roll Express.

Another purpose is to join two wrestlers who bring different talents. A wrestler who doesn't have a gift of gab will be joined with someone with good interview skills. Jesse Ventura was a wild man on the microphone, but was a limited wrestler. When he joined with the technically superior Adrian Adonis, promoters struck gold. Ricky Morton was a great talker who was the spokesman for The Rock & Roll Express. Separately the two would have had short careers. But together, they offered much more.

Some tag teams are born out of necessity. Wrestling thrives on big, powerful types, but sometimes smaller wrestlers find success as a team. Marty Janetty and Shawn Michaels toiled in the land of giants. Together, as The Rockers they became one of the most popular teams of the 1990s. Others who grew from that mold were the Fabulous Ones (Stan Lane and Steve Keirn), the Simpson Brothers (Scott and Steve), and the Fantastics (Bobby Fulton and Tommy Rogers).

In recent years, tag-team wrestling has evolved even further with the advent of wrestling stables. The original Four Horsemen (Ric Flair, Ole Anderson, Arn Anderson, and Tully Blanchard) and the Freebirds (Michael Hayes, Terry Gordy, and Buddy Roberts) were perhaps the first conglomerates. The idea behind these teams was that any member could fight on any night.

Usually, they were the main heel focal point of a show. Others were born out of the Four Horsemen mold. The Radicals (Chris Benoit, Eddie Guerrero, Perry Saturn, and Dean Malenko), Degeneration X (Triple H, X-Pac, Road Dogg, and Billy Gunn), the Disciples of Apocalypse (The Harris Twins and Crush), the Truth Commission (Kurrgan

Jim Cornette was famous with his talented duo, the Midnight Express.

and Bull Buchanan), and others have all seen moderate to great success when joined as a unit. In the 1960s and 1970s, it was popular to bring in a special partner attraction as a novelty partner. Andre the Giant, Verne Gagne, Ernie Ladd, and Bill Watts were often brought in to be special one-time partners to fight off the established heels.

Teams with connections to different parts of the world have been marketable too. The Sheepherders (Luke Graham and Butch Williams) were billed from New Zealand, the Orient Express (Akio Sato and Pat Tanaka) were billed from Japan. Anything to create interest.

Several sets of twins have hit the ring. Perhaps most famous are the McGuire twins, who weighed a combined 1300 pounds and are entered in the *Guinness Book of World Records.* Trained by Gory Guerrero, they were a popular team in the 1970s. The Battens (Brad and Bart) were big in the South in the 1980s. Ron and Don Harris, who look amazingly like Bruiser Brody, wrestled as the Bruise Bros., in the World Wrestling Federation. Current WWE star, Charlie Haas, had a twin brother who was training to be a wrestler when he died in 2001. Both brothers were amateur stars at Seton Hall.

The McMahon family affair

There is an old adage around wrestling circles: Keep it in the family. The profession is one in which who you know and who you are really do count. From grandfathers who promote to daughters who wrestle, and from grandmother ticket takers to wrestling stepsons, wrestling has seen it all.

Thousands have tried their hand at wrestling. In select cases, talent and charisma rise to the top. But having a famous name can help the most.

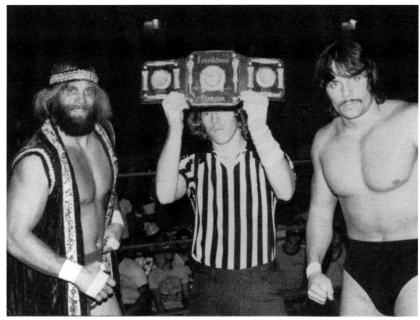

Famous brothers often teamed, such as Lanny Poffo and Randy Savage.

The McMahons are without a doubt wrestling's first family. Vince McMahon Jr., is the chairman of World Wrestling Entertainment, which began as a company his father owned. As the boss of WWE, his accolades include creating Wrestlemania and being a champion performer in the ring. His only son, Shane, oversees new media, but like all the McMahons, has been on the air. Shane McMahon's wife is former on-air talent Marissa Mazolla. Vince's daughter, Stephanie, is in ad sales and television scripts. The matriarch, Linda McMahon, was a college sweetheart of Vince's and has been a steadying force behind the scenes. She has been the company CEO since 1997.

Vince McMahon, one of the Forbes 400 Richest Americans, is reportedly wrestling's first billionaire. His roots are deep in family history. McMahon's father, Vince Sr., was a longtime boxing and wrestling promoter in the East. Vince Sr., who owned Capitol Sports Corp., coordinated wrestling shows from Washington, D.C., to New York up to his death in 1982. Senior learned the ropes from his father, Jess McMahon, who was

One of the great tag-team wrestlers was Michael P.S. Hayes.

Bad Company from Calgary was comprised of Brian Pillman and Bruce Hart.

Adrian Adonis got nationwide attention in the 1980s when he wrestled for Vince McMahon in New York.

Brian Adams, and Bryan Clark as the powerful Kronik.

The super duo, Scott Hall and Curt Hennig.

also a ring sport promoter. Jess McMahon harkens to an era where federations and alliances carved up different territories around the country, and fellow promoters played by those unwritten rules.

In 1971, Vince Jr. went to work with his biological father, Vince Sr. After establishing himself as one of the sport's premiere commentators, he took a crash course in promoting. In 1982, before his father passed away from cancer, McMahon Jr. bought Capitol Sports. He smashed all the rules his grandfather and

Kevin, David, and Kerry Von Erich in a family pose.

father played by and set out to be the best promoter ever.

In September 1983, loaded with a national cable television contract, McMahon raided talent from the established promotions and took the World Wrestling Federation show nationwide. He mass merchandised his product, and forged ahead into the lucrative pay-per-market. Although McMahon's dreams were big, he nearly bankrupted the WWF several times.

Insiders claim that longtime ring announcer Howard Finkel and announcer Gorilla Monsoon allegedly helped the WWF financially during the hard times. Other tight times came for the WWF when it fought a federal steroid distribution charge in 1994. Later, the defections of Hulk Hogan and Randy Savage to World Championship Wrestling and declining ratings saw McMahon fall on hard times.

Other critics remind the soothsayers that the WWE, as well as boxing, had enjoyed glory years and always struggled through the slower times. The WWE had some serious competition

Popular in Toronto, the Fabulous Kangaroos with manager George Cannon pose with Maple Leaf hockey players.

over the years. Paul Heyman's ECW came and went, and even Ted Turner's WCW couldn't stop the McMahons. Ironically, the WWE now owns the rights to both groups. Even more ironic is that once WCW and ECW ceased to exist, the WWE's business declined. As the year 2002 came to a close, the only national promotion came from another family, the Jarretts, who head the NWA-TNA group in Nashville. It may be foolish to say never, but it's hard to say a promoter will ever emerge that was as colorful and multi-talented as the McMahons.

Lots of branches on the family trees

Parents have been known to pass the wrestling torch to their sons and daughters. Every wrestling father believes in their own skills and name value. Every son that follows their pop into the ring believes they can do at least as well. In the case of David Sammartino, Erik Watts, or Greg Gagne, their famous names worked against them. Others like Bret Hart, Nick Bockwinkel, Ted DiBiase, and Curt Hennig all equaled, and even surpassed, their father's ring accomplishments.

In WCW, the Jung Dragons were comprised of Jimmy Yang (left), Jamie Noble, and Kaz Hayashi (right).

Dory Funk Jr., a spitting image of his dad.

In the WWF, Ted DiBiase teamed with Andre the Giant and Virgil.

King Tonga teams with Steve Rickard (right).

Larry Hennig, with his son Curt.

Dory Funk Jr. and Terry Funk were successful in Japan.

Fans loved it when guys like Andre the Giant and Jay Strongbow joined forces.

Promoters also utilize second and third generation grapplers. Fans gravitate to see the famous offspring. Like that proverbial car wreck, they expect the worst and hope for the best. Certainly, second and third generation wrestlers can bring extra appeal to the table.

Some wrestlers prefer to avoid the whole family mess and make it on their own. Greg Valentine didn't want to live in the footsteps of his father, Johnny Valentine, and began wrestling with other names. Randy Poffo distanced himself from his father, Angelo Poffo, and used the name Randy Savage. Brian Christopher tried to hide being Jerry Lawler's son, but in Memphis, there are few secrets.

Texas has been a wildly successful wrestling state over the years. Numerous Texan families have become icons, like the Von Erichs, Blanchards, Funks, and the Ortons. The late Dory Funk Sr. was a top performer in the 1960s. He later began promoting in the Amarillo area. Always concerned with community, the senior Funk gave a Texas safe house for wayward boys 10 percent of every gate and always made sure the local impoverished youth received free tickets to the matches.

By the mid-1960s, Funk Sr., dedicated the majority of his energies to promoting and training newcomers. Two of them were future National Wrestling Alliance champions, Dory Funk Jr., and Terry Funk.

Joe Blanchard typified the tough Texas phenomenon. He toured throughout the U.S. during most of the 1960s, but never garnered super success in the ring. His reputation was as a guy who gave it his all. In his home state he did win a bevy of belts and opened the doors for his son, Tully, to follow in his footsteps during the 1980s.

Papa Joe was a major force behind the first hardcore televised wrestling group, Southwest Championship Wrestling. His promotion was often drenched in blood and bizarre characters like the Sheepherders, Abdullah the Butcher, and Bruiser Brody were at home there. It was thought that Blanchard's promotion was too violent for the airwaves. Southwest briefly appeared on the USA Network but lost its spot in 1983 to Vince McMahon Jr.'s World Wrestling Federation.

Blanchard's son, Tully, like the Funk boys, was a fully developed technical wrestler. He spent the majority of his career in either Texas or NWA rings.

Later on, he and Arn Anderson had a stint as WWF tag-team champions. Blanchard was a terrific tag-team partner. He and Gino Hernandez were a top Texas team and he was also a longtime member of the wildy successful Four Horsemen. After his wrestling career was complete, Blanchard turned to the church where he has done missionary work.

Bob Orton Sr. won numerous titles in the 1960s and also wrestled as the Zodiac. His sons, Barry O and Bob Orton, Jr., followed his illustrious path into wrestling. Barry had regional success, did some time in Calgary as the Zodiac, and sporadically toured the WWF. Bob Jr. was a superior technician. He enjoyed success in the WWF as both a singles and tag-team star. His son, Randy Orton, is an up and coming World Wrestling Entertainment star and celebrates the Orton tradition three generations strong.

The Von Erich (Adkisson) family is the most tragic family story in wrestling history. After a very successful worldwide career, Fritz settled in as a Texas promoter. In the mid-1980s, Fritz's World Class Championship Wrestling group landed a brilliant syndication deal, and the family were superstars in Dallas. But just as the family was getting successful, tragedy prevailed. Four of the five wrestling sons (David, Mike, Kerry, and Chris) died; three of suicide and one from illness. Only Kevin Von Erich, now gone from wrestling, is living.

Before Verne Gagne ruled the roost in Minnesota, a brother tandem planted roots in the Land of 10,000 Lakes. Joe and Tony Stecher were brothers who fared well in the ring. Joe was a top 10 contender in the 1930s, and Tony settled into the promotion business in Minnesota. When Joe passed away in

1954, the business was sold to Wally Karbo and Gagne, who the territory was eventually built around.

The American Wrestling Association was not like any other promotion. Brothers, fathers and sons, and related combos faired well there. The Crusher and Bruiser, the area's top drawing tag team, were billed as cousins. Onetime Gagne protégé Larry Hennig was a top

Mr. X (Dick Beyer) and Mr. XX (Jim Osborne) teamed to create mayhem in the ring.

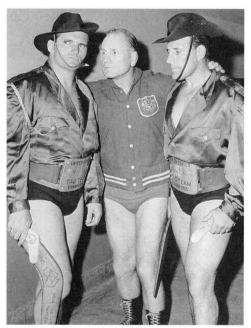

The Fabulous Kangaroos: Roy Heffernan, Red Berry, and Al Costello.

David and Fritz Von Erich.

The East-West Connection, Adrian Adonis and Jesse Ventura, were a durable duo in the AWA.

Twin menaces, Ron and Don Harris.

draw and passed the torch to his son, Curt. The Valiant Brothers, Tolos Bros., Guerrero's, and Wild Alaskans (Jay and Mike York) also fared well in the AWA.

The Gagnes ran a tight business. Verne's only son, Greg, was a superb tag-team wrestler, but never really broke out of his father's footsteps. Daughter Donna Gagne handled publicity for the company. The elder daughter, Kathy, was a noted horse follower and leant a hand in the office. Kathy Gagne actually married the last AWA champion, Larry Zbyszko. The one-time coveted belt was shelved, but stayed in the family.

Top Mexican wrestling families include the Guerreros, Romeros, and Santos. Gory Guerrero fathered Mexican-American super talents Chavo, Armando, Hector, and Eddie. Chavo's son, Chavo Jr., along with Eddie, have been regulars through the late 1990s and early 2000s.

Rocky Romero was a mid-level card star of the 1950s. His oldest son, Steve, struggled with the Romero name, but he headlined as Jay Youngblood. Chris and Mark Youngblood followed their bloodlines and toured with that name in World Class, Mid-Atlantic, Japan, and Puerto Rico. Mexico's biggest wrestling name of all time is El Santo. Rudolfo Huerta wrestled from the 1940s to early 1980s and was a star in film and television. His son, Rudolfo Jr., carried on the family name as El Hijo del Santo. El Santo passed away in 1984.

Few names fill up an American phonebook like Smith and Anderson. It should come as no shock to wrestling fans that a few Andersons and Smiths have made impacts in the ring. The most famous Anderson is Gene Anderson, the founder of the Minnesota Wrecking Crew. His son, Brad, wrestled some in NWA/WCW circuits and is still active, but never reached the status of his father.

Gene Anderson and Ole Anderson (Alan Rogowski) ran roughshod over the

Power and finesse—Dino Bravo and Greg Gagne.

Brutality was common when the Sheepherders entered the ring.

The Von Erichs, Kevin, David, Fritz, and Kerry.

Charlotte and Carolinas regions' babyfaces in the early 1970s. Before that, Lars Anderson (Larry Heinimi) was the Anderson brother. In the 1980s, a Continental-area prelim wrestler named Marty Lunde redefined his career as nephew, Arn Anderson. Lunde epitomized the Anderson name. He was a superb grappler like Gene, and a believable trash talker like Ole. Arn helped keep the name alive, and as a WWE road agent, he continues behind the scenes today.

Aurelian Smith Sr., is better known as "Grizzly." He and Luke Brown won numerous tag belts in the NWA area in the early 70s as the Kentuckians. Always noted for having a good wrestling mind, he worked for Mid South, WCW, UWF, and WWF among other groups for most of the 80s and 90s as a road agent and booker. His son, Aurelian, Jr., is better known as Jake "The Snake" Roberts.

His youngest son Michael wrestles as Sam Houston. Sam's onetime wife, Nickla, also wrestled and valeted as Baby Doll. Her mother Lorraine Johnson was a top female wrestler of the 50s and 60s, and her dad, Nick Roberts, wrestled and promoted in the same era. Smith's daughter, Robin, is a former WWF women's champion, and used the name Rockin' Robin in the late 80s and early 90s.

In the 1980s, a pair of Smith brothers were regional successes. David Smith and his brother, Mark, were territorial stars in Tennessee and Florida. In the middle of the decade, David, who wrestled as Chris Champion, tagged with Sean Royal as the New Breed. When injuries befell Chris, he teamed with his brother in Tennessee as the Wildside. Champion tried several other gimmicks including the Teenage Mutant Ninja Turtle in Memphis and Kung Fu master, Yoshi Kwan, in WCW.

The most famous Smiths were part of the British-Canadian family. Davey Boy Smith turned pro in England at 15. At 16, the middleweight moved to Calgary, where he met and later wed, Diana Hart. Smith's cousin, Johnny

Bruno Sammartino and Dom DeNucci were popular out East.

Tag-team legends, the Fabulous Freebirds.

Gory Guerrero holds up the family. From left to right are future wrestlers, Chavo, Hector, and Mando Guerrero.

Dory Funk Sr. was always comfortable at home on the Double Cross Ranch.

Smith, followed Davey to Calgary and Japan in the late 1980s. Davey Boy Smith died in 2002 at age 39. His son, Harry, wrestles in Canada. Several days prior to his Davey's death, he and his son teamed together for the first time on a small, Alberta independent show.

In addition to the Harts, several wrestling families came from Canada. The most famous have been the Vachons, Martels, Rougeaus, LeDucs, and Singhs.

Montreal's Maurice Mad Dog Vachon turned pro in 1955 after a stellar amateur career, which included a position on the Canadian Olympic team. Had he not lost his right leg in an auto accident in 1987, the always-ready-to-rumble warrior may still be active today. His larger but younger brother, Paul,

turned pro several years after Mad Dog. Their sister, Vivian, was one of the top female stars of all time. Paul's son, Mike, wrestled briefly as Mad Dog Jr. in the 80s, and his daughter, Angelle, continues to keep the Vachon name alive as Luna. Luna has been married to Dick Slater and Gangrel, David Heath.

Frenchy Pierre Martin (Martel) has had several identities and incarnations as both a wrestler and a manager. After headlining in the Grand Prix and Montreal circuits in the 1970s, the French Canadian drifted to Puerto Rico and the WWWF. The youngest Martel, Rick, had a Hall of Fame career. In the 1980s, Martel was a top performer in the WWF and Puerto Rico, and he once held the AWA world title.

Rick Martel and Roddy Piper get ready for action.

The Wild Samoan family is large indeed.

Rick and Scott Steiner.

Chavo Guerrero Jr., far right, with his fellow Misfits in Action: Lash LeRoux, A-Wall and General Rection.

The Briscos, Jerry and Jack.

The late Jos Le Duc was the prototypical bearded, French lumberjack-type. He, like so many Canadian stars, also headlined in Puerto Rico. He is still noted as one of the strongest men to ever wrestle. His younger brother, Paul, also often toured with him. Jos Le Duc wrestled from the 1970s to 1990s.

Dara Singh is one of India's all-time top drawing cards. Not only did he draw record numbers in his homeland, he was also a globetrotter in the 50s and 60s. His son, Tiger Jeet Singh, threw away the rulebook, and became a proficient bleeder and brawler. He relocated to Toronto, where he had a career-long feud with the Original Sheik in the 1960s. His thickly built son, Tiger Ali Singh, became a third generation start in the late 90s. He moved on to Puerto Rico and signed with the WWE.

The Rougeaus have kept Montreal's wrestling fire burning for six decades. Jacques Rougeau Sr. was a Quebec native who main evented and promoted as early as 1950. His sons, Raymond and

In Canada, they came no tougher than Paul and Maurice Vachon.

The flamboyant Valiant Bros. with their manager Lou Albano.

The apple didn't fall far from the tree for Terry Funk.

Jacques Jr., toured globally as the Fabulous Rougeau Bros. Jacques Sr.'s brother, Johnny, may have been the best of the group. His 1971 main event in Montreal netted one of the largest non-WWF gates in Canadian history. Raymond has been involved in WWF announcing for French speaking telecasts and the family is once again promoting in their native Montreal to moderate success.

Afa and Sika Anoia, better known as the Wild Samoans, are arguably the most notable of all the Samoan athletes. They were former WWF tag-team champions and have appeared as attractions all over the world. They originally set up shop in San Francisco, but have since promoted globally, even traveling to Afghanistan in 2002. Now they have a home base of Eastern Pennsylvania.

Their influence is enormous. It's true that upwards of 20 offspring and relatives and family members are tied to the original duo, who actually wrestle full-time. The family tree's branches begin with Afa, Sika, and adopted brother, High Chief Peter Maivia. Peter's daughter married African American sensation Rocky Johnson, who, in turn, spawned Dwayne Johnson, better known as The Rock.

Afa has three wrestling sons. One is the former Headshrinker Samu; the other two are newcomers L.A. Smooth and Afa Jr. Sika has a son who wrestles as one half of 3-Minute Warning in the WWE. When it comes to nephews in the ring, who can keep track? Nephews of both Afa and Sika include the late Rodney

Some odd duos made for fun in the ring. Take Tonga Kid, Dino Bravo, and Rocky Johnson for example.

Anoia (Yokozuna), Rikishi, Rosie and Jamal, Tonga Kid, and The Rock. Also included are newcomers Hamo Solo and Reno, who both figure to make it big someday.

Former WWE tag-team champions and World Class Wrestling standbys, the Samoan Swat Team (Headshrinkers) were Fatu and Samu who are cousins. Extending the tree even further, superstar Jimmy Snuka is the cousin of Afa and Sika. The late Gary Albright, a star in Japan, was Afa's son-in-law.

When it comes to keeping it in the family, those wild-eyed Southern boys are kings. The Lawlers, Jarretts, Fullers, Fargos, Dundees, Armstrongs, and Watts have all led powerful and storied promotions.

Via the WWE, Jerry Lawler may have become one of the sport's most recognizable forces. However, Memphis fans have known him as the King for the past three decades. An artist at heart, the fast-talking Lawler has been the main event in Memphis against the best of the best since the 1970s. His sons, Brian and Kevin, have also donned the trunks. One of the King's ex-wives, Stacey Carter, was a popular WWE valet. Honkytonk Man Wayne Ferris is Lawler's cousin.

Adrian Adonis (center) had several different tag-team partners.

Back in the USSR, Ivan and Karol Kalmikoff.

Throughout much of his career Lawler has either headlined or promoted with Tennessee veteran Eddie Marlin. The fabled Marlin is known as a partner with 1970s wrestler and promotional whiz Jerry Jarrett. Jarret's mom, Christine, was a long-time promoter in Louisville. The threesome, Lawler, Jarrett, and Marlin, organized matches over nearly two decades for various groups.

The Fuller name is synonymous with wrestling in Tennessee and Alabama. As

Bob Roop and Bob Orton Jr. display their tag-team title.

Antonino Rocca and Miguel Perez joined forces to delight crowds.

Rocky Marciano takes a moment with the entire famous Hart family.

Looking like his pop, is the blond-haired David Flair.

The Alaskans, Jay and Mike York.

The Original Interns made for a challenging duo.

Two famous brothers were Mark and Donn (right) Lewin.

Larry Hennig and Harley Race were a fine tag team.

There's Jesse Ventura and Adrian Adonis showing off their tag titles.

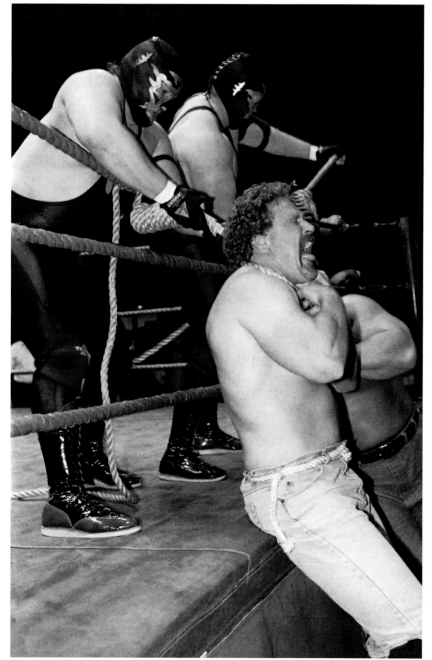

The Texas Hangmen double-team John Nord and Scott Norton.

many as a dozen of their relatives either promoted or wrestled. Roy Welch opened shop in Knoxville in the 1950s, as both a promoter and wrestler. His son, Lester, became noted as the rugged Buddy Fuller. Buddy's sons, Robert and Ron, became third generation promoters and stars. Robert wrestled and managed in WCW using several personas including the Colonel.

Bill Dundee came a long way from his days as being an Australian trapeze artist to setting up a base in Memphis where he worked, trained, and promoted. The 70s and 80s star has a son, Jamie Dundee, who was a star himself in Memphis, the WWF, and ECW as a member of PG-13. The Armstrongs are noted throughout Alabama. Papa Bob wrestled under a mask as the Bullet. The former fireman's real name is James. He has promoted too, and has sons Scott, Steve, Brad, and Jesse James (Road Dogg).

After becoming a major star during most of the 1960s, Bill Watts opened the Mid-South territory. The Cowboy's son, Erik, appeared in WCW and WWF, although stardom eluded him. Eddie Gilbert fared well for Watts in the UWF. The fast-lane-loving Gilbert died at age 32 in Puerto Rico after wrestling in nearly every major group in the country. At one time he was wed to Missy Hyatt. Gilbert's younger brother, Doug, began wrestling in the 1980s, and is still active today. Named after his uncle, Doug used many different hooded gimmicks. Their father, Tommy Gilbert, was a 1960s to 1970s mid-level star and referee.

The Grahams deserve the honor of being Florida's jewels. After a successful career in the 1950s and 1960s, Eddie Graham moved to Florida where he ran a successful promotion for most of the 1980s. As a promoter, Eddie Gossett ran numerous fundraisers for the sheriff's department. His son, Mike, followed in his footsteps as a wrestler and co-promoter. The promotion was successful at using newcomers like Rick Rude and Scott Hall, and combining them with veterans like Dusty Rhodes and Bugsy McGraw. Sadly, Eddie committed suicide in the late 1980s, reportedly over bad investment deals which led to depression. At that point, Mike became a road agent for WCW, where he stayed through most of the 1990s.

There was no love lost when the Love Bros. stepped through the ropes.

Booker T and Stevie Ray are "Harlem Heat."

Stan and Reggie Lisowski are wearing their satin robes.

A definite odd couple, Moondog Mayne and Fred Blassie.

Mulligan and Lanza, the famed Blackjacks, tore up the Midwest.

The Terminators gleefully suplex super fan, Marvin Rubin.

WWWF tag-team champions, the evil Mr. Saito and Mr. Fuji.

The Rock & Roll Express were very popular in the 1980s.

The Scuffling Hillbillies, Rip Collins and Chuck Conley.

Ric Flair often teamed with the Four Horsemen members, Arn Anderson and Tully Blanchard.

CHAPTER 10

WOMEN, VALETS, AND MANAGERS

Women in wrestling have always had the cards stacked against them. Their history in the pros reaches back more than 100 years, yet for many of those years, attaining prominence in the male-dominated business was met with resistence. Women fought for their opportunities. Only recently have their opportunities increased.

Former National Wrestling Alliance world champion Ric Flair wrestled thousands of all-stars around the world. He worked feuds with the best, and rightfully deserved his position. But, like all male wrestlers, if Flair had failed to become a star, he had no one to blame but himself.

It's not crazy to surmise Flair wrestled in more main events annually than renowned women's champion Wendi Richter wrestled over her entire career. To become a top female wrestler in the U.S., one had to be special. Extra special. But when promoters needed a one-time special attraction they thought nothing of calling in one of the "girls."

It's estimated there were as many as 2000 working pros and nearly 500 who made a considerable living in the U.S. during the 1980s. As for the women, it's believed there were less than 100 experienced women wrestlers, and about a dozen who made enough money to be full-time performers. Girls wanted "to have fun," as singer Cyndi Lauper crooned in 1985, but when it came to wrestling, opportunities for women were few.

Up until the 1960s, some state athletic commissions even outlawed women's wrestling, for fear they would injure themselves. But as the years passed, females fought the odds and became the favorites of many. Whether it was yesteryear champions like the Fabulous Moolah, Joyce Grable, Betty Nicolai, Princess Little Cloud, Susan Green, and Richter, or modern-day favorites Molly Holly, Trish Stratus, and Lita, all women deserve an "H" as in "Heroine" next to their name in wrestling's history books.

That's a teenaged Jim Cornette showing off an award from a wrestling fan's convention.

Laughs were plentiful when managers Fred Blassie, Lou Albano, Grand Wizard, and Oliver Humperdink got together.

Luscious Johnny Valiant blows smoke at his opponents.

Lou Albano entertains Blondie lead singer, Debbie Harry.

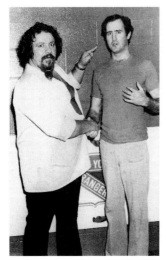

Andy Kaufman has a run-in with manager Lou Albano.

Josie Wahlford of New Jersey is widely regarded as the first recognizable female wrestler. She toured along with her husband, an ex-wrestler, as a vaudeville act. She was seen similar to a human oddity and would challenge the audience to strength contests. Later on, at the turn of the century, Alice Williams and Cora Livingstone picked up the trade. Livingstone is probably the first women's champion on record.

Women have come a long way. Now they play prominent roles based largely around sex appeal. Take Chyna. She became wrestling's true barrier-breaking star. Beautiful enough to pose for *Playboy* and brawny enough to hold a male singles championship, the woman nicknamed the "Ninth Wonder of the World" proved to be a star for the ages.

Long before Chyna lit up television screens, the first woman of prominence in the modern era was Mildred Burke. Burke took women's wrestling out of the sideshow that Williams was stuck in. Born Mildred Bliss of Coffeyville, Kansas, Burke spent hours grooming her movie-star looks and carried herself like a champion. She held major titles from 1936 through her retirement in the late 1950s. She also trained and promoted her own stable of superstars until she passed away in 1988 at age 73.

Vivian Vachon will be remembered as one of wrestling's top female stars.

The Dink managed many monsters like Lord Humongous.

Born and raised in Montreal, Vachon was the sister of the legendary Mad Dog (Maurice) and Butcher (Paul) Vachon. She started wrestling at 20 and toured around the U.S., Japan, and Australia. Although she never dethroned the great Fabulous Moolah, few females competed at her level. Vachon was also a crossover star in Canada as a singer. It was a career she took seriously, and her albums sold well in Canada and Europe. Vachon was also a featured performer in the film, *The Wrestling Queen*, a 1975 documentary also starring Danny Hodge. Sadly, Vachon and daughter Julie were killed in a 1991 auto accident in Montreal.

Few wrestlers, males included, have the credentials of Lillian Ellison, otherwise known as the Fabulous Moolah. As the "Slave Girl" in the 1950s, Ellison was a top wrestler and valet for Buddy Wolfe. As her career progressed, Moolah was to women's wrestling what the great Jackie Robinson was to baseball.

In the 1950s, tight-knit promoters had little interest in putting women in the ring. Even the males felt threatened by the women who they thought would take away their thunder. And many states, New York included, had bans on women's wrestling. Moolah stuck to her guns. She kept working on her craft and, slowly, women's opportunities rose. It wasn't until Ellison changed her name to the "Fabulous Moolah" that she first won the World Wide Wrestling Federation world title.

After years of wanting to join the New York-based WWWF, promoters finally gave Moolah her shot. In 1956 in Baltimore, Moolah beat Judy Grable to win her first title. Amazingly, Moolah held that title for 28 years, over four decades. With New York's Madison Square Garden the home base of the

WWWF, Moolah fought the arena's rule prohibiting women from wrestling there. After much haggling, she was finally allowed to perform at the Garden. Even as a title holder, Moolah rarely settled into a territory to work for an extended period. "Have tights, will travel," became her mantra. She crisscrossed the world fanatically without tiring.

In July 1984, a young Richter defeated Moolah to win the world belt and end the Fabulous One's reign. At the time, Richter was at the top of her game, so promoters gave her a shot. Richter was part of the WWF's coming out party. She was immensely popular and owes her success to her legendary feud with manager Capt. Lou Albano. Richter was hooked up with then-pop star Lauper against Albano. Richter's exposure on MTV and Wrestlemania I, in 1985, gave her the attention that women had long searched for.

Truly, it was a unique time for Richter and women's wrestling. Although women have subsequently never been the subject of attention quite like that, the WWF has given some females an opportunity. In the years that followed, Sherri Martel, Rockin' Robin Smith, Velvet McIntyre, and Lelani Kai held the women's belt until it was shelved in 1990. It did not reappear until 1993, when a whole new era for women emerged.

Before her time in the WWF, Martel was an accomplished performer. In the late 1980s, Martel's role in the American Wrestling Association was expanded as a valet to perennial losers Doug Somers and Buddy Rose. The combination worked and the trio earned main-event positioning. Somers and Rose had a classic feud with the Midnight Rockers (Shawn Michaels and Marty Janetty).

Randy Savage used his wife, Elizabeth, as his manager.

Tull Blanchard with his squeeze, Baby Doll.

Martel was talented at generating jeers from the crowd. The WWF took notice and hired her in 1987. In the WWF, Martel was the women's champion, but was more successful managing Randy Savage and Michaels. As a manager, Martel was incredible. Even though her job was at ringside, Martel worked the match at a pace that most men would not keep even in the ring. Martel was not afraid to take a fall from high places, either. Martel finished her career in the early 1990s in World Championship Wrestling as a manager for Harlem Heat.

Other stars included Madusa Micelli. Once a nurse's aide, Micelli found a spot for herself when Martel originally departed for the WWF. She first managed Nick Kiniski and Kevin Kelly, and later Curt Hennig. But Micelli was

Jackie was popular with fans, even before her time in the WWE.

Bobby Heenan explains to the humanoids the powers of the Masked Superstar.

Oliver Humperdink plots his strategy before a match.

Wit and wisdom from brainiacs, Bobby Heenan and Nick Bockwinkel.

Puerto Rican manager, Hugo Savinovich, with his main charge, Abdullah the Butcher.

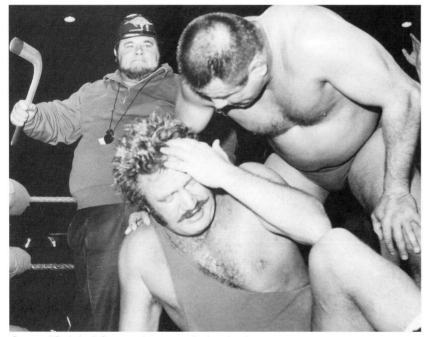

George "Crybaby" Cannon always got the last laugh.

taught how to wrestle and she did not see herself solely as eye candy. So she practiced and trained, and actually became a fine wrestler.

In 1987, opportunity knocked for her. Promoters in Japan wanted the blond-haired maven to come and feud with Chigusa Nagayo. Madusa packed her bags, left for Japan, and matured into a star. While in Japan, Madusa won championships, feuded with Nagayo, and also recorded a pop album. When her Japan tour was over, Madusa returned to America and started in the WWF as Alundra Blaze, and won the singles title. Another stint, this time in WCW, came later on. Generally, Madusa

was a hit wherever she went. But the lack of women wrestlers in the U.S. prevented her from becoming a bigger star here.

Over in Japan, the late 1980s championed a new breed of women wrestlers in a very special blend of fast action and high-risk maneuvers. Women like Nagayo became pop icons appearing on highly rated television shows singing pop songs. Promoters in Japan traditionally give their biggest stars recording deals. The phenomenon worked as arenas were packed and crowds went nuts. Several women from Japan used that momentum in the U.S. The Jumping Bomb Angels (Itsuki Yamazaki and Noriyo Tateno) once held the now-defunct WWF's women's tag-team title in a feud with the Glamour Girls (Judy Martin and Lelani Kai).

Other stars in Japan were born out of the new style. Dump Matsumoto, Devil Masami, Aja Kong, and Bull Nakano even had their own styles by blending the Road Warriors' ring presence with the intensity of Bruiser Brody and Stan Hansen. Masami, Lioness Asuka, Akiro Hokuto, Manami Toyota, and Cutie Suzuki gave stellar performances. No one had seen women perform at this level before.

After this boom period, women's wrestling in Japan slowed. When a wrestler was at her peak physically at age 25, they were forced to quit to make room for new talent. This led some of the women to start their own rival promotions, and circumvent the archaic rules. Fans wanted little part in a watered-down product. After being acclimated to the greatest woman's wrestling ever, fans just went away.

In the U.S., attempts at all-women's groups played second fiddle to the

Japanese promotions. Promoter David McLane had a vision in the 1980s to promote women's wrestling with Gorgeous Ladies of Wrestling, and Tor Berg tried it as well with the Ladies Pro Wrestling Association. Though nationally syndicated, the groups never caught fire.

Of late, the World Wrestling Entertainment has hosted a stable of marketable female wrestlers. Stratus, Holly, Jackie, Jazz, Ivory, Lita, and Torrie Wilson are all trained professionals. Molly is one of their more underrated talents. As Miss Mona in WCW, she was a balanced technician but, like many before her, lacked competition. In the WWE, Molly has shown she can wrestle and be an entertaining personality.

Ivory, meanwhile, has wrestled for numerous types of women's groups during the past decade. She is one of the veterans now, with a true wrestling background. Jackie is sexy and witty and learned her skills as Miss Texas in Memphis for many years, before getting a national break. Of late, Lita has shown flashes of brilliance. She was trained by her real-life beau, Matt Hardy, and takes a page out of his book with flying moves that would make a circus performer proud. Wilson and Stratus, both fitness models-turned wrestlers, probably never figured they would be wrestlers. But they met the in-ring demands of the company and are more than entertaining in their roles.

Enter the valets

Female valets have become a staple in professional wrestling, dating back to the 1950s when Gorgeous George's wife, Betty, accompanied him to ringside while spraying perfume and primping George's hair. Fabulous Moolah also spent many of her first days in wrestling as a valet named "Slave Girl."

Spurts of popularity have surrounded the history of valets. After the 1950s, women valets weren't trendy until the late 1970s and early 1980s. Miss Linda was never far from the exotic Adrian Street. And Brenda Britton seemed to be joined at the hip of "Hustler" Rip Rogers. Both Street and Rogers were territorial stars through the 1970s.

Promoter Sam Muchnick was the man in St. Louis.

The Grand Wizard and his main man, Ken Patera.

Butcher Vachon spends time with the lovely Vivian Vachon.

In the mid-1980s, the World Class area in Dallas caught fire with a bevy of beauties. Raven Rude, Sunshine, Baby

The wily Jim Cornette led the Midnight Express to world titles.

Red Berry guided the careers of Toru Tanaka and Tony Galento.

The fun-loving promoter, Wally Karbo.

Doll, and Precious added new enthusiasm to the company's already explosive television program. Prior to hooking up with Precious, Jimmy Garvin was just another average wrestler chugging away. With Precious, Garvin rejuvenated his career and caused friction with many male fans. The petite blond played the part well and knew how to generate heat at ringside.

Around the same time as Dallas' success, the Universal Wrestling Federation utilized Dark Journey and the incredible beauty of Missy Hyatt. Hyatt was the valet for Eddie Gilbert's entourage, Hot Stuff International. Her valley girl-speak and hussy appearance was a hit. After her stay in the UWF, Hyatt became a star as a television personality in World Championship Wrestling. Visually, Missy had great appeal and in many ways set the stage for the current glitzy females.

Not known as a place for valets, the WWF utilized one woman in the mid-1980s. As the valet for her ex-husband Randy Savage, Miss Elizabeth played a damsel in distress in textbook fashion. She originally met Savage in Tennessee, where Savage was the champion of an outlaw promotion and she was a weather forecaster on a local television station. When they met, it set in motion a top-drawing attraction.

Liz was by the Macho Man's side during his epic battles. Although she was not a great talker, she was an expert at less-is-more. By gasping and by covering her face with her hands in distress, she captivated fans. She may have had her detractors, but her run in the World Wrestling Federation was nothing less than stunning. Later on, she and Savage divorced, but oddly enough, they both found employment together in WCW.

Of late, the WWE has turned up the sex appeal with a new array of valets. Perhaps none was bigger than Reno Mero, formerly known as Sable. She had a short stint, but it was nothing short of fantastic. Sable, the wife of wrestler Marc Mero, had great sex appeal and helped usher in the WWE's "Attitude" ad campaign. She was so marketable, Sable was a multi-time model in *Playboy*. At her peak of popularity, Mero sued the WWE for sexual harassment. After her promises of stardom, she has been virtually unseen ever since.

Terri Runnels came from WCW as Alexandra York to manage her then-husband Dustin Rhodes. Runnels originally played the part of Marlena while Rhodes wrestled as the unforgettable character, Goldust. Her pre-Monica Lewinsky cigar antics and sexy taunts gave the Goldust character an edge. This is one case where a valet was used perfectly. Dustin did his best to make the eerie gimmick work, but Marlena gave the character life. Had it not been for her charm, Goldust may have been another Saba Simba. Later on, she divorced Rhodes, but stayed in the WWE as one of their Divas.

Others who have valeted include the cadre of women from the defunct-Extreme Championship Wrestling. The company was a hotbed for women and produced current stars like Francine, Jasmine St. Clair, and Dawn Marie.

Through its short life span, ECW was home to many valets. Nancy Sullivan, known as Woman, was there in its early days. Tammy Sytch, who once performed as Sunny in the WWE, was there for short periods of time managing her husband, Chris Candido. Sytch began her quick rise to stardom in the disbanded Smoky Mountain Wrestling group in the mid-1990s. She got her break when an opportunity arose to manage the Body Donnas, a team that included Candido and Tom Pritchard.

Before the WCW was bought by the WWE, Kimberly Page, Daphne, Pamela Paulshock, Stacey Keibler, Ryan Shamrock, Aysa, Paisley, and Midaja tried to create a niche for themselves. WCW also branded the Nitro Girls phenomenon but poor management of the troupe, as well as in-fighting, led to its disbandment.

Managers: The ones fans love to hate!

Managers have always been a vital part of professional wrestling. In the early years, Farmer Burns served as Frank Gotch's manager. Burns not only trained Gotch, much in the manner of a drill instructor, but he also helped secure the proper sparring partners and fights for the wrestler. Burns' main job was to

Lou Albano loved taping rubber bands to his face.

Making their way to ringside are Joyce Grable and Princess Little Cloud.

Eddie Gilbert led a stable of wrestlers in the Mid-South.

Sherri Martel out-hustled most men in the ring.

Cora Combs was a championship contender in the 1950s.

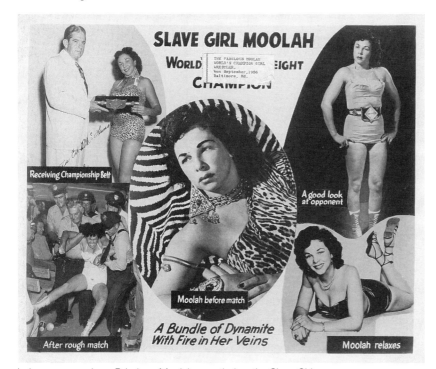

In her younger days, Fabulous Moolah wrestled as the Slave Girl.

finesse the media and be Gotch's mouthpiece. In later years, managers changed. No longer were they legitimate handlers of a wrestler's affairs. They had become part of the show. In time, managers became essential players in a wrestling territory.

Like wrestlers, managers come in all shapes and sizes. A large percentage were traditional heat seekers whose job was to rile up the masses. Not all, though. A few, like Arnold Skaaland (who managed Bruno Sammartino and Bob Backlund) played it straight down the middle. Others, like Tommy Gilbert, Eddie Marlin, Paul Ellering, and Jackie Fargo, were corner men of the fan favorites. While useful, these types of managers were more like glorified cheerleaders. Only a few managers made a national impact helping a fan favorite because, ideally, hometown heroes didn't need help getting cheered. Instead, managers were attached to their heels.

There are only two categories of managers. One is the former wrestler who turned to managing because he was injured or too old to perform in the ring, like Fred Blassie, Johnny Valiant, and Bobby Heenan. Another is the group of fans who broke into the inner circle of wrestling and became characters themselves. The ones that fall into this second category, such as Jimmy Hart, Jim Cornette, and Paul Heyman were, and continue to be, exceptional managers.

As storylines often explain, managers are cast as the sleaziest characters around. They have a propensity toward cheating and always complain about their lack of airtime. In reality, they usually have a great sense of humor. A good manager can actually make a promotion better. A great one can cause sell-out crowds.

Young fans traditionally dislike all managers. But, as we get older, we learn to appreciate the intricacies of their craft. "Wild" Red Berry was one of the first heel managers, when they became part of the show in the 1950s. Berry's presence alone was enough to guarantee jeers for his team, the Fabulous Kangaroos.

As territories strengthened through local television outlets, managers became essential parts to the promoting puzzle. In the 1970s, Sam Bass roughed-up folks in Memphis, "Crybaby" George Cannon bullied foes in Detroit, Tarzan Tyler plagued the Rougeau family in Montreal, and King Curtis riled up life throughout Hawaii.

Without a doubt, 1970 through 1990 were the glory years for managers. During that time, the World Wrestling Federation was a haven for managers. The insanely aloof Capt. Lou Albano and the eccentric Grand Wizard were mainstays there. All guided champions at one time. It was the Wizard who helped dethrone champions like Bruno Sammartino, Pedro Morales, and "Superstar" Billy Graham. Albano still tells anyone within earshot that he managed 17 tag-team champions while in the federation. Rather than retire after his successful career as a tag-team wrestler, Albano became an on-screen mastermind.

Albano was beyond weird. He loved short sleeved, Hawaiian shirts, wore rubber bands on his face, and was not afraid to get beat up. His booming, bizarre voice didn't hurt his image either. One of the most successful teams Albano managed, was the Valiant Brothers. The three men who made up the team weren't much before promoters stuck them with Albano. Johnny Valiant was a floundering veteran, Jerry Valiant was a noted mid-level performer, and Jimmy Valiant was young and had a rock star feel. The Valiants' trademark was their long trunks decorated with catch phrases. Without Albano, the threesome probably would have faded away into obscurity. With Captain Lou, they became famous.

Albano became something of a caricature himself in the 1990s. After his cameo in pop star Cyndi Lauper's music video "Girls just want to have fun," his creative juices were drained. When Albano was in his prime, he generated heat like no other. In the storylines, when he pressured Jimmy Snuka into turning on the fans, Albano became a super heel. Then when Snuka realized Albano was a hindrance, not a help, the muscular islander turned on Albano and became a wildly popular babyface. Without

The Hippie Girl, Miss Flower Power.

Penny Banner was a sexy woman.

Fabulous Moolah has her hands full with Donna Christanello.

Sweet Georgia Brown was successful in the South.

The Grand Wizard shouts out commands at Vince McMahon Jr.

Sunshine was a valet in Texas.

Mildred Burke, as shown in this promotional shot, was a popular star in the 1960s.

Albano as the foil, no matter how great Snuka was, he would never have attained such popularity.

Blassie was much of the same. He knew exactly when to call a fan favorite a "pencil-necked geek" and even recorded a song by the same name. He had the looks of a movie-star heel, and even appeared in various television programs like the "Dick Van Dyke Show." He baffled crowds with words only scholars knew, and was a dirty player. Wearing sequined shirts, bodacious jewelry, and sporting a walking cane, Blassie looked classy as the mouthpiece for such villains as Nikolai Volkoff, Iron Sheik, and even a young Hulk Hogan.

While the Wizard, Albano, and Blassie reigned out East, a young and talented Bobby Heenan split time between Minnesota and Indiana. The eloquent speaking former world champion, Nick Bockwinkel, gave Heenan the now-famous nickname, "the

Brain." Fans, however, preferred to call him the "weasel." In fact, Heenan once lost a series of matches against Buck Zumhoff in the early 1980s, and was forced to wear a weasel suit.

Heenan fit like a glove with Bockwinkel. While the dapper champion teetered on earning the fan's respect, Heenan's taunts would never fail to push them over the edge and made them hate Bockwinkel even more. At times, Heenan was so sharp and so witty, his work would carry an entire 60-minute television program.

He continued to drive Midwest fans crazy until 1983, when he joined the WWF. After managing the greats like the Blackjack Lanza, Pat Patterson, and Ray Stevens, Heenan was ready to appear on the nationally syndicated program. Heenan was right at home in the WWF. At first, he managed Big John Studd and King Kong Bundy against Hogan. Years later, he guided all-star talents such as Ric Flair, Rick Rude, the Brainbusters, and Curt Hennig.

Heenan also broke ground with his position as a heel television commentator. With his partner, Gorilla Monsoon, Heenan was like an act in a comedy club. His barrage of one-liners tapped into Monsoon's role as a straight man. They had undeniable magic together. Heenan played the perfect buffoon at times, and was never afraid to be the butt of a joke.

Ex-wrestlers Paul Jones, Sonny King, and Ellering gave serviceable performances in Georgia Championship Wrestling. But they were no match verbally for the young and enthusiastic Michael Hayes and Roddy Piper. Hayes was the mouthpiece of his own team, the Freebirds. Piper, after ring wars with Greg Valentine and Flair, took a reprieve from wrestling and took to the announcing booth with Gordon Solie. Piper was sometimes linked with the one and only Abdullah the Butcher. The combo was a foundation for mayhem.

Other managers are remembered as solid regional acts. Gary Hart dedicated his life to ruining the life of Dusty Rhodes in Florida. He tried to run him out of the Sunshine State with the Asian Assassins and Dick Slater. He even convinced babyface Bob Roop to face Dusty, but no one could get the job done. Hart spent most of the 1980s in Dallas with Abdullah the Butcher and Kabuki. He also had a run in the NWA with Al Perez and the Great Muta. A lifelong fan, the flashy Oliver Humperdink wreaked havoc in Florida during the 1970s and 1980s. He partnered with a crazed Kevin Sullivan to form a satanic-like wrestling family. It was a host of oddities with only one common goal: ridding the area of Rhodes.

In the 1980s, a new era for managers started when non-wrestlers entered the fray, beginning with Jimmy Hart and Cornette. Hart was knee-deep in the music industry, during the heyday of wrestling's popularity in Memphis, when he and Jerry Lawler hooked up for the first time. Lawler, a talker himself, noticed Hart's gift of gab and brought him into the profession. At first, Hart managed Lawler, and the twosome were as brash and cocky as can be imagined.

Up until around 1984, Hart and Lawler were the main focus in Memphis. Things really took off for Hart when he actually began to feud with Lawler. Every week, Hart would screech on television and bounce around ringside as he rotated in new characters to challenge for Lawler's Southern title. Dutch Mantel, Jesse Ventura, King Kong Bundy, Tommy Rich, Lord Humongous, Austin

Idol, and Eddie Gilbert is just a short list of the foes Lawler tangled with thanks to Hart.

Hart took his mouth and signature megaphone to the WWF in 1984 and guided numerous talents including Terry Funk, Adrian Adonis, Bob Orton Jr., the Hart Foundation, the Rougeau Bros., and the Natural Disasters. He was a regular on WWF television every week, before eventually heading to WCW for a rebirth in the mid-1990s. He's not around on the national scene any longer, but Hart's footprints carved a new trend for the next decade.

Sometimes old fans make the best managers. Cornette is one of them. As a kid in Louisville, young Jimmy bled wrestling. He started as a writer and photographer in the Memphis area in the early 1980s. Twenty-five years removed, he is still active as a coordinator of new talent for World Wrestling Entertainment.

The beautiful Vivian Vachon could wrestle and sing.

Jean Antone strikes a pose for the men.

June Byers once laid claim to the women's world title.

Jimmy Hart was a singer in the band, the Gentry's.

That's the determined Mae Young wrestling a bear!

The undisputed trainer of champions, Eddie Sharkey.

After paying his dues as a photographer, Cornette was bitten by the bug. He began managing in Memphis and did some of his best work there. Later, in Bill Watts' Mid-South area, Cornette guided the Midnight Express to national acclaim. The Express ventured to Dallas for a short time and then broke out in Georgia with the NWA. In the mid-1990s, Cornette went to the WWF where he guided Yokozuna, Owen Hart, and Big Van Vader.

Over the years, Cornette was at his best with wrestlers who could perform in the ring but were not known for their interview skills. Without Cornette's mile-a-minute promises, trademark polyester suits, and tennis racquets, Dennis Condrey, Bobby Eaton, and Stan Lane may never have made it past mid-card status.

With Hart and Cornette enjoying national success, a young Paul Heyman made a name for himself as Paul E. Dangerously. Bold, brash, and carrying a cell phone, Dangerously was the epitome of the new breed of managers riding the

wave of success of Cornette. Heyman payed homage to the past greats.

In his 10-year managing career, Heyman was in the corner of the Original Midnight Express (Condrey and Randy Rose), Jack Victory, Mean Mark (The Undertaker), the Dangerous Alliance (Bobby Eaton & Arn Anderson), Gilbert, Rich, Idol, and many others. Of late, his dream as a kid was realized when he guided Brock Lesnar, Big Show, and Kurt Angle to WWE crowns. Heyman is meticulous, loud, but respectful of the business. That makes him one of the true greats to circle ringside.

Managers always had a life of their own, and fans were never sure where these characters came from. Slick, once a Kansas City street-preacher who was friends with Bruiser Brody, was a big name for the WWF in the 1980s. Donning a turban as a sheik was always a big way to become a manager. Skandor Akbar and Adnan Al Kaissey were two of the finest.

Of late, managing is a lost art. Wrestlers today realize they need to talk on camera themselves and, slowly, managers have become extra bodies that promotions don't need. In the name of Berry and Blassie, let's hope that this important piece of wrestling lore is not lost forever.

Barb Nichols with George Becker.

Manager and trainer, "Pretty Boy" Larry Sharpe.

After she hung up her tights as a wrestler, Sherri Martel went on to become known as the greatest women's manager ever.

Ryan Shamrock shows her worldly side.

World women's contenders, Lelani Kai and Fabulous Moolah.

Manager Gorgeous George works the crowd.

Diamond 'Lil and Little Tokyo tore up the midget scene.

WWF manager Terri.

The flamboyant and energetic, Chris Love.

Manager Francine of the ECW.

ECW manager Dawn Marie sells her gimmicks.

Scandor Akbar guided all types of freaks in Dallas, such as the One Man Gang.

Shane Douglas puts the squeeze on Kristi Myst of XPW.

Manager Jimmy Hart, the "Mouth of the South."

Jerry Jarrett with Memphis pal, Tojo Yamamoto.

Tommy Dreamer and a friend.

ECW manager Fonzie.

Chyna is one of the most prominent women wrestlers in the ring today.

Joyce Grable and Vicky Williams held the world tag-team titles.

Shane Douglas with valet Torrie Wilson.

Japanese women's star Akira Hokuto.

Mom and daughter, Cora and Debbie Combs.

Shane Helms lays a smooch on manager/valet Ryan Shamrock.

Scott Steiner with valet Midajah.

CHAPTER 11

GETTING A HOLD ON THEIR OPPONENT

Like anything in professional wrestling, the holds and maneuvers used in a match have changed greatly over the years. But, as some forms of today's wrestling by products show, even those changes have come full circle.

In the early 20th century, shoot-style wrestling ruled. Shooting, or hooking, as it was sometimes called, referred to legitimate moves born out of submission moves from the martial arts genres. Shoot wrestling is far different than what a fan may see in a match in World Wrestling Entertainment.

The style is more of a slow, plotting, yet painful combination of moves. It is more inclined to look like an amateur

Eduardo Carpentier gets acrobatic on John Vander.

Tiger Mask dropkicks his top nemesis, Black Tiger.

The Spoiler delivers a leg drop on Steve Williams.

Jesse Ventura often resorted to choke holds.

Tito Santana displays his dropkick talent against John Studd.

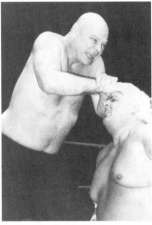

Dusty Rhodes feels the power of the claw from Baron von Raschke.

Billy Robinson, a master technician, forces Josef Zarinoff to submit to an armbar.

Bullrope matches were frequent in the 70s and 80s.

wrestling bout than what the public would consider professional wrestling. Competitors begin from a standing position, but the action usually goes to the mat. Opponents submit or "tap out," usually from painful joint locks or repeated blows to the head. Often, referees will halt the match before serious injury is suffered.

The moves used in this style were leg locks, ankle locks, and arm-bars that saw both contestants on the mat, rather than today's vertical style. The 1908, 3-hour bout between Frank Gotch and George Hackenschmidt, for example, was a match very indicative of the day. Assuming those matches were real, Gotch was said to enjoy hurting his opponents. Most of that match took place on the mat as each man tried to wear down his opponent in a true test of wills. While ropes were used around the ring, wrestling, at this point, had not taken the turn to using them to perform moves.

Wrestling remained in that style well into the 1920s, but as the sport grew into a show, the idea of actually hurting an opponent largely subsided. The public, even back in those days, had questions as to the legitimacy of wrestling. Even so, from the 1920s to 1930s, wrestlers, in an effort to keep the mystique alive that wrestling was real, still used versions of the moves born out of shooting. The headlock and figure-four leg lock, moves still used today, grew in popularity.

By the 1930s, moves were conjured up to fit a particular wrestler's personality. Jim Londos, a noted scientific wrestler, made his trademark move a basic arm lock. Strangler Lewis used to intimidate the audience into thinking his headlock was so powerful, he could literally squeeze a man to his death. Of course, that was just part of the show.

Mankind used the unique mandible claw.

Power was a pleasure for Steve Williams as he press slams Rick Steiner.

Nikolai Volkoff applies a painful nerve pinch on Dusty Rhodes.

Bill Watts performs a flying bulldog move.

As promoters clued in to the show aspect of pro wrestling, maneuvers changed with the times. Gus Sonnenberg used the flying tackle in the 1930s, which connected him to his college football days at Dartmouth. Antonino Rocca was probably the first wrestler to utilize highflying moves in his arsenal. Rocca regularly performed drop kicks and basic moves off the ropes. There was implied danger when a wrestler climbed to the top of the ropes and crashed down on his opponents. Some commissions in different areas of the country even outlawed such moves, not knowing that wrestling was far from real.

From the 1950s to present, wrestling holds and moves evolved significantly. As wrestlers took more risks by performing death-defying feats, there were always others waiting to show off an even more thrilling move. After awhile, outdoing a fellow performer was a way to become known and marketable to promoters.

Few argue that professional wrestlers are pure entertainers with an eye for the dramatic. While the character that a wrestler portrays accounts for much of that, the maneuvers that he or she uses do just as much to create the character as interview style or costume.

The finishing move that a wrestler uses is a big part of their identity. The reason for that is simple. Largely, a finishing move (the move that is used to put away an opponent before a pin fall)

Some moves are just plain brutal, like the forearm smash from Greg Valentine.

Nick Bockwinkel often took to piledriving his opponents.

Jimmy Snuka used the air to his advantage against Mike Sharpe.

is used exclusively by that wrestler. Steve Austin has the "Stone Cold Stunner," Scott Steiner uses the "Steiner Recliner," and Rob Van Dam uses the "Van Terminator."

Greg Valentine levies one of his patented elbow drops.

Finishing moves are one of the most recognizable aspects of a wrestler's personality. Hulk Hogan is synonymous with the leg drop. For much of the 1980s, crowds would cheer and get on their feet when one of Hogan's foes was the victim of that move. The Rock has the "People's Elbow." It was, and still is, rare when an opponent actually gets up after a finishing move is applied or performed.

Some wrestlers have taken great pride in new move innovations. Many of today's highflying moves, like a huricanrana and moonsault were born in Japan and Mexico. Often, an American wrestler will watch videos of matches overseas and try to imitate the move in the United States.

Ron Garvin bridges out from under Arn Anderson.

Jack Brisco has Giant Baba tied up with a leg lock.

In the late 1980s, when Keiji Muto came to the United States for the first time as the Great Muta, he brought with him the moonsault. The move is performed by standing on the top turnbuckle and somersaulting onto an opponent. It was the first time anyone in America had seen the move and fans were electrified. That one move seemingly caused a revolution in professional wrestling. The moonsault is now part of a any wrestler's regular arsenal. Even in his 40s, Terry Funk was performing moonsaults like the best youngsters.

Wrestling now looks more like a high-wire act than a wrestling match. The Hardy Boys, Rey Mysterio, Juventud Guerrera, and Sabu have been genuine innovators by employing the most spectacular moves fans have ever seen. These wrestlers are certainly not afraid of injury. Their arsenals consist mainly of moves in the air, full of twists and turns, and crashing through tables and chairs.

But some of wrestling's old days remain. Kurt Angle is not opposed to using an ankle lock, a move symbolic of his amateur-wrestling career. Ric Flair used the figure-four leg lock well into his semi-retirement in 2002. Even Austin uses the simple Lou Thesz press as homage to the former NWA champion and Chris Benoit is a suplex master.

Barry Windham orchestrates a claw hold on Dusty Rhodes.

In Japan, and the U.S. to an extent, submission moves made famous by Gotch and others in the early 1900s are gaining in popularity. Promotions like Pride F/C and the Ultimate Fighting Championships, are pro wrestling spinoffs and highlight bouts with submission and shoot moves. In Japan, these promotions are generally legitimate and have become immensely popular.

Nearly 100 years after Gotch held the world's wrestling championship, performers of today would make him proud to know his style did not die with the times.

Baron Scicluna finds himself caught in a Bruno Sammartino bear hug.

When tall wrestlers, like Giant Baba, throw dropkicks, everyone better watch out.

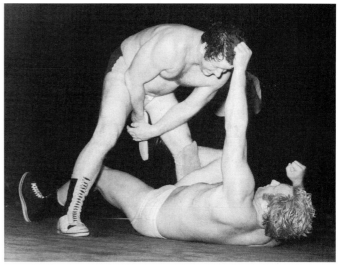

Terry Funk carefully sets Nick Bockwinkel into a spinning toe hold.

Rocky Johnson gets Killer Brooks to submit to a painful arm lock.

Leg locks are commonly used wrestling holds.

Dick Shikat demonstrates the art of applying an arm lock.

The Rock shows Jerry Lawler the way to the ring post.

Rick Martel enjoyed using submission holds, like the Boston Crab.

Technician Karl Gotch using his famed suplex.

Chris Taylor used to send foes packing with his Olympic Plex.

Billy Watson has Lou Thesz wrapped in a headlock.

Mike Graham uses an arm drag.

One of Abdullah's favorite moves is the flying elbow drop.

Bob Backlund sends the Sarge for a ride.

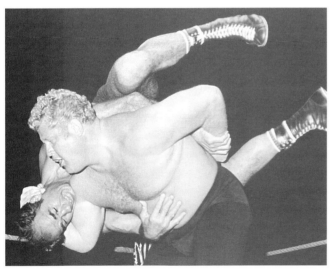

Larry Hennig tosses Lou Thesz as Thesz maintains his arm lock on Hennig.

Power was the name of the game for Hawk.

Sting could wrestle, too, as he applies an arm lock on Animal.

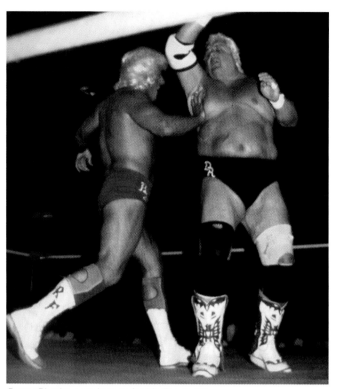

Dusty Rhodes was known for his Bionic Elbow.

One of the early users of somersaults was LePetit, here against Tiger Cat.

The kneelift is a common move.

CHAPTER 12

CONNECTING THE DOTS

Professional wrestling, in all its glory, is arguably the greatest show on earth. No performers work harder at pleasing the crowd, their peers, and themselves than wrestlers. Whether it's in front of 50 people in Any Town U.S.A., or in front of 50,000 at the Tokyo Dome, the industry is spellbinding, thrilling, dramatic, engaging, and, at times, humorous. On any given night in America, hundreds, put their hearts and souls into a wrestling ring.

From humble beginnings to an extravagant present, wrestling has gone through many modifications. Out of the television era in the 1950s, every decade has brought change. Beginning in the 1960s, territories had to exist. The product that promoters offered was simply too good to allow for just one champion to appear in one city each night. Most major cities jumped at the chance to hold live cards. From Portland to San Francisco and St. Louis to Atlanta.

Ric Flair's career has spanned several decades.

Early champion wrestler Harley Race.

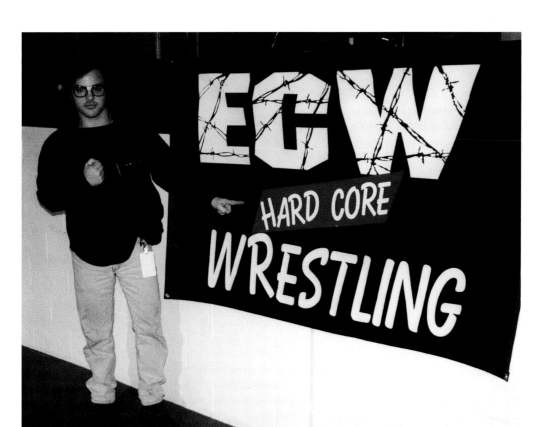

No one stands taller in hardcore matches than Spike Dudley.

Chris Benoit utilizes submissions regularly, just as Frank Gotch, Wayne Munn, and Farmer Burns did back in their day.

At right is a bloodied New Jack after a ladder match.

Sting applies pressure on Ric Flair.

Killer Kowalski, right, and Blackjack Lanza share a moment.

The times were good and hundreds of wrestlers stayed active.

With the advent of cable television in the 1980s, fans turned on the tube. Territories expanded. Dusty Rhodes, Ric Flair, Tommy Rich, the Freebirds, the Junkyard Dog, Buzz Sawyer, Harley Race, and dozens more seemed to jump from the television screens into our lives.

Prior to cable, only Eastern fans were privileged to see the WWF's stars. Whether it was the lure of true champions like Bob Backlund and Bruno Sammartino, or guilty-pleasure favorites like S.D. Jones and Salvatore Bellomo, wrestling fans had an opportunity to see the stars on a national scale. Even smaller promotions had chances on cable. Groups in California, Texas, Oregon, Hawaii, and Louisiana were seen weekly, and had loyal followings.

Then in a flash, wrestling as we knew it was gone.

The explosion of the 1980s gave World Wrestling Entertainment owner Vince McMahon Jr. reason to puff his chest. Wrestling was seen on the networks and his concept called Wrestlemania was a pay-per-view success. The WWF was everywhere.

Smalltime promoters could no longer compete and were run out of business.

By the 1990s, fans grew tired of it all. Whether fans were bored of Hulk Hogan or whether the accusations that McMahon hid a steroid abuse problem in his company took a bigger toll than originally thought. The WWF saw lean years early in the decade. By the end of the 1990s, Steve Austin had picked up where Hogan left off and opened the door for Triple H and The Rock to join in an even bigger boom.

By the late 1990s, Pay-per-views had replaced regularly run territorial shows from two decades earlier. Instead of making plans for monthly shows at their hometown arenas, fans instead made plans to watch monthly pay television programs.

We see wrestlers everywhere. Austin was on network programming, The Rock and Diamond Dallas Page were in movies, and even Rob Van Dam was on film. The new-age wrestlers are simply carrying on the tradition laid by their forefathers. Gorgeous George, Hard Boiled Haggerty, Lenny Montana, Woody Strode, Tor Johnson, Terry Funk, and countless others appeared on film long before Austin or Rocky ever did. It only seems that in a world of Internet and satellite television that today's wrestlers are bigger than ever.

Has wrestling really changed all that much? Hardly. It may have been modernized and it certainly has become a faster-paced event, but what we see now has always been around.

Wrestling continually digs into its 100-year-old bag of tricks. In many ways the Undertaker is a lot like Funk who was a lot like the television cowboys of the 1950s. Austin is never afraid to mix it up and grabs a beer when he wins. Maybe when Austin was a kid he never watched the Crusher. But the only things that separate them are the times and the fact that Austin doesn't smoke cigars like the Crusher did.

Old ideas. New twists. Frank Gotch, Wayne Munn, and Farmer Burns were avowed shooters in the early 1900s. Ninety years later, Japan sells its fans the notion that their matches are real. Chris Benoit, Little Guido, Tazz, and Ken Shamrock utilize submissions regularly.

Highflyers, like Edge and Christian, are simply new versions of the Hart family, who borrowed something from Eduardo Carpentier, who surely owed thanks to the great 1950s star, Antonino Rocca.

You want hardcore? Every week fans get a glimpse of matches with chairs and tables. But in 1910, Tom Chaaker died in Montreal after the beating he took at the hands of Yousouf the Terrible Turk. Twenty-one years after that, Stan Stasiak died from injuries and infection he suffered in the ring against champion Ed Don George in Canada. How's death for hardcore?

Wrestling giants Kevin Nash, Albert, and Kane are large, powerful men. But wasn't President Abraham Lincoln, a wrestler in 1831, remembered as being 6'8"?

Bill Goldberg had a make-believe winning streak that was nothing short of impressive. When Farmer Burns retired, he reportedly had an amazing 6000 wins to his credit.

The first decade of professional wrestling was spectacular. Certainly the names are different, but wrestling just has not changed all that much. In the next century, perhaps matches will be held on floating platforms in outer space, but we can always be certain that someone will get drilled with a steel chair.

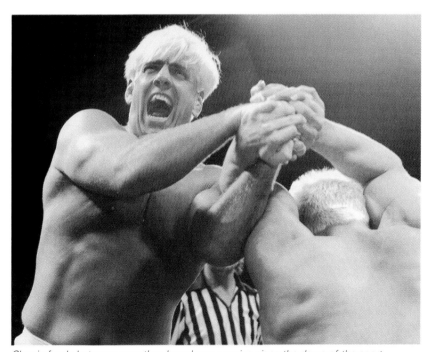

Classic feuds between wrestlers have been ongoing since the dawn of the sport, whether it's Tommy Dreamer and Justin Credible, left; Lex Luger and Hulk Hogan, right; or Ric Flair and Sting, pictured below.

Note: The dates in parentheses denote the decade(s) that wrestler has appeared in; names in brackets following each biography are aliases used by that particular wrestler. Trivia answers are located on page 256.

AAA

One of the main arteries for wrestling South of the Border, this group has produced modern day stars like Rey Mysterio Jr., Konnan, and Juventud Guerrera.

Abbot, Dave (Tank)
(1990s-2000s)

From the mean streets of Ultimate Fighting to WCW, this real-life barroom brawler had the charisma to go far, but he never found his niche in pro wrestling. [Tank]

Abdullah the Butcher
(1960s-2000s)

The scarred forehead is unmistakably Abby. This five-decade star is truly a legend. Born in Montreal and a world traveler ten times over, he's frightened opponents and fans while leaving a wide swath in his wake. His feuds with Bruiser Brody are classics.

Abrams, Herb
(1990s)

Abrams envisioned an empire that would rival Vince McMahon Jr., but his early-1990s UWF promotion based in California was filled with lies and deception. He died of a drug overdose in 1996.

Abuddah Dein
(1970s-1990s)

The son of King Curtis Iaukea, he later made a name for himself, sans his legendary father's name. As Dein, he was a devil-crazed character and had success in the Pacific Northwest. [Rocky Iaukea]

Ace, Johnny
(1980s-1990s)

The real-life brother of Road Warrior Animal, the lanky Ace found stardom in WCW with Shane Douglas (as the Dynamic Dudes) and later in All-Japan. His ability to write believable storylines got him hired by the WWE where he still works behind the scenes.

Acid, Trent
(1990s-2000s)

The East Coast firecracker is short in size but long on talent. Wearer of multiple regional belts, he's found a home in Japan and CZW but his high-flying ability will surely give him a chance in a major league one day.

Adams, Brian
(1990s-2000s)

Hawaii has been the origin of only a few competitors, but Adams still calls it home. He's had many opportunities to shine in WWF, WCW, and the Northwest. He's Antonio Inoki's son-in-law and was once the fourth member of Demolition. [Crush; Kronik]

Adams, Chris
(1980s-1990s)

Adams was a superb Brit wrestler and judo expert who helped the Dallas area boom in the early 1980s. He wasn't flashy, but he always played an important role wherever he went and he helped train Steve Austin. He was murdered in 2001 in a domestic dispute. [Gentleman Chris]

Adias, Brian
(1980s-2000s)

A Dallas-based star who saw minor stardom in the 1980s as Texas champion during the Von Erich era. He can still be found plugging away on the independent scene.

Adonis, Adrian
(1970s-1980s)

A very solid technician who won world tag belts with Dick Murdoch (WWF) and Jesse Ventura (AWA), he had numerous runs as an East Coast bad boy. Later, he appeared in the WWF using a flamboyant homosexual gimmick. Adonis died in a 1988 car wreck. [Adorable Adrian]

Afi, Siva
(1970s-1980s)

This former WWF performer had Hawaiian bloodlines, but he never made it out of the mid-card line-up. [Samoan Warrior]

Aguayo, Perro
(1960s-1990s)

One of Mexico's true warriors, he was one of the few Luchadores who didn't wear a mask; however, he was noted for wearing Mastadonian-styled boots. He also headlined some in Japan.

Aja Kong
(1990s)

When you think of Kong, you think of a female Abdullah the Butcher. A superior brawler when the Japan women's explosion hit the early 1990s, Kong had some of the most memorable bouts, fitting her among the all-time great females.

Akbar, Skandor
(1960s-1990s)

In Dallas, one manager comes to mind: Akbar. A former mid-card attraction turned manager, he helped lead the territory through some of its hottest times, always leading a stable of monsters including One Man Gang and Missing Link.

Albano, Lou
(1950s-1980s)

Passers-by recognize Albano merely by the rubber bands dangling from his face. But Albano was a classic heel manager—after he was a WWWF tag champ in Tony Altimore in 1967—guiding the likes of the Samoans and Moondogs to tag belts.

Albert
(1990s-2000s)

This hairy backed, pierced big man is one of many to get the nod as a WWE star. With a deceptively large 6-5 frame, his namesake comes from the piercing culture and he has mainly a power arsenal. [A-Train; Baldo; Prince Albert]

Albright, Gary
(1980s-1990s)

Albright became an international star in the late 1990s, when he died of a heart attack in 2000 in the ring, after pinning his opponent. The bearded big man had a successful amateur career and was married into the Wild Samoan family. [Vokkan Singh]

Alfonso, Bill
(1980s-2000s)

The pesky former referee switched to managing and found a home in ECW where he led Sabu, Tazz, and Rob Van Dam to many titles. He was also the official interpreter for El Gigante in the WWF.

Trivia

Q. Which wrestler took home a bronze medal at the 1976 Montreal Olympics for Judo in the heavyweight division?

Ali, Muhammad
(1970s-1980s)

Arguably the most famous athlete ever, this boxing legend spent time in the wrestling ring in matches against Kenny Jay and Antonio Inoki. It is said the fast-talking, colorful Ali mimicked Gorgeous George's ring-persona.

Al-Kaissey, Adnan
(1960s-1990s)

Legitimate Iraqi native who played up his connection to Saddam Hussein in WWF storylines. He wrestled virtually every modern-era performer and was also a talented amateur, but is most known for managing Ken Patera, Crusher Blackwell, and Sgt. Slaughter. [Billy Whitewolf; General Adnan; Sheik Adnan]

Allen, Bad News
(1980s-1990s)

When people think of real-life tough men, they often pass over this former Olympic judo team member. He was a top star in Japan in the 1980s and began under Hart family tutelage. He toured Canada and WWF as well. [Allen Coage; Bad News Brown]

Allen, Steve
(1950s-1960s)

The late comedian and former host of the "Tonight Show" began as a wrestling announcer. He later made Wrestlemania cameos.

All-Japan Pro Wrestling

One of the oldest-reigning promotional groups in Japan, formerly headed by the late Giant Baba, its roll call of champions is immense. All-Japan began in 1953 as the Japan Wrestling Association with Lou Thesz holding its first recognized championship, the NWA International title. In 1973, Baba formed All-Japan and used the PWF belt as its championship. In 1989, it recognized the Triple Crown title, which still exists today.

All-Japan Women's Wrestling

This female off-shoot of the men's group in Japan is known for some of its grueling tactics in training future stars. Among them, Minami Toyota and Chigusa Nagayo.

Altimore, Tony
(1950s-1960s)

A mid-level performer who caught on as Lou Albano's partner as the Sicilians. He won regional tag-team belts including the WWWF version in 1967.

Amazing Red
(2000s)

A graduate of Mikey Whipwreck's wrestling gym, he is one of the smaller stars around, but he has raised eyebrows with his mix of Lucha and Japanese styles in NWA-TNA.

TRIVIA

Q. Who was the subject of a late 1980's PBS documentary?

American Wrestling Association
(1960s-1990s)

This now-defunct group based in Minneapolis was run by Verne Gagne beginning in 1960. Gagne and promoter Wally Karbo bought the territory from promoter Tony Stecher. In 1960, the AWA crowned Gagne as its first world champion. One of the original three major promotions to crown a world champion, it closed in 1990 from financial trouble.

Amish Roadkill
(1990s-2000s)

A grad of the Tazz's wrestling school, Roadkill is an agile big man with a quirky gimmick. He and Danny Doring were the last to hold the ECW tag belts.

Anaya, Ciclone
(1970s)

A popular Texas grappler who often held Brass Knux titles, he was noted for his feuds with Jose Lothario.

Anderson, Arn
(1980s-2000s)

Marty Lunde was a preliminary attraction before he caught on as Ole Anderson's fictional nephew in the Mid-Atlantic area. One of the great tag-team wrestlers ever and an original member of the Four Horsemen, he won numerous world tag belts with Tully Blanchard. Injuries ended his career in 1999 and he now works as a WWE agent. [Super Olympia]

Anderson, Billy
(1980s-1990s)

California-based wrestler and trainer who has sent his grads to Japan, most notably the late Louis Spicolli. [The Mercenary]

Anderson, Brad
(1980s-1990s)

This journeyman was trained by legendary father Gene Anderson and wrestled in Georgia and the Northwest, but never hit it big.

Anderson, CW
(1990s-2000s)

Technically-sound WCW Power Plant grad who emulates Arn Anderson in independent rings out East. He was also part of the last crew in ECW before the promotion closed in 2001.

Anderson, Gene
(1950s-1970s)

The late Anderson founded the Minnesota Wrecking Crew and was successful in the Midwest and later the Carolinas in tag teams with Ole and Lars Anderson.

Anderson, Lars
(1960s-1970s)

Capitalizing on the Wrecking Crew fame, Ole "adopted" this man as his brother. He had AWA success and seemed destined for prime time. He eventually landed in Hawaii where he promoted with Lia Maivia. One of the original Andersons, he teamed with Gene in the Carolinas. [Larry Heinimi]

Anderson, Ole
(1960s-1990s)

Along with "brother" Gene, Alan Rogowski made up one-half of the Minnesota Wrecking Crew. He wreaked havoc in NWA and Mid-Atlantic. A rugged performer who brought an air of believability, he later became a talent coordinator for Georgia Championship Wrestling. Later, he was a matchmaker for WCW. [Black Scorpion]

Anderson, Ox
(1960s-1970s)

A big, burly regional character, the 6-foot-2 Ox was a popular contender. He is a former bar owner who toured the Midwest and wrestled in the Northwest, winning the tag-team titles there.

Anderson, Randy
(1970s-1990s)

Georgia amateur wrestling standout who followed best friend Arn Anderson to the pro side where he became a reliable referee. [Pee Wee Anderson]

Andre the Giant
(1960s-1990s)

A true legend in wrestling, during the 1970s, few wrestlers had more world-wide appeal than Andre. A France native, he toured the world and was a special attraction in virtually every corner of the globe. His career climaxed in the 1987 Wrestlemania III main event against Hulk Hogan. He was also considered the King of the Battle Royals. [Eiffel Tower; Giant Machine; Giant Rouisimoff]

Angel of Death
(1980s)

A bald and menacing wrestler from the 1980s, he played a variety or roles regionally in Canada, World Class, and UWF. He won several regional tag-team titles. [Black Scorpion; Russian Assassin No. 2]

Angle, Eric
(1990s-2000s)

Older brother of WWE star Kurt Angle, this wrestler with an amateur background is a trainee looking to hit the mainstream. He's been involved in several WWE and OVW storylines.

Angle, Kurt
(1990s-2000s)

Former 1996 Olympic champion turned pro wrestler, Angle amazingly won every major WWE singles title in his rookie year in 2000. The Pittsburgh native is one of the fastest improving wrestlers ever and is as funny on the mike as he is skilled in the ring. He overcame a near career-ending injury in 2003 and returned to the spotlight.

Animal
(1980s-2000s)

One-half of the famous Road Warriors, this Chicago native trained in Minneapolis and was the stronger member of the legendary team. They are regarded as the most popular tag team ever and held tag titles in every major group they appeared in. [Road Warrior]

Anthony, Tony
(1970s-2000s)

Part old-school, part hardcore, this Southerner had deep roots in Tennessee wrestling. This rugged, all-out brawler was one-half of the Dirty White Boys with Lynn Denton. He's shed blood in Continental, Northwest, Smoky Mountain, and Mid-South. [Dirty White Boy; T.L. Hopper; Uncle Cletus.] See: Dirty White Boys.

APA
(1990s-2000s)

Former college football studs, if the Acolyte Protection Agency had been given the chance in Japan, they may have been one of the great teams ala Bruiser Brody and Stan Hansen. Instead, their WWE run has been highlighted by three runs as tag champions. Is there more to come? [Acolytes.] See: Bradshaw; Ron Simmons.

Apollo, Argentine
(1950s-1960s)

One of the top draws of the Golden Age, he was a high-flying regular when television wrestling first became popular.

Apter, Bill
(1960s-2000s)

The avid fan-turned-editor of *Pro Wrestling Illustrated*, he's probably produced more wrestling magazines than anyone in modern time. His style often sided with promoters' storylines and the entire newsstand wrestling magazine business was coined "Apter Mags" as a result.

Arakawa, Mitsu
(1950s-1960s)

Japanese star who performed in the Midwest and teamed with Mr. Moto to win AWA titles in 1967. Also teamed with Kinji Shibuya in the Midwest and Vancouver areas. In 1969, he held the WWWF International tag title with Toru Tanaka.

Arcidi, Ted
(1980s)

A onetime power-lifting champion, he gave wrestling a try. He was a decent talker, but had trouble in the ring. He is known as the former weightlifting trainer of Triple H.

Arion, Spiros
(1970s)

WWWF tag-team oriented Greek grappler who teamed with, and challenged, Bruno Sammartino. Against Bruno, the scientific Arion hired the help of manager Fred Blassie in storylines.

Armstrong, Bob
(1970s-2000s)

This former fireman loved wrestling enough to leave a week before his pension was secured to become a ring star and molded himself into an icon in the Southeast region. He is the father of wrestlers Brad, Steve, James, and Scott Armstrong. [The Bullet]

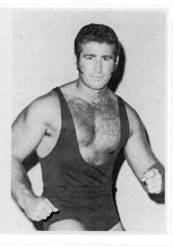

Armstrong, Brad
(1980s-2000s)

A fine technical wrestler who never made it nationally because of his lack of size. Regionally, he was a champion in the 1980s and still had a WCW career in the 1990s. [Arachnaman; Badstreet; Candyman; Fantasia]

Armstrong, Jack
(1980s)

This bruising, wild-haired madman held multiple versions of California championships and was often in bloody feuds. [The Wildman]

Armstrong, Jesse James
(1980s-2000s)

Brian James toiled in Memphis for years before catching a break as Jeff Jarrett's lackey. Then, in 1997, he created the totally unique Road Dogg character and tore the house down with his trademark quotes to win WWF tag titles with Billy Gunn. [B.G. James; Roadie; Road Dogg]

Armstrong, Scott
(1980s-1990s)

Turned pro as a lightweight but trained himself into a main event star in the Southeast. He teamed in WCW with Tracy Smothers. [Southern Boy]

Armstrong, Steve
(1980s-1990s)

The third son of Bob Armstrong, he was a natural cruiserweight. Superb technician who was a Smoky Mountain Wrestling draw. [Dixie Dynamite]

Arquette, David
(2000s)

Something of a new-age Andy Kaufman, this "Ready to Rumble" film star was given the WCW world title in 2000 in a match to draw attention to the failing group. The experiment, which lasted two weeks, is not remembered as an industry highlight.

Ash, Mark
(1980s)

The former 1980 U.S. Jr. heavyweight champion in the Southeast promoted in Georgia and the Gulf Coast area. He's also known as a longtime maker of wrestling boots. [Mean Mark]

Asuka, Lioness
(1980s)

Along with Chigusa Nagayo, she was in the Crush Gals team, the most popular team in Japanese women's history. In a famous feud, Asuka later beat her former partner Nagayo for the WWWA championship. She retired, with belt in hand, in 1989.

Atlas, Omar
(1960s-1990s)

This star from Venezuela was a high flying and powerful force in the Midwest and Texas. With a few Central States titles to his credit, he was a preliminary attraction before his retirement.

Atlas, Tony
(1970s-1990s)

This former smiling, bodybuilding freak was a main event star in NWA, WWF, and AWA rings, winning titles virtually everywhere he went. [Saba Simba; Superman]

Austin Idol
(1970s-1990s)

The Florida-based muscleman was often called a smaller version of Billy Graham, but Idol said different. He claims Hulk Hogan stole his own "Idolmania" and turned it into "Hulkamania," although no one knows for sure. But Idol was quite a star in the South during the 1980s. A gifted talker, he helped draw massive crowds to Memphis for his matches against Jerry Lawler in 1987. Although he never became a national star, Idol was a super regional performer. [Mick McCord]

Austin, Norvell
(1970s-1980s)

Capable African-American who was one-half of the Pretty Young Things with Koko Ware and an early member of the Midnight Express with Dennis Condrey and Randy Rose. Austin was mainly a regional star in the Southeast.

Austin, Steve
(1980s-2000s)

A former blond-haired brawler, Austin broke onto the scene in Dallas in the late 1980s in a feud with his former trainer, Chris Adams. His breakout year was 1993 in WCW when he won the U.S. and tag-team titles. He toiled there until 1995 when the WWF took a chance on him. After an ill-fated push under the management of Ted DiBiase, he carved his own niche as "Stone Cold." The gimmick quickly grew into one of the most profitable in history. Bringing a new style to wrestling, he ushered in a new era for the WWF. The former six-time WWF champion has been involved in huge money feuds with Rock and Vince McMahon, which cemented his place in history. [Ringmaster; Stunning Steve]

Awesome Kongs, The
(1990s)

A heavy-set tag team under masks during the early 1990s, they wrestled out of Dallas but got a short-lived break in WCW.

Awesome, Mike
(1980s-2000s)

A highly unusual wrestler. At close to 7 feet tall, he is huge, but maneuvers like a cruiserweight and has a penchant for high-risk moves. Between shots in WWF and WCW, he's been established in Japan for almost a decade and is also a former two-time ECW champion. [That 70s Guy; Gladiator]

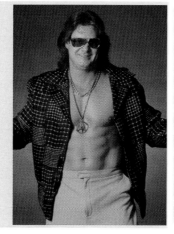

Ayala, Hercules
(1970s-1980s)

Everyone needs a nemesis and in Puerto Rico, Ayala was the No. 1 challenger to Carlos Colon's WWC Universal title in the 1980s. His career began in Boston where he trained with Angelo Savoldi, but his island matches with Colon are remembered most. This very large, menacing foe is a multi-time Universal titleholder.

Baba, Ali
(1930s)

Early era word champion who beat Dick Shikat in 1936 to claim the title. His career spanned to America, Europe, South Africa, and India. Some insist his matches, often hours long, harken to a time when the bouts were real.

Baba, Motoko
(1960s-2000s)

The widow of Japanese legend Giant Baba, she was a force behind the scenes for All-Japan wrestling and reveres old-school ethics and honors loyalty. She is still making an impact as the company's owner since her husband's death in 1999.

Baba, Shohei "Giant"
(1960s-1990s)

One of the true legends of wrestling. A former baseball player, he was a student of Rikidozan in the 1960s. His 7-foot stature made him an instant hit. As the owner of All-Japan wrestling, he was a three-decade headliner. His success followed him to North America where he was a three-time NWA world champion. His passing in 1999 from cancer ended an era, but as the wide audience that watched his funeral on live television shows, he won't be forgotten. [Giant Baba]

Baby Doll
(1980s)

Longtime World Class and NWA valet who guided Dusty Rhodes and Tully Blanchard in some explosive early 1980s feuds. Sporting a Pat Benatar look, she was a sex object for the times. She is also married to wrestler Sam Houston.

Backlund, Bob
(1980s-1990s)

Backlund, a stellar amateur, trained in the same camp as Jesse Ventura. When his career finally brought him to New York, he found himself in a strange situation: being on the small side, he was given the world title after the WWF fans were used to monsters like Billy Graham and Bruno Sammartino. Backlund made the opportunity work and finished as a three-time WWF world champion. He had epic feuds with Ken Patera and Don Muraco, which drew thousands to sell out Madison Square Garden. In later years, he turned to politics.

Bad Company
(1980s-1990s)

In Calgary, Brian Pillman and Bruce Hart used this name for their tag team while winning the Stampede tag-team titles twice. See: Brian Pillman; Bruce Hart.

Badd Company
(1980s)

Tag-team name used by Paul Diamond and Pat Tanaka in AWA and Memphis. The karate-prone tandem, led by manager Dallas Page, beat the Midnight Rockers for the AWA belts in 1988. See: Paul Diamond; Pat Tanaka.

Bagwell, Buff
(1990s-2000s)

Georgia native who discovered his charisma in WCW. He's a former five-time WCW tag-team champion. After wrestling, he ran a wrestling novelty store. [Fabian; Handsome Stranger; Marcus Alexander Bagwell]

Baillargeon Brothers, The
(1940s-1960s)

This wrestling family, a famous troupe of strongmen, boasted six brothers who took their strength to the ring. Charles, Paul, Adrien, Lionel, Jean, and Antonio performed feats of strength in Quebec. In wrestling, their rubbery flexibility wowed crowds across Canada where they are still remembered fondly.

Baker, Ox
(1950s-1980s)

Stop the presses! The famous Ox is one of the scariest looking men to don the tights. If his looks didn't kill, his heart punch did—in 1972, Ray Gunkel died after injuries apparently suffered from Baker's punch. The Ox traveled far and wide as a main event star in the U.S., Canada, and Puerto Rico, but his career never culminated in world title reigns. He also had a role in the flick, "Escape from New York," upon his retirement.

Bambi
(1980s-2000s)

The tanned Southern Belle has toured relentlessly around the country, but her biggest challenge has been finding opponents. She's headlined in various women's promotions like LPWA and WOWW. [Selina Majors]

Banner, Penny
(1950s-1970s)

This women's wrestler was a top challenger for the world title. A true athlete, this blonde bomber was the first AWA women's champion and, after retirement, has been active in the Senior Olympics. She even claims to have dated Elvis Presley in her younger days.

Barbarian, The
(1980s-2000s)

A three-decade star who is considered by some to be the toughest wrestler ever. He was a unique character, using a wild gimmick with face paint and a Mohawk hairdo. For many years, he was the tag-team partner of the Warlord.

Barend, Johnny
(1960s)

Nicknamed "Handsome," he was the tag-team partner of Buddy Rogers. Together, they won the U.S. tag title in the 1960s.

Barr, Art
(1980s-1990s)

Remembered as a rare American influence on Lucha Libre, this son of Portland promoter Sandy Barr was small in size, but was a buzz saw in the ring. When Roddy Piper crowned him with the Beetlejuice gimmick, Barr's career flourished. But it wasn't until he traveled to Mexico as Eddy Guerrero's partner that his true talents emerged. Before he could parlay his talent into American success, he died in 1994 at age 28. [Beetlejuice; Juicer; Love Machine]

Barr, Jesse
(1980s-1990s)

Brother of Art Barr, he wrestled all over the country, including with the WWF, under a Lone Ranger mask in the early 1980s. They called him a Funk, but he had no relation to the Texas family. [Jimmy Jack Funk]

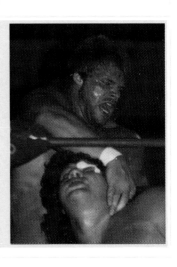

Barr, Sandy
(1970s-2000s)

The father of Art and Jesse Barr was the right-hand man for Portland promoter Don Owen. He later bought the promotion in the 1980s and still runs cards out of the Sandy Barr Flea Market in the Crescent City.

Barrett, Pat
(1960s-1970s)

"Irish Pat" was a popular, but small, European and Canadian heavyweight. In 1975, when Victor Rivera retired as Dom DeNucci's partner, Barrett filled in to help develop the WWWF tag-team titles.

Barton, Mike
(1980s-2000s)

A former tag-team champion with Billy Gunn in the WWF, after his tours there, he found a home in Japan. His career started in the Florida independents, but he made the most of his chances. His credibility blew a fuse when, at Wrestlemania 16, he was demolished by Butterbean in a tough-man fight.

Bass, Don
(1970s-1980s)

This Memphis and Southeastern veteran was a member of the Masked Interns with partner Roger Smith. He also performed with his brother, Ron Bass.

Bass, Nicole
(1990s)

A toned, muscular woman who tried to find a niche as a bodyguard in the mold of Chyna. She had a brief shot in ECW before wrestling in the WWF.

Bass, Ron
(1970s-1980s)

The husky Texan and friend of Dusty Rhodes wrestled in the Southeast, including Florida, where he was the Southern heavyweight champion. Later, he was an opening act in the WWF. [Outlaw Ron Bass]

Bass, Sam
(1970s)

This famous manager guided the Masked Superstars, Don Greene and a young Jerry Lawler. He is remembered as Lawler's first loud-mouthed manager in Memphis. In 1976, Bass perished in a car accident that also killed the Masked Dominoes.

Bassman, Rick
(1980s-2000s)

The California-based impresario brought Sting and Ultimate Warrior into the eyes of wrestling promoters through a group called Power Team USA. In the 1990s, he started recruiting future stars, such as John Cena, and promoted cards in Southern California in his UPW group.

Bastein, Red
(1960s-1970s)

Red was a top draw in the AWA during the 1960s and often teamed with Billy Red Lyons as the Fabulous Redheads. Also a West Coast veteran, he won the AWA tag-team title in 1971 with Hercules Cortez.

Batista, Dave
(1990s-2000s)

The freaky looking bodybuilding phenom was a former OVW champion but got a call-up from the WWE. Has had among his tag-team partners D-Von Dudley and Randy Orton. [Deacon Batista; Leviathan]

Batten Twins, The
(1980s-1990s)

Brad and Bart were never superstars, but they are indeed legit twins. The undersized tandem mainly toured the Southeast and Mid-Atlantic areas, but they once held the WWC tag titles in Puerto Rico.

Battle of the Belts

This Florida supercard series was a live, televised show. Promoter Eddie Graham booked the shows from 1985-86 using NWA talent such as Ric Flair and the Road Warriors.

Battle Royal

Perhaps the most famous, and popular, gimmick match, it dates back to the 1950s when television wrestling was a first-time hit. The object? Pretty easy. A large number of wrestlers climb into the ring and throw their opponents over the top rope to the floor. The last remaining star wins. Over the years, the match evolved some as more wrestlers were added—sometimes as many as 50. Two-ring, and even three-ring, Battle Royals have been staged through the years, too.

Bearcat Wright
(1950s-1970s)

An African American pioneer who broke color barriers to main event in the U.S., he toured the free world and headlined many arenas. In 1963, he defeated the legendary Fred Blassie on the champ's home turf for the WWA world title in Los Angeles.

Bearer, Paul
(1980s-1990s)

Formerly known as Percy Pringle, the Dallas manager performed in the WWF as the guide of the Undertaker. This legit, former funeral director was a great heel in his day, especially in World Class where he led heels like Rick Rude. [Percy Pringle]

Beat the Champ Title
(1950s)

The first-known TV title based in Los Angeles from 1968-82, the idea of the belt was that it would be defended on television exclusively. Some of its holders included George Cannon (its first), Black Gordman, Fred Blassie, and Victor Rivera (its last).

Beefcake, Brutus
(1980s-2000s)

Ed Leslie began his career as Hulk Hogan's cousin in Florida and that relationship served his career well. He reached superstar status in the 1980s as Brutus, winning the WWF tag title with Greg Valentine in 1985. A man of many identities, he overcame a tragic sailing accident that crushed every bone in his face. In his prime, he was a well-sculpted star who performed as a fan favorite and heel and later appeared in WCW as, you guessed it, a friend of Hogan's. [Barber; Butcher; Disciple; Ed Boulder; Man With No Name; Zodiac]

Benjamin, Shelton
(1990s-2000s)

This former amateur standout and teammate of Brock Lesnar's at the University of Minnesota has tried to carve a niche as a high-flyer with mat skills. His earliest success came as the WWE tag-team champion with fellow amateur Charlie Haas. He also held the OVW tag-team title with Lesnar.

Benoit, Chris
(1980s-2000s)

This wrestler from Canada adds an air of believability to the current scene. He trained under the Hart family tutelage in Calgary, but traveled the world to better his skills. A devoted follower of Dynamite Kid, he has emulated the former star's style and taken a nearly identical career path. Benoit's five-star matches in Mexico and Japan still have people raving. He's a former WCW world champ, and WWF tag-team and Intercontinental champion. [Wild Pegasus]

Bergstrom, CW
(1980s-1990s)

A skilled journeyman and independent star, he lacked the charisma to find a national following. He has traveled to Memphis and Portland, and was a former tag-team champion in both areas.

Bernard, Brute
(1950-1960s)

A native of Quebec, he is one of the first big, bad, bald men. He was over 6-feet-tall. Main events never eluded him, as he won tag titles with Skull Murphy and Mike Paidousis.

Berry, Red
(1930s-1950s)

"Wild" Red was one of the sport's first fanatical managers and famously guided the Fabulous Kangaroos team to stardom and championships around the country. Flamboyant to the end, he was a former boxer and light heavyweight wrestling champion before he turned to managing.

Beyond the Mat

Virtually every would-be Hollywood scriptwriter is drawn to the compelling real-life dramas of boxers and wrestlers. Writer Barry Blaustein was the one who did something about it. After success with films like Eddie Murphy's "Nutty Professor," Blaustein spent more than five years compiling "Beyond the Mat," in which he follows the lives of three wrestlers: the legendary Terry Funk; the drug-riddled Jake Roberts; and new star Mick Foley. The film was partly done tongue-in-cheek but it traveled to areas the wrestling industry had long considered off-limits. In that sense, its merits as a documentary were important in many ways.

Big Daddy
(1960s-1980s)

Shirley Crabtree, a 300+-pound English wrestler, was a star in Europe in the 1970s and 1980s. The wrestler with a 64-inch chest had almost a cult following overseas. His persona was said to be a take-off of the late actor, Burl Ives. No doubt, people enjoyed his whimsical approach to wrestling.

Big Show, The
(1990s-2000s)

Once dubbed Andre the Giant Jr., Paul Wight suffers from gigantism as Andre did. Big Show was thrust into the spotlight quickly: his first match was against Hulk Hogan on television. He's appeared in films and TV, but in the ring he's a multiple world champion. In 1996, he won the WCW world title and won the WWF title in 1999 from Triple H. He's also held tag-team titles on three occasions. [Giant; Paul Wight]

Bigelow, Bam Bam
(1980s-2000s)

A former karate fighter, he considered shoot fighting and boxing careers before getting into wrestling through Larry Sharpe's Monster Factory in New Jersey. The agile, big man whose tattooed body led him to main events all over the country, has been a steady star—from his beginnings in World Class in the 1980s to the WCW and WWF in the late 1990s. [Beast from the East]

Bischoff, Eric
(1980s-2000s)

The former AWA ad salesman turned major power broker in WCW in the 1990s. He is credited for turning around that failing company and bringing it to new levels of success. With the NWO concept, which he claims to have started, and the introduction of "Monday Nitro," Bischoff was the first to beat Vince McMahon. With WCW since closed, he was actually employed by McMahon and has been an influence on-screen in the WWE ever since.

Black Bart
(1970s-1980s)

With a name like that, it's easy to guess he played the role of a villainous cowboy. He and Ron Bass were a mid-level card team who wrestled throughout the Midwest. In 1986, he shockingly was awarded a version of the world title in Dallas. Famous for his all-black outfits and bullwhip, he also toured World Class, the UWF, and the NWA in the 1980s.

Black Gordman
(1960s-1980s)

A top Mexican star who often teamed with the Great Goliath in Los Angeles rings, he usually portrayed a rule breaker and was known for a very believable style. He was tough and relentless. Later, he wrestled in Puerto Rico.

Blackhearts, The
(1980s)

A masked touring tag team of David Heath and Tom Nash, they were former Stampede tag champions. They also toured Japan.

Blackman, Steve
(1990s-2000s)

A trained Black Belt, he was schooled in wrestling by Bruce Hart in Canada. He was a role player in the WWF and once held the company's Hardcore title. A late 1990s bout with malaria sadly suspended his career and he never fully recovered enough to return full-time. [Lethal Weapon]

Blackstone, Bonnie
(1980s-1990s)

The real-life wife of Joe Pedicino, Bonnie was a part-time television announcer for the defunct "This Week in Wrestling" and several promotions in Dallas and Georgia.

Blackwell, Jerry
(1970s-1990s)

No one ever said Blackwell looked like a wrestler, but he was one of the few 400 pounders who could move well in the ring. This talented brawler, who also held his own against the technicians, was a main event star in the AWA where he feuded with Mad Dog Vachon. He passed away in 1995 at age 45. [Crusher Blackwell]

Blair, B. Brian
(1970s-2000s)

The Florida native was a mat tactician who reached national appeal as one-half of the Killer Bees team with Jim Brunzell. Trained by Hiro Matsuda, he held many regional titles including the Florida title. In his later years, he's worked for Gulf States independents.

Blanchard, Joe
(1960s-1990s)

After his wrestling career was finished, Blanchard was a successful promoter of Southwest Championship Wrestling out of San Antonio. The group, remembered as a blood and guts free-for-all, ran from 1970-85 before it was sold to the Von Erich family in Dallas. Joe, the father of Tully Blanchard, was also an AWA figurehead commissioner in the early 1990s.

Blanchard, Tully
(1970s-1990s)

A thinking-man's wrestler: that's what Tully's opponents would probably say of this original member of the Four Horsemen. He was a second-generation star and despite his diminutive size, was championship caliber. The former college football star held many regional titles including the Southwest belt eight times. Known as a tight fighter who could brawl and chain wrestle, his famous move was the slingshot suplex. He reached wide acclaim with the Horsemen in the 1980s. Together, with Arn Anderson, he was a three-time world tag-team champion. Blanchard retired from the ring before his prime ended to focus on ministry work.

Blassie, Freddie
(1950-1990s)

"Classy" Freddie Blassie: the name will forever be known in the annals of wrestling. Americans knew him as the "Hollywood fashion plate" and Japanese fans knew him as the "Vampire." Blassie did it all: records, television shows, stunt work, international tours, you name it. His feuds with John Tolos, the Destroyer, and Rikidozan were historic to say the least. He toured the U.S. extensively in the 1950s, including Los Angeles, and later he pushed the envelope in Japan. Seen in Dracula poses, he was known to bite his opponents. After retirement, he switched to managing and coined the nickname, "pencil-necked geek," which he saved for fans and opponents. In 2003, Blassie passed away.

Blears, James
(1950s-1980s)

The "Lord" as he was often known was a distinguished British star who wrestled, announced, and promoted in Hawaii from the 1950s-70s. He also toured North America extensively. [Lord James Blears]

TRIVIA

Q. Before his wrestling days, this wrestler escaped a Japanese submarine takeover while working on an Allied merchant ship during World War II. Who is he?

Bloom, Wayne
(1980s-1990s)

The tall, tough guy was a former AWA world tag-team champion with fellow Minnesotan Mike Enos. A blond haired tough talker, he was a marginal wrestler, but found decent success in the AWA, NWA, and WWF. [Beau Beverly] See: Destruction Crew.

Blue Demon
(1940s-1980s)

In Mexico, few wrestlers have had the type of success that the mask-wearing Demon had. A star in both the ring and in movies, his friendship with El Santo only went so far. In the ring, he and Santo were bitter enemies who drew monster crowds in the 1970s. He feuded with Santo over the NWA welterweight title, which he held solidly during a 4-1/2-year span. Blue Demon retired in 1989, but his legacy is strong—it is also followed by his son, who wrestles as Blue Demon Jr.

Blue Meanie
(1990s-2000s)

This strange gimmick wrestler clad with blue hair found a home in ECW. He had a short-lived shot in the WWF before he left wrestling to get in shape. Constantly improving, he is often paired with Jasmine St. Clair in his independent promotion, 3PW, in Philadelphia. [Blue Boy]

TRIVIA

Q. Which mask-wearing wrestler was a longtime on-screen ally of El Santo?

Bockwinkel, Nick
(1960s-1990s)

Few wrestlers have brought the veracity for words as this second-generation star. One of the more technically sound performers of any era, Bockwinkel was a four-time AWA champion in the 1980s and a longtime tag-team companion of Ray Stevens. The duo won the AWA tag titles three times. As smooth as he was in the ring, he was smoother in interviews in which he'd wrap up his opponent's flaws with wit as spectacular as his wrestling holds.

Bockwinkel, Warren
(1930s-1950s)

This early era journeyman wrestler, the real-life father of Nick Bockwinkel, urged his son to enter wrestling at a young age. Though his offspring truly made the Bockwinkel name famous, Warren held his own across the country.

Body Donnas, The
(1990s)

Managed by Sunny, the blond haired, crew-cut sporting duo known as Skip and Zip (Tom Pritchard and Chris Candido) rode their exercise-addict gimmick to the WWF tag championship in 1996. [Chris Candido; Tom Pritchard]

Boesch, Paul
(1940s-1980s)

Not many people—let alone wrestlers—can boast the life of Paul Boesch. A wrestler, promoter, announcer, WWII soldier, and author, Boesch was a favorite promoter of many wrestlers. His wild and wooly Houston-area shows, which often featured cross-promotion champions, pioneered famous gimmick matches still used today.

Booker T.
(1990s-2000s)

Trained in Texas by Ivan Putski and Scott Casey, Booker grew from the independents to become only the second African American WCW world champion in history, a belt he carried five times. A very gifted and athletic star, he's the real-life brother of Stevie Ray, who he held the WCW tag title with 10 times. He's become a popular WWE singles star, often challenging for that group's world title. [G.I. Bro]

Boone, Brady
(1980s-1990s)

Boone was a talented wrestler with a myriad of abilities and seemed always on the brink of making it. His acrobatic style helped him win titles in Portland and he later wrestled under a mask. He died in a car accident in 1998. [Battle Kat]

Borne, Matt
(1970s-1990s)

Son of Tony Borne, he was a Portland-based star who toured nationally. Matt got a break as Big Josh in WCW and as Doink in the WWF. [Big Josh; Borne Again; Doink]

Borne, Tony
(1960s-1970s)

Father of Matt Borne, he was a tag-team partner of Lonnie Mayne in the Northwest. Lucky for him, he was there during the territory's hottest period.

Bossman, The
(1980s-2000s)

A surprisingly agile man, he began his career as Bubba Rogers, a bodyguard for manager Jim Cornette, but his talent in the ring would emerge later. He was tendered an offer to wrestle in the WWF as the Bossman and his career took off. While not a championship type, he has been a headliner in the WWF and WCW. [Big Bubba Rogers; Guardian Angel; Ray Traylor]

Boston Garden

The grand old building opened in 1928. Shortly thereafter, Bostonians got their first taste of professional wrestling. One of the first matches to be held there was a world title tilt between Gus Sonnenberg and Ed "Strangler" Lewis. They fought over a branch of the world title, indicative of the day, called the Boston AWA title. That night, in 1929, Gus dethroned the Strangler to become world champion. The Garden continued to hold cards until its closing in 1995.

Boyd, Jonathan
(1970s-1980s)

As one of the founding Sheepherders, the ugly faced Boyd was an anti-American heat-seeker throughout the country, most notably in the Southwest and Northwest. A fan of blood and barbed wire, he survived a debilitating car accident to resume his career.

Boyette, Mike
(1960s-1980s)

This wrestler appeared as a California hippie wearing beaded vests. Seen in the Gulf Coast region, he even had a series against the legendary Danny Hodge, which showed the serious and talented side of his career which was often overlooked. He once held the U.S. tag-team title.

Bradshaw
(1990s-2000s)

The West Texas native harkens to the days of Stan Hansen. He played college football and tried wrestling just as Hansen did. A very large character, he searched for a role in the WWF. As Ron Simmons' partner, they won the WWF tag titles three times. [Blackjack Bradshaw; John Hawk; Justin Hawk] See: APA.

Bravo, Dino
(1970s-1980s)

A famous Canadian strongman, his career was overshadowed by his grisly murder at gunpoint in 1993. At his career peak, Bravo was a star in Montreal as well as the WWWF, where he held the tag-team titles with Dom DeNucci. He also held the NWA Canadian title.

Brazil, Bobo
(1940s-1980s)

One of the few wrestlers to perform for more than five decades, this African-American star was very influential in breaking color barriers. Some reports have him turning pro in 1939 and wrestling into the 1990s, which would make him a seven-decade vet. A native of Benton Harbor, Mich., and master of the coconut headbutt, he was a classy champion in the Detroit area and gave that belt respect. He had famous, bloody feuds with Johnny Valentine, Sheik, Killer Kowalski, Fred Blassie, and the Sheik.

Brazo De Oro
(1970s-2000s)

A Lucha Libre celebrity, his whole family, including his wife, sons, brothers, and cousins, all wrestled. He himself lost his prized mask in 1988.

Brickhouse, Jack
(1950s-1960s)

This legendary sports broadcaster from Chicago announced pro wrestling in that city during the 1950s and 1960s and is fondly remembered as one of the classic talkers.

Brisco, Jack
(1960s-1980s)

This multi-talented athlete and wrestler was one of the prides of the 1970s. A former NCAA champion in 1965 at Oklahoma State, he held the NWA world title two times between 1973-75. He dethroned Harley Race and Giant Baba for the crown. A true fighting champion, he defended the title on a six-day-a-week schedule. Outside his title defenses, he and his brother, Jerry, had a career-long feud with the Texas Funk family.

Brisco, Jerry
(1960s-2000s)

Like his brother Jack, he was a talented wrestler in his day, winning three NWA tag-team titles with his brother. The Oklahoma-born Briscos were part Native American. After his wrestling career, Jerry became a valued employee with the WWF, working as a road agent, in addition to his infamous Brisco's Body Shop in Florida.

British Empire Wrestling

From the 1930s to 1980s, Toronto wrestling, under the promotion of the late Frank Tunney's Queensbury Athletic Club, held cards under this banner. Frank's nephew, Jack Tunney, who later took on the group in the 1980s, eventually worked with the WWF. He was even the group's figurehead commissioner.

Brito, Gino
(1970s-1980s)

A Canadian-born wrestler, whose father, Jack Briton, was a Montreal promoter. The younger Brito was known for traveling with the popular midget wrestlers of the day.

Briton, Brenda
(1980s)

The lovely lady was known as the valet-manager of the colorful Adrian Street while in the Continental territory.

TRIVIA

Q. Which pro wrestler, also known as a stock market guru, has appeared on cable financial networks giving his tips?

Brody, Bruiser
(1970s-1980s)

Remembered as one of the hardcore innovators, no fan or wrestler was safe when the 6-foot-8, longhaired wild man was present. A true rebel, Brody was never around any territory long enough to look bad. He usually entered a group like a tornado and left just as suddenly. Born in west Texas, he was a college football player but went to wrestling for the money. In Japan, Brody's status is legendary. As a single's competitor, he drew incredible crowds for matches with Antonio Inoki. He also teamed regularly with friends Jimmy Snuka and Stan Hansen against the top Japanese attractions. Tragically, Brody died from stab wounds he suffered in 1988 while on tour in Puerto Rico. [Red River Jack]

Brooks, Tim
(1970s-1990s)

The "Killer" was the king of Texas ring wars in the 1970s. A former holder of the coveted Texas Brass Knuckles title, he once challenged Muhammad Ali in wrestling magazines.

Brower, Bulldog
(1960s-1970s)

An East Coast heel who also fared well in California and Japan, the barrel-chested brawler barked at the moon, ate announcer's ties, and broke every rule in the book. [Dick Brower]

Brown, Bob
(1960s-1980s)

Nicknamed the "Bulldog," he was a noted star in Kansas City and Calgary. He was no-frills, simply wearing black trunks. His nephew, Kerry Brown, whom Bob even called "son," also wrestled in Canada. Together, the Browns were Calgary tag-team champions.

Brown, Brickhouse
(1980s-1990s)

This sculpted African-American attraction was mainly a mid-card talent in Texas, Louisiana, and Tennessee. He had long feuds with Iceman Parsons and Jerry Lawler and wrestled as both heel and fan favorite.

Brown, Dave
(1960s-2000s)

Dave Brown was a five-decade announcer in the Memphis territory. The Tennessee native first began broadcasting in the late 1960s and has been part of the live Saturday morning broadcasts almost solidly ever since. He's been through a lot of turmoil in the region, but no matter who promoted, Brown added an air of credibility to the Memphis chaos.

Brown, D-Lo
(1990s-2000s)

The hard-working, popular D-Lo began his career as a pudgy member of the Gangsta's, alongside New Jack and Mustafa in Smoky Mountain Wrestling. Later, he worked in the WWF for several years and carried the European championship.

Brown, Kerry
(1980s-1990s)

The real-life nephew of Bob Brown, he was a former Stampede North American champ in Calgary. Some of his frequent tag-team partners included Bob Brown and Duke Meyers. [Rick Valentine]

Brown, Leroy
(1970s-1980s)

A monster in the ring, Brown was 6-foot-2 and 310 pounds. Mostly remembered as a fan favorite, he even had matches against Ric Flair in the Georgia territory. While in Florida, he changed his ring name to Akeem Elijah and teamed with Ray Candy as the Zambouie Express. They won the state tag-team titles. Brown passed away at the young age of 38. [Akeem Elijah]

Brown, Orville
(1930s-1940s)

A real-life bronco rider, he was too big for that sport so he tried wrestling. The Kansas native beat the top ring names of the day. He won a version of the world title from Dick Shikat in 1942. After a car wreck in 1949, he retired but did so with a reportedly unblemished record.

Browning, Jim
(1930s)

A pre-war wrestler, Browning was a former world champion as he defeated Strangler Lewis for the belt in 1933. He dropped it a year later to Jim Londos.

Bruiser Mastino
(1980s-1990s)

A former CWA-European champion, the Midwest amateur standout was trained by Mad Dog Vachon. On the independent circuit, he's one of the better high flyers, despite weighing in at 350 pounds. He also wrestled briefly in the WWF as Mantaur. [Mantaur]

Brunzell, Jim
(1970s-1990s)

This skilled high-flyer made his debut in 1972 and had a very productive career in the AWA, WWF, and Japan. Tag-team wrestling was Brunzell's forte. As the partner of Greg Gagne, the duo was called the High Flyers and won the AWA tag titles two times. In the 1980s, Brunzell sported a Bruce Springsteen look and even recorded a takeoff on one of the pop star's songs called "Matlands." He then crossed to the WWF, where he teamed with B. Brian Blair as the Killer Bees.

TRIVIA

Q. Which wrestling announcer first served Memphis as a meteorologist?

Buchanan, Bull
(1990s-2000s)

This Southern WWF mid-card wrestler has been part of many tag teams, including the Truth Commission and Right to Censor. He has good agility for big man, but has yet to break out on his own. He's also toured in Memphis and OVW.

Budokan Hall

Known as the grandest building in Tokyo, it was built in time for the 1964 Olympics, but it quickly became home to Japanese pro wrestling. In 1966, Giant Baba's All-Japan promotion drew the first-ever sellout to the arena. Ever since, some of the best All-Japan and New Japan shows are staged there.

Bundy, King Kong
(1980s-1990s)

Bundy was a bald, towering presence who, at 400 pounds, was quite speedy. One of his gimmicks was to give opponents a fair chance by allowing a five-count, rather than the traditional three-count. In his prime, he toured virtually every major territory, but was made famous in the WWF for five-plus years. He even challenged Hulk Hogan for the world title in a cage bout at Wrestlemania II.

Burke, Leo
(1960s-1970s)

One of Canada's top junior heavyweights, he carried Calgary's British Commonwealth belt. He didn't avoid the big boys, however, and was a seven-time Calgary heavyweight champion.

Burke, Mildred
(1930s-1950s)

This former women's champion lays claim to more than 5,000 wins against women—and 150 wins against men. A tremendous athlete, her physique was quite unique. She was 5-foot-2, but incredibly tone and strong. Her career began on the carnival tours but it took her around the world many times.

Burns, Farmer
(19th Century)

The mentor of the famous Frank Gotch, he pioneered a new age in wrestling when Greco-Roman and collar-and-elbow styles merged. Remembered as one of the toughest ever, he claimed to have more than 6,000 victories.

Bushwackers, The
(1990s)

Formerly the bloodthirsty Sheepherders, Butch Miller and Luke Williams took off for the WWF using this toned down, kid-friendly gimmick. Overnight, they went from bloodbath wrestlers to funny men. See: Sheepherders.

Caddock, Earl
(1910s-1920s)

An early century grappler, this two-time AAU champion beat Joe Stecher in 1917 for what many think was the last "honest" world wrestling championship. In the two-out-of-three falls match, he won when Stecher quit in the third fall. Like Frank Gotch a decade before him, Caddock was born in Iowa.

Calhoun, Haystacks
(1960s-1970s)

One of the top draws of the 1960s, Calhoun was a pure oddity because of his size. The 600-pounder wore overalls and a scruffy beard. His freakish appeal made him an attraction throughout the world. In pre-cable television days, Calhoun was a must-see and made headlines in the WWWF in a feud with Bruno Sammartino. Photos of Bruno body slamming Calhoun appeared in several American newspapers. He and Tony Garea held the company's tag-team titles in 1973. His poor diet and training habits took a toll and before he passed away, diabetes took his leg. As an annual attraction, few had the power to draw like Calhoun.

Callis, Don
(1980s-2000s)

This Winnipeg native trained to be a wrestler, but found national success as a manager and announcer. In the late 1990s, he followed Edge and Christian to the WWF where he managed the Oddities. He resurfaces from time to time and writes a wrestling column in his hometown newspaper. [Cyrus; Jackyl]

Cameron, Larry
(1980s-1990s)

The former Canadian Football League player had a career in bodybuilding before hitting the rings in the Midwest. Not known on a wide scale in the U.S., Cameron was the last wrestler to hold the Calgary Stampede heavyweight title before the promotion closed. He was a part-time member of WCW's tag-team champions, Doom. While on tour in Germany in 1993, Cameron died; it was later attributed to heart failure. See: Doom.

Canadian Wildman
(1970s-1980s)

Dave McKigney, sporting a beard, looked like a wildman, hence the gimmick. An outlaw wrestler in Canada, he trained novelty wrestling bears and often performed against them in the ring. He wrote the cult book, *Drawing Heat*. He died in 1988 in a car accident that also took the lives of Adrian Adonis and Pat Kelly. [Bearman]

Candido, Chris
(1990s-2000s)

A former holder of the NWA championship, Candido broke off from the East Coast independent groups to get shots in Smoky Mountain, WCW, and WWF. Along with Tom Pritchard in the Body Donna's tag team, he won the WWF tag title in 1996. [Skip]

Candy, Ray
(1970s-1980s)

The 400-pound Candy was a relatively agile Florida native who made up one-half of the large Zambouie Express with Leroy Brown. The tandem was a force in the Sunshine State and once wrestled in the Crockett Cup. [Kareem Muhammad]

Cannon, George
(1950s-1980s)

The "Crybaby" was a wrestler, manager, announcer, and promoter—and he was skilled at all. Best known for his work in Detroit's Big Time Wrestling, the 300-pound Cannon got his nickname from throwing tantrums and "crying" after losses.

Canterbury, Mark
(1990s)

The rough and tumble Southerner found his start in WCW under a mask in a tag team with Tex Slazinger. He went to the WWF with his partner where he became a two-time tag-team champion in the team called the Godwinn Bros. [Henry Godwinn; Shanghai Pierce]

Caras, Dos
(1970s-2000s)

Recognized widely in the Lucha Libre world, Caras is known as an acrobatic wrestler who is also a noted submission artist. Some say he's one of the best ever. His bloodlines certainly have greatness: his brother is the wonderful Mil Mascaras.

Carnera, Primo
(1950s)

Numerous ex-boxers dabbled in wrestling, but Carnera dropped the gloves completely. He was a top draw and held his own. Part of his life story was chronicled in the film, "Requiem for a Heavyweight." He died in 1967.

Carpentier, Edouardo
(1950s-1980s)

Nicknamed the "Flying Frenchman," Carpentier was a strapping high-flyer who used his experience in gymnastics in the ring to delight crowds. He was one of the first to complete somersaults from the top ropes and land on his foes. He held many titles in his prime, including several branches of the world title. He even beat Lou Thesz for the NWA world title in 1957, but the title change was later reversed. His deep career took him into the 1980s in Canada and he also served as a wrestling television commentator. His nephew, Jacky Weicz, also wrestled using the Carpentier name.

Carter, Stacey
(1990s)

The former wife of Jerry Lawler was a valet and host in Memphis before she followed her hubby to the WWF. While there, she wrestled some and once held the company's women's championship. [Kat; Miss Kitty]

Casas, Negro
(1970s-2000s)

One of the legends of modern-day Lucha Libre, Casas is a multiple-time champion in Mexico. His talents have also taken him to Japan, where he is a celebrated junior heavyweight.

Casey, Scott
(1970s-1990s)

The Texan was a popular attraction in Southern territories like Southwest and World Class in the 1980s. Nicknamed "Cowboy," he was a regional champion and was known to shed blood against his opponents. Later, he helped train Harlem Heat.

Casey, Steve
(1930s-1940s)

A star from the early century, this Irish-born grappler, known as "Crusher," even has a song dedicated to him in his native country called "Steven Casey of Sneem." Talk about an athletic family: his father was a known bare-knuckles boxer, his mother was an accomplished rower, and his brothers, Tim and Jim, were wrestlers and Olympic rowers. Steve was a rower himself, but his true acclaim came in the ring, where he won the world championship in 1938 beating Lou Thesz in his adopted American home, Boston.

Castillo Jr., Hurricane
(1980s-2000s)

A second-generation star, Castillo Jr. is a former WWC junior heavyweight champion and has been an island staple.

Castillo, Hurricane
(1960s-1980s)

The Puerto Rican wrestler was one of the first major stars on the island. He held numerous belts, including the NWA Caribbean title and WWC Universal title. He found early success in Montreal in the 1960s, where he was a top heel teaming with Abdullah the Butcher. His son also wrestles as Hurricane Castillo Jr. [Fidel Castillo]

TRIVIA

Q. Who was the first former heavyweight boxing titleholder to totally convert into a full-fledged wrestler?

Caudle, Bob
(1970s-1980s)

This old-school announcer from the Mid-Atlantic territory was first a weatherman and sportscaster before his wrestling days. He also reportedly worked for former Senator Jesse Helms in North Carolina. He worked with Jim Ross in WCW and later for Smoky Mountain Wrestling.

Cena, John
(1990s-2000s)

The Boston-native had dreams of becoming champion one day. He started as a student in Rick Bassman's California group but was quickly snatched up by the WWF. He spent time as the OVW champion in Louisville before heading to the big show, where he's shown the charisma needed to go far. [Prototype]

Central States Wrestling

From the 1950s to 1980s, the states of Kansas, Missouri, Nebraska, and Iowa were run under the banner of this group headed by promoter and owner Bob Geigel. The group boasted many top names including Bob Brown, Roger Kirby, and Harley Race. It was Race, though, who put the area on the map nationally in 1973 after he won his first of six NWA world titles.

TRIVIA

Q. Which Champion is the brother of wrestler Mark Starr?

Champion, Chris
(1980s-1990s)

With revolutionary martial arts moves in the ring, Champion looked to be on the fast track as one-half of the New Breed tag team in the late 1980s, but his stock quickly fell. He toured Florida and Tennessee using a variety of gimmicks, like the Ninja Turtle. [Ninja Turtle; Yoshi Kwan]

Champion, Todd
(1980s-1990s)

The model-looking Champion was seen in many different territories in the mid-1980s, including Portland, where he teamed with Ricky Santana. He got a big break in WCW using a Chippendale's gimmick, but he quickly faded from the scene. [Firebreaker Chip]

Charland, Richard
(1970s-1980s)

A skilled judo artist and amateur wrestler, Mad Dog Vachon discovered him in Canada. He was introduced to wrestling through the Grand Prix territory at age 16. He was a solid scientific wrestler who seemingly got caught between the old ways and new styles of the 1980s. Later in his career, he lost the use of his eye in a ring-mishap against the Sheepherders.

Charles, Tony
(1970s)

An English wrestler, Charles rose to fame in a feud where he competed for the U.S. Junior Heavyweight belt against Les Thornton.

Chase Hotel

Sam Muchnick, the famous old-time promoter in St. Louis, produced a "Wrestling at the Chase" television program from the 1950s-70s noted for being built around the NWA world champion. The weekly 60-minute show was taped inside the Chase Park Plaza Hotel.

Chetti, Chris
(1990s-2000s)

The real-life cousin of WWE star Tazz, Chetti was a graduate of the ECW wrestling camp and tried to rise the ladder in that promotion, teaming with Nova before it closed in 2001. The East Coast native continues to wrestle on the independent scene.

Cholak, Moose
(1950s-1970s)

After a string of wins in the amateur ranks, Cholak turned pro. One of the first 300-pounders seen on television, he was a star from Chicago in the early 1960s. Because of his amateur background, he often wore headgear into the ring.

Chono, Masa
(1980s-2000s)

There is no denying his success in Japan, but Chono was one of the few to "get" American wrestling. He brought that style back to Japan in the 1990s. He broke into the business with Keiji Mutoh and later feuded with him. He wasn't a stranger to championships either: he's a former two-time NWA champ, one-time IWGP champion, and six-time IWGP tag-team champion.

Choshu, Ricky
(1970s-1990s)

One of the recent legends in Japan, Choshu rose through the pros stemming from his standout amateur career which took him to the 1972 Olympic Games. Into the 1980s, he became one of the country's most explosive performers and helped establish Japan's strong style of wrestling. A longtime front office employee in New Japan Wrestling, he's held many world titles, including the IWGP belt three times.

TRIVIA

Q. Who was the announcer for the "Wrestling at the Chase?"

Christanello, Donna
(1960s-1980s)

One of the few female journeymen in wrestling, she was co-holder of the WWF women's tag-team title with Toni Rose in 1970.

Christian
(1990s-2000s)

This Canadian independent star got a shot in the WWF and made the best of it. Although he's not a headliner, Christian employs a classic style and remains one of the more talented workers around. He is a former seven-time tag-team champion with Edge. The duo hit its stride in the late 1990s in a series of ladder matches against the Hardy Boys. [Christian Cage]

Christy, Paul
(1970s-1980s)

Nicknamed the "Golden Boy," Christy was a star in the Gulf States promotion where he wrestled as the "brother" of Ken Lucas. He's a former WWA tag-team titleholder with Roger Kirby and he has the distinction of being the last ICW-Tennessee champion when the promotion closed in 1984. [Chris Lucas]

Chyna
(1990s-2000s)

Brawny and powerful, Chyna is perhaps the most successful WWF female of all-time. Carefully promoted, she never wrestled women until later in her tour. She burst on the scene as a bodyguard, but eventually became one of the group's most recognizable faces. The only female to hold a men's WWF major championship, she beat Jeff Jarrett for the Intercontinental title in 1999, a belt she held twice. [Joanie Laurer]

Clark, Bryan
(1980s-2000s)

At 275 pounds and nearly 6-foot-7, the wrestling industry is a perfect home for a guy like Clark. He's found homes in the AWA, Smoky Mountain, WCW, and WWF. Using mainly power moves, Clark has wrestled almost exclusively as a heel. His major chance as champion came as the partner of Brian Adams in WCW. Together, the duo were two-time tag champions. [Adam Bomb; Night Stalker; Wrath]

Clash of Champions

What began as a one-time free show on cable to combat Wrestlemania in 1988, WCW carried on the tradition on TBS until 1997. Remember the first broadcast? Most die-hards do. It was Sting's coming-out party in which he battled then-NWA world champion Ric Flair to a 45-minute draw.

Cobo Hall

The Detroit-area arena was made famous in wrestling circles as the home of Big-Time Wrestling during the 1960s and 1970s. It was the site of many bloodbaths with the wicked Original Sheik.

Cole, Michael
(1990s-2000s)

A new wave announcer who has caught on with the WWE, he began hosting the company's syndicated shows, but graduated to full-time, lead announcer for a time when Jim Ross recovered from an ailment. Since then, Cole has learned his craft and has formed a decent broadcast team with Tazz on "Smackdown!"

Collins, Ripper
(1950s-1980s)

Remembered as a vicious heel, Collins made Hawaii his home and often teamed with the equally demonic King Curtis. He held the Hawaiian Heavyweight title seven times from 1969-71. Later in his career, Collins tamed a bit and became a TV announcer.

Colon, Carlos
(1960s-2000s)

One name is synonymous with Puerto Rico: Colon. This head of the family never reached fame globally but it wasn't for his lack of trying. He tried his hand on the mainland but success always eluded him. He's been an island hero since the 1960s, most often carrying the World Wrestling Council title. In recent years, Colon was still active, often helping his children, Eddie, Carly, and Stacey, with ring careers of their own. [Carlos Belafonte]

Colon, Carly
(1990s-2000s)

The first son of Carlos Colon, Carly has become a star in his own right in Puerto Rico and has become the new flag bearer for the WWC promotion. In that group, he's held the Universal title eight times.

Colon, Eddie
(1990s-2000s)

The youngest son of Carlos Colon, Eddie has become a popular cruiserweight wrestler in Puerto Rico.

Combat Zone Wrestling
(1990s-2000s)

Since ECW folded in 2001, CZW has tried to pick up where Paul Heyman left off. With Philadelphia as his home base, company owner John Zandig has been a bridge to Japanese hardcore wrestling. Often aligned with Big Japan, CZW has sent its top performers like Nick Mondo and Justice Pain to be involved in wild hardcore matches. See: John Zandig.

Combs, Cora
(1960s-1980s)

One of the modern-day travelers, Combs, a first-generation star from the 1970s, was once billed as the women's U.S. champion. She toured the world to find competition, and often battled the best counterparts of the day.

Combs, Debbie
(1980s-1990s)

The daughter of Cora Combs, she was a journeyman wrestler in the 1980s with visits in virtually every major territory. Some of her tours took her to the WWF where she challenged Fabulous Moolah for the world women's title.

Condrey, Dennis
(1970s-1990s)

A true Southerner, Condrey found a home in Tennessee in his early years but was nothing more than a bit player before he hooked up with Randy Rose as the Midnight Express. When Jim Cornette finally got a hold of the team, Rose was replaced with Bobby Eaton and Condrey's career blossomed. In the early 1980s, Condrey toured World Class, Mid-South, and the NWA, where he was a U.S. and world tag-team champion. Later, he rejoined Rose in the AWA and won that group's tag championship. See: Midnight Express.

Constantino, Rico
(1990s-2000s)

Something of a renaissance man, Rico was a former Las Vegas cop who competed on the TV show, "American Gladiators." In his mid-30s, he tried pro wrestling on a whim. He competed in OVW for several years and his dedication to improving was rewarded when he was offered a WWF contract in 2001. He's been both OVW champion and Southern tag-team champion with John Cena. [Rico]

Continental Championship Wrestling

Originally called Southeastern Championship Wrestling, this Robert Fuller-owned promotion ran out of Alabama and Tennessee. In 1988, the group's name was changed to the Continental Wrestling Federation.

Conway Jr., Tiger
(1970s-1980s)

The son of Texas legend Tiger Conway Sr., he had loads of charisma while wrestling in Mid-South and the NWA among other areas. He was a frequent tag-team partner of Pistol Pez Whatley.

Conway Sr., Tiger
(1950s-1980s)

A skilled tough guy, he was a legend in his home state of Texas. The former Texas champion was a leader in the business community and was even recognized by the state in 1995. His son, Tiger Conway Jr., was a frequent ring partner.

Conway, Rob
(1990s-2000s)

Nicknamed the "Ironman," Conway is a former Ohio Valley Wrestling heavyweight champion. He's been a key member of that promotion and is a favorite of promoter Danny Davis.

Corino, Steve
(1990s-2000s)

Corino does it all: he's been a Dusty Rhodes-like brawler in ECW, a Bobby Heenan-like wise guy, and also takes a page from the Japanese tradition of ring excellence. In 2000, he held the ECW world title. Since then, he has split time between Japan and East Coast independents, always proclaiming to be "old school."

Cornette, Jim
(1970s-2000s)

The insanely witty Cornette began his career as a wrestling photojournalist in Memphis and Louisville but quickly turned his attention to managing where he shined on camera. For the following 20 years, he was one of the industry's highest-profile managers, guiding the likes of the Midnight Express, Bubba Rogers, and Yokozuna in World Class, Mid-South, Memphis, the NWA, and WWF. Often called too old school for his own good, Cornette has stood by his convictions as a wrestling promoter in the now defunct Smoky Mountain territory, as well as Ohio Valley Wrestling. Now with his managerial career over, his value as a talent developer can't be overlooked. Without him, where would upstarts like Brock Lesnar and John Cena be? See: Midnight Express; Heavenly Bodies; Ohio Valley Wrestling.

Cortez, Hercules
(1950s-1970s)

One of the strongest and most muscular wrestlers ever, he boasted a 64-inch chest and 23-inch arms. He won numerous tag-team titles like the AWA tag title with Red Bastein. Sadly, in 1971, he was killed in a car accident en-route to a match.

Costello, Al
(1950s-1980s)

He was the backbone of the famous tag team, the Fabulous Kangaroos. Later, he helped manage another incarnation of the tandem. Costello was popular in many territories including Detroit and Toronto. He generally wrestled as a villain before he concentrated on training newcomers in the 1980s.

Cousin Junior
(1980s)

One of a number of wrestling hillbillies, he wrestled in the WWF as the partner of Cousin Luke, Hillbilly Jim, and Uncle Elmer.

TRIVIA

Q. Which Spanish heavy lifter brought boulders into the ring and challenged foes to carry them?

Cousin Luke
(1970s-1990s)

Like "Uncle Elmer" Gene Lewis, Luke was saddled with a hillbilly gimmick. First he went through multiple personalities. In the WWF, he and Elmer teamed with Hillbilly Jim as the Hillbillies, a throwback to an old 1960s gimmick.

Cow Palace

The famous San Francisco arena began its wrestling life in 1949. Promoter Roy Shire drew monster crowds there from 1961-82. At its peak, the building could seat 14,000 and the arena was famous for its annual 18-man Battle Royals.

Cox, Steve
(1980s-1990s)

A blond-haired wonder boy from the Bill Watts camp, he won regional titles in Watts' Mid-South and later in World Class.

Cpl. Kirschner
(1980s-1990s)

A mildly talented wrestler, he caught on in the 1980s in the WWF as a protégé of Sgt. Slaughter. After that tour, he found a steady career in Japan, despite having spent time in jail there. [Leatherface]

Creachman, Eddie
(1960s-1970s)

Best known as the manager of the Original Sheik, he was used in Toronto, Detroit, and Montreal, where he resided. A very fast talking, pesky con artist who was an entertaining on-air persona, he was seen in the film, "I Like to Hurt People."

Credible, Justin
(1980s-2000s)

Often deemed too small, Credible worked many different gimmicks before settling on this persona. He was a minor hit in the WWF and Memphis but received his big break in ECW. There, he had a six-month run as world champion. He was also a two-time ECW tag champion with Lance Storm. [Aldo Montoya; Man of War; P.J. Walker]

Crews, Art
(1980s)

A veteran from the Portland and Central States areas, he was a multi-time regional champion who later gave up sports for a career in law enforcement.

Crockett Cup

This two-time event held in 1987-88 was a North American one-of-a-kind tag-team tournament promoted by the Crockett family. It was a unique concept: a two-night tourney held at the same location with NWA stars. Dusty Rhodes and Nikita Koloff won the inaugural event in Baltimore in 1987; Sting and Lex Luger won in 1988 from Greensboro.

Crockett, David
(1980s-1990s)

Brother of Jim Crockett Jr., he was a promoter in the Mid-Atlantic area where he was also an announcer and television producer for the cable hit, World Championship Wrestling.

Crockett Jr., Jim
(1970s-1980s)

The oldest son of Crockett Sr., he took over the promotional reigns of the Mid-Atlantic area from his father in 1973 and ran it until he sold the group to Ted Turner in 1988. He was a three-time president of the NWA. Gone from wrestling (despite another failed attempt to promote in the early 90s), he resides in Dallas.

Crockett Sr., Jim
(1930s-1970s)

Patriarch of one of the famous names in North American wrestling history, he promoted the Carolinas and Virginia from 1935-73 until his oldest son took over the family business.

Crush Gals, The
(1980s-1990s)

A famous name in Japanese women's wrestling, this team, comprised of Lioness Asuka and Chigusa Nagayo, were superstars. They had a classic feud with Dump Matsumoto and Bull Nakano and won the WWWA tag titles three times.

Crusher, The
(1950s-1980s)

A complete master of mayhem, Reggie Lisowski was a main event star throughout the world but is most known in the Midwest where his career finished in the early 1980s. At the height of his career, he was a barrel-chested brawler who drove fans wild in the 1950s and 1960s and later he became a popular fan favorite. He feuded feverishly against Mad Dog Vachon and Baron Von Raschke. The innovator of the stomach claw and bolo punch, he was known for his trademark cigars and hilarious interviews.

Cuban Assassin
(1980s-1990s)

No fewer than a half dozen wrestlers used this moniker. Most famous, surely, was David Sierra, a dead ringer for Fidel Castro, who used the gimmick in Florida and Japan. [David Sierra]

Curry, Fred
(1960s-1970s)

Son of Wild Bull Curry, he was the scientific antithesis to his brawling pop. Named "Flying Fred" because he threw a high number of dropkicks, he was a champion in Hawaii and won tag gold with Fritz Von Erich, Bobo Brazil, and Tony Marino.

Curry, Wild Bull
(1950s-1970s)

Born of Lebanese descent, he was a pure wild man in the ring and incited many crowd riots. He made a name for himself in Texas, where he was a constant in the Houston area's Brass Knuckles division. He once boxed Jack Dempsey. Fans from his day still remember his wild, overgrown eyebrows.

Curtis, Don
(1950s-1970s)

The "Buffalo Bomber" was said to have been discovered by Lou Thesz. Not too shabby. He was a two-time U.S. tag champ with Mark Lewin and he also held the WWWF tag title. Later, he promoted in Florida.

Cutler, Charlie
(1910s-1920s)

While he never beat anyone for the world title, Cutler (like many in his day) laid claim to the title in 1915 after the retirement of Frank Gotch. That year, Joe Stecher defeated Cutler in Omaha, despite getting help in training from Strangler Lewis, to claim rightful ownership of the belt.

Dallas Sportatorium

It may have looked like a shack from the outside, but inside, the Dallas arena was magical. The legendary ragamuffin building housed famous concerts (Elvis Presley) and later on, many Texas wrestling promotions. It was the home to the Von Erich's and in the early 1980s, there was arguably no better place to watch wrestling than the Sportatorium.

Damaja, The
(1990s-2000s)

Only a teen-ager when he began his career, this former Ohio Valley singles champion and Southern tag champ is part of the new breed. Often knocked for being small, he combines cruiserweight appeal with solid charisma. [Dan Basham]

Daniels, Christopher
(1990s-2000s)

A very talented East Coast indy wrestler, Daniels is a technically sound attraction. He's found success in Japan, as well as Ring of Honor and NWA-TNA. [Curry Man; Fallen Angel]

Darsow, Barry
(1980s-2000s)

A man of many identities, Darsow carved a nice career out of being a mid-level gimmick performer. He spent some time in Mid-South before catching on with the Crockett's in Georgia. Promoters put him in many roles, but his most famous was as one half of Demolition, a copy of the Road Warriors. Together with Bill Eadie, the face-painted Darsow won the WWF tag-team title three times. [Blacktop Bully; Demolition Smash; Krusher Kruschev; Repo Man.] See: Demolition.

Davis, Danny
(1980s-2000s)

A smallish wrestler who was member of the Nightmares with Ken Wayne, he now busily runs Ohio Valley Wrestling and occasionally wrestles. See: Nightmares.

Davis, Mike
(1970s-2000s)

Davis began his career as a light heavyweight and was considered a fine worker. As wrestling boomed in the 1980s, Davis formed the RPMs with various partners. They were very active in the Southeast and Puerto Rico. After nearly 25 years on the road, he passed away in 2001. [Maniac Mike; Viper.] See: Rock & Roll RPMs.

Death Match

Think of a match sans the rulebook. Houston promoter Paul Boesch probably first dreamt of this match to settle a feud. The rules? Try no time limits, no falls, and no disqualifications. It's simple: when one man cannot continue, he loses. For years, tough Texan Dory Funk Sr. was known as the king of the death matches.

DeBeers, Col.
(1980s-1990s)

After learning his craft in Portland as a technician, he entered the AWA as a brawling colonel. Billed as a member of a South African diamond mining family, he had high profile feuds against Sgt. Slaughter and Derrick Dukes. [Ed Wiskoski; Mega Maharishi]

DeGlane, Henri
(1920s-1930s)

The strapping Frenchman was best known as the world champion among Northeast promoters in 1931 after a title match in Montreal against "Strangler" Ed Lewis. DeGlane complained that Lewis bit him, an accusation Lewis flatly denied, claiming DeGlane bit himself to curry favor with the referee. In a rematch, DeGlane was destroyed, but the title was not on the line. Despite the controversy, Lewis was still recognized as world champ outside Canada and the Northeast.

TRIVIA

Q. Which 1931 wrestler reportedly had a gnawing complaint against Ed "Strangler" Lewis?

Del Rey, Jimmy
(1980s-1990s)

A smallish, Tennessee-based wrestler who wrestled around the Southeast and later teamed with Tom Pritchard as the Heavenly Bodies in Smoky Mountain Wrestling. The tandem was multi-time SMW tag champs. [Gigolo; Jimmy Backlund.] See: Heavenly Bodies.

Demolition
(1980s-1990s)

Vince McMahon needed a quick answer to the Road Warriors who were tearing up the NWA in 1986. His answer seemed simple: copy them. McMahon put Barry Darsow and Bill Eadie in face paint, spikes, and leather and called them Demolition. At first fans weren't fooled. But in time, the Demos created their own identity, were given lengthy runs as world tag champs, and performed admirably. In history, the Roadies are legendary, but at the time, WWF fans were none the wiser. See: Barry Darsow; Bill Eadie.

Demon, The
(1990s)

Son of baseball manager Jeff Torborg, Dale Torborg's character was a short-lived WCW concoction to capitalize on the popularity of the rock band KISS. Pyro, entrance music by the band, and keen makeup surrounded the tall ambassador for music and wrestling. [MVP]

DeMott, Bill
(1990s-2000s)

A stocky brawler in WCW and WWE who seemed to take a page from Jim Duggan's early style of wrestling. He even bares a resemblance to Duggan. He's a two-time U.S. champion. [Capt. Rection; Hugh Morrus]

Denton, Len
(1980s-2000s)

For many years, Denton was the heart of Portland Championship Wrestling. His career spanned nearly three decades as the partner of Tony Anthony in the Dirty White Boys. Nowadays, you'll find him wrestling part time as the Grappler and running an auto shop in Portland. [Dirty White Boy; Grappler]

DeNucci, Dominic
(1960s-1990s)

The Italian-born DeNucci is one of the WWWF's all-time favorites. A technically sound single's star, he was also a talented tag-team wrestler with partners Tony Parisi, Jay Strongbow, Bruno Sammartino, and Spiros Arion. His heavy accent made him popular with East Coast fans.

Destroyer, The
(1950s-1970s)

Dick Beyer was an amateur standout at Syracuse but reached a high level of fame in the pros as a masked man. In his prime in the 1960s, he was a mega-star in Japan and still remains a legend there. He had classic feuds with Fred Blassie and John Tolos, among others. [Doctor X]

Destruction Crew, The
(1990s)

Wayne Bloom and Mike Enos worked hard, stiff, and were legit tough guys as the AWA tag-team champions in the early 1990s. Later, the twosome went to WCW as the masked Minnesota Wrecking Crew before heading to WWF as the Beverly Bros. [Beverly Bros.; Minnesota Wrecking Crew] See: Mike Enos; Wayne Bloom.

Diamond Lil
(1970s)

This was one of the few female midget wrestlers. She toured the country, but had few opponents.

Diamond, Paul
(1980s-1990s)

He was a former pro soccer player from Florida before he headed for the gym to wrestle. He held numerous tag titles with Pat Tanaka and was one-half of Badd Company and the Orient Express [Kato; Maxx Moon]

Diamond, Simon
(1990s-2000s)

This sculptured, East Coast independent wrestler burst on the scene, winning a Delaware cruiserweight tournament before getting the attention of ECW. [Lance Diamond]

DiBiase, Mike
(1950s-1960s)

Popular Omaha-based blue-collar grappler who won belts in Texas, Georgia, and Central States areas. The father of Ted DiBiase, Iron Mike perished in an in-ring accident in 1969.

DiBiase, Ted
(1980s-1990s)

Few wrestlers have the fluidity in the ring like this second-generation star. Long before he was the WWF's Million Dollar Man, he was a gritty fan-fave Mid-South champ. With the millionaire gimmick, he totally lived the part, flying private jets and riding in limos. But he was worth it. [Million Dollar Man]

Dick the Bruiser
(1950s-1980s)

Havoc was the middle name for this rugged ex-football player. He often partnered with the Crusher through the Midwest and co-ran the Indianapolis-based WWA. In the 1960s and 1970s, there weren't many wrestlers who created mayhem like the Bruiser.

Dillon, J.J.
(1970s-2000s)

As a wrestler and manager, Dillon did his best to rile fans. Ironically, the former manager of the Four Horsemen is one of the most respected men in wrestling. He won numerous regional titles as an adequate wrestler, but his true claim to fame was guiding the Horsemen, the pioneering NWA group of wrestlers led by Ric Flair. Since his ringside days ended, Dillon has been a big influence backstage in WWF, WCW, and NWA-TNA.

Dinsmore, Nick
(1990s-2000s)

An energetic, young star from the Ohio Valley group, he held the company's championship and he's also been a long-time partner of Rob Conway.

DiPaolo, Ilio
(1950s-1960s)

Born in Italy, DiPaolo found a surrogate home in Buffalo, where he remains a legend. He overcame polio as a youth to become an athletic star. For most of his career, he was a solid mid-card attraction on the East Coast, but he had flashes of brilliance: among them, a Canadian tag title stint with Whipper Watson and two, 60-minute title bout draws against Pat O'Connor and Lou Thesz.

Dirty White Boys
(1980s-1990s)

A Kentucky and Alabama-based tag team comprised of Tony Anthony and Len Denton, they were territory journeymen over two decades. This heel team held many regional tag belts. See: Len Denton; Tony Anthony.

DiSalvo, Steve
(1980s)

Not all visually impressive stars were successful and DiSalvo showed that. Trained by Californian Bill Anderson, the former Calgary champion had the looks of a superstar, but he ended up as one of wrestling's powerhouse flops. He had brief opportunities in the AWA, WWF, and Puerto Rico, where he was the Universal champion in 1989. He's a talented painter, too. [Billy Jack Strong; Steve Strong]

Dixon, Dory
(1950s-1960s)

A pioneering African-American wrestler, he was an impressive Golden Age grappler. His aerial ability was so solid, it is said to have inspired Mexican legend Mil Mascaras.

Doink the Clown
(1990s-2000s)

Who loves a killer clown? A lot of independent promoters, for starters. The brainchild of the WWF, the original was Matt Borne, but it's since been played by many traveling wrestlers like Steve Keirn and Steve Lombardi, among others.

Doll, Steve
(1980s-1990s)

This well-traveled veteran who, with his Kerry Von Erich looks, has been to virtually every territory. The sensation found a home in Portland and Memphis and later in the tag team, Well Dunn, with Rex King. [Steve Dunn]

Donovan, Chick
(1970s-1990s)

This husky, muscled journeyman had a shot in Georgia Championship Wrestling before he bolted for Puerto Rico where he's been a conniving wrestler-manager for many years. He even guided Abdullah the Butcher for a time.

Doom
(1990s)

A short-lived tag team comprised of a masked Butch Reed, Ron Simmons, and Larry Cameron. Managed by Woman, Reed and Simmons beat the Steiners for the WCW tag titles in 1990. See: Butch Reed; Larry Cameron; Ron Simmons; Woman.

Douglas, Shane
(1980s-2000s)

Widely known for his role as the Franchise in ECW, Douglas is a journeyman who also holds a teaching degree. Always a great interview, he helped build a young ECW into a national promotion. He wrestled in many territories after getting his first break with Bill Watts' UWF. [Dean Douglas; Franchise]

Downtown Bruno
(1980s-2000s)

This pal of Jerry Lawler got a chance in Memphis where he became another in the line of funny heel managers there. He guided virtually every heel to come through the area during the late 1980s. He went to WWF, where he had a major run as manager of champion, Psycho Sid. Never adverse to wrestling himself when needed, he actually held the WWE women's title for one day after beating the Kat. [Harvey Wippleman]

Dr. Wagner
(1960s-1980s)

The original "Evil Doctor," this Lucha Libre star's real name was Manuel Rivera. Under the mask, he was a hated, but charismatic villain. After a car accident in 1986, which killed wrestler Angel Blanco, Wagner retired. His sons have followed his ring exploits using the names Dr. Wagner Jr. and Silver King.

Dr. X
(1960s)

A Midwest masked star named Guy Taylor, he died in the ring after a match, oddly enough, with another Doctor X (Dick Beyer) in 1968.

Dreamer, Tommy
(1990s-2000s)

An ECW legend who has left blood on mats around the country, he was a softy when all of a sudden, the hardcore style hit him like a brick. He had a quiet and controlled, yet crazy, demeanor. He won and lost the ECW title on the same show in 2000. [T.D. Madison]

Drozdov, Darren
(1990s)

The former college (Maryland) and pro (Denver) football player seemed poised for a productive career when he was hired by the WWF which wanted to market his phenomenal talent of vomiting on cue, but the New Jersey native was paralyzed in a freak accident while wrestling D-Lo Brown in October 1999. Despite his disability, he still works for the WWF's Web site. [Droz; Puke]

Druk, Steve
(1960s-1970s)

Following a career as a preliminary bum in the AWA, the Professor became a manager, guiding the Russian Kalmikoff Bros.

Dudley Boys, The
(1990s-2000s)

When the Public Enemy departed ECW, Paul Heyman created this strange gimmick, but it worked. Originally D-Von and Bubba Ray, there were many more Dudleys that popped in, including Dances with Wolves Dudley, Dudley Dudley and Sign Guy Dudley. The original two, who could brawl to no end, held numerous tag-team titles and have gone on to greater heights in the WWF.

Dudley, Big Dick
(1990s)

A very large man, Alex Rizzo was once a partner with Dudley Boys in ECW. He wrestled in California for XPW before he passed away in 2002. [Alex Rizzo]

Dudley, Buh Buh Ray
(1990s-2000s)

A modern-day Dusty Rhodes, Mark Lomonica is one of the original Dudley Boys. Trained by Sonny Blaze, he worked for several East Coast leagues before hooking up with ECW as the bodyguard for Bill Alfonso. When he was given a spot as a wrestler, he and his partner, D-Von Dudley, became eight-time ECW tag-team champions. [Mongo Vyle]

Dudley, D-Von
(1990s-2000s)

This Dudley Boy had more to offer than his funny gimmick would intimate. He's a talented worker, as evidenced in his series of matches against the Hardy Boys. An eight-time tag-team champ with Bubba Ray, D-Von is actually the son of a minister. [Reverend D-Von]

Dudley, Spike
(1990s-2000s)

A former Wall Street stockbroker, he had a passion for wrestling and changed professions to live out a dream. As small as any star in the WWF's history, he makes up for his lack of size by putting his body in harm's way for the crowd's appreciation. He initially found a home in ECW, but he was hired by the WWF where he's teamed with the original Dudleys.

Duggan, Jim
(1980s-2000s)

Three careers make up this Buffalo native's ring life: First, he was a terrific brawler in Bill Watts' Mid-South and UWF in the early 1980s; then, he took the money and had a great run as a comedy act in the WWF; later, he's been a part-time performer who can still get pops from crowds who remember his years on top of his game. In 2000, he showed his courage in a return to the ring after a fight with cancer.

Duncum Jr., Bobby
(1990s)

Looking to make a career for himself, the son of Bobby Duncum was a spitting image of his dad. With long hair, he was a bruiser in Texas independents before getting a look from WCW in the late 1990s. There, he teamed with Curt Hennig and Barry Windham in the funny West Texas Rednecks. Sadly, he died from heart failure in 2000 from drug use.

Duncum Sr., Bobby
(1960s-1980s)

This wild man from Texas who stomped around the ring with long blond hair is known mostly as a brawler and he crashed the AWA, among other territories. Nicknamed "Big Bad Bobby," who fathered wrestler Bobby Duncum Jr., he was very believable in the ring. He was also once a member of Bobby Heenan's first family, as he and Blackjack Lanza won the AWA tag titles in 1976.

Dundee, Bill
(1970s-2000s)

Former Australian tightrope artist who became a wrestling star in Memphis in the late 1970s. He was a longtime foe and friend of Jerry Lawler and he's held numerous Mid-South singles and tag-team titles. At 5-5, he never turned down a challenge: he's known to go toe-to-toe with the likes of Terry Funk, Austin Idol, and Dutch Mantel. His son, Jamie, has carved a career for himself in the ring.

Dundee, Jamie
(1980s-2000s)

The son of Bill Dundee, he is small, but determined. He wrestled in Memphis with Wolfie D as PG-13 for over five years. Along the way, the mouthy attraction has had stopovers in WCW, WWF, and ECW. [Cyberpunk; J.C. Ice.] See: PG-13.

Dupre, Emile
(1950s-2000s)

A longtime Canadian promoter of Maritimes Grand Prix Wrestling in New Brunswick, Nova Scotia. His son, Rene Dupre, is a new star in the WWE.

Duseks, The
(1930s-2000s)

Nebraska was home to this renegade wrestling family, led by renowned shooter, Wally Dusek. Wally and his brothers, Emil, Ernie, Rudy, and Joe, all wrestled from the 1930s to 1950s. For a time, they were called the notorious Omaha Riot Squad. Joe Dusek later promoted the city. Frank Dusek, the son of Wally, did it all in later years as a wrestler, promoter, and television producer in Texas.

Dynamite Kid
(1980s-1990s)

One of the most influential wrestlers of the modern era, Tom Billington helped usher in a style never seen before in North America. The style, learned in Canada, picked from the best from Mexico and Japan. He was a high-flying, suplex machine who was unafraid to hurt his body in the ring. Before he began teaming with Davey Boy Smith as the British Bulldogs, Dynamite was a star in Canada and Japan in the 1980s. He held the WWF tag championship with Smith for eight months. Sadly, his career was shut down from the incredible punishment he sustained through the years.

Eadie, Bill
(1970s-1990s)

A man of many identities, he found his biggest success as a member of Demolition in WWF. He was a multi-time regional champion who was a tough man in the ring and a brilliant talker in Georgia and other Southeast groups in the 1980s. [Ax; Bolo Mongol; Masked Superstar; Super Machine.] See: Demolition.

Eagle, Don
(1950s-1960s)

One of the sport's true Native Americans, Eagle was a very colorful performer who brought pride to his tribe, the Mohawks. He appeared around the U.S. and Canada and even held the AWA version of the world title in 1950. In the ring, he was successful, but his inner demons caught up to him in 1966 when he took his own life.

Eagles, Johnny
(1970s)

One of the typical regional attractions of the day in Texas and Oregon, Eagles wore a huge tattooed eagle on his chest. It seemed to complement his blond hair and acrobatic style. He teamed with the likes of Jimmy Snuka and Terry Latham, who he won the NWA U.S. tag titles with.

Earthquake
(1980s-1990s)

John Tenta was a sumo wrestler in Japan when he switched to the pro side. He trained in Canada and finally got his stateside break in the early 1990s in the WWF. He challenged for the world title and later on underwent a variety of personality changes. [Avalanche; Golga; Shark.] See: Natural Disasters.

Eaton, Bobby
(1970s-2000s)

Quiet and understated, Eaton was regarded as one of the best wrestlers of the 1980s. Technically superior to most of his contemporaries, his fame skyrocketed as one-half of the Midnight Express. Born in Huntsville, Ala., he grew up watching wrestling and graduated to setting up rings before he trained for the ring himself. He had brilliant stints in Mid-South, Dallas, and the NWA. He carried the NWA tag titles three times with three different partners (Dennis Condrey, Stan Lane, and Arn Anderson). [Earl Robert Eaton] See: Midnight Express.

ECW Arena

Head to south Philadelphia and any wrestling fan is bound to have a story about the old, dilapidated building, formerly used as a bingo parlor. It became the home of ECW in the early 1990s and still houses independent groups. Its intimate quarters make it one of the jewels for watching wrestling, as the fans always have up front views of the performers.

Edge
(1990s-2000s)

One of the breakout stars in the WWE, Adam Copeland carries on the pipeline of talent from Canada to the United States. He trained with Dory Funk Jr. after some time on the independent scene and quickly made an impact in the WWE. Very charismatic, he epitomizes the new style of wrestling. He's a four-time Intercontinental champion and seven-time tag-team champion with steady partner, Christian. [Sexton Hardcastle]

Einhorn, Eddie
(1970s-1980s)

Einhorn always had an eye for television. He was a programmer in Illinois and from that experience began the Washington, D.C. area promotion, the IWA. The group tried to diminish the East's WWWF presence using the internationally known Mil Mascaras as its champ. The promotion failed due to poor live gates. He also co-owned the Chicago White Sox for a time and promoted Superclash I in the Windy City.

El Canek
(1960s-1990s)

The masked, high-flying Mexican star was one of the bigger draws in Lucha Libre history. The former UWA world champion had main events after Mil Mascaras departed for the U.S. in the 1970s. Canek is remembered as one of the few to beat Andre the Giant, which he did in 1984. Billed as the brother of Don Caras and Mil Mascaras, he was also a huge star in England and Japan.

El Gigante
(1990s)

An immensely tall, wrestler, Gigante was more than 7 feet. A former basketball player, he joined WCW and later performed in the WWF to marginal success. [Giant Gonzalez]

El Hijo del Santo
(1980s-2000s)

The "son of the saint," he's one of seven sons of Lucha Libre legend El Santo; however, he's the only son of El Santo to follow his dad into wrestling. Like his famous father, he's also acted in Mexican movies. His ring career has taken him all around Mexico and Japan where he's won numerous championships.

El Santo
(1960s-1980s)

A true legend in wrestling, El Santo's role cannot be overlooked. He was a mega-star in Mexico and ushered in a new era of multimedia personalities. In the ring, he stands as the top drawing attraction of all-time. He also appeared in more than 80 feature films, which are still regarded as cult classics.

Elizabeth
(1980s-1990s)

No female played the "damsel in distress" better than Liz, who was a popular WWF ringside attraction in the 1980s. A onetime wife of wrestler Randy Savage, she was part of many super feuds alongside Savage. Later, she appeared in WCW, sometimes with Savage, who she was actually separated from in real life. Sadly, she died in 2003.

Ellering, Paul
(1970s-1990s)

This former weightlifting champion and prelim wrestler (he once held the Southern title) turned his attention to managing in a maniacal, demented role. He first guided the careers of Arn Anderson and Matt Borne in the Southeast, but his real fame came as the manager of the Road Warriors, the top tag team of the 1980s. After his wrestling career waned, Ellering turned to sled dog racing and was even a musher in the Iditarod.

Ellis, Bob
(1960s-1970s)

A muscular man with a cowboy gimmick, he was a fan favorite in many territories. He held tag titles with Johnny Valentine and once held the WWA version of the world title.

Embry, Eric
(1970s-1990s)

With a body never to be confused with a heavyweight, Embry's verbal skills took him around the regional territories of the 1980s. He also relied heavily on his skills as a scriptwriter, especially in Dallas, where he helped the USWA draw big crowds in the later part of the decade. A brawler and bleeder, he was a favorite to fans who enjoyed his underdog roles in the ring.

Enos, Mike
(1980s-1990s)

Known as a rough and tumble journeyman, Enos was a former AWA tag-team champion with Wayne Bloom. He also wrestled with Bloom as the Minnesota Wrecking Crew in WCW and the Beverly Bros. in the WWF. [Blake Beverly; Mean Mike.] See: Destruction Crew.

Equalizer, The
(1980s-1990s)

This Portland-based big man lacked pure wrestling skills but had a few decent runs. After his days in the old Northwest territory, where he teamed with the Grappler, he ventured to WCW before quitting the business. [Evad Sullivan]

Eric the Red
(1960s-1970s)

Sporting a Viking gimmick, he looked the part, weighing more than 300 pounds and wearing horns to the ring. He was used in the Northeast and Canada and beat Johnny Powers for the NWF North American title. In 1978, he was killed in a car accident. [Eric the Animal]

European Greco-Roman Title

By the late 1800s, wrestlers around the world competed for this title. Some historical indications are this was not so much a title, as it was a designation won in an annual tournament. In 1877, American William Muldoon beat French champ, Christol, to be named the Greco-Roman champ. Many sources recognize Muldoon as the first real, pro wrestling champion. While it remains a disputed branch of the world title, its roots in wrestling's history cannot be denied.

Executioners, The
(1970s)

How do you hide an already known 300-pound star and one of the most recognizable bodies in wrestling history? Easy: put a mask on them. It seemed to be that type of logic when John Studd and Killer Kowalski won the WWWF tag-team titles in 1976 from Louis Cerdan and Tony Parisi. Never defeated in the ring, they were stripped of the belts because of the interference from a third partner, the masked Nikolai Volkoff.

Exploding Ring Match

Japanese hardcore legend Atsushi Onita created this match to set his Frontier Martial Arts group apart from the pack in the early 1990s. Exploding pods were set around the ring, which would be ignited when a wrestler fell on them. Little did Onita know the trend he would start as the match is still used in Japan.

Extreme Championship Wrestling
(1990s-2000s)

Formerly Eastern Championship Wrestling founded by Tod Gordon. When Paul Heyman climbed on board the name Extreme was added and wrestling changed forever. At first, the group was a cult favorite for die-hard fans with its penchant for hardcore matches and profanity. Soon, the promotional and television production tactics were used far and wide—even by Vince McMahon. Based in Philadelphia, its list of champions included Terry Funk, Shane Douglas, Cactus Jack, Sandman, and Rhyno, just to name some. The promotion closed in 2001 after a brief time on cable and pay-per-view.

Fabulous Kangaroos, The
(1960s-1970s)

Roy Heffernan and Al Costello founded this top-drawing tag team and later Don Kent was brought into replace Heffernan. Often managed by George Cannon, they had successful runs as the U.S. tag champions and defended those belts in Chicago, Detroit, and the Northeast.

TRIVIA

Q. Lilian Ellison fought state laws for the right to wrestle in the 1960s-1970s. She goes by what name in the wrestling world?

Fabulous Moolah
(1940s-2000s)

A seven-decade performer, who is regarded as the queen of women's wrestling. Moolah held the WWF women's title from 1956 to 1984 and was wrestling well into the new millennium. [Slave Girl; Spider Lady]

Fabulous Ones, The
(1980s-1990s)

After feuding against each other to marginal box office success, Steve Keirn and Stan Lane formed the "Fabs," managed by Jackie Fargo. Heading to the ring as Z.Z. Top's "Sharp Dressed Man" played on the loudspeakers and wearing top hats, the duo shot to stardom in Memphis and the AWA. Classic feuds ensued against the Sheepherders and Moondogs.

Fantastics, The
(1980s-1990s)

Tommy Rogers and Bobby Fulton were a top team in the 1980s in the Rock & Roll Express mold. Skilled technicians, they had memorable feuds with the Sheepherders and Midnight Express. While they had tours of most major territories in the 1980s, they always played second fiddle to the company's top teams.

Fargo, Don
(1950s-1960s)

Playing everything from a wild man to a nature boy, Fargo was a constant around the Southeast. He teamed with Ray Stevens, as well as Jackie Fargo, as the famous Fargo Bros. [Don Stevens]

Fargo, Jackie
(1950s-1980s)

An old-time legend in Louisville and Memphis, Jack Faggart was the leader of the Fabulous Fargo Bros. With beautiful blond manes and a flare for the dramatic, they were one of the South's best drawing teams ever. Jackie was a big-time heel teaming with Don Fargo. He also teamed with his brother, Roughhouse Sonny Fargo.

Fergie, Carl
(1970s-1980s)

Once a member of Jim Cornette's Memphis troupe called the Dynasty, he is the cousin of Jerry Lawler and Honkytonk Man. Fergie held many regional tag-team titles before becoming a referee late in his career.

Fernandez, Manny
(1980s-1990s)

This Southwest star's career took him to many territories, from Texas to Florida. A well-rounded performer, he was most often a fan favorite but hit his stride as a heel in the NWA teaming with Rick Rude, with whom he won the world tag titles.

Finkel, Howard
(1970s-2000s)

One of the throwbacks to the Vince McMahon Sr. days, Finkel was once part owner of the WWWF, but he's best known as the company's four-decade ring announcer. Sometimes he's known as the "Fink."

Finlay, Dave
(1980s-2000s)

Wrestlers don't come any more rugged than Finlay, an English-born wrestler who is known as a "stretcher" by many peers. His career was spent mostly in Europe, trading various belts with Tony St. Clair and Dave Taylor, but toward his later years, he hit the scene in WCW. While there, he suffered a devastating knee injury in a hardcore bout, but rehabilitated himself back to action. With WCW closed, he found a home in the WWE as a road agent. [Belfast Bruiser; Fit Finlay]

Fire Match

Pushing the envelope has been a standard in wrestling, so it came as no surprise when promoters first began lighting ring ropes afire during matches. Many variations have popped up, including the WWF's Inferno match, but the first was likely done in Puerto Rico in 1989 to settle the feud between Carlos Colon and Hercules Ayala. These bouts were later famous in Japan, where they are still used today.

Firpo, Pampero
(1950s-1980s)

Fans keenly remember the wild-haired maniac, who claimed he was from South America, keeping foreign objects in his mop hairdo. It was a heck of a gimmick. Firpo appeared all over the country including Hawaii, Texas, the AWA area, and Puerto Rico. [Ivan the Terrible]

First Blood Match

Traditionally used in Texas, the first wrestler to draw blood is declared the winner. It was widely used between 1960-1980.

Flair, David
(1990s-2000s)

It's always hard to live up to a family name, but David Flair really had great odds to beat: he's the real-life son of former world champion Ric Flair, who is perhaps the greatest of all-time. David, the eldest son, has been learning his craft. He has spent time in NWA Wildside, Ohio Valley Wrestling, and WCW, as well as NWA-TNA. He briefly made an appearance in WWF with his dad in his feud with the Undertaker.

Flair, Ric
(1970s-2000s)

One thing many spectators can agree on is Flair's legacy in wrestling. Often called the greatest wrestler ever, Flair has done it all and has held a world title more times (14) than anyone in history. He learned his craft in the Mid-Atlantic region and helped bridge the old school with the new during the 1980s. Employing a pure scientific style, his charisma and ability to make opponents look great was unparalleled. He beat Dusty Rhodes for his first NWA world title in 1981 and has still provided solid matches in the New Millennium. Flair, although born in Minnesota, is a legend in North Carolina, where he once considered running for governor. Not many wrestlers have had as many feuds as Flair: among his most notable opponents were Roddy Piper, Rhodes, Harley Race, Ricky Steamboat, Sting, and Hulk Hogan. [Black Scorpion; Nature Boy]

Flash Flannagan
(1990s-2000s)

A former Ohio Valley champ, the Mid-South star is an awesome hardcore risk-taker who has had difficulty being accepted as a television star. He has wrestled mainly in the Southern independents in Tennessee and Kentucky.

Florida Championship Wrestling

Based in Tampa, Fla., this promotion was a hotbed for action from the 1960s-80s. Running in towns like Hollywood and St. Petersburg, "Championship Wrestling from Florida" was seen by thousands every week on television hosted by the golden-throated Gordon Solie. Among the many stars who found success there were Dusty Rhodes, the Funks, Briscos, Grahams, and Windhams.

Flowers, Tim
(1970s-1990s)

A throwback to the 1950s, Flowers could put on a clinic and his timing was impeccable. He could also be as extreme as any ECW performer. He was a vet of British Columbia and the Northwest where he won multiple titles. [Street Fighter]

Flynn, Jerry
(1980s-2000s)

A trained kick boxer and former ultimate fighter, he trained with the Malenkos in Florida and later got a break in WCW. Very tall and strong, he's toured Florida and Japan.

Foley, Jonathan
(1970s-1980s)

A pesky manager from Stampede Promotions in Calgary who was often the foil of the Hart family.

Foley, Mick
(1980s-2000s)

Plain and simple, Foley beat the odds. A former independent mainstay, Foley bucked all conventional wisdom about which wrestlers get championship runs when he captivated fans enough to earn a world title run in 1998. Trained under Killer Kowalski, Foley was a pudgy journeyman before getting his first break in WCW. While known for risking his body for the sake of a match, he was never more than a mid-card attraction. His career then veered to Japan and the upstart ECW, where he helped create a new hardcore style. In the WWF, he finally got his chance. After wrestling a few years with the gimmick, Mankind, Foley made his case while the group was in need of new stars. Traditionally, wrestlers who looked like Foley never got the world title, but Foley had charisma like few before him. In feuds with the Rock and Steve Austin, Mankind magically touched the masses and wound up getting three world title stints. In doing so, he rewrote the rules on who can be a marketable champion—and it's been fun watching him. [Dude Love; Jack Foley; Mankind; Super Zodiac No. 2, Cactus Jack]

Four Horsemen, The
(1980s-1990s)

Some say the Horsemen, created in the NWA in 1983, marked the beginning of the groups of today. The originals were Tully Blanchard, Ole and Arn Anderson, and Ric Flair, with J.J. Dillon as their manager. The group changed in later years with others like Sid Vicious, Barry Windham, Paul Roma, and Chris Benoit joining in. Most of the time, the members held title belts, led by Flair and the NWA world championship.

Fralic, Bill

A former football player in college (Pitt) and the pros (Atlanta), he was a mid-card wrestling attraction in Hawaii and Oregon. In football, he was the originator of the pancake block. In wrestling, his career highlight was an appearance in the Battle Royal at Wrestlemania 2.

TRIVIA

Q. Which wrestler and former pro football player was named to the list of 100 Greatest Players of All-Time by *College Football News*?

Francine
(1990s)

Former Queen of Extreme in ECW, the mouthy brunette was the gal pal of Tommy Dreamer and also managed Shane Douglas and Justin Credible.

Francis, Ed
(1950s-1970s)

This former NWA junior heavyweight champion was a big name through the 1970s in Hawaii and helped promote there with Lord James Blears. Francis was a three-time Hawaii titleholder. At one time, because of Francis' help, wrestling on the island was the highest-rated television show on Saturday nights. His two sons, Bill and Russ, also wrestled.

Francis, Russ
(1970s-1980s)

The son of Ed Francis, Russ was a three-time Pro Bowl football player from the 1970-80s. In 1985, the tight end helped San Francisco win a Super Bowl championship. Because of his dad's influence, Russ wrestled in the off-season to stay in shape, in Hawaii and Oregon, where he attended college. He also promoted briefly in Hawaii before running for public office on the islands.

Frazier, Stan
(1970s-1980s)

The mammoth Frazier was close to 400 pounds and played many different characters in his day. In Memphis, he donned an outfit covered in rags and called himself the Mummy. Into the 1980s, he became Uncle Elmer in the WWF, teaming with Hillbilly Jim. [Convict; Mummy; Uncle Elmer]

Freebirds, The
(1970s-1990s)

Michael Hayes was ready to quit wrestling forever when fate stepped in. He took a ride with the equally frustrated Terry Gordy one night after a meager payoff and the two put their heads together and came up with the Freebirds gimmick. With the pesky Buddy Roberts, the trio was brash and groundbreaking. Hayes handled the mike, and Gordy, even as a teen, could wrestle circles around the vets. The threesome went on to heights in World Class against the Von Erichs and in Georgia against all comers and were a classic team. See: Buddy Roberts; Michael Hayes; Terry Gordy.

Fujinami, Tatsumi
(1970s-2000s)

Noble is one word to describe Fujinami, a Japanese star who had success in the U.S. He began his career in New Japan's junior heavyweight division, but his career is marked with hundreds of main event caliber matches against pure heavyweights.

Fuller, Buddy
(1950s-1970s)

Fuller, who passed away in 1996, was part of a true wrestling family. His pop, Roy Welch, was a longtime Tennessee promoter with Nick Gulas from the 1940s-70s. Buddy's real name was Ed Welch and he was himself a wrestler and promoter from 1954-59 in the Gulf Coast region, which promoted in Alabama and Florida. Fuller later sold the territory to his cousin, Lee Fields, who was also a wrestler in the famed Fields Bros. tandems. Buddy Fuller's sons, Robert and Ron Fuller, wrestled and promoted in the Southeast region.

Fuller, Robert
(1960s-2000s)

The "Tennessee Studd" is the younger brother of former Tennessee promoter Ron Fuller. His entire family was involved in wrestling, mainly across the Southeast. Robert Fuller was almost exclusively a heel and he won many tag titles with his partner, Jimmy Golden. On screen, Fuller was a hoot, combining Southern wit with a cocky attitude. He later made appearances in Memphis, with his Studd's Stable, and WCW, managing Harlem Heat. [Col. Robert Parker]

Fuller, Ron
(1960s-1980s)

This longtime Knoxville-based wrestler was a noted promoter and businessman. His uncle, Roy Welch, was a promoter, while his dad, Buddy Fuller, was a Southern grappler and promoter in Alabama and Florida. Ron Fuller co-promoted Southeastern Championship Wrestling during the 1970s and 1980s, which later changed its name to Continental.

Fulton, Bobby
(1980s-1990s)

This energetic ring journeyman was a popular attraction in many areas during the 1980s with tag-team partner Tommy Rogers as the Fantastics. See: Fantastics.

Fulton, Jackie
(1990s)

The younger brother of Bobby Fulton, he was a smaller version of his kin and even wrestled with Bobby as the New Fantastics in the 1990s. See: Fantastics.

Funaki, Sho
(1990s-2000s)

This Japanese cruiserweight was an independent sensation in the Orient, wrestling for Michinoku Pro, when he was brought stateside. He hooked into the WWF as well as Shawn Michaels' training camp in San Antonio.

Funk, Alan
(1990s-2000s)

In the few years of its existence, the old WCW Power Plant produced only a few marketable talents, and Funk is one of them. Mostly a cruiserweight, he also appeared in NWA-TNA. [Kwee Wee]

Funk Jr., Dory
(1960s-1990s)

Scientific as they come, Dory Jr., the oldest son of Dory Funk Sr., had a prestigious career. He was an NWA world champion in 1969, having beaten Gene Kiniski for the title in Tampa, Fla. He also had a prolific career in Japan where he and his younger brother, Terry, were extremely popular draws for All-Japan in the 1970s and early 1980s. There were few, if any, territories he didn't appear in since the 1960s. Still active, he's a respected trainer in Florida. [Hoss Funk]

Funk Sr., Dory
(1950s-1970s)

In Texas in the 1950s and 1960s, Dory Funk was king—king of the death matches. What you saw is what you got with Funk, as he lived the Texas ranch-hand gimmick he brought to the ring. Out of the Amarillo territory, Funk ran a longtime promotion, which was home to his sons, Terry and Dory Funk Jr. He died in 1973. [Texas Outlaw]

Funk, Terry
(1960s-2000s)

This five-decade, road-weary traveler keeps going despite multiple injuries and false retirements. That's been a blessing for fans who remember him from his passionate performances across the globe. Funny thing is, he's still giving fans thrills. Terry's biggest days were the 1970s. He held the NWA world title for 14 months from 1975-77. He was also a legend in Japan where he and Dory Jr., his older brother, were immense crowd pleasers for All-Japan in feuds with Bruiser Brody, Jimmy Snuka, Stan Hansen, and Giant Baba. Amazingly, he was still active into in his 50s while setting new standards—by doing moonsaults and having wild barbed wire matches—for older wrestlers. His career has stopped and started more than anyone in history. Every time he retires, he makes a return only to come back even stronger and crazier. Never one to back down from changes in the business, he helped put ECW and Japan's Frontier Martial Arts group on the map in the 1990s with his daredevil, hardcore performances against Cactus Jack and Atsushi Onita. Many believe he's the uncrowned king of wrestling and nothing in his illustrious career, especially in the last decade, would prove otherwise. [Chainsaw Charlie]

Gadaski, George
(1950s-1970s)

"Scrap Iron" was an AWA preliminary star often teaming with fellow lovable loser, Kenny Jay. But he did have some times in the sun, beating the Texas Outlaws and Adrian Adonis and Dick Murdoch.

Gagne, Greg
(1970s-1990s)

Being the boss' son did wonders for the career of Gagne, a second-generation technician. His pop, Verne, owned the AWA, where he saw most of his success. For most of the 1980s, he was an integral part of the promotion, teaming with Jim Brunzell as the popular High Flyers. The pair had a two-year reign as tag-team champions from 1981-83. When the AWA folded in 1990, he remained in wrestling as a backstage hand in WCW.

Gagne, Verne
(1950s-1980s)

One of the true legends, Verne was a college wrestling star at Minnesota, where he won the NCAA heavyweight title and parlayed that success in the pros. Gagne awarded himself the AWA title, a belt he'd hold nine times until 1980. In fairness, he took on challenges from every corner of the globe and was known by his comrades as a stellar technician. His AWA was at one time one of the most successful promotions in the world, servicing a wide area in the U.S. Virtually every major star walked through his turnstiles. In 1990, after financial difficulties and a changing wrestling climate, the AWA folded. But Gagne remains one of the most prominent fixtures in modern wrestling history.

Galento, Tony
(1930s-1950s)

A double-tough boxer who was often used as a special referee in the 1950s. Although his ring career was sometimes spent wrestling bears in special attractions, Galento, as a boxer, once fought Joe Louis for the heavyweight title.

Gangrel
(1980s-2000s)

David Heath has had many gimmicks, but his most famous was as Gangrel, the blood-sucking vampire in the WWF. The short, power wrestler has been a territorial warrior, taking himself to Canada, Japan, Memphis, and other destinations. [The Blackheart; Vampire Warrior]

Gangstas, The
(1990s)

This team from the early 1990s capitalized on the rap and gang culture. The original was New Jack, a Georgia independent wrestler who played college football at Florida A&M. He joined Mustafa and later D-Lo Brown, and created havoc in Smoky Mountain Wrestling and ECW. All three followed with successful singles careers: New Jack became an ECW regular, Mustafa cruised around the world, and Brown had success in the WWF.

Garcia, Lillian
(1990s-2000s)

One of the WWF's few women announcers ever, Garcia began her career on "Monday Night Raw." Her career has also gotten her work singing the National Anthem at house shows, and even at professional baseball games.

Garea, Tony
(1960s-1980s)

The tall, lanky Italian has been one of the McMahon family's most loyal employees. He was a journeyman in East Coast rings, often in tag-team competition. From 1973-81, he held the company's tag title five times with partners Haystacks Calhoun, Dean Ho, Larry Zbyszko, and Rick Martel. He still works with the WWE as a road agent.

Garvin, Jimmy
(1970s-1990s)

The younger brother of Ron Garvin began his career as a teen-aged wrestling manager, guiding "brother" Terry Garvin and Bobby Shane. Garvin was seemingly everywhere during the cable explosion of the 1980s, traveling to Florida, World Class, and the NWA. Nicknamed "Handsome Jimmy," he was a quality mid-card attraction along with his wife and valet, Precious.

Garvin, Ronnie
(1970s-1990s)

Diminutive, yes; a pushover, no. Garvin portrayed a tough S.O.B. in the ring and often backed it up. Regionally, he was a solid star with adequate ring skills and fans always took to his small-town demeanor and fiery temper. His career reached the pinnacle in 1987 when he defeated Ric Flair for the NWA world title in Detroit. He finished his career with runs in the WWF and Smoky Mountain. [Rugged Ron; Hands of Stone]

Garvin, Terry
(1960s-1980s)

No relation to Ron and Jim Garvin, Terry was a former U.S. tag-team champion with Duke Meyers and later worked as a WWF road agent. He passed away in 1998 at age 61.

Gatorwolf, Steve
(1980s-1990s)

An independent wrestler based in the Southwest, he was a prelim star for the WWF before he turned his attention to running a training facility in Arizona.

Gaylord, Jeff
(1980s-1990s)

Once tabbed as a breakout star, Gaylord had trouble breaking out of the regional mindset. Often compared to the Ultimate Warrior due to his sculpted physique, Gaylord was popular in Memphis and Dallas, where he was promoted as a former football star from the University of Missouri. [The Hood]

TRIVIA

Q. Who is the wrestler that owned the AWA, which was founded in 1960?

Geigel, Bob
(1950s-1990s)

The Central States (Missouri, Kansas) promoter was a top grappler in the late 1950s and early 1960s, especially in tag competition. He was recognized as the AWA tag-team champion with Hard Boiled Haggerty after Gene Kiniski left H.B. without a partner. He also won belts with Otto Von Krupp. By the late 1960s, Geigel slowed and set his eyes on promoting the Central States region. For the next 10 years, he ran a fine territory. Stars like Marty Jannetty, Mitch Snow, and Curt Hennig got their feet wet there. Vets like Ox Baker and Johnny Valentine roughed up the greenhorns. As the 1980s wound down, most territories were closing shop. Although Geigel succumbed to the times, he ran one last super show with Giant Baba. It didn't draw well, but the Texan went down swinging.

George, Ed Don
(1930s-1950s)

A Native American wrestler who hearkens to the days when wrestling was considered a legit sport, George was an Olympic athlete and world wrestling champion. He was said to have been in numerous shoot matches, some against Ed "Strangler" Lewis. One of his matches, in 1934 against Jim McMillen, drew nearly 34,000 to Wrigley Field in Chicago. In 1928, he was an AAU and Olympic amateur wrestler. In 1930, he dethroned Gus Sonnenburg for the world title. That change was noteworthy because Sonnenburg, a famous football star, garnered some unpleasant publicity when he was beaten up in a street fight. The NWA directors, not crazy about seeing their reputable champ disgraced like that, gave the O.K. for George to win the title, and with any luck, restore some credibility to the belt.

George, Mike
(1970s-1990s)

A veteran of the Kansas City, Mo., wars, the bruising George was a four-time Central States champion. He served as the Mid-South North American champion and often teamed with Bob Sweetan there. The stiff George once had an 83-minute draw with NWA world champion Ric Flair.

Georgia Championship Wrestling

This first breakout cable television show emanated from the Georgia studio for WTBS in the early 1980s, which later became the home of the defunct WCW.

Gertner, Joel
(1990s-2000s)

Onetime fan, turned announcer, turned manager in ECW, he was a chubby, foul-mouthed commentator, but never short on providing a laugh or two. He was famous for his double entendres during interviews and as Joey Styles' television co-host after guiding the Dudley Boys to multiple ECW tag-team titles.

Giant Haystacks
(1960s-1990s)

One of England's top draws, the 6-11, bearded behemoth weighed nearly 500 pounds. He and Big Daddy, another UK attraction, drew thousands to matches in Wembley Arena in the 1980s. He died in 1998. [Loch Ness]

Giant Silva
(1990s-2000s)

An immensely large man, the Brazilian native trained under Dory Funk Jr. in Texas and has had trips to WWF, Japan, and Mexico. In the WWF, he was a member of the Oddities with Kurrgan and Golga before finding fame in Lucha Libre.

Gibson, Ricky
(1980s)

Older brother of Reuben (Robert) Gibson, he was a referee and wrestler around Florida. He once wrestled Harley Race for the NWA belt there, but sadly, a car wreck took his life.

Gibson, Robert
(1980s-2000s)

Like his older brother, Ricky, Robert began his career as a referee in the Gulf Coast region before taking to the ring. Robert was a famous tag-team wrestler and part of perhaps the most popular tandem in history, the Rock & Roll Express. Less charismatic than his partner, Ricky Morton, Gibson was the perfect complement and held his own in the ring. Together, the pair toured most major promotions in the 1980s and were four-time NWA tag-team champions. See: Rock & Roll Express.

Gilbert, Doug
(1980s-2000s)

Son of former wrestler Tommy Gilbert and brother of Eddie, he was never far from his older bro in Memphis. He could wrestle if he chose, but he settled into a brawler's mold. He's a multi-time Southern tag-team champion who still shows up in the Southeast to wreak havoc. [Freddy Kreuger; Dark Patriot]

Gilbert, Doug
(1960s)

This Gilbert was one of the few wrestlers who spent the majority of his career as a fan favorite. He's remembered as a solid ground wrestler and demonstrated those skills when teaming with Dick Steinborn. The combo won the AWA tag titles in 1962.

Gilbert, Eddie
(1970s-1980s)

When he wasn't contributing backstage, this second-generation star helped usher in the hardcore era in the ring. The son of Tommy Gilbert was a booker/scriptwriter for ECW, Memphis, Puerto Rico, and Windy City and Continental when he wasn't busy feuding with Jerry Lawler. In the ring, he was very productive. A great talker, he usually led stables of wrestlers called Hot Stuff Int. In Memphis, he called his group the Memphis Mafia and was involved in a famous angle in which he ran down Lawler with a car. Gilbert, in the prime of his career, died in his sleep in 1995 at age 33.

Gilbert, Tommy
(1960s-1990s)

The father of one the all-time great wrestling families, his sons Doug Gilbert and the late Eddie Gilbert followed in his Southeast territory footsteps. Gilbert was a mainstay in the Mid-South region and even wrestled Lou Thesz. In his prime, he was a fabulous interview, which helped him as a drawing card in the 1970s. Into the 1990s, he was still going strong as a manager.

Gilberti, Glenn
(1990s-2000s)

How many have made a career of being a pest? Disco Glenn is one, that's for sure. Sporting a Honkytonk Man-type gimmick, the former WCW cruiserweight and tag-team champion is said to be a creative force behind the scenes for NWA-TNA. He once turned down a lucrative WWF offer to stay in WCW. [Disco Inferno; Disqo]

Gill, Duane
(1990-2000s)

As a Bill Goldberg impressionist named Gillberg, he was a noted jobber who was given air time because of his fun gimmick and even rode that success to the defunct WWF light heavyweight title.

Gilzenberg, Willie
(1950s-1960s)

As a former promoter from Philadelphia, Gilzenberg was successful under the auspices of the NWA. But after having trouble getting the world champion to come to the Northeast, he and New York promoter, Vince McMahon Sr., partnered to form the WWWF in 1963. For that, he's remembered as an integral part of wrestling's history. He died in 1978.

Global Wrestling Federation
(1990s)

Dallas group headed by Joe Pedicino in an attempt to pick up where the Von Erichs and the Jarretts left off. It used the Sportatorium as its home and gave opportunities to Marcus Bagwell, X-Pac, and Jerry Lynn.

Go, Ryuma
(1970s-1990s)

A journeyman wrestler from Japan, Go is credited with helping to start a revolution in that country. In 1989, he promoted Japan's first independent wrestling card with Atsushi Onita. The country, which had long-standing traditions with major promotions, has since seen the independent scene blossom with as many as 30 different groups at one time.

Godfather, The
(1980s-2000s)

Another current-day wrestler with a multiple personality disorder, he began his career in the independents but quickly moved up the ladder due to his size and strength. In the WWF, he took on several gimmicks, like Papa Shango and Kama. But as the Godfather, he was a hit while wearing his patented pimp outfits. [Soul Taker; Papa Shango; Kama; Godfather; Goodfather]

Godwinns, The
(1990s)

As former two-time WWF tag-team champions, Mark Canterbury and Dennis Knight followed in the footsteps of hillbilly gimmick stars Uncle Elmer and Hillbilly Jim.

Goldberg, Bill
(1990s-2000s)

This former college and pro football player was spotted by Lex Luger and Sting in a Georgia gym and urged to try wrestling. At first he was a cult favorite, but to everyone's surprise, his mainstream popularity skyrocketed in WCW, which culminated in a world title win over Hulk Hogan in his rookie campaign. Storylines claimed he had a 175-match win streak. Slowed by injuries, he debuted in the WWE in 2003 and has been searching for the magic that brought him success in WCW.

Golden, Jimmy
(1970s-2000s)

During the 1980s, the Southeast scene was defined by several stars, including this Tennessee-based wrestler who was usually aligned with Robert Fuller. A pure territory performer, he later saw action in WCW. [Bunkhouse Buck]

Golden, Mike
(1980s-1990s)

Known as the "Golden Boy" in the ring, he wrestled throughout the South and Northwest regions and held several minor titles in Florida.

Gomez, Pepper
(1950s-1970s)

Bodybuilding was a passion for Gomez, a Mexican sensation who, without a mask, found success in the United States. He was a major attraction in San Francisco and around Texas and held the San Francisco title and numerous tag-team titles.

Gonzales, Jose
(1980s-1990s)

Only marginally talented as a wrestler, Gonzales was part of the most famous masked tag team in Puerto Rican history, the Invaders. He teamed with Roberto Soto to create the team.

Gonzales, Rey
(1980s-2000s)

This Lucha Libre star is also one of the longest running champions to hold the Universal title in Puerto Rico.

Gordienko, George
(1960s-1970s)

If he had his way, Gordienko probably would have been an artist. In addition to wrestling, he's been a respected painter and many of his works have been sold to collectors. Noted as a shooter in the ring, the Canadian-born wrestler was popular in Calgary where he won titles in the 1970s.

Gordon, Tod
(1990s-2000s)

The original owner of ECW, he sold off his controlling interest to Paul Heyman in 1994. Gordon has been seen on the East Coast independent scene ever since.

TRIVIA

Q. Who was acquitted in the 1988 slaying of Bruiser Brody?

Gordy, Terry
(1970s-1990s)

There are so many memories from Gordy's career that it's sad to think he died so young. Beginning his wrestling journey at the ripe age of 16, he defied his size and was seemingly destined to become a star. He was on the verge of quitting when he and Michael Hayes hooked up to form the Fabulous Freebirds with Buddy Roberts. His real success was realized in Japan where the fans took to his realistic style that made them remember Bruiser Brody. By the late 1980s, his career was cruising. He won two Triple Crown titles in 1990 and in all was a seven-time All-Japan tag-team champion (two with Stan Hansen, five with Steve Williams). He fought through a coma to return to the ring but was never the same and in 2001, he died. Today, his son, Terry Ray Gordy Jr., continues the legacy. [The Executioner; Terry Mecca.] See: Freebirds.

Gorgeous George
(1940s-1960s)

Born George Wagner of Seward, Neb., he was arguably the first must-see star in the history of pro wrestling. With the explosion of television wrestling in the early 1950s, Wagner's flamboyant act—complete with 24k gold hairpins—drew the nation's attention. The stars of today owe the "Human Orchid" a debt of thanks for helping the sport grow into a brand new form of entertainment.

TRIVIA

Q. Which female wrestler was the partner of Wendy Richter in the team Texas Cowgirls?

Gotch, Frank
(1900-1910s)

Regarded as the best American wrestler ever, his legendary status is affirmed. The fact that even today's generation still talks about him is a testament to his celebrity. The Iowa native knew hundreds of holds and was the first American to earn the world's heavyweight title, which he won from Russian George Hackenschmidt in 1908 in Chicago. He died in 1917, in the prime of his life at age 41, from uremia.

Gotch, Karl
(1950s-1980s)

This noted shooter was part of the Legionnaires tag team with Rene Goulet in the early 1970s. Born in Germany, he's still considered a legend in Japan. [Karl Krauser]

Goulet, Rene
(1960s-1980s)

As a lounge-singer lookalike, the French-Canadian was a fairly successful mid-level performer in the AWA where he toured in the 1960s. He made his way to the WWWF where he won the tag titles as the Legionnaires with Karl Gotch. He stayed with the WWF and has been working there as a road agent since retiring in the mid-1980s. See: Legionnaires.

Grable, Joyce
(1950s-1970s)

Known as the "Golden Goddess," she took her nickname from film star Betty Grable. Her mom, Judy, wrestled, too.

Grable, Judy
(1950s)

The mother of Joyce Grable, she toured the country extensively as one of the top names of the day. She also held a version of the women's belt in the 1950s.

Graham, Billy
(1960s-1980s)

Bodybuilding beach bum, Wayne Coleman, adopted the "Graham" name and carried it all the way to the WWWF world title in 1977. The "Superstar" was often a rule breaker but his flamboyant style made him a popular favorite almost everywhere he went. Graham, a known steroid user, was a major influence in wrestlers becoming physically impressive. Unfortunately, that drug use caused numerous health problems prior to his retirement in the late 1980s.

Graham, Eddie
(1940s-1980s)

Regarded by some as one of the greatest wrestlers of all time (certainly of the 1960s), Ed Gossett, a noted "brother" of Luke and Jerry Graham, was a Grade A main-event star throughout the world and successful promoter in Florida. Like most Grahams in the ring, he was flamboyant and sported blond hair. With Jerry, he won three WWWF tag-team championships. When he settled on the business side, his group dominated the Sunshine State in the 1970s and 1980s. Well respected by his peers, his territory was a cross-pollinated concoction on the NWA, AWA, and Mid-South. With regional groups closing in the 1980s, Graham's promotion fell. His personal demons caught up with him and, in 1985, he committed suicide.

Graham, Jerry
(1950s-1970s)

The long-time partner of "brother" Eddie Graham, Jerry was the only real Graham among the famous tag team. He actually founded the famed team and was a frequent headliner at Madison Square Garden. Before his wrestling career, he was a World War II paratrooper. That belied his ring career where he was a villain in every sense of the word. A great heel, he was an opponent of Buddy Rogers and Bruno Sammartino. The elder and "smarter" Graham, known as the "Dr.," was an average single's star but a superior tag-team wrestler. One of the blond innovators of TV's Golden Age, he held the WWWF tag title four times, including the very first crown awarded in 1957. He passed away in 1997.

Graham Jr., Luke
(1980s-2000s)

The heavily scarred son of Luke Graham made a name for himself as a nutty brawler. His smallish size held him back in many cases but he wrestled throughout the South. He has been a vocal backer of starting a union for pro wrestlers. Although he had regional success, he never enjoyed the same amount of success as his father.

Graham Sr., Luke
(1950s-1980s)

"Crazy" Luke was a wacky character in the WWWF and Southwest. Certainly not politically correct, his hijinks were a fun diversion. A tag-team champion with his "brother" Jerry, he ventured through California and Hawaii in the 1960s in addition to his time in the WWWF. Along with Tarzan Tyler, he was a former WWWF tag-team champion. The wild-haired heel also was found in the Central States where he held that company's single's title.

Graham, Mike
(1970s-2000s)

The Florida-based Graham was one of the premier junior heavyweights of the 1970s, primarily in the South. The son of Eddie Graham, he's a second-generation attraction who later joined WCW's booking team with Dusty Rhodes and Kevin Sullivan.

Graham, Troy
(1970s-1980s)

Those who know like to remember Graham as one of the great Southern fast-talkers, blending Dusty Rhodes and Jerry Lawler with his own flare. In fact, few matched the general charisma that he displayed as a regional star in the Southeast. Most of his career was under the hood as the Dream Machine feuding with Lawler over the Southern heavyweight title. Although he never reached beyond the South, he is remembered fondly. He passed away in 2002. [Troy T. Tyler; Dream Machine]

Grand Wizard, The
(1960s-1970s)

One of the quirkiest managers ever to round ringside, he was diminutive, wacky, and all fun. Wearing sunglasses and a turban, he took on a Middle Easterner gimmick while guiding many champions and miscreants in, among places, the WWWF, and is said to have been a favorite of the McMahon family. He passed away in 1983. [Abdullah Farouk]

Great Goliath, The
(1960s-1980s)

Great heel from the old days who often teamed with Black Gordman in California. He also visited the Midwest IWA promotion. Toward the end of his career, he made an appearance in the fun wrestling flick, "Grunt: The Wrestling Movie."

Great Mephisto, The
(1960s-1980s)

Frank Cain wore a turban and professed to be from the Middle East. As a wrestler, he was found in San Francisco where he was a U.S. champ before losing the belt to Pat Patterson. He also held the U.S. tag titles with Dante. Later, he was a famous territory manager in the Southeast where he talked a good game.

Great Sasuke, The
(1980s-2000s)

A tremendous, masked, high-flyer from Japan who has been a constant on the independent scene. His career highlight was in the 1995 Super Juniors tournament. In May 2003, he was elected as a lawmaker in the local council chamber in Morioka, Japan. He has stuck to his wrestling roots by wearing his signature mask while in office.

Green, Sue
(1970s-1980s)

A journeyman ringster, she toured to limited success, but various reports have Green winning a version of the women's championship from Fabulous Moolah in 1976.

Greensboro Coliseum

For many years, the home of Jim Crockett Promotions/Mid-Atlantic was in Greensboro, N.C. The building opened in 1959 and during the 1970s and 1980s, watching wrestling at the arena was a Sunday night tradition. Many major title changes happened there including two NWA world championship switches. The first was in 1983, when Ric Flair dethroned Harley Race at the first-ever Starrcade.

Guerrera, Juventud
(1980s-2000s)

This Lucha Libre star received American fame while in the WCW cruiserweight division. Along with Rey Mysterio and Ultimo Dragon, the crew brought U.S. wrestling to new heights in the mid-1990s. Under a mask, Guerrera was a three-time cruiserweight champ. He also had success in Japan.

Guerrero Jr., Chavo
(1990s-2000s)

A third-generation start, the son of Chavo Guerrero is a cruiserweight who has appeared in WCW and WWF. He struggled to find his own identity, but persevered to win the WCW cruiserweight title. Of late, he's been an important member of the WWE family, winning the tag-team titles with his uncle, Eddy Guerrero. [Lt. Loco]

Guerrero Sr., Chavo
(1970s-1980s)

The eldest son of Gory Guerrero, he was a former Texas champion and popular among Latino fans in U.S. border towns. Like all the Guerreros, he was a talented high flyer and had success in the Mid-South territory. He also teamed with his brothers, Hector, Mando, and Eddy.

Guerrero, Eddy
(1980s-2000s)

A talented high flyer and member of the legendary family (he's Chavo Jr.'s uncle), Eddy's career began to take flight in Mexico where he teamed with Art Barr to wild success in the early 1990s. He also wrestled in Japan but was brought to the U.S. by ECW in the mid-90s. Despite having to recover from a horrific car accident, he has restarted his career in WWE, where he's won the Intercontinental and tag-team titles and is consistently one of the best performers in the world. [Latino Heat; Black Tiger; Mascara Magica]

Guerrero, Gory
(1950s-1960s)

Although this Mexican superstar is best known for fathering four wrestling sons (Hector, Chavo, Mando, and Eddie), he was a true talent in his own right. He was a huge star in Mexico, Japan, Texas, Oregon, and California, where he won numerous singles and tag-team titles, including the NWA world junior heavyweight title.

Guerrero, Hector
(1970s-1980s)

An acrobatic Latino star, the son of Gory Guerrero wrestled mainly in the Southeast. The tallest of the wrestling Guerreros, he brought many Lucha Libre skills, which, at the time, were very new to American fans. He won regional titles and also had a run in the NWA in the junior heavyweight division as Lazor Tron. [Lazor Tron; Gobbledy Gooker]

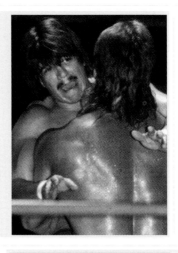

Guerrero, Mando
(1970s-1980s)

Although he's the shortest of the wrestling Guerreros, he may have been the most agile: he utilized in-ring somersaults and high-flying moves. He had regional success and was never far from his brothers.

Gunkel, Ann
(1960s-1970s)

The widow of promoter Ray Gunkel holds a very important distinction in wrestling history. Ray Gunkel ran Georgia Championship Wrestling in Atlanta. When he passed away from a ring injury in 1972, Ann Gunkel split off, taking all the Atlanta-based workers to form All-South Wrestling. Although the company survived only a few years, a bitter war ensued. The NWA directors, knowing the area was key to its success, sent all of its top talent to compete against Gunkel. In 1974, All-South closed shop.

Gunkel, Ray
(1960s-1970s)

A clean-cut and dashing baby-face wrestler-promoter in Georgia, he died in 1972 from injuries suffered in a match earlier one evening against Ox Baker in Savannah, Ga. Baker, known for his heart punch move, administered the move on Gunkel and he inadvertently bruised Gunkel's heart. The injury was reportedly the cause of his death. He was also a noted promoter of wrestling in Georgia and, when he died, his wife, Ann, took over until the promotion closed in 1974.

Gunn, Bart
(1990s-2000s)

Formerly one-half of the Smoking Gunns tag team with Billy Gunn, he was a cowboy character in the WWF after a brief stint on the Florida independent circuit. With Billy, the twosome won three tag-team titles. Bart ventured on his own, winning the "Brawl for All" contest and appeared poised for a UFC career before he was kayoed by Butterbean at Wrestlemania 15. Ever since, he's been in All-Japan trying to escape that embarrassment. [Mike Barton; Bodacious Bart]

Gunn, Billy
(1990s-2000s)

Perhaps no current-day wrestler has been in the right place at the right time more often than Gunn, an average mid-carder who found success in the WWF as one member of Degeneration X after playing a cowboy gimmick with Bart Gunn. Together, they won three tag-team titles. Billy later joined with Road Dogg in DX and claimed five more tag-team titles. He's also a former Intercontinental champion. [B.A.; Bad Ass Billy Gunn; Mr. Ass]

Hackenschmidt, George
(1900-1910s)

Recognized in 1904 as the first world champion in the line of NWA title holders, he earned that recognition after a match with then-North American champion, Tom Jenkins, in New York City. With a chiseled physique, he looked like a dominant force. After dodging American hopeful Frank Gotch for several years, Hackenschmidt was dethroned in a Chicago match in 1908.

Haiti Kid
(1970s-1980s)

A legendary midget wrestler, Kid was a popular WWF attraction when the promotion became a nationwide hit in the early 1980s.

Haku
(1980s-2000s)

Like a cat with nine lives, Haku has been reincarnated many times in many territories with various gimmicks. He's been everything from a king to a warrior, but this legendary tough guy is multi-talented. The kick-boxer and martial artist has wrestled in New Zealand, Canada, Australia, Singapore, Canada, and all over the U.S. Not known to hold many titles in his career, he has won the WWF tag belts (with Andre the Giant) and WCW hardcore belt. [Meng; King Tonga; Tonga Warrior; King Haku]

Hall, Scott
(1980s-2000s)

Known mostly for his blockbuster role in the New World Order with Kevin Nash and Hulk Hogan, Hall was originally a territory star from the Florida scene in the early 1980s. After trips to the AWA (where he was tag-team champion with Curt Hennig) and WCW, he received a new look in the WWF as Razor Ramon. He had a brief run as Intercontinental champion, but the company cut him and Nash loose in 1995. With a chip on his shoulder, he went to WCW where he was part of the hot NWO gimmick, which drew capacity crowds for nearly two years. Unfortunately, his personal demons derailed his career, despite numerous second chances. [Gator Scott Hall; Razor Ramon]

Halme, Tony
(1990s)

This Swedish-born star has boxed and wrestled. Large and powerful, he had a brief stint in the WWF but wrestling wasn't his forte. He tried boxing unsuccessfully and in 2003, he was surprisingly elected to the Finnish Parliament. [The Viking; Ludvig Borga]

Hamilton, Jody
(1970s-1990s)

After a career as one-half of the Masked Assassins, Hamilton became a talent scout and agent for the WCW. He's said to have been the person who discovered Kevin Nash. [The Assassin]

Hansen, Stan
(1970s-2000s)

A true Texas legend, he is known for being one of the most rugged wrestlers ever and many would-be opponents have run from him in the ring. But his true success came in Japan where he has been a two-decade attraction on the singles and tag-team scene. His list of accomplishments include four All-Japan Triple Crown titles from 1990-95, eight All-Japan tag-team titles, and the AWA world title in 1985.

TRIVIA

Q. Which famous wrestler appeared in more than 25 films and countless cameos oh hit televison shows such as "The Love Boat," "Happy Days," and "Get Smart?"

Hanson, Swede
(1950s-1980s)

Teamed up with Rip Hawk, Hanson was a feared tag-team wrestler in the Carolinas. He was a husky heel who exhibited great chemistry with Hawk, with whom he was a multiple tag-team champion. Hanson passed away in 2002 at age 68.

Happy Humphrey
(1950s-1960s)

Was he the largest wrestler ever? Some say yes. At more than 700 pounds, he was from the circus circuit and wrestled as a special attraction through the 1960s, but he never achieved the success of his fellow big man friend, Haystacks Calhoun.

Hard Boiled Haggerty
(1950s-1960s)

Not to be confused with Mr. Clean, this big, bad, and bald-headed warrior parlayed his mid-card AWA career for a prolific acting stint. In the early 1960s, Haggerty was a two-time AWA tag-team champion with Lenny Montana and Gene Kiniski.

Hardy, Jeff
(1990s-2000s)

Hardy is the type who gives all backyard wrestlers hope. The North Carolina native trained himself to wrestle and, along with his brother, Matt, he was determined to hit the national scene. With stints in various independents, the daredevil was given a shot in the WWF where he was a tag-team champion five times with Matt. His interest in wrestling waned, which led to his early retirement in 2003. [Willow the Wisp; The Wolverine]

Hardy, Matt
(1990s-2000s)

Like his brother, Jeff Hardy, Matt went from backyard wrestling to main event star in short time. He helped orchestrate some classic matches with Jeff against Edge and Christian including a series of eye-popping ladder matches. With Jeff's career on the fritz, Matt went solo and has been successful, winning the WWE cruiserweight title. [Surge]

Harlem Heat
(1990s)

Ray and Booker Huffman began their careers in the Texas independents before getting a call from WCW in the early 1990s. At first they were heels, but there was no denying their popularity. Together, the duo won the world tag titles 10 times. See: Booker T.; Stevie Ray.

Harris Bros., The
(1990s-2000s)

Inseparable, the real-life twin brothers and Bruiser Brody look-alikes were found in the Northwest and Mid-South before heading to the WWF. [Bruise Brothers (Ron and Don); The Blu Bros. (Ely and Jacob); Disciples of Apocalypse (Eight Ball and Skull)]

Hart Foundation, The
(1980s-1990s)

Bret Hart and Jim Niedhart, managed by Jimmy Hart, made up this tag team in the WWF's early-1980s era. Brokered to the WWF from Calgary Stampede, they blended perfectly as Niedhart provided the power while Hart provided the technical skills. In the beginning, they were glorified mid-carders but eventually caught the attention of Vince McMahon Jr. Their feuds with the Rockers and British Bulldogs showcased four-star matches nightly. The Foundation won two WWF tag-team championships, in 1987 and 1990. See: Jim Niedhart; Bret Hart; Jimmy Hart.

Hart, Bret
(1980s-2000s)

One of the most gifted wrestlers of the modern era, Bret blended a distinct style that combined Japanese, American, and Mexican styles and was key in bringing wrestling into a new era with his creative flair for moves and tremendous work ethic. In Calgary, the home base of his family's promotion, he was a five-time Stampede North American champion. In the U.S., he became a WWF icon, winning the world belt five times from 1992-97 and the Intercontinental title twice, from 1991-92. With his career in high gear, he broke ties with the McMahon family on ugly terms, a feud that is still ongoing. He ventured to WCW where he was a two-time world champ in 1999. His career's final years were not pretty, as he was forced to retire from post-concussion syndrome, stroke, and stress stemming from his brother Owen's death in 1999.

Hart, Bruce
(1970s-2000s)

Extremely intelligent wrestler who is credited with bringing the Japanese style to North America. In the Hart family, Bruce has been the mastermind behind the scenes. He helped his father, Stu, operate Calgary Stampede's training center for many years. In addition, he held the Stampede British Commonwealth belt five times. In the late 1980s, he trained and teamed with Brian Pillman. Bruce remains active with hopes of a Calgary revival.

Hart, Dean
(1970s-1980s)

Like the entire Hart family, Dean possessed an intelligent wrestling mind. He wrestled briefly, refereed, and promoted. Family members knew him to march to his own beat. This Hart member passed away in 1990 at the age of 21.

Hart, Gary
(1970s-1990s)

This ex-wrestler reached stardom as a manager in Florida, Dallas, and the NWA. He has had classic feuds with Dusty Rhodes in which he managed foes like Kabuki and the Great Muta against Rhodes and a host of heroes.

Hart, Helen
(1950s-1990s)

The matriarch of the Hart family, Helen was a motherly influence behind the scenes. Well liked and fondly remembered, she passed away in 2001. Always the gracious host, Helen was mom to four daughters and eight sons, all of whom took part in wrestling in one form or fashion.

TRIVIA

Q. Who went by the nickname "Mouth of the South?"

Hart, Jimmy
(1980s-2000s)

Hart was a famous heel manager who started in Memphis with the help of Jerry Lawler. His best years were in the early 1980s, when he was at the center of the Lawler-Andy Kaufman feud. He went on to the WWF, and later WCW, where he managed multiple tag-team and single's champions. Before wrestling, he was a singer in the band, the Gentrys. He still has his hands in the business as a promoter.

Hart, Keith
(1970s-1980s)

One of the lesser-known Hart family members, Keith was popular in Canada, Hawaii, and England. He won numerous belts, including the Calgary Mid-Heavyweight and tag-team titles (with brother Bruce). He was considered too small for a major market but, just like all the Harts, he was a technically sound grappler.

Hart, Owen
(1980s-1990s)

One of the special performers of the modern era, he died tragically at age 34 performing a stunt in 1999. Owen, the baby of the Calgary Hart family, was a high flyer in Canada and Japan, who was destined to become a star. He wanted to be an Olympic wrestler, but the pro ranks always called out to him. In Calgary, he teamed with brother, Bruce, and held the Calgary Stampede title in feuds with Makhan Singh. Sometimes deemed too small, he broke into the WWF twice as the Blue Blazer. When he finally had a chance to be himself, Owen shined, winning the WWF Intercontinental title, European title, and tag titles three times.

TRIVIA

Q. Which wrestler broke his neck while trying his signature move, the lionsault?

Hart, Ross
(1970s-2000s)

Like every one of Stu Hart's sons, Ross wrestled. Although he enjoyed wrestling as much as any of his brothers, he was more successful on the business side than in the ring. One of the smaller Hart boys, he had success wrestling in Hawaii and Calgary.

Hart, Stu
(1940s-1980s)

He's the man who started it all for the Hart clan. A former amateur standout, he turned pro in the 1940s and his imprint is still felt today. His family run promotion, Calgary Stampede, has, since 1948, been the home of pioneers, rebels, and miscreants, many of which have graduated from his training center to become some of wrestling's biggest stars. Only the toughest of the tough survived his training camps in his dreaded dungeon. Alums? How about Davey Boy Smith, Dynamite Kid, Bad News Brown, not to mention his all-star roll call of sons. Countless Japanese stars have also passed through his mitts. In 1986, he stepped into the ring for the last time at age 70. An icon in Calgary, Canadian wrestling will likely always be remembered for Hart's massive contributions.

Hase, Hiroshi
(1980s-2000s)

One of the great junior heavyweights from Japan, Hase crafted a pro career after wrestling as an Olympic amateur in 1984. The former two-time IWGP champ held the WCW International title after a 1993 win against Rick Rude. An active wrestler today, he's one of several wrestlers to hold public office in Japan. Hase was elected to the Upper House in 1995 and later elected to the Lower House in 2000. [Viet Cong]

Hashimoto, Shinya
(1980s-2000s)

The bulky, Japanese star has been on top since the mid-1980s. Aligned with Keiji Mutoh and Masahiro Chono, he was part of the country's strong style and was arguably the nation's top draw in the 1990s. His accolades include the IWGP title three times from 1993-96 and the NWA world title in 2001.

Hass, Charlie
(1990s-2000s)

Twin brother of Russ Haas, he wrestled at Seton Hall in college before looking to the pros. He and his brother, former independent tag-team champions, were often compared to the Briscos. But sadly, Russ passed away in 2001. Charlie has fought through the adversity of losing his brother and has built a nice career in the WWE as the partner of fellow collegiate star, Shelton Benjamin, as Team Angle. Together, they were tag-team champions in 2003.

Hass, Russ
(1990s)

The twin brother of Charlie Haas, Russ, also a Seton Hall grad, was on the fast track with his brother when he passed away in 2001 from heart failure.

Hawk
(1980s-2000s)

Not particularly talented in the ring, Hawk had one thing going for him that made him a sure thing: a gimmick. As one half of the Road Warriors, Hawk (born Mike Hegstrand) had loads of charisma when he burst on the scene in the early 1980s with his partner, Animal. Perhaps the hottest tag-team creation ever, the Road Warriors were in high demand for much of the 1980s and helped usher in a new era of big men. See: Road Warriors.

Hawk, Rip
(1960s-1980s)

The long-time partner of Swede Hanson, Hawk was a big-time talker in the Mid-Atlantic region. A super drawing card, he was Ric Flair's first partner. In 1984, the duo won the Mid-Atlantic tag-team title.

Hayabusa
(1980s-2000s)

Courage defines Hayabusa. Eiji Ezaki learned his trade in the Frontier Martial Arts promotion in Japan as a masked sensation with a flair for the air. During the 1990s, he was one of FMW's top attractions and never shied from taking part in exploding ring matches. His injuries forced him to retire, although he's vowed a come back. [H]

Hayashi, Kaz
(1990s-2000s)

A top-flight Japanese cruiserweight who had some success in America, this competent, but small, performer dazzled crowds in the WCW tag-team, Jung Dragons. [El Gringo, Shiryu]

Hayes, Alfred
(1970s-1990s)

His Lordship was one of the most likeable figures in wrestling. Famous for his days as television host of "Tuesday Night Titans" with Vince McMahon, he was an accomplished wrestler in England and the AWA employing a dapper and suave aristocrat persona. [Lord Alfred Hayes]

Hayes, Michael
(1970s-2000s)

One of the greatest interviews in wrestling history, Hayes can make you laugh, cry, and scream all in one interview. As the famed leader of the Fabulous Freebirds, he was a main-event star wherever he went through the 1980s. Some of his exploits took place in World Class, Georgia Championship, and the Mid-South region. Along with Terry Gordy and Buddy Roberts, they were genuine heat seekers and are fondly remembered. [Dok Hendrix]

Haynes, Billy Jack
(1970s-1990s)

The well-chiseled Haynes traveled to Florida and the Central States but he rose to the top in Portland. With his regional days behind him, he took an offer to wrestle in the WWF in the early 1980s. It proved to be a mistake. Despite a Wrestlemania III match against Ken Patera, he never caught on. After that tour, he began promoting in Oregon, where he has been ever since. [Black Blood]

Headbangers, The
(1990s)

Chaz Warrington (Mosh) and Glen Ruth (Thrash) were East Coast independent stars when they turned a stint in Smoky Mountain Wrestling into a WWF contract. Riding high, using a grunge-rock gimmick, they held the WWF tag titles for a month in 1997. [Flying Nuns; The Spiders (Mosaic and Tarantula)]

Headhunters, The
(1980s-2000s)

Are they twin sons of Abdullah the Butcher? They sure look it. Manuel and Victor Santiago sure were a sight to see. Who could forget 400-pound men flying off the top rope? They rode their gimmick to titles in Japan and Mexico. With the exception of a tiny stint in the WWF managed by Jim Cornette, U.S. stardom eluded them.

Headshrinkers, The
(1980s-1990s)

In the long tradition of Samoan warriors, Samu and Fatu (Rikishi) were mid-level stars in World Class and the NWA as the S.S.T. before hitting the WWF, where they earned tag-team gold in 1994. [Samoan Swat Team]

Heavenly Bodies, The
(1990s)

When Jim Cornette opened Smoky Mountain Wrestling in the early 1990s, he needed a tag-team in the mold of the Midnight Express. The Bodies, comprised of former Express member Stan Lane and newbie Tom Pritchard, picked up the slack. Later, when Lane quit, Jimmy Del Ray was brought in. They didn't make people forget about the Midnights, but for a regional throwback team, they fit the bill.

Hebner, Dave
(1980s-2000s)

Earl Hebner's brother has been active in the old NWA and WWF. Like his brother, he has worked in many high profile pay-per-view events. Nowadays, he's hung up the ref shirt for a clipboard backstage as a road agent in WWE.

Hebner, Earl
(1980s-2000s)

Known as the dean of referees, few striped shirts have earned accolades like Hebner. He's usually put in a Mills Lane-styled law and order role. When Andre the Giant feuded with Hulk Hogan in 1987, it put Hebner on the map when he, along with his brother, Dave, was involved in a "twin brothers" angle that left Hogan stripped of his title. Earl was also the ref of record in Montreal when Bret Hart lost the WWF title to Shawn Michaels in a whirlwind of controversy.

TRIVIA

Q. Which big bruiser (a.k.a. Axe) spent his last days in wrestling as tag-team partner with his son Curt?

Heenan, Bobby
(1960s-1990s)

Few men in wrestling have had the access to their wit as Bobby Heenan, the finest manager to ever live. Heenan began his career as a wrestler in Indiana but used his wit and interview ability to build up stables of wrestlers. In the AWA and WWF, he was an all-purpose show stopper and behind-the-scenes genius whose ability to draw fans into the matches was unparalleled. He helped lead the careers of Blackjack Lanza, Nick Bockwinkel, Curt Hennig, and Rick Rude and has had a career-long, onscreen feud against Hulk Hogan that culminated in Hogan's Wrestlemania III match against Andre the Giant at the Pontiac Silver Dome.

Hennig, Curt
(1970s-2000s)

Considered to be the perfect athlete while with the WWF in the 1990s, he was the son of Larry Hennig. Curt won the AWA world title in 1987 and later grabbed the WWF I-C belt. One of the best workers in his heyday, he was known as a prankster backstage. Hennig lost his life in 2003. [Mr. Perfect]

Hennig, Larry
(1960s-1980s)

The "Axe" began his career as Verne Gagne's protege and eventually Hennig turned on his mentor. With Harley Race, Hennig formed a famous blond-haired tag team. He is the father of wrestlers Curt and Jesse Hennig.

Henry, Mark
(1990s-2000s)

The agile big man was an Olympic weightlifter in 1996. Based on that success, the WWF signed him to a multi-year contract, but wrestling has been a tough transition for Henry. A former European champion, he was used in OVW for a time and resurfaced on the main stage in a strongman-type role. [Sexual Chocolate]

Herman, Hans
(1940s-1960s)

Another in a long line of German gimmick wrestlers to come along after World War II, he was a powerhouse sort and often teamed with Fritz Von Erich. Hans was also a tag-team wrestler in Portland in the 1950s.

Hernandez, Gino
(1970s-1980s)

Gino, a major player from the Southwest, was a phenomenally gifted athlete who seemed destined for superstardom when he died in 1986. In hindsight, he was one of wrestling's first drug tragedies. A quarterback in college, his flamboyant style wowed fans as Chris Adams' partner in Dallas in their epic feud against the Von Erichs.

Hernandez, Hercules
(1970s-1990s)

Wielding a chain, he was formerly a territory star of the late 1970s. The native Floridian, with broad shoulders and a mean look, took off for the WWF after stints in Texas and the Central States. Usually a mid-card single's star, he teamed briefly with Paul Roma.

Heyman, Paul
(1980s-2000s)

What else can be said of Heyman. He's been a jack-of-all-trades in wrestling, going from fan, photographer, and manager to booker, commentator, television director, and creative genius. He ventured to many promotions, including Memphis, the AWA and NWA. After his ECW group closed its doors in 2001, he settled into an on-again, off-again role with the WWE, managing Brock Lesnar and Big Show. [Paul E. Dangerously]

Hickerson, Phil
(1970s-1990s)

An extra-large Southeast star who made a career in the Memphis/Louisville/Nashville areas. [P.Y. Chu Hi]

Hildebrand, Brian
(1980s-1990s)

A talented manager and referee who died of cancer in 1999, he was integral behind the scenes in Smoky Mountain Wrestling and was a regularly used referee in WCW. Trained as a wrestler, he would often get involved in matches, to the crowd's delight. Among his charges were Abdullah the Butcher and Eddie Gilbert. As a manager, he wasn't widely known, but some say he was one of the best ever. [Mark Curtis]

TRIVIA

Q. Who was the first wrestler to grace the cover of *Sports Illustrated*?

Hillbilly Jim
(1970s-1990s)

Spotted in Memphis, he was called by the WWF in the early 1980s, where he became a fun-loving, fan-friendly gimmick wrestler. He also worked for Stu Hart's Calgary group. [Harley Davison]

Ho, Dean
(1950s-1970s)

The barefooted Japanese star, a fan favorite in Calgary, Japan, and Hawaii, was a precursor to today's high flyers. He also looked great—he was a Mr. Hawaii bodybuilding champ in the 1950s. He was also a Mr. America finalist in 1956. In 1974, he and Tony Garea won the WWF tag-team titles. [Dean Higuchi]

Hodge, Danny
(1950s-1970s)

Regarded by some as the greatest "wrestler" to ever live, Hodge remains a legend in his native Oklahoma. A multi-talented athlete, he's the only man to win both boxing and wrestling amateur titles. In wrestling, he was a highly regarded light heavyweight, but he also beat most heavyweight challengers.

Hoffman, Horst
(1970s-1980s)

A talented European shooter who was feared and jeered by fans in the 1970s. Often aligned with partner Baron Von Raschke, he made waves in Japan.

Hogan, Horace
(1990s-2000s)

The nephew of Hulk Hogan, he sowed his oats in Japan in the bloody FMW group. He was brought into WCW in the late 1990s, courtesy of Hogan, where he was a marginal star. [Horace Boulder]

Hogan, Hulk
(1970s-2000s)

A true superstar, few can argue he made the biggest impact on wrestling. As a television personality, he captured the attention of fans globally in the early 1980s, which enabled the WWF to rule the roost. He was a 12-time world champion in WWF and WCW (six times in each promotion). Many fans got their start in wrestling from watching Hogan. [Terry Boulder; Hulk Machine; Hollywood Hogan; Mr. America]

Holliday, Jonathan
(1980s-1990s)

A light heavyweight wrestler and manager from the Calgary, British Columbia, and Oregon promotions, he had a brash, mouthy, and fun gimmick.

Holly, Bob
(1980s-2000s)

Few wrestlers can pull it off, but Holly's lack of personality has been an asset. But he could work. He worked in Southeast independents before getting a chance in WWF courtesy of Jim Cornette. After a trial run with an auto racer gimmick and even a shot as the New Midnight Express with Bart Gunn, his role finally was established in a feud with Big Show when Bob became Hardcore Holly. He's a two-time hardcore champion and carried the WWF tag titles twice (1-2-3 Kid and Crash Holly). [Sparky Plugg; Bombastic Bob; Hardcore Holly]

Holly, Crash
(1990s-2000s)

This West Coast independent wrestler, despite his small frame, reached fame in the WWF as Bob Holly's "cousin." At 5-6, it would seem the deck is stacked against him, but he found a niche as a hardcore/comedy act. He won the WWF hardcore belt a record 13 times. He's also a former European and tag-team champion with Bob. [Erin O'Grady]

Holly, Molly
(1990s-2000s)

In an era when women's wrestling is often a joke, the short sweetheart has tried to bring some respectability to the division. A native of Minnesota, she trained in Florida. She used her connections with Randy Savage as a springboard to WCW in the late 1990s. From there, she hit the WWF and has been a staple ever since, even winning the women's title. [Miss Madness]

Hollywood Backlot Brawl

At Wrestlemania XII in Anaheim, the feud between Goldust and Roddy Piper came to a head. In this match, staged outside, it was highlighted by a car chase with Piper driving an O.J.-like white Bronco and 'Dust driving a gold Cadillac. After some entertaining brawling, Piper scored the win once the match made it back into the arena.

TRIVIA

Q. After failed attempts at stardom, this wrestler used the Elvis gimmick and hit pay dirt in the WWF. Who is he?

Hollywood Blondes, The
(1970s-1990s)

The name of several tag teams of the past, one of the originals were Buddy Roberts and Jerry Brown. Even Steve Austin and Brian Pillman called themselves the Blondes in WCW in the early 1990s. In Memphis, Ken Timbs and Dusty Wolfe used the name. In Puerto Rico, Larry Sharpe and Jack Evans used the Blondes gimmick.

Honkytonk Man, The
(1980s-2000s)

Wayne Ferris is a Memphis-area legend, who borrowed from Elvis Presley's image to create this gimmick. Wrestling is in his family. His cousins are wrestlers Jerry Lawler and Carl Fergie. [The Moondog]

Horner, Tim
(1980s-1990s)

A talented light heavyweight, his smallish size prevented him from reaching true stardom. Even so, Horner made a nice career in the UWF and NWA in the early 1980s, teaming with Brad Armstrong. He always had decent runs, but the main event was elusive although he was a multi-time regional champion. Later on, he also was Jim Cornette's business partner in Smoky Mountain.

Horowitz, Barry
(1970s-2000s)

Known widely as a jobber from the WWF, the entertaining Horowitz was actually a talented worker who traveled to many regions in the early 1980s. So go ahead, Barry, give yourself a pat on the back. [Bret Hart; Jack Hart; Barry Hart; Red Knight]

Houston, Sam
(1980s-2000s)

Second-generation wrestler and brother of Jake Roberts, he was a tall, lanky Texan on Southeast cards. The opening cat once held the defunct NWA Western States title, among other regional belts.

Huber, Spike
(1970s-1980s)

This ex-construction worker hailed from Indiana and saw action in World Class and (father-in-law) Dick the Bruiser's WWA. He wore a hard hat to the ring and sometimes teamed with Wilbur Snyder.

Hughes, Curtis
(1980s-1990s)

Clad with sunglasses and a fedora hat, Hughes is a decent talent who never caught on. With trips through the Central States, AWA, WCW, and WWF under his belt, he's a consistent veteran with an arsenal of power moves. [Big Cat]

Humperdink, Oliver
(1970s-1990s)

Red Sutton was a journeyman wrestler in the Mid-Atlantic (where he held the TV title) and Central States area, but found his calling as a manager in Florida, WCW, and the WWF (where he guided Bam Bam Bigelow) in the 1980s. A career nemesis of Dusty Rhodes, Humperdink always had a beefy stable to call on to do his dirty deeds. [Sir Oliver Humperdink; Big Daddy Dink]

Hurricane, The
(1990s-2000s)

Super heroes come in all sizes, right? Hurricane may be small, but he's large on talent. After breaking into wrestling in the Carolina independents with Shannon Moore, Shane Helms caught on in the WCW cruiserweight division. There, he teamed with Moore and Evan Karagis. When he finally got to the WWE, he was anointed with the Hurricane gimmick, based loosely around his interest in comic book characters. With a marketable name, Helms has settled into his popular cruiserweight role. [Shane Helms; Sugar Sean]

Hutchison, Ron
(1970s-1980s)

Once considered one of Canada's young guns, he won numerous regional titles before opening a wrestling school in Toronto with Sweet Daddy Siki.

Hutton, Dick
(1940s-1950s)

A member of the National Wrestling Hall of Fame, this former three-time NCAA champion at Oklahoma State turned pro. In 1957, he dethroned Lou Thesz for the NWA world title, a belt he held for two years before losing to Pat O'Connor.

TRIVIA

Q. Which wrestler is currently active in promoting New Japan Pro Wrestling, and holds public office in Japan?

Hyatt, Missy
(1980s-1990s)

Pure eye candy, that's what Missy Hyatt was. A fast talker and loose walker, Hyatt began as a valet in World Class and Mid-South and welcomed a new era for women in wrestling. After a few years as a broadcaster for WCW, she returned to valet work on the indy scene.

Iaukea, Curtis
(1950s-1990s)

Once considered a hardcore legend, Iaukea was an odd-looking character with a scarred bald head. He won numerous regional belts while tearing up foes in Hawaii, Australia, and the WWF. Also, he is said to have influenced Bruiser Brody. [King Curtis; Master]

Iaukea, Prince
(1990s)

No relation to King Curtis, this Polynesian wrestler was a mid-card sensation in the WCW cruiserweight division. [The Artist]

Infernos, The
(1970s)

Wearing hoods and terrorizing the Florida circuit in the 1970s, this team comprised of Frankie Cain and Rocky Smith were once that state's tag-team champions.

Inoki, Antonio
(1970s-2000s)

Like his one-time friend and partner, the late Giant Baba, Inoki reached legendary status in Japan. After training under Rikidozan, Inoki quickly became a star and retained his success all the way to his retirement in the 1990s.

Inoue, Mighty
(1970s-1990s)

An accomplished star from Japan, Inoue was a main tag-team attraction in the 1970s. Over his career, he won the All-Asia tag titles on four occasions with three different partners.

TRIVIA

Q. Which wrestler, while at the WWF, won the Intercontinental title from Ricky Steamboat in 1987?

Iron Sheik, The
(1970s-2000s)

Born Kosrow Vaziri, this former WWF world champion is said to have been a bodyguard for the Shah of Iran. He had a background in weightlifting and he used his power in wrestling. After hitting many areas around the country, he settled in as a controversial figure in the WWF in the 1980s. In December 1983, he surprisingly beat Bob Backlund for the title in New York only to lose it a week later to Hulk Hogan. [Great Hossein; Col. Mustafa]

Irwin, Bill
(1970s-2000s)

Brother of the late Scott Irwin, Bill was first a tag-team wrestler with Scott as the Super Destroyers and Longriders. Later, he used a cowboy gimmick in virtually every major area including World Class, AWA, and NWA. [The Goon; Super D]

Irwin, Scott
(1970s-1980s)

Along with brother Bill, they made up the Longriders and masked Super Destroyers before Scott, a talented wrestler, passed away in 1987 from a rare ailment. [Super D]

Island Death Match

In October 1987, New Japan's hottest feud was Antonio Inoki versus Masa Saito. To settle the feud, the two staged a match on Ganyru Island: one ring, no fans, no refs, no time limit. The wrestlers were brought to the island by boat. After the drama built for several hours, Inoki won the match.

Ivory
(1980s-2000s)

Positiveness pours from Ivory, who toiled in glam women's groups in the 1980s before she landed a gig in the WWE. The former GLOW women's champ, she revitalized her near-dead career and captured the WWE belt. A fitness guru at heart, Ivory fits the WWE idea of Diva to a tee. [Tina Morelli]

Jacqueline
(1980s-2000s)

The spunky spitfire, trained in Texas under Skandor Akbar, made her debut in 1989. Since then, she's been to WCW, the WWE as a valet and manager, and the USWA, where she won a record 14 women's titles from 1993-96. [Sweet Georgia Brown; Jackie; Miss Texas]

Jaggers, Bobby
(1970s-1980s)

This gruff-talking Southerner was a regional performer. In Southwest Championship Wrestling, he filled in for Jonathan Boyd as a member of the Sheepherders. Later, he teamed with Dutch Mantel in the Kansas Jayhawks. [Bobby Mayne]

Jannetty, Marty
(1980s-1990s)

Known as a high-flying technical star, the Kansas-based Jannetty began in Bob Geigel's Central States group. Too small to be a heavyweight, he teamed with Shawn Michaels. Capitalizing on the MTV generation, the duo, named the Midnight Rockers, blitzed the AWA and won the world tag titles. Later, the duo maxed their potential in the WWF as the Rockers. With Michaels seen as the next superstar, Jannetty, not to be outdone, relaunched his singles career and even won the WWF Intercontinental title in 1993. See: Rockers.

Japan Wrestling Association
(1950s-1970s)

Japan's first recognized body for wrestling, it was alive from 1953-73 but its heritage is kept alive through All-Japan Wrestling. Rikidozan was this group's first champion.

Jarrett, Jeff
(1980s-2000s)

Second generation star from Memphis, Jeff started his career in his teens. Initially he looked like a beanpole, but through hard work, he matured into a top U.S. star. He has always fought the label of being too "regional" looking, but defied the critics and served time as the WWF Intercontinental and tag-team champion. In 2000, he won the WCW world title from Dallas Page in Chicago. Of late, he's been trying to revitalize the NWA-TNA promotion based in Nashville. [Double J]

Jarrett, Jerry
(1960s-2000s)

Long considered a wrestling genius, Jarrett has been an astute businessman in the Memphis region. He was a better-than-average wrestler in the 1970s, but found his true calling as promoter of Memphis wrestling. Alongside Jerry Lawler, the territory survived most changes in the business and was, for a time, considered a time-warp promotion. By the 1990s, Jarrett had sold off the group and left wrestling altogether, but resurfaced in 2002 as the owner of NWA-TNA. He's hopeful he has some old magic left to make the new group a success.

Jay, Kenny
(1960s-2000s)

The "Sodbuster" was a legendary jobber in the Midwest in the 1960s and 1970s. In his heyday, he held surprising victories over Harley Race and Bobby Heenan, both of which made him famous with fans. His career high was wrestling Muhammad Ali in an exhibition match in Chicago as Ali geared up for his match with Antonio Inoki. Well into his 60s, Jay still wrestled on independent cards.

Jazz
(1990s-2000s)

Probably as tough as any women's wrestler, she started her career in 1999 as Justin Credible's manager in ECW. But Jazz sought higher ground and continued to train for wrestling. That diligence paid off: in 2003, she became the WWE champ. [A.C. Jazz]

Jericho, Chris
(1990s-2000s)

Often compared to Roddy Piper (for his gift of gab) and Shawn Michaels (for his ring style), Jericho has bucked the odds. His pop, Ted Irvine, was a pro hockey player, and that athleticism runs in the family. Chris trained with the Hart family in Calgary before setting off for Japan and Mexico to learn his trade. He went to ECW and WCW before nabbing the spotlight in the WWE, where he became the promotion's first Unified world champion in 2001, in addition to the Intercontinental and tag-team titles. [Lionheart]

Jindrak, Mark
(1990s-2000s)

Tall and muscular, this former WCW partner of Sean O'Hare won the world tag title two times in his rookie year in 2000. Agile for his size, Jindrak has been working his way back to the top in OVW and hopes to return to the main roster.

Johnson, Ahmed
(1990s-2000s)

This former quick-rising WWF star won the Intercontinental title in 1996 and appeared poised for a world title run, but his stock dropped fast. A large and powerful specimen in his prime, he worked in WCW briefly before retiring. [Tony Norris; Big T]

Johnson, Rocky
(1960s-1980s)

The "Soulman" may be best known as the Rock's pop, but he was a top drawing wrestler the world over. He had strong ties to boxing and had an Ali-like foot shuffle. Promoters hoped to cash in on his African-American Superman look, and he and Tony Atlas once held the WWWF tag belts in 1983.

Johnson, Tor
(1930s-1960s)

As freaky looking as they come, this balding menace wrestled as the Swedish Angel in many territories. He even parlayed his looks into a spot in the Ed Wood cult classic, "Plan 9 From Outer Space." He also had bit parts in more than 25 films, including ones starring Abbott & Costello and Bela Lugosi. [Swedish Angel]

Jones, Nathan
(1990s-2000s)

This legit Aussie strongman champion crossed over to wrestling in the late 1990s in the WWE and various independent groups. His skills have been questioned, but he has a look. Is it enough?

Jonathan, Don Leo
(1950s-1960s)

The 6-7 monster earned a rep as one of the best big men around. Because few wrestlers of his day carried his girth, he wrestled a lot against the likes of Andre the Giant and Ox Baker. But his matches against Gene Kiniski, Bruno Sammartino, and Lou Thesz have earned him elite status. He was adept at both technical wrestling and brawling, and won numerous titles in his prime.

Jones, Paul
(1960s-1980s)

Before he became a manager, Jones was a highly successful wrestler in the Mid-Atlantic, Florida, and Georgia areas. His top years were in the mid-1970s when he held the Florida and Southern titles simultaneously. Nicknamed "No. 1," the quick-witted Jones also won two Mid-Atlantic tag-team championships. Later, as a heel manager, he guided a myriad of bad guys including Rick Rude, Ivan Koloff, and Manny Fernandez.

Jones, Rufus R.
(1960s-1980s)

Kansas City was home to the "Freight Train." At 6-5 and 250 pounds, you couldn't argue with that nickname. He was often billed as having one of the hardest heads in wrestling. In the Central States, he often teamed with fellow hardhead Bobo Brazil. In 1993, Jones passed away at age 60 in his home state.

Jones, S.D.
(1970s-1980s)

"Special Delivery" Jones was a prelim favorite in the WWF. His claim to fame was getting squashed by King Kong Bundy at Wrestlemania 1 in a "record" 8 seconds.

Jovica, Victor
(1970s-1990s)

One of the founding fathers of wrestling in Puerto Rico, Jovica helped create the World Wrestling Council in the early 1970s. In the ring, he was involved in multiple blood baths.

Jumping Bomb Angels
(1980s)

Following the success of Japan's Crush Gals, All-Japan Women's promoters promoted Noriyo Tateno and Itsuki Yamazaki as the Angels to mega-stardom. They were even victorious in a brief stateside stint in the WWF in 1988, winning the now-defunct women's tag-team titles from the Glamour Girls.

Junkyard Dog, The
(1970s-1990s)

After hitting most regions of the country, Sylvester Ritter was the biggest star in Mid-South in the early 1980s. As an African American, he had a loyal following in New Orleans. Riotous crowds watched him in explosive feuds against Ted DiBiase and Butch Reed. While there, he won the Mid-South title four times. Later on, he traveled to the WWF and helped take the group national. His career over, he died in 1998 from injuries suffered in a car wreck. [Big Daddy Ritter; Stagger Lee]

Kabuki
(1970s-1980s)

One of manager Gary Hart's assassins from Florida to battle Dusty Rhodes, Kabuki was shrouded in mystery. He spewed green mist at his opponents and also during his pre-match ritual. As a wrestler, Kabuki was talented and appeared in other U.S. territories like World Class.

Kai, Lelani
(1970s-1980s)

This journeyman wrestler, along with Judy Martin, formed the Glamour Girls in the WWF during the 1980s

Kalmikoff Bros., The
(1950s-1960s)

Ivan and Karol were five-time AWA tag-team champions from 1957-63 using a controversial Russian gimmick.

Kamala
(1970s-2000s)

James Harris was a territory journeyman who had one thing going for him: his size. The 350-pounder adopted the Ugandan headhunter gimmick and gave his career life. He's often been a main event monster in Memphis, World Class, and the WWF. [Bad News Harris]

Kane
(1980s-2000s)

Glenn Osborne has been an underrated performer in the WWF, but his time on a national level shows his uniqueness to the company. After several failed gimmicks, he went to the minors to learn. By the late 1990s, he was back in the WWE as Kane, Undertaker's "brother." A former world singles and tag-team champion, he's been one of the better big men in recent memory. [Fake Diesel; Unibomb; Isaac Yankem; X-Mas Creature]

Kanemura, Wing
(1990s-2000s)

A true-blue blood and guts performer, Kintaro Kanemura made a name for himself by scarring up his body on the Japanese independent scene. Portly but strong, he's been to FMW and WING in Japan. His mid-1990s match against Kevin Sullivan in Smoky Mountain Wrestling was even voted bloodiest match of the century.

Kanyon, Chris
(1990s-2000s)

Innovation has defined Kanyon's career. Through his trips to SMW, ECW, WCW, and WWE, he's taken pride in his friendship with Dallas Page and his ability to invent moves. He's also worked in Hollywood, as he wrote the wrestling choreography for Jesse Ventura's TV bio-flick. [Mortis; Kanyon]

Karagis, Evan
(1990s-2000s)

Few ready-to-work stars were born from the old WCW Power Plant, but this cruiserweight was one. Small but quick, he was a member of 3-Count but has struggled since WCW's closing.

Karbo, Wally
(1950s-1980s)

An all-time favorite for old-time Midwest fans, Karbo was the quirky promoter for Verne Gagne's AWA for four decades. Tapes of his on-screen commish role still leave people in stitches.

Karras, Alex
(1950s-1960s)

One of the biggest pro football stars to wear the tights, Karras was an All-Pro with the Detroit Lions. His biggest moment came in a feud with Dick the Bruiser, which drew a reported 16,000 fans in the Motor City.

Kashey, Abe
(1930s-1950s)

Always rough, the "Syrian Assassin" bit his opponents throughout the Midwest. In many main events of the day, he is noted for being Verne Gagne's first opponent. [King Kong Kashey]

Kazmaier, Bill
(1990s)

Short-lived in pro wrestling, this legend of strength contest was a pet project in WCW in the early 1990s. He teamed with Scott Steiner, but his strongman gimmick wasn't enough to keep fans interested.

Keirn, Steve
(1970s-2000s)

The Floridian reached wide appeal as the Fabulous Ones with Stan Lane in the early 1980s. The team, managed by Jackie Fargo, was a spin-off of the popular 1960s team, the Fabulous Fargos. Keirn, always a solid presence in the ring, was a fine single's performer with runs in Florida and the WWF. [Skinner]

Kelly, Kevin
(1980s-1990s)

Kelly, a former bodybuilding pal of Hulk Hogan's, was a bleached-blond, big-talker who could back it up. After touring World Class, AWA, and Windy City, he caught on briefly in the WWF as Nailz. After his career, he became a real-life bounty collector. [Mr. Magnificent; The Convict; Nailz]

Kent, Don
(1960s-1970s)

A.K.A. the "Bulldog," this Central States journeyman was also a brief partner of Norman Charles III in the Royal Kangaroos.

Kent, Roger
(1960s-1980s)

This old-time AWA television announcer was bombastic, but precise. He also served as one of the group's promoters and road agents before retiring.

Kentuckians, The
(1970s)

This tag-team, comprised of Grizzly Smith and Luke Brown, were Mid-South's U.S. tag champs in 1971. The duo played off their rugged, backwoods style rather than the comedy of some gimmick wrestlers like Hillbilly Jim.

Keomuka, Duke
(1950s-1970s)

The father of Pat Tanaka, Duke was a staple in the 1960s throughout the U.S. and Japan. He was one of the first Japanese to enjoy success in the U.S. One of his career feuds was against the maniac, King Curtis, in Hawaii.

Kernodle, Don
(1970s-1980s)

Recruited by Sgt. Slaughter to be his Private, Kernodle was an NWA star, particularly in the Carolinas. Skilled in the ring, he had feuds with Ricky Steamboat and Jay Youngblood. He and Slaughter were NWA tag champs in 1982. His brother, Keith Larson, wrestled as Rocky Kernodle.

Khan, T-Joe
(1980s-1990s)

With a Mohawk and karate pants, Khan was a mid-card heel menace in Florida, Memphis, AWA, and NWA where he teamed with Pez Whatley and Paul Jones.

Kid Kash
(1990s-2000s)

Introduced to wrestling by Ricky Morton, this Kid Rock look-alike wrestled in the Southeast for many years before getting a break in ECW. A spectacular high flyer, he's also been an integral part of NWA-TNA, winning the X-Division title. [Dave Cash; David Taylor; David Morton]

TRIVIA

Q. How long did Ivan Koloff hold onto the WWF world championship belt after ending the eight-year reign of Bruno Sammartino?

Kidman, Billy
(1990s-2000s)

Trained by the Wild Samoans in Allentown, Pa., this acrobatic star became a cult hit in WCW first as a member of Raven's Flock. He's tried hard to reach beyond the cruiserweight level (he even feuded with Hulk Hogan), but his true calling is wrestling against other flyers like Rey Mysterio Jr. and Juventud Guerrera. To his credit, he's a former WWE and WCW cruiserweight champion. [Kid Flash; Kidman]

Killer Khan
(1960s-1980s)

Khan was a career-long villain with a wild-eyed gimmick. A premier brawler in his day, he was a top draw around the country and had several high profile feuds in the WWF with Andre the Giant and Hulk Hogan. Later, in World Class, he had bloodbaths with the Missing Link and Terry Gordy.

Killings, Ron
(1990s-2000s)

An energetic wrestler with quick striking moves, Killings began in Memphis, but quickly hit the WWF as a rapping performer. After a stint as Jesse James' partner, he took off for the NWA. He won that belt in 2002 and has been called the first-ever black NWA world champion. [K-Krush; K-Kwik]

King, Sonny
(1960s-1970s)

Although he never set out to be a champion of civil rights, he is recognized as the first African American to hold a major belt. In 1972, he and Jay Strongbow defeated Baron Scicluna and King Curtis for the WWWF tag-team titles. He later ventured to Georgia, where he adopted the Isaac Hayes look and became a manager.

Kiniski, Gene
(1950s-1970s)

Generally considered one of the more accomplished wrestlers in history. In 1966, he shocked the world by beating Lou Thesz in St. Louis for the NWA world title which he held for three years. He was also an AWA world champion. He was rough and smug in the ring, a style enjoyed by his Japanese fans. His legendary status leaves some to believe he was one of the top 10 greats of all time. He left a family legacy as well, with his wrestling sons Nick and Kelly Kiniski.

Kirby, Roger
(1970s)

The Central States bodybuilder/wrestler laid claims to U.S. leg-lifting records. As a wrestler, he called himself the "Nature Boy" and was a regular around the Midwest.

Knight, Denn
(1990s-2000s)

He began his national career as a jobber in WCW with Mark Canterbury. When the two were hired by the WWF, they won tag-team gold using the Godwinns' gimmick. He also worked solo for several years. [Naked Mideon; Mideon; Tex Slazinger; Phineas Godwinn]

Knobbs, Brian
(1980s-2000s)

Formerly of the Nasty Boys tag team, Knobbs never professed to be a great wrestler. Doesn't matter. His fun, brawling gimmick was good enough to give him a career. He's a former AWA and WWF tag-team champ, as well as a former WCW hardcore champion. See: Nasty Boys.

Kohler, Fred
(1940s-1960s)

Long-time Chicago fans know Kohler best. For 20 years, he promoted the city and he also served as AWA president in the early 1960s. His televised shows from the old Marigold Arena on the DuMont Network were beamed to more than 65 cities in the early 1950s. Because of that, he was a powerful broker of talent for the entire country. Before he sold the group to Dick the Bruiser, he promoted the famous Buddy Rogers-Pat O'Connor match in 1962.

Koloff, Ivan
(1960s-1990s)

One of the few Russian-born wrestlers, he was feared but also admired for his skills. He held the NWA tag title four times, but his shining moment came in 1971 while winning the WWF world championship from Bruno Sammartino, which ended Bruno's eight-year reign. Despite the win, Koloff only held the belt for 21 days before dropping it to Pedro Morales.

Koloff, Nikita
(1980s-1990s)

Wrestled as a Russian but he was really from the Midwest. He was a very stiff competitor, but a tremendous heel. In the NWA Mid-Atlantic area, he won tag titles and singles titles teaming with Ivan Koloff. He reached super-star status when he turned baby face and teamed with Dusty Rhodes. These days, he owns a franchise of gyms in the Mid-Atlantic area.

Konnan
(1980s-2000s)

Discovered in San Diego where he was a Navy man, he was a huge hit in every major Mexican promotion in the 1990s before getting a spot in WCW. In 1993, his match with Cien Caras drew nearly 50,000 in Mexico City. Has held the AAA and EMLL world titles, as well as WCW tag and U.S. title. [El Centurion; Max Moon]

Koshinaka, Shiro
(1970s-2000s)

An outstanding junior heavyweight from Japan, he's a former three-time New Japan junior champion. Consistent in the ring, the bearded man is known for his hip blocks.

Kowalski, Killer
(1950s-1970s)

Master of the claw hold, he was a two-time WWWF tag-team champion. A devout vegetarian, he's trained Cactus Jack and Triple H at his Massachusetts wrestling school.

Kowalski, Stan
(1950s)

Stan Kowalski toured Canada and won numerous belts in the 1950s, including the AWA tag title with Tiny Mills. Often called "Big K," he remains a community activist in Minnesota.

Kox, Karl
(1950s-1980s)

A famed Brass Knuckles contender from Texas, he was tough, cocky, and always ready for a fight. A main event star in every territory of the day, he feuded with Tony Borne and Bull Curry over the Brass Knux title in the 1960s.

Kroffat, Dan
(1980s-2000s)

The well-traveled Kroffat had the goods, but superstardom wasn't in the cards. Canadian born, he was a top flyer in Japanese rings. He formed a popular tag team with Doug Furnas in Japan. The duo toured WWF briefly, but their style was better suited overseas. [Phil Lafon; Phil LeFleur]

Kronus, John
(1990s-2000s)

This East Coast wrestler, who teamed with Saturn as the Eliminators in ECW, is a four-time tag-team champ. His size belies his ability, as he's one of a few who can do a 450 splash. His style was progressive, but he never got a big break.

Kung Lee, Kato
(1960s-2000s)

The rope-walking, karate-kicking high-flyer was a main-event star in Mexico and Japan.

La Parka
(1980s-2000s)

This very entertaining Mexican star with a skeleton outfit made a name for himself in WCW with his flair for throwing chairs. He remains a star in Lucha Libre.

TRIVIA

Q. Which great heel of the 1950s severed the ear of Yukon Eric in a 1954 match after a knee-drop?

Ladd, Ernie
(1960s-1980s)

An extremely influential African-American wrestler who was prominent in the NFL before crossing over to wrestling. At 6-7, the Big Cat was a huge presence. He toured the world winning numerous regional titles, particularly throughout the Mid-South and Georgia.

Landel, Buddy
(1980s-2000s)

Destined for stardom, bad luck and poor timing were Landel's biggest foes. This pure Southern performer used his Nature Boy gimmick well. In 1985, when Ric Flair needed time off, promoters were set to give the NWA belt to Landel, but he no-showed. Later, he honorably battled back from drug abuse and was offered a gig in the WWF, but he injured himself before the match and was never seen again. That's wrestling's loss, since he was a great talker and entertaining performer wherever he went.

Lane, Stan
(1980s-2000s)

Lane, with a dashing, made-for-television look, has been a fine tag-team wrestler. Trained by Ric Flair, he was one-half of two very successful teams, the Fabulous Ones (with Steve Keirn) and the Midnight Express (with Bobby Eaton). With those teams, he was a Southern and NWA world tag-team champion. Lane also found regional success with Tom Pritchard as the Heavenly Bodies in Smoky Mountain Wrestling. See: Midnight Express; Heavenly Bodies.

Lanza, Blackjack
(1960s-1980s)

He began his career as a fan favorite, but once he turned heel, his career blossomed. A good worker, he met Bobby Heenan. Once they went to the AWA, they were stars. He had a year-long run as tag-team champion with Bobby Duncum and later he teamed with Blackjack Mulligan. Since the early 1980s, he's been a steady agent in the WWE.

Lawler, Brian
(1980s-2000s)

The real-life son of Jerry Lawler, he has his pop's gift for interviews and has been a fun heel wrestler. He began as a light heavyweight jobber in Memphis, but quickly rose through the ranks thanks to his dad's influence. In fairness, he was worth promoting. He had numerous main event feuds in Memphis, even a few against his dad. By the late 1990s, he finally got a chance in the WWF. Teamed with Scott Taylor as Too Cool, the duo electrified crowds with big moves and break dancing. They also won the tag-team titles in 2000. [Brian Christopher; Grandmaster Sexay; New Kid Brian]

Lawler, Jerry
(1970s-2000s)

Few wrestlers over the course of a career have had as many different opponents as the King. He holds wins over Hulk Hogan, the Rock, Steve Austin, and just about every contemporary wrestler around. For most of his career, he has been a part owner of various wrestling companies based in Memphis and has held the Southern Heavyweight title more than anyone. The Southern icon has wrestled relentlessly since the 1970s and has survived the many changes of the industry. A true renaissance man, Lawler is also an artist, a former disc jockey, would-be politician, talk show host, color commentator, and singer. He held the first unified world title in 1988 in a bloody win over Kerry Von Erich. One of the quickest wits in the world, Lawler's influence is still felt as a broadcaster. His sons, Brian and Kevin, both have had wrestling careers. [The King]

Layton, Lord
(1940s-1970s)

Athol Layton was called the Lord of the Ring. He played the heel Englishman to a tee (although he was Australian) and had a fine career in Canada. Before wrestling, he was in the Aussie military and even boxed. As a wrestler, he even feuded against Rikidozan and the Sheik.

LeBell, Gene
(1950s-1980s)

"Judo" Gene has done it all. From judo to wrestling, he has also been a wrestling referee, promoter, author, and trainer. Away from the ring, the California legend has also been in numerous films from the 1950s and 1960s and helped choreograph fight scenes.

LeBell, Mike
(1960s-1980s)

Brother of Gene LeBell and son of Los Angeles promoter Aileen Eaton, he helped run the territory in its popular days in the 1970s from the great Olympic Auditorium, where he wrestled, too.

LeDoux, Scott
(1980s)

The one-time heavyweight boxer, who had fights against Leon Spinks and Ken Norton, started in wrestling as a troubleshooting referee in the AWA. He wrestled briefly in matches against Larry Zbyszko. In later years, he became an ESPN boxing analyst.

LeDuc, Jos
(1960s-1990s)

With eyes beaming, he was one of the wildest stars ever. His heyday saw him play the crazy Canadian lumberjack and he was involved in many bloodbaths. Once, he cut his own arm on live TV with an axe. With tours all over the Southeast, fans will never forget him. He passed away in 1999 at age 55.

LeDuc, Paul
(1950s-1970s)

The "brother" of Jos, he caused riots across Canada in feuds with the Vachons in wild matches. Trained by Stu Hart, Paul's son, Carl LeDuc, also wrestled.

Lee, Brian
(1980s-2000s)

The 6-7 Lee is actually related to the Harris twins. A Southerner, he had his best years in Memphis and Smoky Mountain but also has been to WCW and WWE, where he played the replacement Undertaker. [Primetime; Undertaker No. 2]

Lee, Tiger Chung
(1960s-1980s)

The Korean-born villain appeared in many countries, as well as most promotions in the U.S. In addition to wrestling, he was a popular character actor in Hollywood who even served as the foil in one of Jackie Chan's action flicks. [Kim Duk]

Legend, Johnny
(1980s-1990s)

A renegade at heart, this wild-bearded manager from California produced Andy Kaufman's "Breakfast with Blassie" film in addition to his regional duties as a manager and promoter.

Legionaires, The
(1970s)

Sgt. Jacques Goulet led this team with various partners winning both the WWWF and WWA tag titles. Sometimes he used partner Karl Gotch, a known shooter, in the WWWF and other times Goulet used soldier Zarinoff Le Beouf. See: Rene Goulet; Karl Gotch.

LeRoux, Lash
(1990s-2000s)

Louisiana-born, this redhead climbed the ladder in WCW, going from the Power Plant to cruiserweight hero in short time. He also held the WCW tag titles with Chavo Guerrero. [Cpl. Cajun]

Lesnar, Brock
(1990s-2000s)

Even as a college wrestler at Minnesota, Lesnar seemed destined for the pro ranks. After winning the NCAA heavyweight title, he signed a WWE contract. Built like a truck, Lesnar is power personified. Combined with his amateur background, he's a new-age force. Shortly after his debut, he beat the Rock, winning his first of what should be many world titles.

Lewin, Donn
(1950s)

The middle brother in the famed Lewin family, Donn was a regional star in Georgia, where he often teamed with brother, Mark.

TRIVIA

Q. Who wrote the book, *I Was A Teenage Pro Wrestler?*

Lewin, Mark
(1950s-1980s)

Longevity has been the word for this strongman who began his career in the 1950s. He toured around the globe, from New Zealand and England to Japan, Canada, and the U.S. From 1978-80, "Maniac Mark" was a five-time Brass Knux champ and his feuds with the Sheik in Detroit are classics. His brothers, Ted and Donn, also wrestled.

Lewin, Ted
(1960s)

Brother of Mark and Donn, in addition to his wrestling career, Ted is an accomplished writer and painter. In fact, he wrestled to pay for his tuition for art school.

Lewis, Dale
(1960s)

One of the few Olympians to cross over, he was a two-time NCAA champ at Oklahoma State and two-time Olympic team member as a heavyweight. In the pros, he won the AWA tag belts with Bobby Graham in 1961 and he was a Florida champ in 1969.

Lewis, Ed
(1920s-1940s)

The Roaring '20s belonged to "The Strangler," who was said to have debuted in the 1900s as a teen. Over his career, he held five different versions of the world title. Part of the Strangler legend says that his neck was a massive 21 inches around. His famous move was the blistering headlock.

Lewis, Evan
(19th Century)

Before Ed Lewis, the original "Strangler" Lewis was this man from the late 1800s. In 1893, while he held the U.S. Catch-as-catch-can championship, he reportedly defeated Ernest Roeber for the U.S. Greco Roman title in New Orleans to merge the championships.

Liger, Jushin
(1980s-2000s)

Like Tiger Mask before him, this Japanese star got his gimmick from a cartoon spin-off. Before becoming a star in Japan, he wowed fans in Mexico and Canada. In New Japan, he was an 11-time junior heavyweight champ and had classic matches with Chris Benoit, Owen Hart, and Ultimo Dragon. He wrestled briefly in the U.S., winning the WCW cruiserweight title. Though his success came a world away, for much of the 1990s, he was arguably the best on the planet.

Ligon, Gene
(1970s-1990s)

Although main event status never came his way, he reached regional success as the Masked Thunderfoot. For many years, he was an NWA Mid-Atlantic mainstay. [Thunderfoot]

Lindsay, Luther
(1950s-1960s)

Legendary shooter who won numerous global honors. This African American star won titles, like the Negro American titles, and others in Canada, England, and Australia. His compact body made it difficult for opponents to get an upper hand. He is said to have been one of Stu Hart's favorites.

Lipscomb, Gene
(1960s)

A former Baltimore Colts defensive lineman from 1953-62, "Big Daddy" was an AWA wrestler on the rise when a drug overdose took his life in 1963 at age 31.

Lita
(1990s-2000s)

Amy Dumas trained with the Hardy Boys and found herself as a valet in ECW before hitting the road in WWE, where she set new heights for women wrestlers. The former women's champ is also the girlfriend of Matt Hardy. [Miss Congeniality]

Little Beaver
(1960s-1980s)

Canadian-born, Lionel Giroux was a famous midget wrestler who used a Native American gimmick. At 4-4, he was a favorite of many and even appeared at Wrestlemania III. He passed away in 1995.

Lizmark
(1970s-2000s)

Part of a new revolution for flyers in Mexico, he was one of the first to use a flying dropkick. He also was the first to use a more modern mask. His sons, Lizmark Jr. and brother Lizmark II, also wrestle.

Londos, Jim
(1930s-1950s)

The name "Golden Greek" surely fit Londos, as he looked like a Greek god. He was said to have been introduced to wrestling through the circus, where he was an acrobat. Regarded as one of the best of his day, he held two versions of the world title (1934 and 1950) and was a big hit on the East Coast, where he was a frequent opponent of Ed "Strangler" Lewis.

Long, Teddy
(1980s-2000s)

The one-time NWA referee later managed Doom (Ron Simmons and Butch Reed) in WCW. He has a unique interview style that leaves people thinking "Johnny Cochrane." He likes to rile fans, despite being called "Peanut Head." In recent years, he's been a referee and manager in WWE, guiding Rodney Mack and Jazz.

Longson, Bill
(1930s-1940s)

"Wild" Bill always kept crowds in a frenzy. Promoters capitalized on his appeal and gave him the world belt three times from 1942-48. Big in St. Louis, he invented the piledriver. He passed away in 1982 at age 66.

Lord Littlebrook
(1950s-1980s)

This Brit is arguably the greatest midget wrestler of all time. He used a nobleman gimmick and claims to be the first to do a somersault off the top rope. He often held the midget world title and feuded with Sky Low Low and Little Beaver.

Lothario, Jose
(1970s-1980s)

A solid technical star who made a name for himself in the Texas region, he often held the Brass Knux title in the 1970s before his retirement. After he left the ring, he opened a wrestling school in San Antonio, Texas. His most famous student was future world champion Shawn Michaels.

Louis, Joe
(1950s-1960s)

Remembered as a legendary boxer, he's only one of three former pro boxing champs to get into wrestling. Louis won the hearts of Americans with a victory over German Max Schmeling. During World War II, Louis enlisted in the military where he boxed some exhibition fights for the troops. In all, he defended his world boxing title 25 times, but because of severe tax debt, he was forced to make some easy money in wrestling and appeared as a special attraction, both as a wrestler and referee in Detroit, among other areas.

Louisville Gardens

Home to the Fabulous Fargos and Fabulous Ones, the famous smoke-filled arena (even in its last days) was last used in 2001 for an Ohio Valley card. Built in 1905 as an armory, it was renamed the Gardens in 1973 and was the Tuesday night home for wrestling for more than 20 years.

Love Bros., The
(1970s)

Hartford and Reginald Love were the first, bonafide flower children of the wrestling world. True hippies, they were. Together, they won the International tag championships in Toronto, clad in tie-dye and mutton-chop sideburns.

Low-Ki
(1990s-2000s)

The Brooklyn-born shooter combines Lucha Libre, martial arts, and traditional wrestling into a compact package. He has been to many regional groups and frequents Japan's Zero-One, too. He's won numerous independent belts.

Lowrence, Marc
(1980s)

The perfect straight-man announcer on television, this cult favorite was one of the voices for World Class in Dallas in the 1980s. After wrestling, he became a minister in Texas.

Lubich, Bronco
(1960s-1980s)

This bulky Texas wrestler won many regional titles over his career. When he wasn't tearing up opponents in singles competition, he teamed with many partners like Chris Markoff and Angelo Poffo. Among his titles were the NWA Mid-America tag title with Markoff and the Southern tag title three times with Aldo Bogni. Later, he worked as a referee in World Class.

Luce, Bob
(1960s-1980s)

While working for Dick the Bruiser's WWA in Indianapolis, Luce was the company's promoter at Chicago's grand old arena, the Amphitheater.

Luger, Lex
(1980s-1990s)

This muscled Florida native was pegged to be the next superstar after a Sunshine State tour. He indeed became WCW world champ in 1991, but his days on top were average. He was a high profile employee for 10 years in WCW and WWF. After a long buildup to win the WWF belt, he was sent packing. He had decent matches with Sting and Ric Flair. Before wrestling, he was a football player at Penn State. [Total Package; Narcissist]

Lynn, Jerry
(1990s-2000s)

This technically sound athlete is capable of any style around the world. Cast aside for most of his career because of his size, his talent was finally recognized when he had memorable feuds with Rob Van Dam and Justin Credible, and beat Credible for the ECW world title in 2000. The WWE saw some of his potential and gave him a shot as the lightweight champion in 2001, but that stint was short. Today, Lynn remains a viable talent on the independent scene and in NWA-TNA. [Mr. J.L]

Mabel
(1990s-2000s)

The temptation is too great. Promoters are always suckers for big men. This 1995 King of the Ring winner (over Savio Vega) began in Memphis as a tag-team wrestler with Mo in the Harlem Knights. In the WWF, they were Men on a Mission and held the tag titles for two days in 1994. [King Mabel; Viscera]

Madison Square Garden

Often called the Mecca for pro wrestling, its roots in wrestling can be traced to the 1880s with such legends as William Muldoon to Frank Gotch. No wonder every wrestler's dream is to work there one day. Today, it's still home to the WWE.

Madril, Al
(1970s-1990s)

Never far from a witty retort, this funnyman has been to many regions and held many titles. Although he was a comedy act late in his career, he was actually a skilled junior heavyweight. He held the NWA Jr. title in 1978.

Maeda, Akira
(1970s-1990s)

One of the sport's legit tough guys, he was trained by Karl Gotch. Displeased with American-style wrestling, he started the shoot-fighting group UWF in 1988 under the premise its matches were "real." The group started a revolution in the sport, continued with promotions like UFC and Pride. In the pro style, he had a distinct realness about him that drew many new fans to the sport. [Kwik Kick Lee]

Magnificent Mimi
(1980s-1990s)

One of wrestling's brunette beauties, she crossed over into small-time Hollywood films after a career in the ring. The former AWA women's champ started her career in the West Coast women's promotions.

Magnum T.A.
(1970s-1980s)

Also known by his real name, Terry Allen, this handsome wrestler was a Tom Selleck look-alike whose career was cut short due to paralysis from a car wreck. Most fans still remember his tearful comeback in the early 1990s as an announcer. As a wrestler, Allen was popular in Florida, the NWA, and Mid-Atlantic territories where he often teamed with his pal, Dusty Rhodes. He had a good look and was adept in the ring, winning the U.S. title two times in 1985.

Magnum Tokyo
(1990s-2000s)

As the top student from Ultimo Dragon's Japanese dojo, Magnum has been a very popular independent star in Japan, especially with females. He faired well in WCW in the late 1990s, but he has been the talk of the cruiserweight division while wrestling in Dragon's T2P group to begin the decade.

Mahoney, Balls
(1980s-2000s)

After meager beginnings in Smoky Mountain, this native New Jersey brawler patterned his career after Cactus Jack. He's been slammed on fire, thumb tacks, and tables in ECW and continues to work in Puerto Rico and East Coast independents. In ECW, he was a three-time tag-team champion. [Abbudah Singh; Boo Bradley]

Maiava, Neff
(1950s-1960s)

Recognized by the Hawaiian Samoan community in 1995 for his service in the ring. He was a hero in his heyday, wrestling at the Honolulu Civic Auditorium. Called the "Prince," he teamed with Billy Whitewolf and Peter Maivia. His favorite move was the coconut head butt.

Maivia, Lia

As the wife of late wrestler Peter Maivia (which makes her the Rock's grandma) and business partner of Lars Anderson, she was a Hawaii-based promoter from 1982-88 after Peter passed away.

Maivia, Peter
(1960s-1980s)

A real-life Hawaiian chieftain who brought fame to the island as a main event star the world over, he was heavily tattooed, as are all tribal leaders, and very muscular with a million dollar smile. In the ring, he was a fun performer who, in addition to wrestling in Hawaii, was always at home in New York for the WWWF. The father-in-law of Rocky Johnson. He also promoted Polynesian Pro in Honolulu from 1980-82 before he died in 1982 from cancer.

Malenko, Boris
(1950s-1990s)

Larry Simon was a superb technical wrestler and trainer. Considered the originator of the Russian chain match, he was never shy by a microphone. His illustrious career took him all over the world, including Japan, where he was treated like a demigod in his matches with Antonio Inoki. His sons Joe and Dean had fine careers themselves. Later in his career, he became a trainer in Florida, producing talent like X-Pac and Norman Smiley.

Malenko, Dean
(1980s-2000s)

A master of submission and counter holds, the son of Boris Malenko was just as tough in real life as his TV persona. Although he had great matches in Japan, the former WCW cruiserweight champ also had five-star bouts in ECW with Chris Benoit and Eddy Guerrero.

Malenko, Joe
(1970s-1990s)

As the older brother of Dean Malenko and son of Boris, he, too, was a master of submission holds and made a name touring in Japan in the late 1980s. He was an All-Japan world junior champion. [Jody Malenko]

Malice
(1990s-2000s)

Tall and strong, he began his career in WCW as Alex Wright's bodyguard. He broke off on his own and has been a steady independent star ever since. [The Wall; Sgt. A-Wall; Snuff]

Mamaluke, Tony
(1990s-2000s)

Anyone who trains with the Malenkos will have a solid technical understanding of wrestling, and this star is no exception. He worked the independents until a call from ECW landed him a national role. He once held the ECW tag title with fellow Italian Little Guido.

Managoff, Bobby
(1930s-1960s)

The son of wrestler Bob Managoff Sr., this star was an early NWA champion in 1942, which he won from Yvon Robert. Later on, he trained wrestlers including Jimmy Valiant. Remembered as a legend, Managoff died in 2002 at age 85.

Mansfield, Eddie
(1970s-1980s)

He'll forever be remembered dubiously. Known as a renegade, mid-level star, he exposed wrestling's "secrets" in 1985 on the news show "20/20," which got him blackballed from the business. It was a shock to many old-time promoters. Later, he tried his luck as a promoter, but he could never escape the notoriety he brought on himself.

Mantel, Dutch
(1970s-2000s)

Named after an early century grappler of the same name, Dirty Dutch was a pure hell-raiser. Southern-based, the hairy-backed, bullwhip-wielding hellion had classic feuds with Jerry Lawler and Bill Dundee in the Mid-South region. He's been everywhere—from the NWA and WCW to SMW and WWF—and has been entertaining in all. [Uncle Zebekiah]

Mantell, Johnny
(1970s-1990s)

The younger brother of Ken Mantel, he was a Texas roughneck who possessed strong technical skills. [The Hood]

Mantell, Ken
(1970s-1980s)

After a career in World Class, he became best known as a Dallas-based promoter. He started Wild West Wrestling in 1987 to go up against his former employer, the Von Erichs, but the group faded quickly.

Maple Leaf Gardens

No longer an operating arena, it was a legendary downtown Toronto hangout for "Maple Leaf Wrestling," promoted by Frank Tunney. It opened in 1931 and matches were staged there that year. The building closed in 1999, but the ghosts of Toronto's past linger.

TRIVIA

Q. Which High Chief is the grandfather of The Rock, Dwayne Johnson?

Marciano, Rocky
(1950s-1960s)

The Rock was billed as the hardest punching boxer of all time. Retired with an undefeated heavyweight record, he spent a large part of the 1950s and 1960s touring the U.S. as a special, trouble-shooting referee in pro wrestling.

Marino, Tony
(1960s-1970s)

From 1966-68, the television show "Batman" was all the rage. Marino, a journeyman East Coast attraction, believed if he used the name, he could make it work. It did. He wrestled using the name Battman, and remarkably, he was never sued. His multiple accolades include tag titles with Tony Parisi, Fred Curry, and his buddy, Bruno Sammartino. [Battman]

Maritato, James
(1990s-2000s)

This small, Italian-American wrestler is large in wrestling skills. A known shooter, Maritato hit the scene in Japan's shoot-fighting promotions. The well-conditioned star ventured to ECW where he teamed with Tommy Rich and Tracy Smothers as the Full Blooded Italians. The former ECW tag champion has been a regular cruiserweight in WWE as well. [Little Guido; Nunzio]

Markoff, Chris
(1960s-1980s)

The thick-bodied Markoff had solid runs in the AWA, WWA, and other Midwest groups throughout the 1960s. Yugoslavian-born, he entered the AWA as a singles star managed by Prof. Steve Druk and gained main-event status. His feuds against the Crusher drew large crowds. Later he teamed with Angelo Poffo in Indianapolis and finished his career as a Russian sympathizer.

Marlin, Eddie
(1970s-2000s)

Many remember Marlin as the on-screen matchmaker in Memphis during the 1970s and 1980s. In fact, that was his real-life job. As the business right-hand man for promoter (and son-in-law) Jerry Jarrett, he was an integral part of the territory in the 1980s. After that stint in wrestling, both he and Jarrett got into real estate.

Marshall, Everett
(1920s-1930s)

With dashing looks, this youngster won the NWA championship in 1936, beating Ali Baba. He lost it to Lou Thesz in 1937 and the following year, with Steve Casey unable to defend the title, Marshall was given the belt by the NWA. In 1939, he lost it again to Thesz. Sadly, the talented wrestler was robbed of his fame early on due to injuries suffered in a car accident.

Martel, Pierre
(1970s-1990s)

This Canadian manager fared well in the corners of Rick Martel, the Legionnaires, Quebecers, and Dino Bravo. Throughout his career, he was predominantly found in the WWF and Montreal areas. [Frenchy Martin]

Martel, Rick
(1970s-1990s)

Martel, widely known for his WWF gimmick as the Model was actually a gifted technical star in the 1980s and a former AWA world champion. Trained by the Rougeaus, he won numerous Canadian belts before hitting the AWA in the early 1980s. In 1984, he beat Jumbo Tsuruta for that group's title. Few threw dropkicks with the proficiency of Martel. He ventured to the WWF where he teamed with Tom Zenk and Tito Santana, winning the world tag titles in 1987, before resuming a singles career. [The Model]

Martel, Sherri
(1980s-1990s)

One female wrestler who, by all accounts, was better than most men in the ring was Martel, a former AWA women's champion who trained under the Fabulous Moolah. Wonderfully talented, she shelved her wrestling career to become a valet in the AWA and WWF, guiding Buddy Rose, Doug Somers, and later, Shawn Michaels.

Martin, Harvey
(1980s)

The former Super Bowl MVP from the Dallas Cowboys performed in the Wrestlemania II battle royal in Chicago and was also a commissioner in World Class. He died from cancer in 2001.

Martin, Judy
(1960s-1980s)

After plying her trade in the AWA and Mid-Atlantic areas, she caught on with the MTV/Cyndi Lauper craze in the 1980s. This long-time ally of Fabulous Moolah had numerous title shots against Wendi Richter for the WWF title.

Martin, Pepper
(1950s-1960s)

A journeyman performer, Martin was found in territories such as Texas, the Northwest, and Hawaii. He also was a co-announcer for Roy Shire's promotion in San Francisco.

Martinez, Pedro
(1960s-1970s)

This former promoter of the IWA (based in Cleveland) was a popular attraction in that region during the 1960s. His son, Pedro Martinez Jr., also wrestled.

Martinez, Luis
(1950s-1970s)

Often seen in the Midwest, this veteran was a fine junior heavyweight. He was usually a tag-team wrestler with partners Wilbur Snyder and Tony Parisi.

Mascaras, Mil
(1960s-2000s)

Aaron Rodriguez was a bodybuilder chosen by an entertainment firm to play Mil in Mexican movies. Based on that success, he became an international draw in the 1970s. In the U.S., he was used as a special attraction. In the mid-1970s, he had his biggest chance at American stardom as the champion of the IWA. His name, loosely translated as "Man of a thousand masks," underscored his legend: He's reportedly never worn the same mask twice.

Masked Assassins, The
(1960s-1980s)

Although nearly every territory has at one time in the past used some sort of Assassins gimmick, the most famous twosome was Jody Hamilton and Tom Renesto Sr. The two were capable in the ring and performed in Mid-Atlantic, Mid-South, and Florida. Don Bass was also a short-term member of the team.

Masked Interns, The
(1960s-1970s)

Wearing plain white outfits, this was a popular tag-team based out of California managed by the silver-tongued Ken Ramey. They feuded with teams consisting of fan favorites Pepper Gomez, Dean Ho, Pepper Martin, and Victor Rivera.

Masked Wrestler, The
(19th Century)

Was he the first masked wrestler ever? Most seem to think so. Believed to be a Frenchman, he wore a white mask in the ring as a novelty act in France in the late 1870s.

Matsuda, Hiro
(1960s-1980s)

On of his era's top light heavyweights and trainers, Matsuda was a Florida-based U.S. and NWA junior heavyweight champion. One of the earliest Japanese to find stardom in the U.S., he trained Lex Luger and is credited with introducing Hulk Hogan to wrestling. After his wrestling career ended, he was a long-time NWA board member.

Matsumoto, Dump
(1980s-1990s)

One of the all-time great names in wrestling, she was a monster heel that helped bring women's wrestling in Japan to new heights. She spent a few high profile years entwined in bloodbaths against fan favorite rival Chigusa Nagoya.

Maxx Bros., The
(1980s)

Through the 1980s, promoters were infatuated with finding the next Road Warriors. Led by Sam DeCero, the Maxx Brothers fit the bill. Regionally successful, they never caught on nationwide. DeCero later founded Windy City Wrestling in Chicago.

Maynard, Earl
(1960s-1970s)

An all-American looking good guy, the muscular Mr. America contestant headlined in Los Angeles in the 1970s. With Rocky Johnson, he won the Americas tag-team title. He was also a "Beat the Champ" titleholder in 1971.

Mazurki, Mike
(1930s-1950s)

Called "Iron Mike" in his wrestling days, he used his character-filled face and Hollywood connections to get himself (and fellow wrestlers of the 1950s and 1960s) coveted roles in television shows, "Charli'_s Angels," and "Bonanza," and in films like *Blood Alley*, and *MurderMy Sweet*." The Austrian-born Mazurki also co-founded the honorable Cauliflower Alley Club for retired wrestlers.

Mazzola, Marissa
(1990s-2000s)

Now you see her, now you don't. This on-air hostess of WWE programming is the wife of Shane McMahon. Mazzola still works behind the scenes in a variety of corporate roles.

McClarity Brothers, The
(1950s-1960s)

This brother tag-team comprised of Roy and Don toured the U.S. and Canada. Don McClarity also held the U.S. tag title in the mid-1960s with Argentina Apollo.

McDaniel, Ed "Wahoo"
(1960s-1990s)

Regarded as the finest Native American star to ever wrestle, McDaniel was a pro football star for the New York Jets and Miami Dolphins and trained for wrestling part time in the off-season with the Funks in Texas. Determined to bring respect and honor to his heritage, he was a proud fighter across the Mid-Atlantic, NWA, and AWA regions. He passed away in 2002 at the age of 63.

McGhee, Scott
(1970s-1980s)

This one-time prelim star had a short run in NWA arenas and was a Florida Southern titleholder. He even had a few world title matches in his prime.

McGraw, Bugsy
(1970s-1980s)

A crackpot, Bugsy broke in as a rule breaker, but later evolved into mainly a comedy act. He had success in many areas, but mostly in Florida, where he teamed with Jimmy Valiant and Dusty Rhodes. [The Brute]

McGraw, Rick
(1970s-1980s)

Onetime rookie of the year and Florida star, he was once the Alabama champion, playing an underdog role. He died at age 34 in 1985.

McGuire Twins, The
(1970s)

Found in *The Guinness Book of World Records*, Benny and Billy weighed a combined 1,300 pounds in the ring. Pure novelty, they actually trained under the Guerrero family in Texas. Following a brief, but fun career, Billy died from heart complications at age 34 in 1979. Benny, who had quit wrestling, passed away in 2001 at age 54.

McGuirk, Leroy
(1950s-1970s)

A wrestler and promoter from the Oklahoma area, his daughter later became an announcer in the WWF in the mid-1980s.

McIntyre, Velvet
(1970s-1980s)

This tireless world traveler caught on as part of the WWF's mid-1980s angles on MTV. She was a championship contender in the AWA and WWF. Among her opponents were Wendi Richter and Judy Martin.

McKenzie, Tex
(1960s-1980s)

The always-gracious McKenzie was a top-tier main event attraction wherever he appeared. He may not have had the skills or size of his fellow cowboys, but he found success nonetheless in California, Texas, Michigan, and other Midwest states. He was never without his cowboy hat.

McMahon, Jess
(1950s-1960s)

The grandpop of the WWE family line, Jess was a boxing and wrestling promoter on the East Coast and taught his son, Vince Sr., the ropes of running a promotion.

McMahon, Linda
(1980s-2000s)

The matriarch of the McMahon-opoloy, Linda was Vince's college sweetheart before their nuptials. Linda has been a powerful person behind the scenes. She has climbed the ladder of success herself and currently holds the position of CEO of World Wrestling Entertainment. Her assets are best used in the boardroom and not as a TV personality.

McMahon, Shane
(1990s-2000s)

A fourth-generation wrestling mastermind, Vince McMahon Jr.'s only son is destined to take over the company reigns one day. He graduated from Boston College. He never trained to be a wrestler, but his forays in the ring have been nothing short of fantastic and he has held his own against Kurt Angle and even has been something of a risk taker—he once dived 40 feet off a stage in a match with Steve Blackman.

McMahon, Stephanie
(1990s-2000s)

Her early days were spent as a fumbling girl, but Stephanie has grown into a respectable on-screen personality. She's been linked romantically with Triple H, and in addition to her roles on television, she is in charge of WWE's advertising unit.

McMahon Jr., Vince
(1970s-2000s)

Is he the greatest wrestling promoter of all-time? History will likely remember him that way. Vince took over the reigns of his father's company in the early 1980s and molded it into a Fortune 500 company. McMahon was once listed as a legit billionaire. His family has a rich tradition in wrestling. Despite his age, McMahon is a well-conditioned fitness fanatic and he held his company's world title in 1999 and has had ring feuds with Steve Austin, Triple H, Hulk Hogan, and his son, Shane McMahon.

McMahon Sr., Vince
(1960s-1980s)

Vince Sr. adopted Vince Jr. and sold his company to his son in the early 1980s. Before the current WWE product, Vince Sr. supplied the Washington and New York markets with consistent regional acts like Killer Kowalski and Bruno Sammartino to tremendous success. The New York icon passed away in 1984 from cancer.

McMichael, Debra
(1990s-2000s)

The vivacious former wife of football player Steve McMichael said she was destined to be a star. She began as a valet for her ex-hubby and also Jeff Jarrett in WCW. Later, she performed in the WWF and married—and later separated from—Steve Austin.

McMichael, Steve
(1990s)

Mongo, as he was nicknamed, was a Super Bowl champion with the Chicago Bears and is remembered in football as one of the toughest ever. That style didn't translate well to wrestling, where he was a mid-card attraction in WCW before bowing out.

McShane, Danny
(1960s)

The "Bulldog" was a popular baby face in Oklahoma. He ventured to most territories in the 1960s including the AWA, where he was a prelim act.

Meltzer, Dave
(1970s-2000s)

As the founder and editor of the *Wrestling Observer* trade newsletter, he revolutionized the industry by being the first to write about the truth behind pro wrestling. In his early days, veteran wrestlers thought, by revealing what had been considered secret, he was the ruination of the industry. Slowly, the vets followed along and with a new generation of wrestlers who grew up reading the *Observer*, Meltzer's rep was established.

Men on a Mission
(1990s)

This duo, formerly called Harlem Knights, were comprised of the short Mo and extra-large Mabel. Together, they captured the WWF tag-team championship in 1994—a title they held for two days.

Menaker, Sam
(1940s-1980s)

Slammin' Sam did it all. In addition to wrestling, he was a pro ballplayer in the Yankees organization, but after World War II, he turned his attention to wrestling promoting and managing. He helped promote Dick the Bruiser's WWA from 1964-87. In Chicago, he was a wrestling play-by-play announcer with baseball legend Joe Garigiola and Hall of Fame announcer Jack Brickhouse. Menacker also made his way to Hollywood, where he had parts in "Alias the Champ" and "Mighty Joe Young."

Mendoza, Ray
(1950s-1990s)

Mexico is famous for its masked stars, but Mendoza is one of the few legends who never wore one. He was a six-time NWA light heavyweight champion and eventually became a power broker behind the scenes. A star in Los Angeles, he retired from wrestling in 1982, but his five wrestling sons carry on the tradition.

Mercer, Bill
(1970s-1980s)

A legendary wrestling announcer for the Von Erich's World Class group in Dallas, Mercer was a renowned sports announcer in Texas. To his credit, he has announced on radio for Texas pro teams, the Cowboys and Rangers (as a partner with Don Drysdale). He also called two Super Bowls and was inducted into the Texas Radio Hall of Fame.

Mero, Marc
(1990s-2000s)

Formerly an amateur boxer, he was discovered in the early 1990s and trained to wrestle in WCW as a novelty act. Funny though, his Johnny B. Badd character worked. Rather than stay in WCW, he took the money and ran for the WWF. But with a new gimmick, he failed to live up to the hype, although in 1996 he won the Intercontinental title. Perhaps he's best known for doing something away from wrestling: He married Sable. [Johnny B. Badd]

Mero, Rena
(1990s)

From trailer park to millionaire diva, the ex-wife of Marc Mero never wanted to get into wrestling, but couldn't resist the offer the WWF made her. With her runway model looks, she became a major player and Playboy pinup. In her few wrestling appearances, she actually fared well for someone without formal training. But it all crumbled for her when she departed the company claiming sexual harassment. However, in 2003, she made her return and apparently all was forgotten. [Sable]

Micelli, Madusa
(1980s-2000s)

The Midwest beauty was once a valet in the AWA, but determined to be a wrestler, she began training. She hit it big in Japan and recorded an album there. She's a former WWF and WCW women's champ, who once held the WCW men's cruiserweight title. Madusa left wrestling in the late 1990s and took up monster truck racing. [Alundra Blaze]

Michaels, Shawn
(1980s-2000s)

The Heartbreak Kid has been a tremendous showman in the WWF, but it wasn't a role that came easy. The San Antonio native, trained by Jose Lothario, broke in as a scrawny lightweight in the Central States area. Going nowhere fast, he teamed with Marty Jannetty and took off for the AWA. Looking like teens, they captured hearts with exciting moves and won the tag title in 1987. After hitting the WWF with Jannetty, Michaels dreamed of being a singles star. Determined, Michaels set out to prove himself in every match, often having four-star bouts with Bret Hart, Mr. Perfect, and Razor Ramon. He was a three-time Intercontinental champ and three-time world champion. After early retirement, he came back in 2002 to win the world title again.

Michinoku, Taka
(1990s-2000s)

This skinny, Japanese high-flying star lives for wrestling. He was an independent wrestler overseas, but went unnoticed by the major companies, so he headed for the States. He was a former member of Kaientai in the WWF, where he held the light heavyweight title briefly.

Mid-Atlantic Wrestling

This old-time region encompassed the Carolinas and Virginia, but was actually the birthplace of WCW. Promoted by Jim Crockett Sr., the area's legend extends to the 1940s. Jim Crockett Jr. took over in the early 1970s and eventually the territory was merged with Georgia Championship Wrestling in 1985. Later, it was sold to Ted Turner in 1988 and became WCW soon thereafter.

Midnight Express, The
(1980s-1990s)

In the early 1980s, up-and-coming manager Jim Cornette needed a team that would send him to success. In Memphis, all the parts were around him. Dennis Condrey, Randy Rose, and Norvell Austin, teaming as the Midnight Express, had feuded with teams led by Stan Lane and Bobby Eaton. It was then that Cornette had a eureka moment. He put Condrey and Eaton together as the Express and the rest was history. Although Cornette's version of the Express also included Lane, his tandems won tag-team titles in Mid-South, World Class, and the NWA, where they were two-time world champs. All four components had something to offer: Eaton was a superior worker; Condrey was a great heel; Lane had the persona of a used car salesman; and Cornette was a top interview. Often viewed as the greatest tag team ever—in part because of Cornette's verbal skills—they had epic feuds and matches against the Rock & Roll Express.

Mid-South Coliseum

The Memphis arena was the home of weekly matches from the 1970s up to the 1990s featuring Jerry Lawler, Dutch Mantel, Bill Dundee, and a host of worldwide challengers and stars.

Mid-South Wrestling

Most famously known as Bill Watts' promotion, the earliest titles from the Louisiana-Oklahoma region date to the late 1960s. The Spoiler was the first Mid-South North American champion in 1969. It stayed that way until the company was renamed the Universal Wrestling Federation in 1986. Just one year later, Watts, the owner, sold his territory to Jim Crockett. It was quickly dissolved into the NWA.

Mighty Igor
(1960s-1980s)

Billed as the world's strongest man, this Polish strength fiend starred in the AWA, Puerto Rico, and the rebellious IWA. To prove his might, he sometimes staged strength stunts before live crowds. He was voted Mr. Michigan in 1954 and legend has it he was ready to compete in the Mr. America pageant, but his arms were deemed "too large." He passed away in 2002.

TRIVIA

Q. Which wrestler was the second man to use the famous Tiger Mask gimmick in Japan?

Miller, Bill
(1950s-1960s)

Miller had a strong career using his own name. But to enhance his marketability, he invaded the AWA under a mask as Mr. M. In 1962, he beat Verne Gagne for the world title, but he was stripped of the belt eight months later when his true identity was revealed. [Mr. M]

Miller, Ernest
(1990s-2000s)

An accomplished black belt, Miller was a top-level competitor on the karate and kick boxing circuit. In wrestling, his mouth did the work. He had marginal success in WCW and has also worked in the WWE broadcast booth. [The Cat]

Miller, Freddie
(1970s-1980s)

A noted Georgia-based announcer on the WTBS Superstation, the bespectacled Miller coined the phrase, "Be there!" when hyping upcoming shows and was a constant for two decades on television.

Mills, Tiny
(1950s-1970s)

Sometimes called the king of the lumberjacks, he was an Alberta, Canada, native who teamed in the Midwest with Stan Kowalski as Murder Inc., and is a former world tag champ with Kowalski.

Minneapolis Auditorium

This building no longer remains, but its memories are alive. It was the home to the Minneapolis Lakers basketball team and wrestling, including the AWA, from the 1930s until its closing in 1987.

Misawa, Mitsuhara
(1980s-2000s)

Ascending out of the Jumbo Tsuruta days in All-Japan, he was widely regarded as the best pure wrestler in Japan of the 1990s. After serving as a three-time Triple Crown champion, and elevating wrestling's history there, he defected in 2000 to start his own group, NOAH. [Tiger Mask]

Missing Link, The
(1970s-1980s)

Dewey Robertson broke into wrestling comparatively late in life and performed well into his 40s. His career took on new meaning as the Missing Link, a strange gimmick that saw him paint his face green and blue. He energized crowds in Mid-South, World Class, and WWF. [Dewey Robertson]

Missouri Mauler, The
(1960s)

Larry "Rocky" Hamilton toured the Midwest before returning to the Central States region. A multiple winner of the Brass Knux title, he excelled as a roughhousing bully.

Missouri Title

When the crown jewel of the NWA, the world title, wasn't being defended in St. Louis, promoter Sam Muchnick topped his Gateway City cards between 1972-86 with defenses of this title. Harley Race was the first —and last—to hold it and other notable champions included Jack Brisco, Gene Kiniski, Dick the Bruiser, and Ted DiBiase.

Mitchell, Jim
(1990s-2000s)

A life-long fan, he originally caught on as a manager of Wrath and Mortis in WCW. With an eye toward the occult, and sharpened fingernails, he's managed many dastardly foes in ECW and NWA-TNA. [Sinister Minister]

Modest, Mike
(1990s-2000s)

A no-nonsense technician from San Francisco who is considered to be a valuable unsigned free agent. The compact blond has held California independent titles and has also faired well in Japan. He was also seen in the documentary, "Beyond the Mat."

Mondo, Nick
(1990s-2000s)

One of the new generations of hardcore wrestlers, Mondo is not averse to taking falls on broken glass. Has held titles in CZW and Big Japan. He held CZW's Iron Man title and was part of one of the company's bloodiest matches in history in 2001.

Mongols, The
(1960s-1970s)

Namesake of the bad, bald, menacing tag team which held the WWWF International tag belts in 1970. Bolo was played by Bill Eadie and Bepo was played by Nikolai Volkoff. Yet another was Geeto, played by Newton Tattrie.

Monsoon, Gorilla
(1960s-1990s)

Before he died in 1999, Gorilla was the television face of the WWF. He was a wrestler, booker, road agent, announcer, and even co-owner of the WWF. As a wrestler in the 1960s and 1970s, Monsoon was billed as being from Mongolia, but his roots were in New Jersey. He had runs as champion in Los Angeles, Japan, and Australia, and later in his career, he and Bobby Heenan were a popular broadcast duo.

Montana, Lenny
(1950s-1960s)

Montana was a perennial semi-main event star who played a big-shouldered bully. He won numerous regional titles in the 1950s as the masked Zebra Kid. His lasting legacy comes from his part as Luca Brazzi in the classic film, "The Godfather." [Zebra Kid]

Moondogs, The
(1970s-2000s)

Is the Moondog one of the most emulated gimmicks ever? Carrying bones, wearing mangy outfits, and barking at the moon, no fewer than 10 Moondogs have hit the scene at one time or another. The most famous, the white-haired, bearded Lonnie Mayne, was a star in the Northwest and California. The Memphis area has been home to its share of Moondogs. Larry Latham and Wayne Ferris wrestled there and were noted for out-of-the-ring brawls. Southeast star Randy Colley was another. Well into the 1990s, the gimmick was still used and it's likely to stay for years to come.

Moore, Shannon
(1990s-2000s)

This spitfire cruiserweight began his career in Southern NWA groups, but got a break in WCW as part of the tag team, 3-Count. From the Hardy Boys mold, Moore likes to use aerial moves to wow crowds and has taken his act to the WWE prelims.

Morales, Pedro
(1960s-1980s)

The first major Puerto Rican star to become champion of a major U.S. group, Morales lit up crowds in New York to win the WWF world, Intercontinental, and tag-team titles. He was the first ever to win that promotion's three main belts. The fiery performer is remembered as a top star of the 1970s who held his own as a main event attraction. His most famous match was a remarkable 75-minute draw with Bruno Sammartino at Shea Stadium in 1972.

Morella, Joey
(1980s-1990s)

The son of Gorilla Monsoon, Joey was a standout WWF referee. He was killed in a car wreck en route to a show in 1994.

Morgan, Rip
(1980s-1990s)

Bruiser Brody look-alike who, in addition to his wrestling days, served as a flag bearer for the Sheepherders. He and Jack Victory also teamed as the New Zealand Militia in WCW.

Morley, Sean
(1980s-2000s)

The sculpted Morley, a.k.a. Val Venis, wrestled in Mexico extensively—even winning the world title there—before signing with the WWF in 1997. He came to the group with an adult film star gimmick, but he is actually a multi-talented wrestler. He hasn't seen a lot of main event matches, but he did hold the Intercontinental title two times. [Val Venis; Big Valbowski; Steel]

Morrell, Frank
(1960s-1980s)

After his days as The Angel in the Southeast, this bald-headed monster was a longtime referee in Memphis for the Jarrett family. [The Angel]

Morrow, Jerry
(1960s-1980s)

The always-ready "Champagne" Jerry wrestled in Canada for Stampede. A multi-time tag-team champion there, he joined the Cuban Assassin on many occasions.

Morton, Ricky
(1970s-2000s)

Morton, in his day, was a super ring tactician with a fabulous feel for the crowd. With throngs of teens backing him, he was a terrific underdog. His career blossomed as the partner of Robert Gibson in the Rock & Roll Express. The team was a four-time NWA tag-team champion. Their feuds with the Midnight Express and Four Horsemen were classics, thanks to the ability of Morton. [Richard Morton] See: Rock & Roll Express

Mortier, Hans
(1950s)

Another of the great German gimmick wrestlers of the war era, he often came to the ring with a cape and monocle, looking like a refugee from "Hogan's Heroes."

Morton, Todd
(1980s-1990s)

The cousin of Ricky Morton, Todd was a little small for the big-time but he found regional success in Mid-South as a light heavyweight, sporting a blond mullet like Ricky.

Mosca Jr., Angelo
(1980s)

Unlike his hulking father, this second-generation fan favorite from Canada and Florida was adept at aerial moves and had a solid dropkick.

Mosca Sr., Angelo
(1960s-1970s)

Mosca, a former Canadian Football League legend and Canadian Hall of Fame inductee, wrestled throughout Canada and the U.S. as a main event attraction. His career was mostly spent as a heel. At 6-3, 270 pounds, he often looked like a character from "The Sopranos." [King Kong Mosca]

Mr. Fuji
(1960s-1990s)

Contemporary fans remember this cane-wielding Japanese manager from the WWF, but Fuji was once an accomplished wrestler. Along his career, he was a five-time WWF tag-team champion—three times with Toru Tanaka and twice with Mr. Saito. His broken English was a hoot in interviews.

Mr. Hito
(1950s-1970s)

Primarily found in Canada, this star was a former Calgary Stampede North American champion in the early 1980s, as well as tag champion with Tarzan Goto in Florida and the Central States areas.

Mr. Moto
(1950s-1960s)

This was the name used by a bevy of Asian stars that was taken from a black and white Peter Lorre film. The most famous version teamed with Mitsu Arakawa and won numerous tag titles, including the AWA version in 1967. [Dr. Moto]

Mr. Pogo
(1980s-1990s)

Wild, face-painted Japanese star who loves to cut open his opponents with assorted metal objects. The hardcore standby even used a power drill and chainsaw to cut foes. His feuds with Atsushi Onita and Tarzan Goto are things to behold—if violence is desired.

Mr. T.
(1980s-1990s)

Larry Tero made the most of every break he got. The former "A-Team" star was discovered during a tough-man contest and recruited to Hollywood. He crossed over to wrestling in 1984 as Hulk Hogan's training buddy for Wrestlemania. Since then, Mr. T has made numerous cameos in WWF and WCW as a wrestler and referee.

Mr. Wrestling
(1960s-1980s)

This masked star, named Tim Woods, followed in the masked Destroyer's footsteps. He was a staple in Georgia and Florida. His plain white mask, trunks, and boots were his trademarks. He also had a memorable feud with Ric Flair.

Mr. Wrestling II
(1960s-1980s)

Johnny Walker replaced Woods in the Georgia territory using his gimmick—despite being more than 40 years old at the time—and became even more popular than his predecessor. It is said one of his matches on cable was the first to draw more than a million viewers. [Rubberman; The Grappler]

Muchnick, Sam
(1930s-1980s)

A legendary promoter from St. Louis, his shows had strong NWA ties but he used a wide array of talent. For years, St. Louis wrestling was regarded as the best found anywhere and Muchnick made sure of that. Legends like Pat O'Connor, Dan Hodge, Lou Thesz, and Harley Race usually saved their best performances for Muchnick. His television shows, "Wrestling from the Chase Hotel," are still considered classics.

Muldoon, William
(19th Century)

One of the first recognized wrestling champions, he claimed the U.S. Greco-Roman title in 1883 after beating Edwin Bibby. Before his wrestling days, the Irish-born Muldoon was a Civil War soldier and later settled in New York. He once fought the famed John L. Sullivan in the first-ever wrestler vs. boxer match. The match was stopped before a victor was decided and years later, he ended up traveling with Sullivan around the country. So, it begs the question, did they fix their famous fight?

Mulkey Brothers, The
(1980s)

Bill and Randy Mulkey played the meager tag team perfectly. Perennial losers, their career high was an appearance in the Jim Crockett Memorial Tag Team Tournament in 1987.

Mulligan, Blackjack
(1970s-1980s)

Mulligan was a former football player with the New York Jets and set out for a career in wrestling. Eventually, he took on this Texan gimmick and cruised to a successful career. At 6-8 and 250 pounds, he and Blackjack Lanza were WWWF tag-team champions and he's the father of Barry and Kendall Windham. [Big Machine; Big Bob Windham]

Munn, Wayne
(1920s)

An early-era warrior, he caught Ed "Strangler" Lewis in 1925 for the NWA world title. He had a short, three-month reign. Munn passed away at age 35 in 1931.

Munroe, Sputnik
(1950s-1960s)

One of wrestling's civil rights pioneers, after working himself to main event status in Memphis, Munroe, a white man, refused to wrestle unless African American fans were allowed access to sit on the main floor. In the ring, he was a rough and tumble type, winning numerous titles in Tennessee, Texas, and Alabama.

Muraco, Don
(1980s-1990s)

He began as a Tom Selleck wannabe from Hawaii, but he turned rule breaker and bulked up considerably. He was an abrasive heel in Florida and Georgia and later a WWF Intercontinental champion before retiring with his wit intact.

Murdoch, Dick
(1960s-1990s)

A take-no-prisoners tough guy from Texas, he teamed with Dusty Rhodes as the inseparable and unbeatable Texas Outlaws. Over his career, many of his matches were in Florida, the NWA, and WWF. Murdoch, known to never turn down an after hours offer, was a main event star in Japan, too. He died in 1996.

Murphy, Skull
(1950s-1960s)

One of the meaner looking bald men of his era, he briefly held the WWWF tag titles with Brute Bernard, who he toured with regularly.

TRIVIA

Q. Which Asian star's trademark moves included throwing salt in his opponent's eyes?

Mutoh, Keiji
(1980s-2000s)

Mutoh is one of the few Japanese stars to break through in the U.S. After he turned pro, he ventured to North America. Wearing face paint, Ninja pants and spewing green mist, he was a hit as the Great Muta. With stints in Puerto Rico and World Class, he was ready for WCW in 1989. He wowed crowds with his moonsaults and beat Sting for the TV title. Frustrated, he headed back to Japan as a star and won the prestigious IWGP title on two occasions. [Great Muta; Super Black Ninja; White Ninja]

Mysterio Jr., Rey
(1990s-2000s)

A second-generation star from San Diego by way of Tijuana, he has been a spectacular junior heavyweight with cat-like responses. He was active in Mexico and Japan before getting a break in 1996 in WCW, where he held the cruiserweight title. His uncle is Rey Mysterio Sr.

Mysterio Sr., Rey
(1970s-2000s)

Uncle of Rey Mysterio Jr., this family leader has been a star in Mexico for more than three decades.

Nagasaki, Kendo
(1950s-1980s)

Named for the city made infamous in World War II, several wrestlers used this name. The first one primarily worked Europe in the 1950s. The second one toured the U.S. in the 1970s and 1980s in World Class. He was famous for his tippy-toe style around the ring. In Florida, he was a main event nemesis of Dusty Rhodes.

Nagayo, Chigusa
(1980s-1990s)

Chigusa was the idol of thousands of young Japanese female fans. Wrestling for All-Japan Women's Pro Wrestling, she was a crossover star as part of the legendary Crush Gals team and recorded several pop singing albums. She had riveting feuds with Dump Matsumoto and American Madusa Micelli. See: Crush Gals.

Nagurski, Bronko
(1930s-1950s)

Hall of Fame football player of Chicago Bears fame, he became world wrestling champion in 1939. He is long considered one of the toughest ever, since he wrestled and played football year-round. A huge attraction in the Midwest, he often said he disliked wrestling, but did it because it paid the bills.

TRIVIA

Q. Which announcer penned the book, *Stranglehold*?

Nakano, Bull
(1980s-1990s)

Originally part of Dump Matsumoto's band of degenerates, this Japanese female star had success as a singles wrestler, including a two-year run as All-Japan WWWA women's world champion. In the 1990s, she held an intense feud with Aja Kong. In all, Nakano held world titles from three different countries (Japan, Mexico, and U.S.). With wild hair and face paint, she was a classic heel.

Nash, Kevin
(1990s-2000s)

Discovered in a Georgia cannery and summoned to try wrestling, the nearly 7-foot-tall Nash had already played college hoops at Tennessee. Once in wrestling, he masterminded his way to the world title in WWF and WCW. But first he worked his way up the ladder as a prelim bum and bodyguard before breaking out on his own. In 1996, he was lured to WCW with Scott Hall where he formed the mega-successful NWO. [Master Blaster; Oz; Vinnie Vegas; Big Daddy Cool; Diesel]

Nashville Fairgrounds
(1970s-2000s)

It doesn't look like much from the outside, but this quaint building, which seats about 600, has been the weekly home to wrestling for over three decades. Now it's home to Jerry Jarrett's NWA-TNA.

Nasty Boys, The
(1980s-1990s)

Brian Knobbs and Jerry Saggs made up this strange duo. Originally, they were unorthodox and clumsy, but under the tutelage of Brad Rheingans, they improved and won world tag-team titles in the WWF and WCW and numerous regional groups. Wearing black T-shirts spray painted with their names, they were a grubby-looking team with a penchant for throwing chairs and using foreign objects. Knobbs went on to a singles career after Saggs retired due to an injury. See: Brian Knobbs; Jerry Saggs.

Natural Disasters, The
(1990s)

Earthquake John Tenta and Typhoon Fred Ottman were the prototypical mid-1990s WWF performers: large, plodding, and reliant on gimmicks. After singles runs, they combined to win the tag belts in 1992, managed by Jimmy Hart. See: Earthquake; Tugboat.

Negro, Cyclone
(1960s)

One of the great Mexican nicknames of the 1960s, he traveled the Southwest, often feuding with Jose Lothario over the Brass Knux title. He also held the Florida title in 1979.

Neilson Bros., The
(1950s-1960s)

Stan and Art formed a successful Golden Age tag team. They often headlined in Chicago, where they held the U.S. tag-team belts. They also held the AWA tag belts in 1962.

Nelson, Larry
(1980s)

Announcers are most often wacky, and Nelson certainly was for the AWA. His facial mannerisms were priceless.

Neu, Paul
(1980s-1990s)

A 300-pound Pacific-area rapping wrestler, who never caught on with fans in major groups, he was a jovial star who found some success in WCW and Germany. [Avalanche, P.N. News]

New Age Outlaws
(1990s)

Billy Gunn and Jesse James were toiling as singles competitors when they joined forces. As members of Degeneration X with Triple H and X-Pac, they revolutionized the WWF. With quippy catch phrases, they captured the attention of fans and won tag-team titles five times. See: Jesse James Armstrong; Billy Gunn.

New Jack
(1990s-2000s)

Never ashamed of exploiting his past, New Jack played the street thug perfectly. After a few years in tag-team action with the Gangstas, the risk-taker changed to singles action. He enjoyed using foreign objects—even stop signs, computer keyboards, and cheese graters—to bash his opponents. See: Gangstas.

New Japan Pro Wrestling
(1980s-2000s)

In the early 1980s, Antonio Inoki broke off ties with long time partner Giant Baba and began his own promotion. The group has been home to some legends: Riki Choshu, Genichiro Tenyru, Bruiser Brody, Mitsuhiro Misawa, and Great Muta have all battled for the group's famed IWGP Grand Prix title.

New World Order
(1990s)

Arguably, one of the most lucrative creations in wrestling history, the original trio of Scott Hall, Kevin Nash, and Hulk Hogan set WCW ablaze and gave the promotion life, with more than a year's worth of feuds and angles. They invaded "Monday Nitro" in 1996 and the company took off. When the NWO faded, so did WCW's run.

Nick the Greek
(1910s-1930s)

This early-era Turk migrated to America and became a U.S. citizen. He wrestled through the 1930s as the Terrible Turk and Louis LeChene.

Niedhart, Jim
(1980s-2000s)

Nicknamed the "Anvil," he trained under the Hart family in Calgary. Known for his trademark goatee, he traveled to regional territories like Calgary and Mid-South in the early 1980s, but was a hit in the WWF as Bret Hart's partner in the Hart Foundation, winning the tag-team championship twice. See: Hart Foundation.

Nightmares, The
(1980s)

Danny Davis and Ken Wayne were two mid-card wrestlers deemed too small to be money players. When put together as the masked Nightmares, things clicked. They were ahead of their time using a cruiserweight style. Together, they won the Continental and Southern tag titles. Davis is still in wrestling as co-owner of Ohio Valley Wrestling.

No DQ

A phrase meaning a variation of an anything-goes bout, competitors can do anything in the ring. Most of the time, it meant wrestlers could use "banned" moves like Jerry Lawler's piledriver in Tennessee without reprisal.

No Holds Barred

Also the name of a feature film starring Hulk Hogan, NHB matches in pro wrestling are used as a gimmick to allow wrestlers to use weapons in the ring. NHB matches are also promoted in mixed martial arts, such as Ultimate Fighting and Pride.

Noble, Jamie
(1990s-2000s)

A hard-working cruiserweight, he began his career in NWA Wildside, but hit paydirt with a WCW contract. He wrestled under a hood as part of the Jung Dragons, but moved on to WWE where he is a multi-time cruiserweight champ using a white-trash gimmick along with valet, Nidia.

Nobunaga, Shima
(1990s-2000s)

Japanese spark plug from the Toryumon promotion, he trained with Ultimo Dragon and had a stint in WCW's cruiserweight division before heading back to a successful career in Japan.

Nomellini, Leo
(1950s-1980s)

The popular ex-NFL player was known as the "Lion." He never missed a game in 14 seasons en route to the Hall of Fame. He began his wrestling career as a troubleshooting referee, but once he started wrestling, he was a popular attraction in many territories. He and Wilbur Snyder won the AWA tag title in 1961.

Nord the Barbarian
(1980s-1990s)

After several years as a prelim bum, John Nord adopted the Barbarian gimmick ala Bruiser Brody. The bearded madman went to Mid-South and AWA and later joined the WWF in the early 1990s to mild success. [John Nord; The Berzerker; The Lumberjack]

North American Title

Several territories from the 1950s to 1980s named their main belt the North American title, including Honolulu and Mid-South. In Hawaii, Nick Bockwinkel was the first to hold it in 1962; in Louisiana, Bill Watts promoted the belt with stars like Junkyard Dog and Ted DiBiase.

TRIVIA

Q. Which two-time IWGP winner had a bit part in Sylvester Stallone's film, *Over the Top*?

Norton, Scott
(1980s-2000s)

Former bouncer and arm wrestler turned ring wrestler, his success can't be denied. This bulky bruiser saw good times in Japan winning the IWGP title two times (1998 and 2001). He trained with the Gagne family's AWA and had success there in addition to WCW.

Nova
(1990s-2000s)

This East Coast wrestler was an ECW prelim standby and has also worked with a WWE developmental deal. This innovator of moves is a former Ohio Valley Wrestling heavyweight champ.

O'Connor, Pat
(1950s-1960s)

This famed NWA champion hailed from New Zealand. He won the belt in 1959 from Dick Hutton. He was a shooter-type wrestler who always played the good guy and his matches were commonly 45- to 60-minute performances. He had epic battles with Lou Thesz and Gene Kiniski in St. Louis.

O'Haire, Sean
(1990s-2000s)

WCW Power Plant grad who was a former tag-team champ of that group. He's very tall and has a super look that makes people believe he has a tremendous future in his current home, WWE.

O'Mahoney, Danno
(1930s-1940s)

A favorite among promoters of his day, O'Mahoney survived as champion during several promotional wars and splits. His wins over Jim Londos and Ed Don George solidified his post as champion in 1935.

O'Neill, Marty
(1950s-1970s)

The announcer was one of the most revered men of the AWA. Though he was small and wore glasses, he never cowered and always stood his ground when interviewing the wrestlers.

Oates, Jerry
(1970s-1980s)

A Southeastern journeyman, he had a run in Oklahoma as the North American champion, as well as stints in Georgia and the Gulf States. He and his brother, Ted Oates, were Central States tag champions. [Jerry O]

Oates, Ted
(1970s-1980s)

Less active than his brother, Jerry Oates, Ted also promoted and trained wrestlers in the Mid-Atlantic and Gulf regions. In the ring, he was the Alabama junior heavyweight champ in 1982.

Ohio Valley Wrestling
(1990s-2000s)

Originally an independent training center run by Dan Davis, OVW has become the home of the WWE developmental wrestlers. Brock Lesnar, John Cena, and Shelton Benjamin all learned the ropes in the Louisville-based group.

Okerlund, Gene
(1970s-2000s)

The mustached "Mean Gene" was an ad executive who shared office space with the AWA when he was discovered to be a super pitchman on television. From the AWA, he leaped to the WWF and became famous for his interviewing chemistry on-screen with personalities like Hulk Hogan and Bobby Heenan.

TRIVIA

Q. Which announcer coined the phrase, "Run, don't walk," when pitching the upcoming cards?

Oliver, Rip
(1970s-1990s)

Oliver was a heel mainstay in the Northwest for promoter Don Owen. He also toured Canada and World Class, but his real success came in Portland where he feuded with Billy Jack Haynes. He held the Pacific Northwest title 11 times and the tag belts 15 times with various partners including the Assassin.

Olsonoski, Steve
(1970s-1980s)

The baby-faced "Steve O" was a popular mid-level attraction in the Midwest. He was similar to Jim Brunzell with a high-flying style, but stardom never followed him. In the late 1970s, he visited Georgia and feuded with Roddy Piper. In 1981, he held the Georgia National title. Steve was also a television analyst alongside legend Gordon Solie.

Olympic Auditorium
(1920s-2000s)

This historic downtown Los Angeles arena was the site of many wrestling and boxing bloodbaths. Its first card, in 1925, pitted Strangler Lewis versus Jim Londos. The building was refurbished in the mid-1990s and is still used for Lucha Libre and independent wrestling.

Omni, The
(1970s-1990s)

Once the home base in Atlanta for NWA wrestling beginning in 1972, weekly cards were held there until the early 1980s. It was still the home for WCW until the Omni was torn down in 1997 after hundreds of title matches.

One Man Gang
(1980s-1990s)

A 350-pound brawler who has been to many territories, the Gang once held the UWF heavyweight title. He had many wars with Jim Duggan and Steve Williams and was a plodding big man with a fun gimmick. He also had WWF success as a tag team with Big Bossman. [Akeem; Crusher Broomfield]

Onita, Atsushi
(1980s-2000s)

Crazy Japanese star who, through his Frontier Martial Arts group, pioneered the hardcore style used today. Rarely is there a match with Onita in which he doesn't bleed. That resulted in his cult status and helped him land a position in public office. [Great Nita] See: Frontier Martial Arts.

Onoo, Sonny
(1990s)

Once the liaison between American and Japanese promotions, he managed for a short period in WCW. He was a public relations consultant backstage, but onscreen played a 1950s Japanese stereotype, which was, ironically, something he sued the now defunct company over.

Orndorff, Paul
(1970s-1990s)

Legit tough guy with a football background with the Atlanta Falcons, the rugged Orndorff plied his trade throughout the country with stops in Florida and Georgia before heading to WWF in the early 1980s. There, he feuded with Hulk Hogan to numerous sell-out crowds. A former two-time WCW tag champ with Paul Roma, he remained active well into the late 1990s, despite an injury which severely limited his arm strength.

Orton, Barry
(1980s)

Also the son of Bob Orton Sr., Barry was mainly an opening act in the WWF. After touring as Barry O, he donned a mask in Calgary as the Zodiac, a gimmick his pop once used. [The Zodiac; Barry O]

Orton Jr., Bob
(1970s-1990s)

An underrated second-generation technician, Orton was a steady tag-team partner and talented enough to be a single's threat, although major singles titles always eluded him. A former NWA tag champ with Don Kernodle, he was a valuable part of the WWF's explosion in the 1980s, as he teamed with Roddy Piper and Adrian Adonis. His father is Bob Orton Sr.

Orton Sr., Bob
(1950s-1970s)

The Texas-bred cowboy main evented throughout the world. He's the head of a three-generation household; his sons, Bob Jr. and Barry, and grandson, Randy, have all wrestled. Bob Sr. found most of his success in Texas, California, Canada, and the Gulf States, also as the masked Zodiac. In Kansas, he won the NWA Heart of America title in the early 1950s. [The Zodiac]

Orton, Randy
(2000s)

A former military man, this slick-looking third-generation star has been climbing the ladder in the OVW and WWE since he debuted in 2001. Unlike his dad, he has shown tremendous athleticism.

Oulette, Pierre
(1990s-2000s)

This stocky Canadian had success as a tag-team wrestler in the WWF. He and Jacques Rougeau were three-time WWF tag-team champions in the early 1990s, and he's still actively wrestling in Montreal. [Carl Oulette]

Outback Jack
(1980s)

With a gimmick taken from "Crocodile Dundee," Jack was a failed gimmick wrestler used in the WWF in the early 1980s. He came in with a bang, but left with a whimper.

Outsiders, The
(1990s)

Close buddies from their WWF days, Scott Hall and Kevin Nash burst into WCW in 1996 with incredible steam. As members of the NWO, they were four-time WCW tag-team champions and brought WCW out of the dark ages. See: Scott Hall; Kevin Nash; New World Order.

Owen, Alton
(1950s-1970s)

Promoter Don Owen's outspoken son, ran the family's Portland area cards. The gravelly voiced Alton was often the victim of wrestler's pranks, but it was all in fun.

Owen, Don
(1950s-1990s)

The proud pig farmer was the driving force behind Portland wrestling for five decades. Owen was an icon in Portland and continued to stick to his territorial ways, even in the promotion's last years. For many years, Portland was a member of the NWA and Owen served as a board member. People knew him on-screen as the ring announcer, a role he served well into his 80s. He stayed active in wrestling until his death in 2002. See: Pacific Northwest Wrestling.

Pacific Coast Wrestling
(1940s-1950s)

Before Don Owen took over the area, Portland and Vancouver promoted matches with old-timers like George Wagner, Jack O'Reilly, and Frank Stojack.

Pacific Northwest Wrestling
(1950s-1990s)

The famous territory was simply known as Portland Championship Wrestling and was usually filmed at local bowling alleys or flea markets. A small but popular area, it was promoted nightly in Oregon and Washington state by Don Owen. The stars who graduated from there include Jesse Ventura, Buddy Rose, and Roddy Piper. Sadly, the group closed in 1992 and is remembered as one of the last vestiges of the territorial days.

Page, Diamond Dallas
(1980s-2000s)

A miraculous person who started as a manager but rode his desire all the way to the world title, Page ran a nightclub in Florida when he was bit by the wrestling bug. He eventually managed stars like Badd Company in the AWA and Scott Hall in WCW. In the mid-1990s, he began wrestling and worked his way up the ladder. In 1999, he beat Ric Flair for his first of three WCW world titles. He retired in 2002.

Palumbo, Chuck
(1990s-2000s)

This tall, sculptured, newcomer had quick success, winning the tag titles in WCW with Sean O'Haire. He ventured to WWE where he has been a bit player, teaming with Billy Gunn, and Nunzio in a "Sopranos" gimmick.

Parade of Champions
(1980s)

From 1984-86, World Class promoter Fritz Von Erich promoted memorial cards in Dallas-Ft. Worth for his fallen son, David Von Erich. The most famous card, from Texas Stadium in 1984, saw Kerry Von Erich defeat Ric Flair for the NWA world title before more than 30,000 fans.

Parisi, Tony
(1960s-1970s)

Popular Pennsylvania Italian who was the quintessential tag-team partner, he made a name for himself in the WWWF. In 1975, Parisi and Louis Cerdan shocked the world by winning the world tag belts over the powerful Blackjacks, Mulligan and Lanza. [Tony Pugliese]

Parks, Reggie
(1960s)

In tests of strength, the straight-ahead strongman was known for allowing cars to drive over his iron-like stomach. He was a top AWA draw and remains active today as a championship belt maker.

Parsons, Iceman
(1980s-1990s)

An African American star who received international exposure in the 1980s in World Class and UWF. He was a perennial semi-main event performer whose style made him a favorite with fans. Always entertaining, he held the Texas title and UWF TV title several times. [King Parsons]

Patera, Ken
(1970s-1990s)

A former competitive weightlifter, Patera was discovered in televised strongman contests. He broke into wrestling in the AWA and traveled around the country. He often headlined Madison Square Garden and was the WWF Intercontinental champion in 1980, a title he held for eight months.

Patterson, Pat
(1960s-2000s)

Patterson, a top singles draw from Canada, had success in San Francisco in the 1960s. Widely known for his ring ability, he was a longtime tag partner with Ray Stevens. He once held the WWWF North American title in 1979, before it was renamed the Intercontinental championship. Famous for his classic Boot Camp match with Sgt. Slaughter, he stayed with the WWE and has been a booker and road agent since his retirement from the ring in the early 1980s.

Patterson, Peggy
(1970s-1980s)

This women's blond bomber was billed as Pat Patterson's sister and was often the holder of versions of the women's title. She was well-schooled and had some matches with Madusa Micelli early in Madusa's career.

Patterson, Thunderbolt
(1970s-1980s)

A talented prelim star who was more famous for his lawsuit against Georgia promoters that sought to open the doors for more minority talent. He feuded with Ole Anderson in the early 1980s.

Patton, Tank
(1970s)

Great name, not so great talent. He was a serviceable, rugged guy who toured Florida and feuded with the likes of Dick Slater and Dusty Rhodes. [Big Mac]

Payne, Maxx
(1980s)

Darryl Peterson was a top-flight amateur who looked destined for mainstream success. He was big, agile, and had a versatile personality: he could either be a rocker or a monster. His career fizzled after stints in Memphis and WCW.

Pazandak, Joe
(1930s-1940s)

This Midwest attraction, trained by George Gordienko, was a frequent star for promoter Tony Stecher. He was most famously known as the man who trained future Hall of Famer Verne Gagne. Pazandak died in 1983.

Pedicino, Joe
(1980s-1990s)

Pedicino was an adequate announcer who first became known for his syndicated show, "This Week in Pro Wrestling." He and co-host (and wife) Bonnie Blackstone built on that success and worked for WCW. Adept at television production, Pedicino took over the USWA in Texas, renamed it the Global Wrestling Federation, and tried his hand promoting on the ESPN Network. In later years, he was still working on a wrestling radio show from his native Georgia.

Perez, Al
(1970s-1980s)

This Latin star was from Texas and became a Florida mainstay in the 1980s. He looked like a pure junior heavyweight, but never shied from the super powers. After early success, Perez and manager Gary Hart ventured to NWA Mid-Atlantic and Dallas, where he held the World Class world and TV titles. His younger brother, Lou, also wrestled.

Perez Jr., Miguel
(1980s-1990s)

Miguelito worked hard in both Capitol Sports and Puerto Rican indies. The second-generation star caught on with the WWF in the Los Baricuas tag team with Savio Vega.

Perez Sr., Miguel
(1960-1970s)

He was a popular tag-team partner of Argentina Rocca throughout the East and Puerto Rico. Though he was a fine technical star, most of his success came via tag competition.

Perry, William
(1980s)

The former Chicago Bears player, known as the "Fridge," was a onetime WWF attraction at the Wrestlemania 2 Battle Royal in 1986.

Pesek, Jack
(1940s-1960s)

Omaha-based promoter and son of wrestler, John Pesek, he played football at Nebraska before his wrestling days and was strong enough to tear phone books with his bare hands.

Pesek, John
(1920s-1940s)

Known as the Tigerman, he was considered a "ripper." A ripper was known to demolish his opponents in quick order. Though he never held a world title, he is widely remembered as a fabulous pure wrestler in his day. In addition to wrestling, he had an interest in greyhound racing. His son, Jack, wrestled and promoted in Nebraska.

Peterson, D.J.
(1980s)

Once a "can't miss" prospect of the 1980s, he had athleticism and a great look. After a successful run in the Central States area, he followed Marty Janetty to the AWA where his success ran thin. He passed away at age 33, in 1993.

TRIVIA

Q. Which rowdy wrestler played a lead role in the movie *They Live*?

PG-13
(1990s)

This tag team comprised of Bill Dundee's son, Jamie, and Wolfie D, who tore up the Memphis territory through the 1990s. Too small for national appeal, they fit perfectly in the Southern scene. They were multiple time USWA-Power Pro tag-team champions before heading to ECW and WWF for brief stints. See: Wolfie D; Jamie Dundee.

Philadelphia Spectrum
(1970s-1980s)

Still standing but no longer used for wrestling, the old Spectrum, built in 1967, was the secondary home for the WWF. For more than two decades, the real Broad Street bullies bore names like Bruno and Pedro after wars there.

Phillips, Mel
(1970s-1980s)

One of the few African-American ring announcers in history. A friend of the McMahon family, he hosted WWF cards from the Philadelphia Spectrum.

Pierce, Boyd
(1960s-1980s)

The longtime voice of Mid-South wrestling (before Jim Ross), and a close ally of Bill Watts, Pierce was a vet on television for more than three decades and 100 percent old-school.

Pillman, Brian
(1980s-1990s)

After a pro football stint, Pillman trained in Calgary, where he was taken in by the Hart family. He was a potent flyer and teamed with Bruce Hart as Bad Company in Stampede. He was signed to WCW in 1988, where he won the WCW tag titles (with Steve Austin) and also was the group's first cruiserweight champ. After a devastating car accident, Pillman's career faded. He was one of the most well-liked wrestlers when he passed away in 1998. [Yellow Dog; Flyin' Brian]

Piper, Roddy
(1970s-2000s)

The "Rowdy Scot" turned pro at age 16 after spending time homeless as a teen. That proved to be his calling, as Piper, born Roderick Toombs, is one of wrestling's most bombastic personalities ever. From his beginnings in Oregon and California, he was the No. 1 heel in Georgia and the WWF for almost a decade. He's a two-time Northwest and three-time U.S. champion. Some say, without Piper, the WWE would not have been what it is today.

Pit Bulls, The
(1990s)

This short, muscled tag team from the East Coast are former ECW tag-team champions, and both carried the group's TV title on separate occasions. Pit Bull No. 1 is now retired, but No. 2 is still wrestling in independents like 3PW in Philadelphia.

Poffo, Angelo
(1960s-1980s)

The father of Randy Savage and Lanny Poffo, this patriarch was one of the most well-conditioned athletes of any era. He even claims numerous world records for push-ups and sit-ups. His ring career peaked in the 1970s, but despite his age, he wrestled until the 1980s. In addition to his ring duties, he founded the ICW in the 1970s and battled over promotional turf with rival Memphis promoters Nick Gulas and Jerry Jarrett. Jarrett ended up buying the group, leading to an ICW-CWA angle.

Poffo, Lanny
(1980s-1990s)

This second-generation performer didn't have success like his father or brother, Randy Savage, but he had a lengthy career. Lanny was the polar opposite of his mouthy, flamboyant sibling. With Savage, he held the Southern tag-team title in Memphis and had memorable bouts with the Nightmares and Rock &Roll Express. Poffo bolted for the WWF in 1985 and was used as an opening act. He also had a penchant for reciting poems when he later managed Curt Hennig. [The Genius]

Poisson, Gilles
(1970s-1980s)

A burly, lumberjack-gimmick wrestler who hailed from Canada, the French-Canadian Poisson spent the bulk of his career in Montreal. Nicknamed the Fish, he traveled briefly to the WWF. In Montreal, he was a tag-team champion with Sailor White and Killer Kowalski. As a singles star, he went on to succeed in Calgary and won the Stampede title in 1976. Sometimes he was known as Giles the Fish. [Louis Cyr]

Polynesian Wrestling
(1980s)

One of the main groups in Hawaii was this one run by Lai Maivia that showcased a bevy of styles. Most often, the cards were held at outdoor venues. The group crowned a variety of Polynesian Pacific Title holders, including Siva Afi (its first) in 1980; Jerry Lawler and Tui Selinga (its last) in 1988.

Portz, Geoff
(1960s-1970s)

One of England's legitimate shooters and top amateurs, it was hard for promoters to translate his skills to the box office. Despite that, he wrestled in Japan, Canada, Texas, and the AWA, where he helped fellow Brit Billy Robinson battle Nick Bockwinkel.

Powers, Johnny
(1960s-1980s)

Employing all styles of martial arts—from judo to kick boxing—he famously holds the distinction of wrestling Joe Louis and Rocky Marciano. Later in his career, he was a Buffalo-based promoter.

Precious
(1980s)

This dainty 1980s valet (and wife) of Jimmy Garvin sprayed the ring with disinfectant prior to Garvin's arrival. She was the source of much mayhem while in Dallas and the NWA.

Prentice, Bert
(1980s-2000s)

Kind of a renaissance man, Prentice has been a manager, announcer, singer, and promoter who always lands on his feet. He's been a matchmaker in Memphis, the AWA, and Nashville (just to name a few) and has been a part-time manager, too. [Chris Love]

Price, Rod
(1990s)

A former football player with the San Diego Chargers, he settled in the Dallas area. Price was a massively built star who wasn't as impressive in the ring as he looked. He made some appearances in ECW in the late 1990s to marginal success.

Pritchard, Bruce
(1970s-2000s)

Brother of wrestler Tom Pritchard, Bruce never wrestled, but he's been a behind-the-scenes genius. He began in Bill Watts' Mid-South area and migrated to the WWF where, in addition to his television production duties, he played the role of goofy Bible-thumper Brother Love. [Brother Love]

Pritchard, Tom
(1980s-2000s)

With a wit like Roddy Piper, he was a classic Southern pest and was a consummate tag-team wrestler. After wrestling well over a decade, including time in the WWF, he has become a WWE talent coordinator. [Zip; Dr. of Desire] See: Heavenly Bodies; Body Donnas.

Public Enemy, The
(1990s)

Rocco Rock and Johnny Grunge made up this odd duo. Not particularly skilled, they bounced around the ring like ping pong balls and started a trend of breaking tables in their matches. They were four-time ECW tag champs and also held the WCW tag belts. See: Rocco Rock; Johnny Grunge.

Putski, Ivan
(1960s-1980s)

This powerful weightlifter became a top WWWF mainstay in the 1970s using the nickname, "Polish Power." He had two careers: one as a bearded, happy-go-lucky fan favorite and the other as a trimmed down, ripped hero. He toured the country, but his home was certainly the East Coast.

Putski, Scott
(1980s-1990s)

The son of Ivan Putski, he is incredibly muscular, but most promoters found him too small for the big-time. He performed regularly for Texas independents.

Quebecers, The
(1990s)

Snobby but tough, Jacques Rougeau and Carl Oulette had history on their side. Both Montreal natives, and throwbacks to the 1960s, they were a quirky WWF tag team in the early 1990s. In 1993-94, they held the company's tag-team titles three times.

Queen Kong
(1980s)

One of the largest and strongest women ever, she toured Japan, Puerto Rico, and a host of women's groups as a gimmick performer. In addition to wrestling, she was a popular talk show guest and a part-time Hollywood performer.

Quinnones, Victor
(1980s-2000s)

Kind of a renaissance man, Quinnones has been linked with hardcore-styled promotions in Japan and has worked as a talent agent for American talent. Always seen with his trademark cigar, he's also one of the few ringside managers in Japan.

Quintero, Jose
(1960s)

A perennial Puerto Rican jobber, Quintero worked the AWA and Puerto Rico. He is known by fellow wrestlers to compete in amateur talent contests and sing in his broken English.

Race, Harley
(1950s-1990s)

The Kansas City native was a classy, eight-time NWA world champion. Before Ric Flair, the NWA was identified by Race's skills. His wrestling career began in the 1950s and along the way he held titles in nearly every region of the country. A three-time Missouri champion, he wrestled Ric Flair at the first Starrcade in 1983. He moved on to the WWF, where he wrestled as the King, but he never duplicated his NWA success. [King Harley Race]

Raimey, Ken
(1970s)

The tuxedo-clad Raimey was a top heel manager. A lifelong fan of wrestling, Ramey called himself "Dr." and managed the Masked Interns to titles in California.

Raines, Dick
(1950s-1960s)

A rugged brawler who had most of his success as a tag-team wrestler, he seemed to be just on the brink of stardom. He performed during a time when having the nickname "Dirty" was enough to rile fans.

TRIVIA

Q. Who found early success in the Midwest as Larry Hennig's partner, together winning the AWA tag belts three times?

Rambo, John
(1980s-1990s)

A few indy wrestlers have used this name, but the most famous was one who fared well in Germany's CWA group, where he feuded with Larry Cameron and William Regal.

Ramos, Bull
(1950s-1970s)

"Wild" Bull was a stocky brawler who toured British Columbia, Texas, California, and Hawaii. He is most known in Portland, where he carried the Northwest title four times in feuds with Dutch Savage and Moondog Mayne. When he retired, he sold cars in the Portland area.

Rapada, Mike
(1990s-2000s)

A former two-time NWA heavyweight champ in 2000, this young Kerry Von Erich-look-alike has been all over the South. He was also a brief holder of the USWA title, which he took from Jerry Lawler in 1996. [Colorado Kid]

Raven
(1980s-2000s)

Originally a bratty heel, Raven has gone through many changes in his career. In Portland, he was a mile-a-minute talker. He won that title three times. He had a brief early stint in WWF, but didn't hit his stride until hooking up with ECW in the early 1990s. He transformed himself into the loner, Raven, and the feuds with Tommy Dreamer and Sandman still have fans talking. [Scott Levy; Scotty the Body; Johnny Polo]

Ray, Stevie
(1990s)

Originally from the Texas independents, Ray was the powerful partner to his real-life brother, Booker T, in their team, Harlem Heat. He developed most of his skills on live TV. When Booker took off for greener pastures, Ray was left out. Before WCW closed, he tried his hand at television commentary. See: Harlem Heat.

Red Cloud, Billy
(1950s-1960s)

A cruiserweight before his time, this Native American mastered the chop. The Mohawk-sporting wrestler was a popular prelim and tag-team performer.

Reed, Butch
(1970s-1990s)

This former rodeo circuit performer and football player turned to pro wrestling in the late 1970s. A super heel in Central States, Calgary, Florida, and Georgia with dyed hair, he turned to the WWF in the mid-1980s and then to WCW, where he teamed with Ron Simmons to win the world tag titles. [Bruce Reed; Hacksaw Reed; The Natural] See: Doom.

Regal, Steve
(1970s-1980s)

Jesse Ventura dubbed this light heavyweight, "Mr. Electricity." He campaigned in Chicago, Central States, and in Indianapolis. But in the AWA, he and Jimmy Garvin shocked the world, "ala Ventura," by taking down the Road Warriors for the world tag titles in 1985. Never a star, he is remembered as being capable of 60-minute matches.

Regal, William
(1980s-2000s)

This well-schooled European wrestler began on the carnival circuit in England. He was lured to America by WCW and had quick success there in 1993, winning the TV title. He eventually won the belt three times. Known for his witty facial expressions, he fit right in with the WWE. There, he won the European title twice and admirably fought back from a public fight with substance abuse. [Lord Steven Regal]

Renegade, The
(1990s)

Independent wrestler Richard Wilson got the break he always wanted as a knock-off of the Ultimate Warrior. Promoters believed in him and in 1995, he beat Arn Anderson for the WCW TV title. With his flash-in-the-pan career seemingly over, his inner demons sadly led him to commit suicide in 1999.

Resnick, Ken
(1980s)

The blond-haired car salesman from Minnesota got his first announcing gig as an upcoming-events pitchman for the AWA. Like Gene Okerlund before him, he eventually high-tailed it for the WWF.

Rheingans, Brad
(1980s)

A very talented wrestler who had ties to Japan. His career was best served as a trainer 10-plus years. In U.S. rings, he was never more than a prelim guy in the Midwest and WWF, thanks to his vanilla personality. But as a trainer, he shined, with Jerry Lynn and Brock Lesnar his most famous students. He also works out many rookie Japanese stars.

Rhodes, Dustin
(1980s-2000s)

Few wrestlers today have a connection to the outlaw days of Terry Funk and Dick Murdoch, but count Dustin, the son of Dusty Rhodes, as one of them. His Texas roots have served him well. Although he was never a mega-star, his consistency has been a benefit. Dustin moved to WCW at a young age, but hung in there, winning the U.S. and world tag titles. Even outlaws are susceptible to changes, and since the late 1990s, he's played the face-painted Goldust character in WWE.

Rhodes, Dusty
(1960s-2000s)

One of the most beloved and jeered men in wrestling history. Fans of his early work know him as one of the most dramatic and fiery interviews ever. Named for a 1950s baseball hero, Dusty played football and baseball in college and pined to be a pro wrestler. Big money feuds have followed him to every territory and he was famous for his bull-rope matches. In Florida, from 1973-82, he held the Florida Southern title nine times. But in NWA country, Rhodes earned icon status, and in 1979, he won his first of three world titles. In the mid-1980s, he added matchmaking to his resume. He's credited with creating the War Games cage matches and the Great American Bash summer series. However, some of his match results still have fans scratching their heads. His legacy is surely in the ring and even into his 50s, he was still active on the independent circuit. [Midnight Rider; American Dream]

Rhyno
(1990s-2000s)

The last wrestler to carry the ECW world title in 2001, he is an ECW grad who reminded some of Tazz. Both were compact and bruising wrestling machines. In ECW, he was also a two-time TV champion and his feud with Sandman was so controversial, it was censored from television. In the WWE, Rhyno has struggled to find an identity, but his potential is still great. [Rhino]

Rich, Tommy
(1970s-2000s)

"Wildfire," has been one of the more passionate performers of the last 25 years. In 1981, he shocked the world by becoming the youngest man ever to hold the NWA world title when he dethroned Harley Race. Although he held the belt for only a week, the win cemented his legend. Known for a wide array of scientific moves, he also held the Georgia National title. Since the 1980s, Rich has had an on-and-off career in the Mid-South and Memphis areas. Tommy's brother, Johnny, also wrestled.

Richards, Steven
(1990s-2000s)

Once billed as a can't-miss star, Richards found a home in ECW where he was Raven's ring lackey. The lightweight was a player there, but struggled to find his own identity. The former ECW tag-team champion took off for WCW and then WWE, where he's played everything from a censorship advocate to a Cactus Jack-impersonator.

Richter, Wendi
(1980s-1990s)

The former Dallas cowgirl was an overnight sensation in the mid-1980s thanks to MTV and Cindy Lauper. Fiery and fun loving, Richter dethroned the Fabulous Moolah from her 30-year reign as world women's champion as part of the "Rock & Wrestling" explosion of the early 1980s.

Riggs, Scotty
(1990s-2000s)

The husky playboy had everything going for him but luck. He had good skills, but promoters never had confidence in him to go far. He was a WCW tag-team champion with Marcus Bagwell before heading to ECW, where he teamed with pal Rob Van Dam.

Rikidozan
(1950s)

Long considered the father of pro wrestling in Japan, the Korean-born wrestler named Sin-Nak Kim had "pro" exhibitions for a nation accustomed to sumo. Thousands would see the exhibitions and "poof!" a new sport was born. He brought in larger-than-life foes like Lou Thesz, the Destroyer, Fred Blassie, and the Sheik, and his fan base grew incredibly. His understudies, Giant Baba and Antonio Inoki, went on to prominence after Rikidozan's murder in 1963 at age 39.

Rikishi
(1980s-2000s)

One of many Samoan wrestlers in the WWE, he was originally a member of the Samoan Swat Team and Headshrinkers in World Class, WCW, and the WWF. For a 400-pound man, he has the quickness of a cruiserweight. As a singles star, he always struggled, before landing headlong into the Rikishi character. After some initial trepidation, he committed to the part and never looked back. [Fatu; The Sultan]

Rivera, Victor
(1970s-1980s)

Well-versed as a heel and baby face, Rivera was a prelim star most of his career. But in 1975, he and Dominic DeNucci beat the Valiants for the WWWF tag-team titles. He was a mainstay in California, where he worked through many changes in the business, and had many main-event matches with the Sheik out West.

Road Warriors, The
(1980s-2000s)

When then-Georgia promoter Ole Anderson wanted a new gimmick for the 1980s, little did he know his request would result in the Warriors. Hawk and Animal, with characters based around the movie "Road Warrior," revolutionized wrestling with their persona and power. The entire decade belonged to them, as virtually every arena they appeared in drew thousands to see their unique style. Managed by Paul Ellering, they were the first team to capture all Big Three (AWA, NWA, and WWF) tag titles. [Legion of Doom; LOD]

Robert, Yvon
(1930s-1950s)

The French-Canadian star may have been the prototype for Ric Flair. In his day, he lived like a champion 24/7, as he enjoyed wining and dining after his contests. He was popular in his home base of Montreal and had high-profile matches with Lou Thesz, Whipper Watson, and Bobby Managoff.

Roberts, Buddy
(1970s-1990s)

Dazed and confused as a singles star, he found a niche as a tag-team worker. Roberts teamed first with Jerry Brown as the Hollywood Blondes; he then joined Terry Gordy and Michael Hayes as the Fabulous Freebirds. He was a bit small and not overly charismatic, but as part of a team, he was a fine complement. [Dale Valentine]

Roberts, Jake
(1980s-2000s)

The son of Grizzly Smith, Roberts has lived a very public life filled with drug addiction, as chronicled in the film, "Beyond the Mat." In his heyday, Roberts was known as the great ring psychologist and storyteller. Few wrestlers cut more believable promos than Roberts. He wrestled all over the country before reaching superstar status in the WWF during the 1980s. Although he never carried a major belt there, he was often as popular as Randy Savage and Hulk Hogan—perhaps even more so.

Robinson, Billy
(1950s-1980s)

The English shooter was a regional titleholder in Britain, Japan, Canada, and Texas before settling in the AWA. There, he held the tag titles with Verne Gagne and the Crusher. He even had some 60-minute matches with Gagne. In Japan, he feuded with Rikidozan. He's remembered as one of the toughest wrestlers to go up against.

Robley, Buck
(1970s-1980s)

This renegade from the Mid-South region managed, wrestled, and promoted. With a military gimmick—he called himself Sgt. Buck—he often guided Kimala. At various times, he was a thorn in the side of Jerry Lawler and Bruiser Brody. [Sgt. Buck]

Rocca, Antonino
(1950s-1960s)

The Argentinean was one of wrestling's first, and most innovative, high flyers. The barefooted wrestler was prolific at singles and tag-team wrestling and was a legendary figure in Puerto Rico and in the East.

Rocco Rock
(1980s-2000s)

Ted Petty was a longtime East Coast independent star who never saw a national break. After wrestling over a decade, his career gained new life in ECW as one-half of Public Enemy. Together with Johnny Grunge, they were four-time tag-team champs and brought hardcore wrestling into the national spotlight. In 2002, he passed away. [Komodo Dragon; Cheetah Kid] See: Public Enemy.

Rocco, Mark
(1970s-1990s)

A tremendously skilled British star, his technical ability was praised worldwide in the 1980s. Although he didn't have a career in the U.S., Rocco was a terrific heel in the U.K. and his reputation was cemented in a series of matches in Japan as the Black Tiger against the original Tiger Mask (Satoru Sayama). In England, he feuded with Sammy Lee (Sayama) and Keiji Yamada (Jushin Liger). In the early 1980s, he was a three-time world heavy middleweight champion and often teamed with Fit Finlay. [Rollerball Rocco; Black Tiger]

Rock & Roll Express, The
(1980s-2000s)

Two prelim light heavyweights, Ricky Morton and Robert Gibson, were lost as singles stars when Jerry Lawler combined them as this rocking tag team. In 1984, everyone wanted a piece of them. They were the precursors to today's faster-paced teams like the Hardy Boys. Gibson was a solid worker, but the team revolved around Morton, who had tremendous skill and popularity. The duo could wrestle anyone, from the Russians to the Four Horsemen to the Midnight Express. They rode that success to Memphis, Mid-South, Mid-Atlantic, and the NWA, where they were four-time NWA tag-team champions.

Rock & Roll RPMs, The
(1980s)

Formed by Tommy Lane and the late Mike Davis, this tag team was popular in Alabama, Texas, and Puerto Rico, often holding regional tag belts in the Southeast. See: Mike Davis.

Rock, The
(1990s-2000s)

Dwayne Johnson quickly established himself as one of the most talked about wrestlers of all time. He's a third-generation star, as his father Rocky Johnson and granddad Peter Maivia were ring stars from the 1950s to 1980s. He's done everything, from winning the world title to starring in a motion picture, and sitting next to President George W. Bush. But it started innocent enough for Rocky. A football player at the University of Miami, he abandoned his sports career to be become a wrestler. His early trainers knew he had potential, and soon he was sent to Memphis to learn the ropes. After less than a year, he was sent to the WWF, where he molded himself into the character he is today. He claims he'll always be a wrestler, but the demands of Hollywood may be too great for the Great One. [Flex Cavana]

Rockers, The
(1980s-1990s)

A high-energy tag team that turned the undersized Marty Jannetty and Shawn Michaels into international superstars. Alone, both wrestlers were floundering in the early 1980s when they were matched together in the AWA as the Midnight Rockers. There, they won the AWA tag-team titles and feuded with Buddy Rose and Doug Somers. The lure of the WWF was too great and by the late 1980s, they departed the AWA. In the WWF, and renamed The Rockers, the duo had classic matches with The Brainbusters and The Hart Foundation. See: Marty Janetty; Shawn Michaels.

Rodman, Dennis
(1990s)

Basketball's king of *National Enquirer* gossip, the tattooed party animal made a $1 million payday by wrestling in the 1998 WCW pay-per-view, "Bash at the Beach." Rodman was respectable in his tag match with Hulk Hogan against Dallas Page and fellow NBAer Karl Malone. Rodman appeared once more for an independent pay-per-view in 2000, wrestling Curt Hennig in Australia.

Rodz, Johnny
(1960s-2000s)

This Puerto Rican star has been a New York staple since he began as a prelim wrestler for the WWF. He always was the star on the independent circuit, but mainstream stardom was elusive for the barrel-chested bruiser. Later in his career, he opened a training gym in New York City.

Roeber, Ernest
(19th Century)

This pre-1900s attraction was christened U.S. Greco Roman champion in 1892 by previous champion, and friend, William Muldoon. It was a title he held for several years. He once battled Youssuf the Terrible Turk in New York in 1898 in a match that ended in a near-riot after Roeber was thrown into the crowd by a furious Turk. Well into his 70s, he was still active as a referee.

Rogers, Buddy
(1950s-1970s)

Rogers, the first "Nature Boy," was also the first-ever WWWF champion in 1963, as well as a former NWA world champion (1961-63). He was proficient at roughhousing and submission holds, but was also known for his sense of timing. He was one of the great blond-haired heels of his day. His look took him to Hollywood, where he found work on several TV shows. After his WWWF title loss to Bruno Sammartino in 1963, Rogers was forced to retire from heart trouble. He died in 1992 at age 71.

Rogers, Rip
(1970s-1990s)

A highly conditioned prelim star who had regional fame in the 1980s, his blond hair and pink outfits were always a sight to see. He had runs in Continental and Memphis and always remained old school. Since his wrestling days, he's been a trainer at the Ohio Valley Wrestling facility near his home state, Indiana.

Rogers, Sonny
(1980s)

A noted Midwest jobber named after a Chicago bluesman, he appeared in Windy City, AWA, and WWA sometimes as the partner of fellow beach bum Jonnie Stewart.

Rogers, Tommy
(1980s-1990s)

One-half of the Fantastics with Bobby Fulton, they were a Chippendale-type team in the Mid-South. As a singles star, Rogers was lost. Always well-conditioned, he bopped around the independents in the early 1990s, finally stopping in ECW.

Roma, Paul
(1980s-1990s)

Roma had better-than-average talent and a movie-star look. In the 1980s, he was a young up-and-comer who teamed with Jim Powers as the jobber team, the Young Stallions. He finally had a chance to hold a major tag title in the early 1990s as the tag-team partner of Paul Orndorff in WCW. Very athletic, he tried his hand at boxing and retired with a 2-1 pro record.

Roop, Bob
(1970s-1980s)

A legendary AAU figure, he had difficulties moving to the pro ranks. His career was spent in the South, where he won many regional titles in Georgia and Florida.

Rose, Buddy
(1970s-1990s)

A noted mid-card performer, the rotund Rose was a talented worker and eight-time Portland champion where he also feuded with Roddy Piper and Jay Youngblood. Always good for a laugh on interviews, he is a former AWA tag-team champion with Doug Somers.

Rose, Pete
(1990s)

Major League Baseball's hit king, Rose was comic fodder at two Wrestlemania's in which, after some verbal jousting, he succumbed to piledrivers from Kane.

Rose, Randy
(1970s-1980s)

Little do some fans know that Rose was an original member of the Midnight Express, along with Dennis Condrey and Norvell Austin, in the early 1980s in Memphis. Rose, a gangly sort, was a brawler and had a nice career in the Southeast. In 1987, managed by Paul E. Dangerously, he and Condrey won the AWA tag titles. Shortly after, the team had another run against Jim Cornette's Midnight Express in the NWA.

Ross, Jim
(1970s-2000s)

Even Ross would likely tell you his success couldn't have been predicted. The former college football announcer first joined Bill Watts' Mid-South group to supplement his income. The wrestling business would be his home for the next 20 years, where his influence can't be undervalued. Held in the highest regard, along with Gordon Solie and Jack Brickhouse, he's been the standard-setter for new announcers. He's called hundreds of NWA and WWE world title matches and has been the lead host for the WWE since 1997. Excitable and dramatic, even a severe case of Bells Palsy, which forced to him to relearn his verbal skills, couldn't hide his talents.

Rotten, Axl
(1980s-2000s)

A toned-down version of his brother, Ian, Axl is very hardcore, nonetheless. Based out of the Mid-South, the rotund punk rocker won the Global tag-team titles with Ian, and then feuded with him. He struggled to become a household name, but nearly became mainstream while in ECW as the partner of Balls Mahoney. But is there life after hardcore for Axl?

Rotten, Ian
(1980s-2000s)

Not as well-known nationally as his brother, Axl, this Rotten has led an infamous independent career. He runs a hardcore promotion in Kentucky-Indiana that takes garbage wrestling to new heights. Rotten is usually at the center of all the mayhem.

Rotunda, Mike
(1980s-2000s)

A former Syracuse star who had a long and productive ring career. Always seen as a capable, technical star without a lot of flair, he spent many years in Japan and was a star in Florida and later the NWA and WWF. In 1985, he and Barry Windham won the WWF tag belts twice; in 1989, he and Steve Williams won the NWA world tag-team title. By the early 1990s, his career seemed on the downside, when he was rejuvenated. His stock rose and he was given another chance in the WWF. With Ted DiBiase, he was a three-time world tag champion from 1992-93. [Michael Wallstreet; Irwin R. Shyster]

Rougeau, Jacques, Jr.
(1970s-1990s)

Second-generation Canadian star who wrestled with his brother, Raymond, in the WWF. Jacques later went on to a successful singles career, winning the WWF Intercontinental title from Bret Hart in 1992. He also captured the WWF tag titles three times with fellow Montrealite, Pierre Oulette. [The Mountie] See: Quebecers.

Rougeau, Raymond
(1970s-1990s)

French-Canadian brother of Jacques Jr., Raymond was a successful tag-team wrestler in the WWF after spending many years in Canada. After his wrestling career was done, he became a broadcaster for the WWF's French-speaking shows and he's also been successful in promoting independent cards in his native Montreal.

Rougeaus, The
(1950s-1960s)

Johnny and Jacques were a legendary Montreal-based brother tandem who later became promoters in Canada. Johnny held the Montreal version of the North American title many times.

Royal Rumble
(1980s-2000s)

This match, a spin-off of the Battle Royal, was a WWF concoction, which debuted in 1988 as a free television show. The rules are easy: 30 wrestlers would enter the ring at two-minute intervals; elimination occurs when a wrestler is thrown over the top rope, and the last man standing wins. Since then, it's become an annual tradition for the WWF on pay-per-view.

Royal, Nelson
(1960s-1980s)

This top NWA junior heavyweight carried that title for several years. Also a trainer and promoter, he claims to have invented the Bunkhouse Stampede match.

Rude, Rick
(1980s-1990s)

Tough amateur arm wrestler and boxer, who was discovered as he was working as a nightclub bouncer. Rude, who was tall and had the most ripped abs of any modern-day wrestler, took pride in improving in the ring. With early success in Mid-South, World Class, and the NWA (where he was a world tag-team champion with Manny Fernandez), Rude bolted for the WWF. Good move. He became a viable main-event star who carried the company's Intercontinental title in 1989. In 1993, he held the WCW International title, which at the time was the company's lead belt, on two occasions. In 1998, in the midst of a comeback, he died at age 40.

Runnels, Terri
(1980s-2000s)

The ex-wife of Dustin Rhodes, she was a secretary for Ted Turner and broke in as a valet in WCW. With her ex-hubby, she took off for WWF where she guided Goldust. Since then, the beautiful Terri is a loyal WWE employee who has found a niche as an announcer and diva. [Alexandra York; Marlena]

Russell, Lance
(1960s-2000s)

Ask any longtime fan in the South their favorite memory, and this classy Memphis announcer will likely be part of it. Since the 1960s, the golden-throated Russell has been going strong as the voice of Memphis wrestling. He played a wonderful straight man to the heel Jerry Lawler in the King's formative years there. He's worked almost exclusively in Memphis; however, he did some work for WCW in the early 1990s.

TRIVIA

Q. Which wrestler was a 1948 Olympic silver medalist in weightlifting?

Russian Chain Match

Made famous by some of the earliest wrestlers with Russian gimmicks, this gimmick match saw two wrestlers joined together by a 15-foot chain, which can be used as a weapon. Wrestlers like Ivan and Nikita Koloff claim to be masters of the chain match.

Russo, Vince
(1990s-2000s)

Russo was a fan working at a video store in New York when he was given the chance of a lifetime to work as a writer for the WWF. Based on his success building the careers of Steve Austin and the Rock, Russo leveraged a job as booker for WCW. That stint failed, but he's resurfaced in NWA-TNA as a booker and on-screen talent.

Sabu
(1990s-2000s)

Terry Brunk, the pioneering table breaker from Detroit, is the nephew of the Sheik, Ed Farhat. Taking a wild page from his uncle, Sabu is nothing short of a wildman himself. He first found a home in Japan's FMW and ECW, where his suicidal tendencies were nurtured en-route to two-time ECW world singles and three tag-team titles. Although he never found major-league success—is he too wild?—he's never been one to bow to risks and is still active despite many injuries suffered over the years.

Saggs, Jerry
(1980s-1990s)

Thought to be unorthodox in the ring, he made a career as the tag-team partner of Brian Knobbs in the Nasty Boys. He very rarely wrestled in single's competition, but his career was fairly successful. After runs in the AWA and WCW, they won the WWF tag-team titles in 1991. Saggs retired early from injuries. See: Nasty Boys.

Saito, Masa
(1970s-2000s)

A classic Japanese star who was as stiff as they come, Saito had success in Japan and the U.S. His real fame came as part of the New Japan group, where he was a major star in the late 1980s, alongside Antonio Inoki and Tatsumi Fujinami. He had tours of the WWF (where he was a two-time tag champion with Mr. Fuji) and AWA, where he teamed with Ken Patera and Jesse Ventura. Later, in 1990, he returned to the group and won the world title from Larry Zbyszko. [Mr. Saito]

Sakaguchi, Seiji
(1970s-2000s)

A top judo and wrestling star in Japan, he was often known as the figurehead president or commissioner of different promotions. His influence strengthened as Antonio Inoki's promotional partner in New Japan Pro Wrestling. He's even starred in several Japanese and American movies.

Sakata, Harold
(1950s-1960s)

What a noteworthy career this Hawaiian-born wrestler had. He was a hated Japanese character in wrestling and parlayed his image into a spot in the 1964 James Bond flick, "Goldfinger," as the top-hat wearing Oddjob. Many Asian stars wisely copied his tuxedo image, but none had his success. [Tosh Togo]

Sam Houston Coliseum

The original home to Paul Boesch's legendary Houston-based promotion, it was the site for wrestling for almost 50 consecutive years. Built in 1937 and torn down in 1988, Boesch (the second promoter there) ran cards featuring stars from Mexico and the NWA. Also notable, the Coliseum was one of the first buildings that saw people of all races watch harmoniously.

Sammartino, Bruno
(1960s-1980s)

The man from Abuzzi, Italy, was at one time the most popular champion in the world. Though he toured occasionally through the AWA, NWA, and Japan, Bruno spent almost his entire career with the WWWF. A tireless weightlifter, he was a wrestling ambassador and was treated by the New York media like major sports heroes Joe Namath and Mickey Mantle. He sold out Madison Square Garden regularly, as well as arenas in Philadelphia, Boston, and Pittsburgh, while defending the world belt against all challengers. He was the first world champion of the company and held the belt continuously from 1963-71. His second run stretched from 1973-77. Old school to the end, Sammartino broke ties with the company he helped build because he disagreed with the new direction wrestling took in the early 1980s. But by then, Bruno's legacy had been set.

Sammartino, David
(1970s-1980s)

Like father, like son, sort of. David followed his pop's footsteps, but unfortunately never lived up to the name. He toured the country and even worked in the WWF with his father, Bruno. Because he was short and stocky, promoters didn't feel he had the goods to be a star. Eventually, he got burned out on wrestling and left the business entirely.

Sanders, Mike
(1990s-2000s)

A WCW Power Plant grad with a gift for gab, he is not your prototypical wrestler. Without a wrestling look, he burst on the scene as leader of Vince Russo's henchman and rode early success to the WCW cruiserweight title. Since then, he's been working for NWA-TNA in 2003.

Sandman, The
(1990s-2000s)

With a gimmick for the times, Sandman was the king of hardcore on the East Coast during the 1990s. He cemented his legacy in ECW with his cigarette smoking, cane-winging gimmick. He won the company's world title five times from 1992-2001 and attained a cult following after his feuds with Raven and Tommy Dreamer. [Hardcore Hak]

Santana, Ricky
(1970s-1990s)

This Latino star was always close to stardom, but stateside success eluded him. Capable as a high-flyer and technical star, he had success in Puerto Rico, Japan, Florida, and Portland. He was also a mid-level star in the NWA Mid-Atlantic area. [Hood; U.S. Male]

Santana, Tito
(1970s-1990s)

One of the great baby faces, Merced Solis was a precursor to today's high flyers. In college, he played football at West Texas with Tully Blanchard and his athleticism was shown in his drop kicks. His wrestling stardom reached its pinnacle in the 1980s. After success in the AWA, he went to the WWF where he was both the Intercontinental and tag-team champion (with Rick Martel). Some say he never had a bad match. [El Matador; Merced Solis]

Sasaki, Kensuke
(1980s-2000s)

Short, stocky, and powerful, Sasaki was a tag-team wrestler in Japan when he broke out in single's competition. In the late 1990s, he was a big-time headline attraction there, winning the IWGP title three times. In all, he held New Japan's tag-team belts seven times, two with Road Warrior Hawk as the Hellraisers. He's also toured Stampede and Puerto Rico, and is a former WCW U.S. champion. [Kendo Sasaki; Power Warrior]

Sato, Akio
(1980s-1990s)

One of the few present-day Japanese stars to see almost all of his success in the U.S., Sato started humbly in the Central States. He was a complementary tag-team wrestler, as evidenced by his time with Pat Tanaka in the AWA and WWF (as the Orient Express). In Japan, he's a former two-time All-Asian tag-team champion. Still living in the U.S., he's married to wrestler Betty Niccoli. [Mr. Sato]

Saturn, Perry
(1990s-2000s)

A well built, but short, ring veteran of WCW, ECW, and WWF, his career took off as the partner of John Kronus in the Eliminators tag team. They were three-time ECW tag champions. He broke out as a singles star during the late 1990s, but he's been limited to mid-card oddball gimmicks.

Savage, Dutch
(1960s-1980s)

The bearded Savage was the prototype for Billy Jack Haynes' career. In Portland, Savage won the Northwest title seven times and was a staple there most of his career.

Savage, Randy
(1980s-2000s)

Family ties to wrestling and pure athleticism helped Savage grow into a superior talent in the late 20th Century. He was a minor league baseball player when his family ties came calling. As the son of legend Angelo Poffo and brother of Lanny Poffo, Savage was ready for prime time. His grinding voice and flamboyant Macho Man persona earned him a shot in the WWF in 1985, and he's been one of the most recognizable faces ever since. Promoters believed in him, as he earned both the WWF and WCW world titles. He's also headlined Wrestlemania. For much of his career, he was accompanied by his ex-wife, the late Miss Elizabeth.

Savage, Ripper
(1980s-1990s)

An underused talent, Don Ross was a journeyman whose entertaining interviews were the hallmark of many short-lived California groups. His wrestling skills lacked, but he made up for it in style.

TRIVIA

Q. Which wrestler nicknamed "Powerhouse" played football at Ohio State before wrestling?

Savannah Jack
(1980s)

A master of the superkick, Ted Russell joined Bill Watts' UWF after a tour with the Midwest independents. In the Mid-South, he was a brief popular attraction and battled Iceman Parsons and Buddy Roberts over the TV title. The former black belt in karate was also a Golden Gloves boxing champ. He retired early from poor health.

Savinovich, Hugo
(1980s-2000s)

Who's that man at the Spanish announcing table? One of them is usually Savinovich, a famed Puerto Rican wrestler, manager, and promoter. A jack of all trades, he's settled in as a liaison between the WWE and island-based talent.

Savoldi, Angelo
(1950s-1990s)

This dad has been a constant on the Massachusetts scene, including in his own group, ICW, which was founded in 1985. The group closed a decade later, but his legacy is strong. As a wrestler, he was an NWA junior heavyweight champ. As a promoter, he had a unique pipeline to Puerto Rico and sometimes brought in Carlos Colon and Hercules Ayala to the Northeast. As a trainer, he's helped Ayala and his sons (Joe, Tom, and Mario) become wrestlers.

Savoldi, Joe
(1930s)

Controversy seemed to follow the original Joe Savoldi. He was an accomplished football player, having played at Notre Dame for Knute Rockne from 1928-30. He was expelled from the school for being married. In 1930, he played for the Bronko Nagurski-led Chicago Bears, but bolted the team after three games. With his famous dropkick, he turned to wrestling. In a famous 1932 bout with Jim Londos, Savoldi double-crossed Londos and laid claim to the world title. Savoldi eventually gave the belt back, but the controversy caused such uproar, wrestling was banned in Chicago for a brief time.

Savoldi, Joe
(1980s-1990s)

Jumpin' Joe, the son of Angelo Savoldi, was a regular attraction for the family's ICW promotion. He rarely ventured outside the Northeast (he had a brief tour with Mid-South), but he did win the ICW belt three times. He teamed and feuded with Vic Steamboat there.

Savoldi, Mario
(1980s-1990s)

The son of Angelo Savoldi, he was also a part-time wrestler. Mainly, he worked as a co-promoter in the family's ICW group in Massachusetts.

Sawyer, Bart
(1980s-1990s)

A small journeyman, this fan favorite cruised the territories in Tennessee and Oregon. In Portland, he was a hit after cutting his hair like the cartoon character, Bart Simpson. [Brett Sawyer]

Sawyer, Buzz
(1970s-1980s)

This former amateur star lived fast and died young. At his best, he created a mad dog-like character. The suplex master, remembered as a short, fast-paced maniac who utilized the top rope well, his best years were in the early 1980s in Georgia, where he feuded with Tommy Rich over the Georgia National title.

Sawyer, Rip
(1960s-1970s)

Along with partner Rip Hawk, he was a staple early 1970s tag-team wrestler based out of the Mid-Atlantic area.

Schmidt, Hans
(1940-1960s)

He was one of the better-known wrestlers sporting a German gimmick to emerge prior to World War II. He was a main event throughout the U.S., but focused his attention on Chicago land wrestling.

Scicluna, Baron Mikel
(1960s-1970s)

A longtime WWF performer, the tall, freaky-looking performer was a star in New York where he won the tag-team titles with Smasher Sloan in 1966. He spent his entire career with a rule-breaking German gimmick.

Scorpio
(1990s-2000s)

A superb high flyer with Japanese training, Scorpio seemed destined for stardom. He had runs in WWF, WCW, and ECW and has had tremendous bouts with Chris Benoit, Dean Malenko, and Eddy Guerrero. A top competitor, he was once considered one of the best workers in the world. In 1993, he captured the WCW tag title with Marcus Bagwell. [2 Cold Scorpio; Flash Funk]

Scott Bros., The
(1950s-1980s)

The great Scotts—George and Sandy—were a successful tag team in the U.S. who did their best work in the Carolinas where they later trained and promoted. Ken Shamrock and Chris Chavis both had some of the earliest bookings for George Scott's 1980s promotion.

Severn, Dan
(1990s-2000s)

This ultimate shoot-fighter crossed over to pro wrestling after he was a UFC champion. The submission specialist, who had legendary UFC matches with Ken Shamrock, wrestled in Japan and held the NWA world title from 1995-99 and had a brief WWF stint. [The Beast]

Sexton, Frank
(1930s-1950s)

This good-looking Ohio native had tons of title matches. Having come along at the same time as Lou Thesz likely limited his success. Nevertheless, he was billed as world champion for several disputed branches of the belt. [Black Panther; Masked Marvel]

Sgt. Slaughter
(1980s-2000s)

Few wrestlers would have fit the bill as the "Sarge" as well as Bob Remus. Whether he was the half-crazed drill sergeant or the flag-waving fan favorite, he never lost a step. Remus began his career under a mask as the Super Destroyer. In the early 1980s, he established himself with the military gimmick while in the Mid-Atlantic area, often teaming with Don Kernodle. He toured with many groups as both a heel and fan favorite, winning many titles along the way. None were bigger than the WWF crown, which he grabbed from the Ultimate Warrior in 1991 in a controversial Gulf War-inspired angle. [D.I. Bob Slaughter; Super Destroyer]

Shamrock, Ken
(1980s-2000s)

Prior to his days in Ultimate Fighting, he was a pro wrestler based in the Carolinas. As a pro, he studied the style of Boris Malenko and toured Japan and Florida. His shootfighting stardom earned him big money. At the peak of his career, he went back to the pros in the WWF Intercontinental title there and, at one time, was in line for a run as world champion. [Vince Torelli]

Shane, Bobby
(1960s-1970s)

Beautiful Bobby was a top heat seeker in the U.S. The junior heavyweight was also a manager in his later years.

Sharkey, Eddie
(1960s-2000s)

As a wrestler, Sharkey was a top light heavyweight from the Midwest. He won the Kansas City U.S. title in 1968 and had 60-minute matches with Danny Hodge. After his wrestling days, he began training a successful stable, which included Jesse Ventura, Rick Rude, and the Road Warriors.

Sharpe Bros., The
(1950s-1960s)

The Ontario, Canada, tough guys, Ben and Mike, were big in the West. In San Francisco, they held the NWA tag titles 16 times. At nearly 7-feet-tall, they were a formidable team indeed. They also wrestled as the Harris Bros. Ben also had singles success as the NWA Hawaiian champ and Pacific Coast champion. They also wrestled together in Japan during the Rikidozan era.

Sharpe, Larry
(1970s-2000s)

The blond bomber was a capable junior heavyweight and general rulebreaker who had success on the East Coast and Japan. He is known most famously for his wrestling school, which helped kick off the careers of King Kong Bundy and Bam Bam Bigelow.

Sharpe, Mike, Jr.
(1970s-1980s)

A borderline star with good size (6'5, 260 pounds) and lineage to boot. He was managed by Fred Blassie and the Grand Wizard during his WWF stints in the 1970s, but main-event status eluded him. After touring Canada, he returned to the WWF in the 1980s using a "loaded" wrist guard and nicknamed "Iron Mike."

Shavers, Ernie
(1980s)

An ex-boxer from Cincinnati, some say he was the hardest-punching heavyweight in recent memory. He had gimmick boxer vs. wrestler matches and later served as a referee in wrestling.

TRIVIA

Q. The Monsteer Factory was a wrestling school owned by whom?

Sheepherders, The
(1960s-1980s)

The Sheepherders were one of the most violent and bloody teams of any era. Lord Jonathan Boyd founded the group with Luke Williams. Their original matches bordered on R-rated exhibitions. When Boyd retired, Williams took on Butch Williams as his partner and the two picked up where Boyd left off. Feuds with the Fantastics, the Invaders, and the Samoans—actually anyone who dared to enter their world—are still considered classics.

Sheik, The
(1950s-1990s)

Although he never held a major world recognized title in the AWA, WWF, or NWA, he was a top attraction in the 1960s and 1970s. Ed Farhat began his career as the Sheik and settled into a rulebreaking style. His matches were short on science and long on blood. He used concealed weapons, fire, and chairs to dismantle his opponents. He mainly wrestled out of Detroit, but Farhat was a star in Los Angeles, Toronto, and Tokyo. In Detroit, his feud with Bobo Brazil spilled into the aisles for nearly 10 years. Revered in Japan, he wrestled at age 65 with his nephew, Sabu, in a ring of fire match. After suffering severe burns, it proved to be the last match from the hardcore icon. But what other way would we expect the Sheik to end his career? In 2003, Farhat passed away. [Original Sheik]

Shiavone, Tony
(1970s-1990s)

The announcer began his career as a radio sportscaster for former NWA promoter Jim Crockett's minor league baseball team in Charlotte, N.C. Crockett heard his golden voice and brought him into the wrestling business. He's announced many world title matches in both NWA, WCW, and WWF and was once the host of "Monday Nitro."

Shibuya, Kenji
(1960s-1970s)

The barefooted iron man from Japan was a heel who used World War II tension as a storyline motivator. Known in the AWA and California, he knew karate and often teamed with Toru Tanaka, Mitsu Arakawa, and Mr. Fuji.

Shikat, Dick
(1920s-1930s)

This early century wrestling star had a legendary feud with Ali Baba in the late 1930s. In 1929, he won his first NWA world title beating Jim Londos. Then, in 1936, he dropped the belt to Baba in Detroit.

Shire, Roy
(1950s-1960s)

Known best as a promoter, he was also a former wrestling partner of Ray Stevens (who wrestled as Ray Shire). Shire was synonymous with San Francisco. He staged top-drawing events at the Cow Palace with stars like Pat Patterson, Gorilla Monsoon, Pepper Martin, and Stevens in that city's biggest days.

Shultz, David
(1970s-1980s)

Dr. D. was a trucker and bounty hunter before hitting wrestling rings in the 1970s. He was a classic territory wrestler who worked a major program with Hulk Hogan in the AWA in the 1980s. Playing the role of a redneck, he wrestled as he lived. [Dr. D]

Sicilians, The
(1960s)

Lou Albano's tag teams won more WWF tag titles than any other manager in history. But as part of the Sicilians, Albano actually held the belt. He and Tony Altimore were the champs in 1967. Shortly after, Altimore retired and opened a wrestling school and Albano went to become a Hall of Fame manager and commentator. See: Lou Albano; Tony Altimore.

Simmons, Ron
(1980s-2000s)

Simmons, an All-American football star from Florida State, was the first African-American to hold the WCW/NWA world title, which he won 1992 from Vader. After football, he began his career in the Florida circuit, but he quickly moved to the NWA/WCW. Before his singles run, he held the world tag belts with Butch Reed as Doom. As his career wound down, he found a home in the WWE. [Farooq] See: APA.

Simpson Bros., The
(1980s)

Steve and Scott, from South Africa, were part of the World Class 1980s explosion. In the mold of the Von Erichs, these sons of foreign promoter Sam Cohen were a smallish, rocker tag team who left as quickly as they arrived.

Singh, Dara
(1940s-1970s)

The father of Canadian-Indian main event star, Tiger Jeet Singh, he was well versed at European and shoot-style wrestling. He remained the Indian version of Hulk Hogan even into the 1970s and wrestled many years in Japan.

Singh, Gama
(1980s)

One of many Singhs to tour in North America, he was a three-time British Commonwealth champion in Calgary, where he teamed with the other Singh cronies.

Singh, Makhan
(1980s-1990s)

Some consider Singh, along with Vader, as the best working big man in history. The 350-plus wrestler was a hard worker in Canada in his feuds with the Harts. A multiple-time tag-team champion, he was the leader of a crew of Singhs in Calgary. The three-time Calgary champ had five-star matches against Owen Hart. In the early 1990s, he had popular runs in WCW as Norman the Lunatic and also spent time in the WWF. [Bastion Booger; Norman the Lunatic; Trucker Norm]

Singh, Rhonda
(1980s-1990s)

Think of a female John Tenta. Singh was a large roughneck wrestler who had to visit Japan to find competition. At 300-plus pounds, she had amazing speed. She did have short rides in WWF (winning the women's title) and WCW before she passed away in 2001 from heart failure. [Bertha Faye]

Singh, Tiger Ali
(1990s-2000s)

This third-generation star and son of Tiger Jeet Singh was set to get a big-time WWF push with a heel gimmick like his dad's, but it never materialized. Since then, the big man has wrestled in Canada and Puerto Rico with minimal success.

Singh, Tiger Jeet
(1960s-1980s)

Although Singh was a marginally talented ring worker, his bloody and maniacal style earned him main-event status the world over. The turban-wearing East Indian rulebreaker was linked to the Original Sheik as both partner and enemy. His epic wars harken to the days of Rikidozan. He was never a mainstream performer in the U.S., but he remains a mythical cult figure in Japan.

Skaaland, Arnold
(1950s-1980s)

The "Golden Boy," made famous in the East through the 1950s and 1960s, was one of wrestling's only non-heel managers. He played an Angelo Dundee-like coaching role while leading Bruno Sammartino and Bob Backlund to WWF titles in the 1970s and 1980s.

Skipper, Elix
(1990s-2000s)

A talented African American cruiserweight, Skipper has made a name for himself as a star with a lot of potential. His asset is his charisma, which draws comparisons to former football star Deion Sanders. He is a former WCW cruiserweight champion.

Sky Dome

This two-time site of Wrestlemania opened in 1989 and drew its largest crowd of 68,237 in 2002 for Wrestlemania X-8. In 1990, for Mania No. 6, 67,678 fans showed up.

Sky Hi Lee
(1950s-1960s)

At nearly 8 feet tall and 300 pounds, he was a short-lived novelty attraction, appearing in the Northeast and Canada. After wrestling, he found work in the Paris follies.

Slater, Dick
(1970s-1990s)

Tough as a Funk and ugly as George Steele, this Southern wrestler trained under Hiro Matsuda in Florida. In the 1980s, he was a widely used star in Florida and Mid-Atlantic. Not a headliner, he was a regular semi-main attraction. As tough as any wrestler to come from Texas, he often teamed with fellow Texans Dick Murdoch and Dusty Rhodes.

Slick
(1980s)

The hustler, turned street preacher, was a jive-talking manager in the WWF during the early 1980s, guiding the careers of Butch Reed and Akeem. After several years on top, he retired to Dallas and returned to his ministry work.

Slinker, Ron
(1980s)

A marginally talented wrestler, Slinker, a former karate champion, used his vast martial arts skills in the Southeast region's mat wars.

Smasher Sloan
(1960s)

One of the all-time great wrestling names, Sloan was a former WWWF tag-team champion with Baron Scicluna.

TRIVIA

Q. What tag team, nicknamed the Kiwis left carved foreheads behind as calling cards?

Smiley, Norman
(1980s-2000s)

A noted shooter with Virgin Island ties, the skinny, smiling Norman found success in Japan and Mexico before finding a spot with WCW. He trained with the Malenko family and is considered a legit tough guy. [Black Magic]

Smirnoff, Alexis
(1970s-1980s)

Originally from Quebec, he ventured to California in the 1970s where he ultimately made his home. He was a regional champ winning the Montreal title in 1973, U.S. title in San Francisco in 1977, and Georgia tag belts in 1980 with Ivan Koloff. [Michael DuBois]

Smith, Davey Boy
(1980s-2000s)

Most know the Brit as a bulky WWF heavyweight, but Smith actually has roots as a junior heavyweight. In the beginning, he weighed around 160, but later bulked up to more than 250 pounds. His main fame came as one-half of the British Bulldogs with Dynamite Kid. The twosome were WWF tag-team champions in 1986. A fantastic, fast-paced tag-team wrestler, Smith had success as a singles star, after Kid retired, by winning the WWF Intercontinental title in 1992. He was also the first European champion in 1997. Before he died in 2002, he left the family legacy in the hands of his wrestling son, Harry Smith. [British Bulldog]

Smith, Grizzly
(1960s-1980s)

Father of Jake Roberts, Sam Houston, and Rockin' Robin, Aurelian Smith was a tag-team wrestler with Luke Brown in a team called the Kentuckians. In the 1980s, Smith worked as a road agent for the UWF and WCW.

Smith, Johnny
(1980s-1990s)

This Calgary-based performer was billed as the cousin of Davey Boy Smith and was even considered a British Bulldog. Although he never caught on stateside, he successfully toured Singapore, England, Europe, Canada, and Japan. His Japan bookings gave him a reputation as a hard worker. Those foreign influences served him well once back home, as he carried the British Commonwealth title three times in Stampede.

Smith, Robin
(1980s-1990s)

The lineage was there, for sure, as was talent. The fiery daughter of Grizzly Smith and sister of Jake Roberts and Sam Houston, Robin's biggest moment came in 1988 when she took the WWF women's title from Sherri Martel. [Rockin' Robin]

Smoking Gunns, The
(1990s)

Billy and Bart Gunn, who are unrelated, were wrestling in Florida when the WWF came calling. With a cowboy gimmick, the duo became three-time tag-team champions. When the act wore thin, each went on to productive singles careers. See: Billy Gunn; Mike Barton.

Smoky Mountain Wrestling
(1990s)

Jim Cornette was determined to bring wrestling back to its territorial days and gave it a shot with SMW based out of Knoxville, Tennessee. Legends like Terry Funk, Dirty White Boy, and Paul Orndorff were found there, as well as future stars Chris Jericho, Lance Storm, Chris Candido, and New Jack. After some memorable cards and shows, the promotion closed in 1994.

Smothers, Tracy
(1980s-2000s)

A friendly, Southern wrestler, Smothers made contributions in the Kentucky-West Virginia region. Closely aligned with the Armstrong family, he teamed with Steve Armstrong as the Southern Boys in WCW. As a singles star, Smothers held the Smoky Mountain title during the early 1990s. [Freddy Joe Floyd]

Snow, Al
(1980s-2000s)

This WWE employee can wrestle all styles. With gimmicks, he can be a psycho, goof ball, or father figure. A disciplined performer, he stuck to his guns until he was given a chance. After struggling in the independents, Snow found a home in Smoky Mountain and WWF with a variety of personas. He's a five-time hardcore champion and held the WWF tag title with Mick Foley in 1999. [Avatar; Leif Cassidy]

Snow, Mitch
(1980s)

The undersized, acrobatic jobber had a several-year career in the Central States region. He wrestled in the AWA, but never caught on nationally.

Snowman, The
(1990s)

This flash-in-the-pan monster held the USWA world title after a series with Jerry Lawler. In the feud, he recruited the help of boxer Leon Spinks. He was stripped of the belt two months later. Rumor has it he took the belt for real and never returned it.

Snuka, Jimmy
(1970s-2000s)

The "Superfly" is easily one of the most recognizable stars of his era. The buffed, part Hawaiian was one of the first to use rope leaps to dazzle fans. He had success in Hawaii, Portland, and Japan, but his biggest success came in the WWF. Had Vince McMahon not had access to Hulk Hogan, Snuka was the promoter's second choice to take the WWF national in 1984. Even so, Snuka was closely aligned with the group's early national success. His feud with Roddy Piper still gets fans talking and his leaps.

Snyder, Wilbur
(1950s-1970s)

Although Snyder was always one of the most technically perfect wrestlers in any territory he appeared in, he was never a "must-see" performer. He settled into the Midwest and in 1961, he and Leo Nomellini won the AWA tag-team title. Six years later, he and Pat O'Connor defeated the Crusher and Bruiser for the belts.

Solie, Gordon
(1960s-1990s)

Often called the dean of wrestling announcers, he was the voice of Florida and Georgia wrestling for many years. He could make the biggest sceptic think the match was real. A grizzly throated announcer, Solie was a tremendous influence on current-day announcers like Jim Ross. He passed away in 2000 but in his prime, no one could sell a match like Solie.

Somers, Doug
(1970s-1980s)

While touring through virtually every promotion, the blond-haired wrestler created a rep as a solid worker but never rose to the top. A fine tag-team compliment, he and Buddy Rose won the AWA tag-team title from Scott Hall and Curt Hennig in 1986. The team also had classic matches with the Midnight Rockers.

Song, Pak
(1960s-1970s)

A native of Korea, he wrestled across the South and was an early partner of a then-heel Dusty Rhodes. On television, he would break wood and cement with his bare hands. After holding titles in Florida, he is remembered for putting Rhodes on the map. In a classic feud, Song turned on Rhodes, which gave Rhodes (renamed the American Dream) an amazing run as a fan favorite. Their feud drew sellouts in the Sunshine State for nearly half a year.

Sonnenberg, Gus
(1920s-1930s)

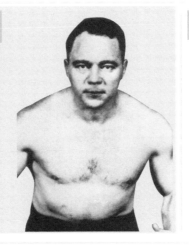

A Larry Zbyszko-looking wrestler, the former college football player helped solidify wrestling's image in the early days. He was immortalized after winning the NWA world title in 1929 from Strangler Lewis in Boston. He held the belt until losing it to Ed Don George in 1930.

Southwest Championship Wrestling

Regarded as one of the bloodiest promotions in memory, this Joe Blanchard-run group ran on the USA Network in the early 1980s before it was deemed too violent and yanked from the air. Its home base was San Antonio and stars like the Sheepherders, Tully Blanchard, Gino Hernandez, Manny Fernandez, and others shined there. Initially, it was a partner with World Class but in 1978, Blanchard set out on his own. In 1985, the group went out of business.

Spicolli, Louie
(1980s-1990)

He appeared to be on the verge of breaking it big when he died of a drug overdose in 1998. The California native was trained by Bill Anderson and he visited Mexico, Japan, WWF, and ECW before hitching a ride to WCW. He was all set for his first pay-per-view match and a new career when his life was cut short. [Mercenary; Rad Radford]

Spinks, Leon
(1970s-1990s)

After only nine boxing matches, the onetime Marine was picked out of nowhere to fight Muhammad Ali for the world title. After dethroning Ali, Spinks' career fell apart. Looking for a payday, he turned to wrestling. He headlined a Japanese show versus the icon Antonio Inoki, and visited the Orient later for additional matches against various foes.

Spivey, Danny
(1980s-1990s)

This tall, blond-haired wrestler had trips to WCW and WWF, where he teamed with Mike Rotunda and Sid Vicious. He was a monster in the ring, but was not seen as a world singles contender, so most of his career was spent in tag teams.

Spoiler, The
(1970s-1980s)

Not many Americans were legendary masked wrestlers, but Don Jardine had his best years courtesy of a hood. For the better part of a decade, he was a Mid-Atlantic mainstay. Some of his titles were won in World Class, Florida, and Georgia. He often feuded with Mr. Wrestling, Wahoo McDaniel, Ted DiBiase, and Dory Funk.

St. Clair, Tony
(1970s-2000s)

A famed British technician, he was a five-time British heavyweight champ and frequent player in the Japanese super juniors tournaments.

Stanlee, Gene
(1940s-1960s)

A pre-television star, he was right in the mix when wrestling on the tube caught on. He often challenged Lou Thesz for the world title and he himself was a Florida Southern heavyweight champ in 1951. He sometimes wrestled with "brother" Steve Stanlee and also wrestled Antonino Rocca in a series at Madison Square Garden. [Mr. America]

Starr, Chicky
(1970s-1990s)

After trying to make a dent in the talent-rich Georgia area, the junior heavyweight found a true home in Puerto Rico. Multilingual in real life, he was fearless in his attacks on island fans, who sometimes threw bottles at him.

Starr, Mark
(1950s-1980s)

Several Mark Starrs appeared over the years: one 1950s-era version was a West Coast attraction; in the 1980s, another Starr, who was the brother of Chris Champion, appeared in Florida and Memphis rings.

Starr, Ricky
(1950s-1960s)

One of wrestling's only trained ballet stars, he toured the world and was a top draw in England. Built like a cruiserweight, he was perfect for the Golden Age times he performed in, using his ballet talent as a gimmick in the ring.

Starr, Ron
(1970s-1980s)

This two-time NWA junior heavyweight champion wrestled in many regions including California, Louisiana, Georgia, and the Gulf States. [Mr. Wrestling; Rotten Ron]

Stasiak, Shawn
(1990s-2000s)

Formerly an amateur wrestler, this second-generation son of Stan Stasiak cut his teeth in Memphis after training with the Funks. With Lex Luger looks, he visited WCW and WWF before fading into the sunset. [Meat; Perfectshawn]

Stasiak, Stan
(1960s-1970s)

The master of the heart punch, he shocked the world by defeating Pedro Morales for the WWWF world title in 1973. Although his reign was only nine days long—he dropped the belt to Bruno Sammartino—his name will forever be remembered. During the 1960s, he was a top Northwest attraction and had a rep as a tough tag-team wrestler. The old school roughneck is the father of Shawn Stasiak.

Stasiak, Stan
(1920s-1930s)

Although not related to the other "Stasiaks," he was a successful wrestler when he passed away in 1931, allegedly from blood poisoning suffered in a match with Ed Don George in Canada.

Steamboat, Ricky
(1970s-1990s)

The Verne Gagne-trained performer, born Richard Blood, was a fan favorite virtually his entire career. His training days were spent with another future star, Ric Flair. Ironically, the two would forever be known for their matches against each other. Capitalizing on the Steamboat name, Ricky was a compelling 1980s wrestler who added a fiery tone and karate tactics to his matches. He concentrated his time in the Southeast and Mid-Atlantic regions. In 1989, his series of matches with Flair over the NWA world title put him in Hall of Fame contention. In 1989, they traded the NWA world title in a series that also boasted 60-minute draws around the country. Fans aren't likely to see that again, so wrestling's debt to Steamboat (and Flair) is large indeed.

Steamboat, Sam
(1950s-1960s)

A Hawaii-based barefooted master of the dropkick, he toured extensively around the world. Not related to Ricky Steamboat, he was a popular attraction and occasionally a main-event star.

Steamboat, Vic
(1980s-1990s)

The younger brother of Ricky Steamboat, he was a popular cruiserweight wrestler on the East Coast in ICW, where he held that company's singles title and feuded with Joe Savoldi.

Stecher, Joe
(1910s-1930s)

One of the NWA's first champion and toughest wrestlers, Stecher ultimately was a three-time world champion in the late 1910s to 1920s. When the legend Frank Gotch retired, Stecher beat the recognized champion, Charlie Cutler, and was christened world champ by promoters in 1915. Promoters tried to line up a Gotch-Stecher match but before it could be made, Gotch died. In 1916, he went to a classic five-hour draw with Strangler Lewis in Omaha. Stecher later beat Earl Caddock in 1920 and some 10 years removed from his first belt, he dethroned Stanislaus Zbyszko. Sadly, he spent the last 30 years of his life institutionalized with mental illness and passed away in 1974.

Stecher, Tony
(1940s-1950s)

The Minneapolis-based wrestler and promoter was bought out of his territory in the 1960s by Verne Gagne and Wally Karbo. At the time of the sale, Tony and his son were in the process of re-establishing the Midwest as a hotbed, but it was picked up by Gagne, who founded the successful AWA.

Steele, George
(1970s-1990s)

The former high school wrestling coach led an amazing pro-wrestling career. The hairy-bodied lunatic would eat turnbuckles, shout gibberish, and dye his tongue green. A true oddity, he was later used as a fan favorite in the WWF to rousing success.

Steele, Ray
(1920s-1940s)

Born in Russia of German descent, Ray (aka Pete Sauer) was an early 1900s attraction, who helped train and mentor Lou Thesz. In the U.S., he was based out of Omaha. His skills included judo and martial arts. In 1940, he beat Bronko Nagurski for the NWA world title, a belt he held for one year and four days before losing it back to Nagurski in Minneapolis. Steele died in 1949.

Steinborn, Dick
(1960s-1980s)

Son of legend Milo Steinborn, he was a regional star in Texas, Florida, and Georgia, and captured the AWA tag title with Doug Gilbert in 1962. In addition to wrestling under his real name, he donned a mask in Tennessee as one of several Mr. Wrestling's. [Mr. Wrestling; White Knight]

Steinborn, Milo
(1920s-1950s)

One of the great strength legends of all time, his exploits were unparalleled. He was even invited to the 1950 World's Fair in Chicago to lift an elephant. In addition to wrestling, he booked and promoted and also managed boxer-turned-wrestler Primo Carnera. He finally settled in Florida, where he promoted into the 1950s.

Steiner, Rick
(1980s-1990s)

A graduate of Brad Rheingans' camp, Rick hit the road early and found success in Bill Watts' UWF. There, he was a maniac teaming with Sting and Eddie Gilbert. With the sale of the UWF to the NWA, Steiner became a staple for the major group. Eventually, he teamed with Steve Williams, Mike Rotunda, and his brother, Scott, who he enjoyed his greatest success with. In all, Rick has been an eight-time world tag champion with his brother.

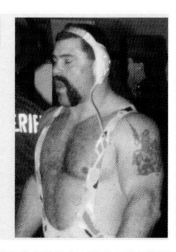

Steiner, Scott
(1980s-2000s)

The younger brother of Rick Steiner, he was a standout at the University of Michigan where, in 1986, he finished in sixth place at the NCAA national championships in the 190-pound division. Closely aligned with his brother during his career, Scott has been a world title contender for more than a decade. He won eight tag-team titles with Rick. Once tabbed as the heir apparent to Ric Flair, he won the WCW world title in 2000 from Booker T. When he was smaller, he helped bring numerous aerial moves to the U.S. including the huricanrana. [Big Poppa Pump]

Stevens, Ray
(1960s-1980s)

After carving a niche as a rodeo rider and car racer, Stevens tried wrestling. His career began to evolve in the Memphis and Mid-South territories in the 1960s. Although he was a world traveler, he made a home in California where he met Pat Patterson and created a classic heel team. By the 1970s, the "Crippler's" career reached a new level. He was a four-time AWA tag-team champion with Nick Bockwinkel (3) and Patterson (1). Stevens is remembered as a legend in the industry. He died in 1996. [Ray Shire]

Stewart, Jonnie
(1980s-1990s)

The flamboyant, blond-haired Stewart began wrestling out of Chicago's Windy City promotion with Sonny Rogers. He toured Memphis briefly before breaking off on his own in the AWA, where he feuded with Buck Zumhoff over the AWA light heavyweight championship.

TRIVIA

Q. After floundering for many regional groups with no real gimmick, which wrestler struck gold as the "Animal?"

Stewart, Nell
(1940s-1960s)

The late Stewart was one of the top female draws of the 1950s. The statuesque blond was a five-time Texas women's champion.

Sting
(1980s-2000s)

Steve Borden was discovered in California as part of Power Team USA, a weightlifting squad, and quickly broke off to Bill Watts' UWF with his original partner, the Ultimate Warrior, as the Blade Runners. When Warrior bolted, the face-painted Sting climbed the ladder in the NWA. An immediate fan favorite, he was given main-event status and positioned for a world title run. Despite a near-career ending knee injury, he recovered to beat Ric Flair in 1990 for his first of seven world titles.

Stomper, The
(1960s-1980s)

Archie Gouldie was one of the most well-conditioned athletes of any era. The former football player once set a world-record 2,800 sit-ups in one hour. Legend has it he once rode a bicycle from Arizona to Calgary, where he was an eight-time Stampede champion. He also toured around the South, including Tennessee, where he was a tag champion with Jos LeDuc, and Georgia, where he was a National title holder. [Mongolian Stomper]

Storm, J.W.
(1980s-1990s)

This Midwest monster boxed and wrestled professionally in the same day, a first. He ventured to WCW as a singles star after reaching regional success in Minnesota and Oregon as Art Barr's tag-team partner. The duo won the Portland tag-team championship. His career fizzled after that. [Big Juice; Jeff Warner]

Storm, Lance
(1990s-2000s)

The proud Canadian, a fitness fanatic, broke into wrestling as Chris Jericho's friend and partner. He was at his best as a tag-team wrestler in ECW. Straight-laced, he's also held the WCW U.S. title. Fewer stars today can say they passed through the Hart family dungeon, but Storm can. In that sense, he's part of a dying breed.

TRIVIA

Q. An athletic star, this wrestler acted in many features including the classic western, *Once Upon a Time in the West*. Who is he?

Stratus, Trish
(1990s-2000s)

Former fitness model turned WWF valet and wrestler, Trish hails from Toronto. At the behest of Vince McMahon, she began training to be a wrestler. Determined to make it work, she worked her way to the WWE women's title and did so admirably.

Street, Adrian
(1970s-1980s)

Exotic Adrian was a genius whose gimmickry and ideas live today. Realizing his career was going nowhere, the Brit became the "Exotic One," a face-painted androgynous oddity. Part Alice Cooper, part Gorgeous George, he was an attraction in the Southeast including Florida and Alabama. The fine tactical wrestler even recorded several albums.

Strike Force
(1980s)

When Tom Zenk left the WWF leaving Rick Martel without a partner, Tito Santana stepped in with the Canadian to create this combo. Highly energetic, they were consummate favorites and feuded with the Hart Foundation over the WWF tag title, which they won in 1987. See: Tito Santana; Rick Martel.

Strode, Woody
(1950s-1960s)

The former UCLA football star is the quintessential African-American hero. Before the Rock, he was the only man to main event a wrestling card and also star in a motion picture.

Strongbow, Jay
(1960s-1980s)

The good Chief was going nowhere fast as Joe Scarpa. Once he donned the feathers and adopted a war dance in the ring, he developed into a top tag-team wrestler. In all, he won four WWWF tag-team titles from 1972-82 with Sonny King, Billy Whitewolf, and Jules Strongbow. [Joe Scarpa]

Strongbow, Jules
(1970s-1980s)

After the Oklahoma Native American Frankie Hill toured the Midwest and AWA, he made his way to the WWWF, where he teamed successfully with his "uncle" Jay Strongbow. Jay had already been successful there, but this new team won two tag-team titles in 1982. [Frankie Hill]

Stubbs, Jerry
(1970s-1980s)

Stubbs surely lived two lives in the ring. As the bald-headed Stubbs, he was a dreaded heel. But he had masked, heroic, alter egos named Mr. Olympia and The Matador. In all, he was a four-time Alabama heavyweight champion, four-time Southeast tag-team champion (three won with Arn Anderson), and a four-time Continental tag-team champ during a prolific career. [Matador; Mr. Olympia]

Studd, John
(1970s-1980s)

One of the sport's legends, he was also considered a true gentleman despite being a heel in the ring. The protégé of Killer Kowalski, he won the WWWF tag title with Nikolai Volkoff as the masked Executioners in 1976. Studd, at 6-8, 350 pounds, was very impressive visually. He also feuded with Andre the Giant in the early 1980s. He died in 1995 at age 46 after a long illness. [Capt. USA; Executioner]

Styles, A.J.
(1990s-2000s)

One of the new breed's top flyers, Styles, a Georgia native, has been the focus of regional groups like Ring of Honor, NWA-TNA, and NWA Wildside. He turned down a WWE contract to remain a renegade in TNA. It paid off: in 2003, he won the NWA world title, a deserved honor.

TRIVIA

Q. Which valet was married to the Task Master before divorcing him and marrying another wrestler, Chris Benoit?

Styles, Joey
(1980s-1990s)

Allegedly, he's a trained wrestler, but Styles was on the fast track as ECW's lead announcer. In his prime, he was a throwback announcer to the days of the soloist. Truly, his strongest work was calling the match by himself, as he blended an old style with new catch phrases for a younger audience.

Sullivan, Kevin
(1970s-2000s)

The Bostonian has had a career full of twists and turns. He's been a wrestler more than four decades, but his biggest contributions have been backstage. He began as a muscular hero in Georgia, but soon thereafter adopted a demonic gimmick in Florida. He's the brainchild of gimmicks like the Dungeon of Doom and has been the matchmaker in Florida, WCW, and Smoky Mountain. Has also managed a bevy of sordid characters over the years. [Dungeon Master; Task Master]

Sullivan, Nancy
(1980s-2000s)

Nancy broke into wrestling as a valet for Ron Simmons and Butch Reed in WCW and was often aligned with the occult. With an Elvira-like demeanor and a model's looks, she was very successful on air. [Robin Green; Woman] See: Doom.

Sunshine
(1980s)

This blonde was entrenched in the valet emergence out of World Class in the early 1980s. She started her career with Jimmy Garvin, but eventually ended up siding with fan favorites, the Von Erichs. She had a brief run in the NWA feuding with Baby Doll.

Super Crazy
(1990s-2000s)

This eye-popping Mexican star is a fine high-flyer who's had success outside his home country. He lost his mask as a youngster in Mexico, but has been a valued entertainer in Puerto Rico, Germany, and ECW, where he held the TV belt.

Super Destroyers
(1980s)

The name of a masked band of wrestlers from the early 1980s in the Midwest, Sgt. Slaughter was the first to don the name, followed by Bill and Scott Irwin.

Super Dome

As cavernous as any building in America, the New Orleans spectacle first held wrestling in 1976, a year after it opened, with a card promoted by Bill Watts and Leroy McGuirk. Some cards of theirs drew more than 30,000 fans and it was the site for a famous cage match in 1980 as Junkyard Dog got revenge on Michael Hayes. Into the 1990s, both WWE and WCW promoted there.

Sweet Brown Sugar
(1980s)

This African-American bodybuilder-type appeared in Memphis and World Class to mid-card success.

Sweet Daddy Siki
(1960s-1980s)

One of the first African Americans to dye his hair blond, he was a consummate showman. A former Calgary Stampede champion, he opened a Toronto wrestling school, in addition to spending time as a nightclub singer. [Big Daddy Siki]

TRIVIA

Q. Which wrestler was known as "Mr. Piledriver"?

Sweetan, Bob
(1960s-1980s)

This Central States wrestler, who weighed more than 300 pounds, and was involved in many bloodbaths. He also visited Mid-South and Texas.

Swenson, Jeep
(1980s)

Wearing battle fatigues, the bearded madman from Dallas feuded with Bruiser Brody in World Class. Their matches usually began and ended outside the ring, much to the fans' delight. He died in 1997.

Sytch, Tammy
(1990s-2000s)

One of the prettiest women to circle ringside, she began as a television announcer in Smoky Mountain Wrestling in 1992, but quickly ascended the ladder to the WWF in 1995 where she managed her boyfriend Chris Candido and Tom Pritchard (as the Body Donnas). More than any female before her, she showed Vince McMahon Jr. how valuable sex appeal could be in wrestling. Her success led to personalities like Sable and Torrie Wilson. [Sunny]

Szabo, Sandor
(1930s-1950s)

This accomplished Hungarian amateur dethroned Bronko Nagurski for the NWA world championship in 1941. Also a former European champion, he was popularly used in the West and was a 13-time San Francisco champion. In addition to wrestling, he was in many Hungarian-made movies, as well as several U.S. releases.

Tajiri
(1990s-2000s)

He was just one of the pack in Japan, so native Yoshihiro Tajiri came to the U.S. in the late 1990s via ECW. It proved to be a smart move. Perhaps no other Japanese has had as much American success in the early part of this century as this buzz saw. He brought several innovative moves with him and used them to win the ECW tag-team title with Mikey Whipwreck. Once in the WWF, he has been a solid addition to the cruiserweight division, winning the belt in 2001. [Yoshihiro Tajiri]

Takada, Nobuhiko
(1980s-2000s)

A widely recognized shooter from Japan, the tall star was a middle of the pack heavyweight and tag-team partner of Akira Maeda in New Japan when he broke off with the renegade Maeda to form the shoot-fighting group, UWF. He saw great success there, but eventually went back to his roots in 1996 in winning the pro wrestling IWGP championship from Keiji Mutoh. He's also appeared in Pride Fighting Championships.

Takano, George
(1970s-1990s)

One of the more underrated juniors in Japan, Takano had a fabulous series in the early 1990s with Dynamite Kid. He's held the Calgary British Commonwealth title two times and was an IWGP tag-team champion with Strong Machine in 1989. [The Cobra]

Tanaka, Masato
(1990s-2000s)

With a forehead of steel, Tanaka made a name for himself in Japan as part of the hardcore group, FMW. Known to take multiple blows to the head, he always gets back up. He's a short, stocky, fireplug.

TRIVIA

Q. Which wrestler went to the ECW where he won the world title in 1999 from Mike Awesome, as well as the tag title with Tommy Dreamer in 2000?

Tanaka, Pat
(1980s-1990s)

A short, karate expert, he wrestled barefooted and was an exciting star in his prime. He teamed with Paul Diamond in many areas, including the AWA and Memphis as Badd Company. He got a big break in the early 1990s when he teamed with Akio Sato in the WWF as the Orient Express. See: Badd Company.

Tanaka, Toru
(1960s-1980s)

One of the most powerful Asian grapplers, he won numerous U.S. tag-team titles in the 1970s. The barefooted wrestler settled in Los Angeles and wrestled into the 1980s. In addition to wrestling, he was a veteran of many feature films, including "The Running Man." [Prof. Tanaka]

Tarzan Goto
(1980s-2000s)

Few wrestlers sport as many scars on their body as Tarzan, an insane hardcore wrestler from Japan. Legs, arms, you name it—Goto's got them scarred. His career began in the U.S. Central States area, where he trained with Mr. Pogo. He feuded with Onita through much of the 1990s and bounced around to virtually every hardcore territory in Japan. He and Onita wrestled in the first barbed wire explosion match on FMW's debut card in 1990. Later, he trained Hayabusa. In the early 2000s, he was still carving his body.

Tatanka
(1980s-2000s)

The bulky performer got a chance as a Native American star in the WWF during the early 1990s after beginning in the Carolina independents. With the WWF, he capitalized on the popularity of the movie, "Dances with Wolves." His push took him to the WWF Intercontinental title. [Chris Chavis]

Tatum, John
(1980s-1990s)

Tatum was a hard working mid-card heel in the South for much of his career. Fans remember him for his hilarious facial gestures. It seemed no other wrestler had his ability to find valets. He's rumored to have had discovered the lovely Missy Hyatt—at a strip club. He was a fun heel in the Mid-South region, aligned with Eddie Gilbert and Jack Victory, and also did time in World Class.

Tau, Akira
(1980s-1990s)

Since the 1980s, one of the best tag-team champions in Japan has been Tau, a six-time All-Japan tag champ (five times with Toshiaki Kawada; once with Jumbo Tsuruta). Stardom found him early: his debut match saw him partnered with legend Giant Baba. Singles success eluded him until 1996, when he finally won his first major singles title, the Triple Crown belt, from Mitsuhara Misawa.

Taylor, Terry
(1980s-2000s)

Should Taylor have been an NWA champion? Some think so. But just as his career was on the rise, this tactician inherited the worst gimmick of all time—the Red Rooster—and it ruined his career. In Mid-South, Taylor lit up crowds in performances against Chris Adams, Eddie Gilbert, Steve Williams, and Ted DiBiase. Despite his size, he seemed destined for greatness. He took the money in the WWF and he never recovered. A former UWF TV champion, he split from the WWF and returned to WCW to try and recapture what was lost. Since then, Taylor has been a road agent for all major groups. [Red Rooster; Terrence Taylor]

Taylor, Chris
(1970s)

One of the first wrestlers to sign a guaranteed contract, Taylor, a collegiate wrestler from Iowa State, was nabbed by Verne Gagne for $100,000 to be the next baby-faced superstar. At 400-plus pounds, he was the biggest Olympic wrestler on record when he won the Bronze freestyle medal in 1972. Tons of promise, his size eventually caught up with him. After time in the AWA, he died in 1979 at the age of 29.

TRIVIA

Q. This Calgary villan was earned his nickname by proclaiming, "The birds made me do it!" Who is he?

Taylor, Dave
(1990s-2000s)

This English wrestler was usually aligned with Steven Regal and Fit Finlay. Stardom eluded him in the U.S., but he has stayed active as a trainer and talent assistant for the WWE. [Squire Dave]

Taylor, Lawrence
(1990s)

The New York Giants football icon battled Bam Bam Bigelow at Wrestlemania XI. He never was a wrestler, but trained vigorously for this match. In a better-than-expected bout, Taylor beat the experienced Bigelow in less than 12 minutes.

Taylor, Scott
(1990s-2000s)

This light heavyweight reminds fans of Eddie Gilbert and Buck Zumhoff. It's hard for any small wrestler to get a break, so Taylor needed to invent some fun. As Scotty Too Hotty in the WWF, he formed a tag-team with Brian Lawler and Rikishi called Too Cool and won the tag-team championship. As a singles wrestler, he won the company's lightweight title from Dean Malenko in 2000. [Scotty Too Hotty]

Tazz
(1990s-2000s)

Too short, too dull, too quiet to make it. Those were the knocks on Tazz before he was unleashed by Paul Heyman in ECW. For several years, he toiled in the independents because of size, but Heyman saw something more. He underwent a personality transplant and became the street thug, Tazz. With carefully crafted interviews, he caught fire and won two ECW world titles and two tag-team titles. Before ECW folded, he bolted for the WWF and began another career as a television broadcaster. [Tasmaniac; Taz]

Tenyru, Genichiro
(1970s-2000s)

The Great Tenyru has earned his rep as a Japanese hero. He's been a promoter and booker and has headlined singles and tag-team matches. Although he seemed to play second fiddle in Japan with Baba and Inoki roaming in the 1980s, he was always at the top of every group he wrestled in. He's held the prestigious All-Japan Triple Crown title two times, beating Jumbo Tsuruta and Toshiaki Kawada. In 1999, he beat Keiji Mutoh to win the IWGP Grand Prix belt. [Great Tenyru]

Test
(1990s-2000s)

Andrew Martin debuted as a "roadie," but quickly rose through the ranks. One of many tall, muscular stars, he's tried hard to distinguish himself. An early angle where he was supposed to marry Stephanie McMahon gave him a career jumpstart. He's held three belts in the WWF: the European, hardcore, and tag-team title.

Texas Stadium

Historic site of the David Von Erich Memorial Parade of Champions shows from 1984-86. At the first, on May 6, 1984, Kerry Von Erich enjoyed a tearful victory over Ric Flair for the NWA world title.

Texas Tornado Rules Match

The precursor to modern day tag-team matches, Mo Sigel promoted the first in Houston. The match, featuring strongman Milo Steinborn, saw all four men in the ring at one time, similar to current-day tag bouts.

Thatcher, Les
(1960s-2000s)

In his day, Thatcher was a top Mid-Atlantic junior heavyweight. Since retirement, he's been an announcer for many promotions in the Southeast. Since the early 1990s, he's owned and operated the Heartland Wrestling Association in Ohio, which for a time, was a WWE training facility.

Thesz, Lou
(1940s-1990s)

Is he the best of all time? That's often a topic of great debate, but no one questions the legacy and importance of Thesz, a six-time NWA world champion. Born of Hungarian ancestry, he turned pro in the 1930s and won his first title at age 21 by defeating Everett Marshall. Equally as impressive, his sixth belt was won in 1963 at age 46. His list of past challengers are literally a "who's who" of wrestling legends. He was revered in Japan, which oddly enough, supported him more than Americans. A conditioning freak, he wrestled his last match in his 70s. Born Lajos Tiza, he died in 2002 at age 86.

Thomas, Art
(1950s-1970s)

The Milwaukee-based strongman was one of the few to fight stereotyping in the wrestling industry. A main-event star, the handsome Thomas held belts in Canada, Los Angeles, and Indianapolis. He died in 2003. [Sailor Art; Seaman]

Thompson, Curtis
(1980s-1990s)

The strong independent wrestler traveled from Atlanta to Portland to learn his craft. He won the Northwest tag-team titles with Ricky Santana as the U.S. Males and also performed in Memphis. After a brief stint in WCW with the awful gimmick, Firebreaker Chip, he bowed out of the business. [Firebreaker Chip]

Thornton, Les
(1970s-1980s)

An accomplished amateur boxer and wrestler, the Manchester, England, native carried the NWA junior heavyweight title five times in the 1980s. He was trained in Calgary and won the North American title there in 1971.

Three-Minute Warning
(2000s)

Jamal and Rosey are two more wrestlers in the long succession of Samoan grapplers. They began their careers in Pennsylvania, but showed enough agility and poise to get a WWE contract early in their careers.

Tiger Mask
(1980s-2000s)

This oft-used wrestling gimmick, based after a children's cartoon, has become legendary in Japan. Satoru Sayama, the first to use the mask, turned pro in 1980 and amazed crowds with his revolutionary dives and cat-like reflexes. On one of his first U.S. tours, he won the NWA and WWF junior heavyweight belts on consecutive nights. His legendary matches with Dynamite Kid, Black Tiger, and Davey Boy Smith are classics and inspired people like Jerry Lynn, Chris Benoit, and the late Owen Hart. The Japanese star truly revolutionized the industry and today's business owes him a debt of thanks.

Tillet, Maurice
(1920s-1940s)

The original French Angel, he was a human oddity. Weighing more than 300 pounds with an enormous head and set of hands, he held one version of the world title. He died in 1951 at age 54.

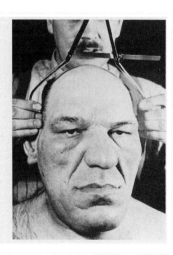

Timbs, Ken
(1970s-1980s)

A bleached-blond light heavyweight out of Georgia and Alabama, he often teamed with another golden-hair, Eric Embry, and had respectable regional success.

TNT
(1980s)

One of Vince McMahon's ideas that should have worked, the show called "Tuesday Night Titans" was a fun program on the USA Network. Think of Johnny Carson meets wrestling: McMahon and co-host Lord Alfred Hayes were joined by WWF stars. It was over the top and outrageous, like the time Butcher Vachon got married and the Wild Samoans taught a cooking lesson.

Tolos, Chris
(1950s-1970s)

With his brother, John Tolos, he was a tag-team wrestler and won the WWWF U.S. tag title in 1963 over Gorilla Monsoon and Killer Kowalski. Though he didn't have the singles success of John, he had a memorable feud in the AWA against the Crusher.

Tolos, John
(1950s-1990s)

The "Golden Greek" was an accomplished star and the ideal traveling heel who would invade a new territory, create a stir by wrestling the top hero, and then leave for another territory. He often used the stomach claw as a finisher. During the 1960s, he was noted for his bloodbath feuds with Fred Blassie and the Destroyer. In the early 1990s, long after retirement, he managed Curt Hennig briefly in the WWF. [Coach; Golden Greek]

Tomasso, Joe
(1950s-1970s)

Remembered as a great villain in Calgary, "Tweet Tweet" Tomasso was a fun preliminary attraction and provided entertaining interviews. The Montreal native teamed with Earl Black and Gil Hayes to win the Stampede tag title four times.

Tomko, Al
(1960s-1980s)

The British Columbia promoter, based in Vancouver, also wrestled in the 1960s and 1970s with a military gimmick. As a promoter, he gave opportunities to the likes of Roddy Piper.

Tonga Kid
(1980s)

A high-flying 200-pounder one day, a 300-pound monster the next, this Samoan family member was one-half of the Islanders tag-team in WWF. Other areas he appeared in are Continental, the AWA, and Japan.

Tori
(1980s-2000s)

Known for her bodybuilding prowess, this former women's wrestler-turned-valet wrestled from Japan to the Northwest, LPWA, and WWF. She held regional women's belts, but departed wrestling altogether. [Terri Powers]

Tormenta, Fray
(1970s-1980s)

Tormenta was a mid-card performer from Mexico who found international acclaim after *Sports Illustrated* wrote a long feature about a minister by day, wrestler by night. It turns out the story was about Fray.

Toyota, Minami
(1990s-2000s)

Often recognized as the greatest female wrestler ever, this Japanese star was very fast paced in the ring. She won four WWWA women's championships in Japan and her match with Kyoko Inoue, which ended in a 60-minute draw, was voted the 1995 Match of the Year by the *Wrestling Observer*.

Tragos, George
(1930s)

The esteemed mentor of Lou Thesz, he taught the future six-time NWA world champion the importance of "hooking," the art of tight wrestling holds and submissions.

Trailer Park Trash
(1990s-2000s)

Sometimes called the heartbeat of Ohio Valley, this Southern performer was a two-time Southern tag-team champion and OVW's first-ever heavyweight champion in 1997. Not especially talented, but able to connect with fans, he's able to wrestle all styles. He's also carried the OVW hardcore title and Puerto Rican junior heavyweight belt.

Triple Crown Title

The crown jewel of the All-Japan promotion, this title has roots in the Japanese Wrestling Association. In 1989, Stan Hansen, who held the PWF and NWA United National titles, was defeated by the NWA International champion, Jumbo Tsuruta, to unify all three, hence the name, "Triple Crown."

Triple H
(1990s-2000s)

From wayward wannabe to bonafide star, Triple H's rise through the ranks has been impressive. Originally a bodybuilder, he looked to Killer Kowalski for wrestling training. After a failed start in WCW, he's consistently improved since his WWE debut in 1995. Known as a backroom politico, he's gone from the goofy aristocratic character Hunter Hearst Helmsley to the modern HHH, a six-time world champion. He was a member of the revolutionary group Degeneration X, which helped the WWE regain its fan base in the late 1990s. In WWE, he's held every major belt and has been ingrained in main events since 1999. And he's still found time to pose for the cover of *Flex Magazine* and find love with the boss' daughter. [The Game; Hunter Hearst Helmsley; Jean Paul Levesque; Terra Ryzin]

Tsuruta, Jumbo
(1970s-1990s)

One of Japan's most revered wrestlers until his death in 1999 after complications following a kidney transplant, he was an Olympic wrestler in 1972 and based on his fame, Giant Baba signed him to an All-Japan deal. During the 1980s and 1990s, few wrestlers were as big as Tsuruta. In the U.S., he trained with the Funk family in Texas. His main-event status was highlighted with three runs as the Triple Crown champion and multiple runs as tag-team champ. His success followed him to the States, as well. In 1984, he defeated Nick Bockwinkel for the AWA world title. While the names Baba and Inoki loom large in Japan, the name Jumbo lies not far behind.

Tugboat
(1980s-1990s)

This extra-large wrestler, discovered by Dusty Rhodes, found a home in WWF and WCW in a variety of roles. After debuting in Florida, he surfaced in WWE and after a heel turn, he won the tag title with Earthquake. [Big Steele Man; Shockmaster; Typhoon]

Tunney, Frank
(1930s-1980s)

One of the legends in promoting, Toronto and Tunney were synonymous. Tunney began running cards in the 1930s and he was the man who put Maple Leaf Gardens on the wrestling map. Before his death in 1983, he passed along the business to his son, Jack Tunney, who kept the tradition alive.

Tunney, Jack
(1980s-1990s)

The son of promoter Frank Tunney, Jack took over in the early 1980s. He accepted an exclusive offer to promote Toronto for the WWF and the McMahon family. That relationship was golden, as Tunney was named the on-air WWF commissioner and stayed in that role through the early 1990s. He also co-promoted Wrestlemania 7 at the Sky Dome in Toronto.

Turner, Ted
(1970s-1990s)

The cable television baron long believed pro wrestling was the anchor of his network, WTBS. For 20 years, the show garnered consistent ratings. When WCW, then owned by Jim Crockett, teetered on bankruptcy, Turner bought the group. When Turner's companies were swallowed by AOL-Time Warner in the early century, wrestling was axed. Some say Turner shed a tear for ol' WCW— and given the chance to start his own network again, he may return to his old friend, rasslin'. See: WTBS.

Tyler, Buzz
(1970s-1990s)

This journeyman, known as the Avalanche, had his best days in the early 1980s, as he saw time as the Mid-Atlantic champion in 1985, as well as several runs with the Central States tag titles.

Tyler, Tarzan
(1960s-1980s)

He was a staple of Montreal wrestling who also enjoyed WWWF fame as well. Together with the equally nutty Luke Graham, he rose to the top of tag-team competition winning the WWWF tag titles. Later, he returned to Canada for a feud with the Rougeau family and he also managed some before dying in a car accident in 1985.

Tyson, Mike
(1990s)

For years, the hardest-hitting heavyweight boxer had offers to hit the wrestling ranks. He never did until 1998, when he accepted an offer to serve as guest referee at Wrestlemania 14 for a Shawn Michaels-Steve Austin main event. Was it worth the wait?

Ultimate Warrior, The
(1980s-1990s)

Jim Hellwig, one of the most controversial figures behind the scenes, started his career as Sting's partner in a Mid-South team called the Blade Runners. The two were discovered during their involvement in the California-based Power Team USA bodybuilding squad. Hellwig took off for World Class where, with his face paint, he won the Texas title as the Dingo Warrior. The WWF came calling and he soon became the Ultimate Warrior, winning the Intercontinental and world titles, the latter by beating Hulk Hogan at Wrestlemania 7 in Toronto. But turmoil followed. Hellwig, with a spiritual calling, left wrestling and after some name calling, sued the WWF to use his ring name. In the end, he was able to call himself The Warrior. Even after the suit, he returned briefly to WWF and WCW but for now, is only a memory. [Dingo Warrior; Warrior]

TRIVIA

Q. Who served as the NWA president from 1960-1961?

Ultimo Dragon
(1980s-2000s)

Having trained in the New Japan dojo, great things were there for the taking for Dragon. Through the early 1990s, he helped bring a sensational style to American wrestling after stints in Mexico. The U.S. scene first glimpsed Dragon in the mid-1990s in WCW, when he captured the cruiserweight title from Dean Malenko. A botched elbow surgery left him retired for several years, but he miraculously came back in 2002. He's also been a pioneering promoter in Japan with his independent group, Toryumon.

Undertaker, The
(1980s-2000s)

Born from the mold of tough Texans such as the Funk and Rhodes families, Mark Calloway bided his time before finding the right gimmick at the right time. He toiled in USWA and WCW with nondescript personalities when, in 1990, he was brought to the WWF to work with the Undertaker gimmick. Rather than balk at the gimmickry, he brought life to the character, which has become one of the most successful concoctions in WWE history. Skilled for a big man, he's able to walk the ropes ala old-timers before him. Despite constant injuries, he's held the world title three times since his debut. [American Badass; Master of Pain; Mean Mark; Punisher]

Ustinov, Soldat
(1980s)

A onetime AWA tag-team champion with Boris Zukoff, the American-born wrestler certainly looked like a Russian. The 6-6, bald menace was managed by both Adnan Al-Kaissey and Chris Markoff before he retired to work as a security specialist.

Vachon, Luna
(1980s-2000s)

Not only does she look the part, she's lived a life on the edge. Luna, short for Lunatic, has played a post-apocalyptic wrestler with face paint and a wild demeanor. This female member of the Vachon family began wrestling in the late 1980s as part of the GLOW group, but kept her career moving and eventually made it to the WWF.

TRIVIA

Q. Which wrestler was nicknamed the "Boogie Woogie Man?"

Vachon, Maurice
(1940s-1980s)

An Olympic wrestler from the 1948 Canadian National team, Vachon struggled to crossover to the pros until he met up with Portland promoter Don Owen who dubbed Vachon the "Mad Dog." From there, Vachon became a legendary wrestler and brawler who employed an aggressive, no-nonsense style. He was a main event star from the 1940s to 1980s and knew two styles in the ring: fast and faster. Along with his brother, Paul Vachon, they won many tag-team titles. Mad Dog even won the AWA world title twice in the 1960s. [Mad Dog Vachon]

Vachon, Paul
(1960s-1980s)

Although he was larger than his brother, Maurice, Paul Vachon's career was not quite as hot. Even so, he was a reliable, solid competitor who performed in the AWA, WWF, WWA, and Canada. He shaved his head and wrestled with a full beard, a distinct look indeed. His feuds against Harley Race, Larry Hennig, the Crusher, and Bruiser drew large crowds in the AWA. [Butcher Vachon]

Vachon, Vivian
(1970s-1980s)

The daughter of Paul Vachon, Viv was one of the most revered and respected women wrestlers of her day. In addition to her ring work, she was a popular French-Canadian vocalist. Sadly, she died from injuries suffered in a car accident in 1991.

Vader
(1980s-2000s)

Leon White began as an AWA mid-card wrestler in the 1980s, but there was little demand for a 30-ish, balding, ex-football player—that was, until he fell into the Big Van Vader gimmick. Reportedly, New Japan and Disney trademarked the name and a signature mask worn by White that blew smoke as he entered the arena. It was quite a spectacle. The smoke left Japanese crowds going nuts. He's known as the only wrestler to hold world titles from four countries simultaneously: Mexico, Germany, U.S., and Japan. Equal to his gimmick was his ability in the ring. Though he was more than 300 pounds, he could do moonsaults and brawl with the best. Among his accolades: two-time Triple Crown champion, three-time IWGP champion, and three-time WCW world champion. [Big Van Vader; Leon White]

Valentine, Greg
(1970s-2000s)

The legit son of 1960s star Johnny Valentine, he originally wrestled as Johnny Fargo so not to be lost in his dad's footsteps. He eventually became a world star as Valentine. He toured the NWA and WWF feuding with and against Roddy Piper. The beefy Valentine was a former Intercontinental champion and tag-team titleholder with Brutus Beefcake. [Blue Knight; Johnny Fargo]

Valentine, Johnny
(1960s-1970s)

Valentine was known for being a rough ring bully and backstage prankster—often going over the line. He was sometimes alienated by his peers, but he was always in high demand with promoters. The father of Greg Valentine could make an entire arena erupt on the drop of a dime. He toured Mid-Atlantic extensively, winning many titles there, until his early retirement in 1975 from injures suffered in a plane crash. He died in 2001.

Valiant, Jerry
(1970s-1980s)

Guy Mitchell was one of many Valiants to wrestle alongside Jimmy and Johnny during the 1970s. Often part of a three-man tag-team, Jerry was once managed by Lou Albano.

Valiant, Jimmy
(1970s-1990s)

This talented and blond rock 'n' roll wrestler was an ideal tag-team wrestler. He had a swagger, adequate skills, and later, was a great interview. Since the mid-1980s, he teamed with "brothers" Johnny and Jerry in the WWWF. In 1974, Jimmy and Johnny were crowned world tag-team champions. As a single's star, he won the Memphis Southern title four times in the late 1970s. [Charlie Brown]

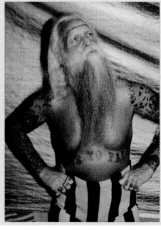

Valiant, Johnny
(1960s-1990s)

The 1970s were a powerful time for tag teams and Johnny, along with Jimmy Valiant, made up one of the most colorful. His real name is Johnny Sullivan and he was a ring veteran who took on numerous names and identities. With his skills waning, he took on Jimmy as his partner and together they were magical. They won the WWWF tag-team titles in 1974 in a win over Tony Garea and Dean Ho. When his wrestling career ended, Valiant went on to managing in the WWF, leading such stars as Greg Valentine, Brutus Beefcake, and Bob Orton Jr.

Vampiro
(1980s-2000s)

Once homeless in Los Angeles, he had designs on a music career when, virtually on a whim, he took off for Mexico. With limited ring experience under his belt, Vampiro hooked up with the EMLL promotion in Mexico City. He was an immediate hit, performing to sold-out crowds with his unique style and misfit appearance. He rode the success to the UWA world title in 1992, and later the WCW tag titles with the Great Muta. [Canadian Vampire]

Van Dam, Rob
(1980s-2000s)

You can't say Van Dam hasn't marched to his own beat. The Michigan native didn't look to have a future in wrestling as a television jobber for WCW in the late 1980s. His Jean Claude Van Dam appearance and martial arts flexibility weren't enough to bring him success. But when he was approached by ECW, everything changed and he was allowed to be himself. His following gave the fledgling promotion life. He had classic matches with Sabu, the Public Enemy, and Jerry Lynn, winning the TV and tag-team titles. Since then, he's become an integral part of the WWE family.

Van Hammer
(1980s-1990s)

With WCW searching for new talent in the late 1980s, the company brought in Hammer. He had a good look (think cross between Sammy Hagar and Lex Luger), but he was never able to put the whole package together. He returned to WCW in the late 1990s, but later disappeared. [Hammer]

Varga, Billy
(1950s-1960s)

He was a U.S. heavyweight who often feuded with Gene LeBell. Varga was a staple in California promotions and appeared in cameos and stunt roles for various television shows. [Count Billy Varga]

Vega, Savio
(1980s-2000s)

A longtime Puerto Rican crowd pleaser, Vega was a main-event star on the island as the masked TNT. He also took that gimmick to Japan, where allied with Abdullah the Butcher. Later in the 1990s, he took off the mask and bolted for WWF, but now makes his home in Puerto Rico. [Kwang; TNT]

Ventura, Jesse
(1970s-2000s)

The only American politician with razor-blade marks on his forehead, Jesse has really done it all. He's been in the military, he's taken body slams in small-town America, he's been to Wrestlemania, and he's had face-to-face meetings with Cuban dictator Fidel Castro. His election as Minnesota governor in 1998 is the crowning achievement for this Minnesota native, but his wrestling career was filled with twists and turns. After debuting in 1979 in the mold of his favorite wrestler, Billy Graham, Ventura's personality-plus gimmick helped solidify him as one of the great entertainers ever. As a wrestler, he left something to be desired. No matter, it was "The Body" everyone craved for. After runs in the Northwest and AWA, he bolted for the WWF in 1983. It was his home for the next decade. An illness in 1984 ended his wrestling career, but he rejuvenated himself as an announcer and Hollywood actor. Little did filmmakers know the real movie should have been of Ventura's largely lived life. [Surfer Jesse]

Vicious, Sid
(1980s-2000s)

This monster has been to the mountain and back again. Seen in VFWs in front of 10 people, he's also headlined Wrestlemania. At 6'7", he looked like a promoter's dream. He began his career in the Continental area, and then took off for WCW, where he teamed with Dan Spivey. Eventually he made his way to WWF, where he was a two-time world champion; he also won the WCW world title twice. A major knee injury ended his career in 2000. [Lord Humongous; Psycho Sid; Sid Justice]

Victoria
(2000s)

This vibrant brunette is a former fitness model who was discovered in Southern California. Part crazy but all beauty, she's been a WWE women's champ with feuds against Trish Stratus and Jackie.

Victory, Jack
(1980s-2000s)

A man of a million gimmicks, the pudgy Victory has been to almost every territory, in roles like a secret serviceman, bodyguard, and militiaman. He's a very complementary wrestler to several tag partners, but he was best as Jack Victory in which he held the UWF tag title in 1986 with longtime partner John Tatum.

Virgil
(1980s-1990s)

Mike Jones began in Memphis in the early 1980s. Shortly after, the well-built African American moved to the WWF where he became Virgil, Ted DiBiase's servant. Was the gimmick a rib on Dusty Rhodes, whose real name is Virgil? Some say so. Virgil was never a major champion, but he held prominent roles. Later, he was renamed Vincent in WCW. Another coincidence? [Vincent]

Volkoff, Nikolai
(1960s-1980s)

This mammoth-sized European wrestler visited many territories under a variety of gimmicks before settling in as the Russian Bear in WWF. Many tag-team partners to his credit, he was a longtime partner of Iron Sheik and nemesis to virtually every hero to come down the pike. [Boris Barishnikoff; Executioner; Mongol]

Von Brauner Bros., The
(1950s-1960s)

A German "brother" team, Kurt and Karl were managed by Saul Weingeroff. In Amarillo, Texas, they were tag-team champions. They also performed for Roy Shire in San Francisco.

Von Erich, Chris
(1980s)

The smallest and youngest of the Von Erich family, Chris, at 5'4", seemed to be jinxed from the get-go. He tried to follow his successful brothers into the wrestling business by wrestling for World Class in its waning days, but he couldn't rally beyond his height. Sadly, he committed suicide in 1991 at age 21.

Von Erich, David
(1970s-1980s)

Each Von Erich family member had something to offer and David was no exception. Considered the best wrestler in the family, the tall and popular commodity was hot not only in Dallas, but in Japan as brother Kevin's tag-team partner. In his home state, he was a four-time Texas champion. He appeared poised for an NWA title reign when he died suddenly in 1984 while on tour in Japan from an intestinal disorder, although drug use was suspected. He was 25.

Von Erich, Fritz
(1950s-1990s)

Fritz Adkisson had a big, menacing ring style using a German gimmick. He held numerous belts with his "brother" Waldo and he held the World Class American title 11 times from 1966-82. The master of the iron claw, Fritz turned his success into a powerful family business in Dallas. All five of his children became wrestlers and sadly, four died in their primes. But in his family's heyday—the late 1970s and early 1980s—their company in Dallas was the hottest wrestling territory in the country. Fritz passed away in 1997.

Von Erich, Kerry
(1980s-1990s)

The most recognized name in the Von Erich family, Kerry was an accomplished high school athlete from Denton, Texas. His dad saw him as having the most mainstream potential, too. So, in 1984, Kerry won the NWA world title from Ric Flair. Surely, it seemed he was well on his way. After a dynamic career in Dallas, where he won the WCCW world title three times, Kerry took off for the WWF, where he won the Intercontinental title in 1990 from another second-generation star, Curt Hennig. Unbeknownst to people around him, Kerry had a portion of his foot amputated after a motorcycle crash, yet he continued to wrestle valiantly despite the use of a prosthesis. Very endearing on the outside, he was cursed by inner demons and drug use from chronic pain. While in the depths of depression and a certain jail sentence for forging prescriptions, he committed suicide in 1993 at age 33. [Texas Tornado]

Von Erich, Kevin
(1970s-1990s)

The only Von Erich son still alive, Kevin was a four-time Texas champion and five-time American champion. Through the early 1980s, like the entire Von Erich family, he was consumed by his family's feud with the Freebirds. Often, Kevin shared the ring with his brothers in six-man tag matches against the "Birds." After Kerry's death in 1993, Kevin wrestled briefly but retired in 1995. Today, he has tried to move on from the pain his family endured and is settled in with his family on their Texas ranch.

Von Erich, Mike
(1980s)

No one would have envied Mike's position following his brother David's death in 1984. He was thrust into Dave's spot, but Mike, at age 20, clearly wasn't ready. In six-man competition, he faired well helping his brothers win the world titles four times. He also had a run as the American champ. While on tour in Japan, he contracted toxic shock syndrome, an illness he barely recovered from. Unable to perform to his own standards, he took his own life in 1987 at age 23.

Von Erich, Waldo
(1950s-1960s)

Most often associated with his "brother" Fritz, the wrestler with a German gimmick teamed with Gene Kiniski to win the WWWF tag title in 1964 and was a widely used regional attraction.

Von Hess, Kurt
(1960s-1980s)

An old-day territory star, Von Hess was a fine heel and teamed with another German, Karl Von Schotz, while in Detroit, winning the NWA tag-team titles. In Canada, he performed as the heel, Bill Terry, and he also had a stint in the Carolinas. [Big Bill Terry]

Von Raschke, Baron
(1960s-1990s)

Jim Raschke was an all-star who wrestled and played football at Nebraska when Verne Gagne discovered him. Using his real name, he failed to catch on. Like many in his day, he became a goose-stepping German in the ring. That was smart, as he became a singles star throughout the U.S. He toured the world using his gimmick, but eventually settled right where he had begun—in the Midwest.

TRIVIA

Q. Which barefooted Von Erich son was a four-time Texas champion?

Von Schotz, Karl
(1970s-1980s)

John Anson got his start in Calgary, where he debuted as a baby face. But he saw dollar signs in his future and decided to shave his head and wrestle as a German, frequently tagging with partner Kurt Von Hess.

Walcott, Joe
(1970s)

"Jersey Joe," a former light heavyweight and heavyweight boxing great, led the New Jersey Athletic Commission and was a part-time special referee in pro-wrestling matches. He even donned the tights in 1963 in a loss to the great Lou Thesz.

Wanz, Otto
(1980s-1990s)

For a brief five-week period, the 400-pound Wanz held the AWA world title. In the history of that group, Wanz (pronounced Vaants), was the first non-American to hold the belt. On television, he would tear phone books in half to show his power. After his time in the U.S., he returned to Germany, where he became a local legend, winning titles and later promoting cards for his CWA group.

War Games
(1980s-1990s)

One of the many mid-1980s innovations, the NWA began promoting two-ring cage matches with this name that pitted five-on-five competition. Usually, two men would start, and one more from each team was added in intervals. Often bloody, usually exciting, and always entertaining.

Ware, Koko B.
(1970s-1990s)

The popular Mid-South prelim attraction broke out nationally as a WWF fan favorite in the early 1980s. Once a tag-team member of the Pretty Young Things, he painted his hair like a rainbow and carried a pet parrot, in the WWF. [Koko Ware; Sweet Brown Sugar]

Warlord, The
(1980s-1990s)

Terry Szopinski was a muscular tough man known for his power moves. He found success in the WCW and later the WWF as the Barbarian's partner in the Powers of Pain tag team.

Watson, Billy
(1940s-1960s)

Toronto-based main-event star who was a former two-time world champion. Despite his Canadian appeal, he found success in the U.S. After a series of matches against Lou Thesz for the Canadian title, Watson was deemed the No. 1 challenger to the NWA world title. In 1947, he beat Bill Longson for his first title. He later beat Thesz for the world belt in 1956. [Whipper Watson]

Watts, Bill
(1950s-1990s)

This rough cowboy from Oklahoma was a major player as a wrestler and promoter. He had a short-lived pro football career with the Houston Oilers in 1961. After being welcomed to wrestling by Leroy McGuirk and Danny Hodge, his biggest days in the ring were in the 1960s. Popularly used around the Midwest and Mid-South, he was a five-time North American champion. By the time he retired, his new career began. He promoted the Mid-South/UWF region, using top caliber stars like Ted DiBiase and Steve Williams, up until he sold the territory in 1986 to Jim Crockett Jr. He was briefly the matchmaker for WCW in the early 1990s, but by then, his style wasn't considered current enough to be profitable.

Watts, Erik
(1990s-2000s)

A second-generation star, this son of Bill Watts played college football at Louisville. With his pop running WCW in 1992, he was thrust into a main-event spot before he was ready. He's struggled to find an identity ever since, but is still active in NWA-TNA.

Watts, Joel
(1980s)

Another of Bill Watts' sons, Joel, was considered a master television producer in his family's Mid-South territory. He also served as an announcer and video choreographer.

Wayne, Ken
(1980s-1990s)

Diminutive but talented, "The Nightmare" was a frequent partner of Danny Davis in several tag teams. Across the Southeast, Wayne performed under tag-team names like the Nightmares, Galaxians, and Masters of Terror. See: Nightmares.

Weaver, Johnny
(1960s-1980s)

A wrestler, announcer, and promoter, Weaver was a staple in the Mid-Atlantic and Florida areas. In 1967, he held the NWA Southern title in Florida. In the early 1980s, he was a regular television announcer and is also noted for his marriage to female wrestler Penny Banner.

Weazal, Abdul
(1980s)

An oddball created by Bruce Hart in Calgary, Weazal was a campy version of manager the Grand Wizard. The 5-4, 125-pounder babbled incoherently and was accompanied to the ring by his henchman, the 350-pound Mahkan Singh.

Weingeroff, George
(1970s-1980s)

A legally blind wrestler who switched to the pro side after a standout amateur career, he had moderate success in Kansas City, Dallas, and Puerto Rico. He also wrestled some with a Sheik gimmick.

Weingeroff, Saul
(1950s-1960s)

A wrestler-referee who made his real impact as a manager, he often aligned himself with the Sheik and Tiger Ali Singh.

Wells, George
(1980s)

This rarely known African American was a football star in college at New Mexico and later in the Canadian Football League. Despite lots of promise and athleticism, he never panned out. [Master G]

Wepner, Chuck
(1970s)

The "Bayonne Bleeder" was Sylvester Stallone's inspiration for the film, "Rocky," following Wepner's boxing fight against Muhammad Ali. The onetime boxing contender entered wrestling's history books by losing to Andre the Giant on the Ali-Inoki undercard in 1976. Wepner tried hard in the mixed martial arts match, but was defeated by Andre via count-out.

Whalen, Ed
(1960s-1990s)

This announcer from Stampede Promotions was on television for four decades. Whalen's appeal was somewhat regional, but he did everything in Calgary, from radio to TV. Remembered fondly for not ever budging when a wrestler grabbed for the microphone, he passed away in 2002.

Whatley, Pez
(1970s-1980s)

Wearing a top hat and tails, this smiling man was a popularly used attraction in Texas and in Mid-South. Mainly a heel in his career, the onetime Florida Southern champion was a tag-team partner of the large Ray Candy and second-generation star, Tiger Conway Jr (as the Jive Tones). [Shaska Whatley]

Whipwreck, Mikey
(1990s-2000s)

Trained by Sonny Blaze, this lovable loser from ECW shocked the world when he defeated Sandman in 1995 for that company's world title. Weighing less than 200 pounds, he constantly got beat up until he was helped in storylines by Cactus Jack. He's also a two-time TV champ and three-time tag-team champ, once with Cactus.

Wild Alaskans, The
(1970s-1980s)

There have been a few different incarnations of this tag team, but the most famous was the brother team of Jay and Mike York. They were bearded, donned plaid shirts, and toured various territories including the AWA, Toronto, Texas, and Indiana. Into the 1980s, the AWA featured a prelim team of Alaskans comprised of Dave Wagner and Rick Renslow.

Wild Samoans, The
(1960s-1980s)

Afa and Sika were a wildly successful oddity team and are actually brothers. They ruled the East Coast and were hardcore before hardcore was cool. In addition to winning the WWF tag titles three times from 1980-83, they toured Japan, Puerto Rico, and Canada. They've left a tremendous legacy as nearly a dozen relatives and family members have broken into wrestling including Rikishi, Tonga Kid, Three Minute Warning, the Rock, and the late Yokozuna. Now retired, they operate an independent group out of Pennsylvania.

Wilkes, Del
(1980s-1990s)

After going nowhere, the well-sculpted baby face took Chris Love's advice and donned a mask to become the Patriot. He traveled to Global (where he was champion), the AWA, and even had a shot in the WWF when an injury ended his career. [Patriot; Trooper]

Williams, Steve
(1980s-2000s)

A native of Oklahoma, he was a natural in Mid-South. After wrestling and playing football for the Sooners—he was a three-time Big 12 conference wrestling champion—and in the defunct USFL pro-league, he debuted for Watts in 1982. He was a mean-looking bruiser and brawler. He won several titles for Watts. After a stint in the NWA, winning the world tag titles with Mike Rotunda, he headed for a prolific career in Japan in the mold of Bruiser Brody. In the 1990s, he and Terry Gordy were arguably the top Americans there. Likely, there won't be another like Williams again. [Dr. Death]

Wilson, Torrie
(1990s-2000s)

Fitness modeling just wasn't enough for the Idaho native. Lured to wrestling by WCW, she's been a valet, manager, and wrestler in WWE. Her popularity and appeal led to lots of face time on TV. [Miss NWO; Samantha]

Windham, Barry
(1970s-2000s)

This second-generation wrestler has had several gimmicks, but always did best as Barry. He's led a career full of highlights despite some dull years. In 1993, the son of Blackjack Mulligan won the NWA world title from the Great Muta. In his youth, he had the grace of a true technician despite his 6-7, 240-pound frame. In the WWF, he won the world tag title with Mike Rotunda, before heading back to WCW. He won the Florida title four times and his series with Ric Flair during that period was phenomenal and have people remembering him as a modern-day great. [Blackjack Jr.; Stalker; Widowmaker]

TRIVIA

Q. Which wrestler won five All-Japan tag belts together with Terry Gordy during the 1990s?

Windham, Kendall
(1980s-1990s)

The less-accomplished son of Blackjack Mulligan, he was a beanpole when he started in Florida in the early 1980s. Even so, he trudged on and had minor success in that state and in the NWA, where he sometimes teamed with brother, Barry.

Wolfe, Billy
(1920s-1950s)

Wolfe was a wrestler, carnival wrestling promoter, and founding board member in the NWA. He was also a pioneering promoter of women's wrestling. Although the sport was banned in some states, Wolfe pressured his buddies to legalize it for women. He promoted an entire group of females, including his wife, former world champ Mildred Burke.

Wolfe, Buddy
(1970s)

A rugged looking outdoorsman from the Midwest, he often teamed with Lars Anderson. Wolfe, at one time, was married to the late Vivian Vachon.

Wolfie D
(1990s-2000s)

A journeyman from a young age, he's been to most independent groups, as well as WWF and WCW, as Jamie Dundee's partner. [Slash] See: PG-13.

World Championship Wrestling

Originally the name of Jim Crockett Jr.'s Saturday television show on WTBS, when Crockett sold his promotion to Ted Turner in 1988, Turner officially renamed his promotion WCW in 1993 after splitting from the NWA. Based out of Atlanta, it continued the tradition of NWA wrestling's title roots until its sale to Vince McMahon Jr. in 2001.

World Class Championship Wrestling

Fritz Von Erich promoted the Dallas area from 1960-87, but his group wasn't officially named WCCW until 1982. The promotion was sold by Von Erich in 1988 to Jerry Jarrett, who renamed the area the USWA.

World Greco-Roman Championship

A turn-of-the-century "title," the lineage of the NWA world title traces back to this championship. It was originally a European title first held by Tom Cannon in 1894. It was converted into a "world" title when then-champ George Hackenschmidt beat American champion Tom Jenkins in 1902. From there, greats like Lewis, Thesz, and Flair carried on the tradition all the way to the new Millennium.

World Wrestling Council

With roots dating to 1974, this has been the home of wrestling in Puerto Rico. Carlos Colon, Gorilla Monsoon, and Victor Jovica founded Capitol Sports as the exclusive home to island wrestling. It was renamed WWC in 1982 and remains so today.

World Wrestling Federation

Born as the World Wide Wrestling Federation in 1963 when promoters Toots Mondt and Vince McMahon Sr. broke from the NWA, McMahon Sr. sold his ownership to his son, Vince Jr., in 1983. Its name was shortened to WWF in 1978. In 2002, it was renamed World Wrestling Entertainment, after the company fell victim to a lawsuit by the World Wildlife Fund.

World's Women's Title

Before Fabulous Moolah, Josie Wahlford of New Jersey was considered by many to be the very first women's champion. Her life was spent as an attraction on the vaudeville circuit. In the late 1800s, women like Alice Williams and Cora Livingstone picked up the slack. For the next few decades, the title disappeared but it resurfaced in the 1930s with Clara Mortenson and Mildred Burke. Then, in the 1950s, Moolah, June Beyers, and Penny Banner firmly established the women's title in wrestling history.

Wright, Alex
(1990s-2000s)

This German phenom could use the ropes with the best of them. In WCW, he was a cruiserweight, television, and tag-team champion, and popular attraction at that. [Berlyn]

WTBS
(1970s-2000s)

For four decades, the Ted Turner-owned network showcased wrestling. Many of the greatest stars and moments the industry has ever seen were on this network's Saturday shows. Ric Flair, Bruiser Brody, the Freebirds, Roddy Piper, Dusty Rhodes, and a virtual "who's who" of wrestling had career-defining moments on the Atlanta cable channel. Georgia Championship Wrestling was the first local hit the station aired. Through the years, the industry went through numerous changes and WTBS stayed with it in step. By the 1990s, Turner had sold off his empire but WTBS and sister network TNT remained home to WCW. It battled for ratings with the WWF until 2001, when Vince McMahon Jr. bought the company. With the sale, wrestling fans bid adieu to ring action from Atlanta as TBS/TNT cancelled the programs.

TRIVIA

Q. What was the name of Koko B. Ware's pet parrot?

X-Division

The NWA-TNA group needed something to set itself apart and this division was the answer. Using the best independent cruiserweights, the division belt has been battled for by Jerry Lynn, Chris Daniels, Shark Boy, Low-Ki, Paul London, Kid Kash, Amazing Red, and A.J. Styles, to name a few.

X-Pac
(1980s-2000s)

Sean Waltman began his career at age 15 at the Malenko school in Florida before moving to Minnesota. There, he combined styles from Japan, Calgary, and Mexico. Has he always been in the right place at the right time? That's what put him in the middle of two revolutionary angles, the New World Order and Degeneration X. Among his titles: one WCW cruiserweight title, two WWF lightweight titles, and four WWF tag-team titles. [1-2-3 Kid; Kid; Lightning Kid; Syxx; Syxx-Pac]

XPW

This promotion, run from Los Angeles, is run by adult filmmaker Rob Black, and tries to pick up where ECW left off. With mostly hardcore bouts, it's often a gore-fest, catering to a niche audience. Champions have included Shane Douglas, Vic Grimes, and the Messiah.

Yamaguchi, Wally
(1970s-2000s)

Longtime Japanese referee and matchmaker, Wally has been known in the U.S. for years and has acted as a go-between for talent in Japan and the U.S. For a time, he was even the manager of Kaientai in the WWF.

Yamamoto, Tojo
(1960s-1980s)

Although he wrestled the world over, the Japanese wrestler was a fixture in Tennessee, where he wreaked havoc for three decades. He sometimes teamed with Jerry Jarrett as a wrestler. By the late 1980s, he was a regularly appearing manager guiding a cadre of miscreants.

Yatsu, Yoshiaki
(1980s-2000s)

A participant in the 1976 Olympics, he missed the boycotted 1980 Games in the Soviet Union. Without an amateur career, he switched to the pros and has been with every major group in Japan. He was a five-time PWF tag champion with Jumbo Tsuruta. Ultimately, he craved to return to his roots and left the pros to try mixed martial arts groups such as Pride.

Yokozuna
(1980s-1990s)

Rodney Anoia, a revered member of the Samoan wrestling clan, lived large. His uncles were the great Afa and Sika. A two-time WWF champion and tag-team champion with the late Owen Hart, he wrestled in the AWA, Mexico, and Japan before hitting the WWF in 1992. His size—at one point he weighed more than 600 pounds—was his livelihood, but it also caused his early death. He was once named Kokina Maximus as a joke, which referred to his large backside. Despite efforts to lose weight, he died in 2000 from heart failure at age 34. [Great Kokina; Kokina Maximus]

Young, Gary
(1980s)

A Texas and Mid-South-based mid-card star, who won regional titles in World Class and Memphis. He is most known for a feud with Eric Embry in Dallas. [Super Zodiac]

Young, Mae
(1930s-2000s)

Although she never won the world title herself, Young is an amazing eight-decade performer. A good friend of Fabulous Moolah, she even turned up in the WWF since 1999 and has provided many laughs.

Youngblood, Jay
(1970s-1980s)

The late Youngblood was an up-and-coming star in the 1970s in Mid-Atlantic, where he was a popular tag-team wrestler winning belts with Wahoo McDaniel and Ricky Steamboat. In 1985 at age 30, he passed away from a heart condition.

Youngbloods, The
(1980s-1990s)

Mark and Chris Romero were second-generation talents who fought to catch on outside the Kansas-Missouri region. With an eye to the future, they adopted the Youngblood name and with it, became known in many promotions. Although very small, they wrestled out of the Mid-Atlantic and Texas promotions using a Native American gimmick to minimal success. Later on, they found success in Puerto Rico and Japan.

Youssuf the Terrible Turk
(19th Century)

One of the great mysteries in wrestling history, few can agree who the Terrible Turk really was. Was he a dock worker from France? Or was he really a monster from Turkey? The man weighed nearly 250 pounds and legend has it a Frenchman brought him to France to wrestle in the late 1800s. Some consider him one of the first brawling wrestlers, as evidenced by his near-riotous match against Ernest Roeber in New York in 1898. One thing most can agree on is how he died: he was a victim on a shipwreck off the coast of Nova Scotia at age 35. Known to be careful with his money, he refused to remove his heavy money belt and he drowned from its weight.

Yukon Eric
(1940s-1960s)

The man with the 60-inch chest was known famously for losing part of his ear in a match with Killer Kowalski. In 1965, he killed himself at the age of 48.

Zandig, John
(1990s-2000s)

The self-proclaimed innovator of "ultra-violent" wrestling, John Corso trained with Larry Sharpe in New Jersey before opening Combat Zone Wrestling in 1999. Using weed whackers and light bulbs as weapons, it is considered one of the goriest promotions in the world. They've toned it down, but its wrestlers still have ties to Japan's garbage groups.

Zbyszko, Larry
(1970s-2000s)

As Larry Whistler, few fans appreciated him until he was "adopted" by Bruno Sammartino in WWF storylines. Eventually, he feuded with his mentor Bruno and the two met at Shea Stadium in 1980. From that feud, he called himself the "Living Legend." Known for his fine interview skills, he was a multi-promotion champion and the last to hold the AWA world title in 1990.

Zbyszko, Stanislaus
(1910s-1930s)

Born in Poland, he was a two-time world champion in the 1920s. Said to be the first wrestler billed as the "8th Wonder of the World," legend has it he was the first to earn $1 million from wrestling. He died in 1967.

Zbyszko, Wladek
(1920s-1940s)

The younger brother of Stanislaus Zbyszko, he also laid claim to the world title, although it was never officially recognized. A noted bodybuilder, he helped a teen-aged Harley Race enter the wrestling profession. He died in 1968.

Zenk, Tom
(1980s-1990s)

This former Mr. Minnesota in 1981 surprisingly quit wrestling in the prime of his career. He debuted in 1984 for the AWA and seemed destined for stardom. Handsome and talented, his critics say he burned bridges. After tours in Japan, he debuted in the WWF in 1987 and wrestled at Wrestlemania 3 as Rick Martel's partner. He landed in WCW and won the U.S. tag-team and TV titles there before retiring. [Z-Man]

Zeus
(1980s-2000s)

He had a short career but it's hard to forget him. The scary looking Tiny Lister is from Orange County, California. After the film was released, Zeus took off around the horn and headlined several shows with Ted DiBiase against Hogan. Since then, he's been in dozens of B-grade action flicks.

Zukoff, Boris
(1980s-1990s)

A goofy-looking Russian-gimmicked wrestler from the 1980s, he was mainly a jobber, visiting World Class, the AWA (where he was tag-team champion) and the WWF (where he teamed with Nikolai Volkoff).

TRIVIA

Q. Which wrestler broke into wrestling as Hulk Hogan's nemesis in the movie *No Holds Barred*?

Zumhoff, Buck
(1970s-2000s)

This four-decade light heavyweight worked his way from ring crew to referee to titleholder in the AWA. Known as the "Rock & Roller," he carried a boom box to the ring in his heyday and rode that gimmick to success in the Midwest and Texas.

INDEX

W

TRIVIA ANSWERS

PAGE	ANSWERS		PAGE	ANSWERS
155	Bad News Allen		206	Peter Maivia
156	Ox Anderson		210	Mitsuhara Misawa
163	James Blears		213	Mr. Moto
164	Blue Demon		214	Larry Nelson
165	Bradshaw		215	Scott Norton
166	Dave Brown		216	Marty O'Neill
168	Primo Carnera		219	Roddy Piper
169	Top: Chris Champion		221	Harley Race
169	Bottom: Joe Garigiola		223	Jake Roberts
171	Hercules Cortez		226	Harold Sakata
173	Henri DeGlane		228	Frank Sexton
179	Fabulous Moolah		229	Larry Sharpe
181	Bill Fralic		231	The Sheepherders
183	Verne Gagne		235	Top: George Steele
185	Jose Gonzales		235	Bottom: Woody Strode
186	Joyce Grable		236	Nancy Sullivan
189	Hard Boiled Haggerty		237	Top: Bob Sweetan
190	Top: Jimmy Hart		237	Bottom: Masato Tanaka
190	Bottom: Hayabusa		238	Joe Tomasso
192	Larry Henig		241	Frank Tunney
193	Danny Hodge		242	Jimmie Valiant
194	The Honkeytonk Man		243	Jesse Ventura
195	Top: Antonio Inoki		245	Kevin Von Erich
195	Bottom: The Honkeytonk Man		247	Steve Williams
199	Ivan lost it to Pedro Morales after only 21 days.		248	Frankie
200	Killer Kowalski		250	A. Zeus
202	Ted Lewin			